M000239944

Stories of women

MANCHESTER
1824

Manchester University Press

Stories of women

Gender and narrative in the postcolonial nation

ELLEKE BOEHMER

Manchester University Press
Manchester and New York

distributed exclusively in the USA by Palgrave

Copyright © Elleke Boehmer 2005

The right of Elleke Boehmer to be identified as the author of this work has been asserted
by her in accordance with the Copyright, Designs and Patents Act 1988.

Published by Manchester University Press
Oxford Road, Manchester M13 9NR, UK
and Room 400, 175 Fifth Avenue, New York, NY 10010, USA
www.manchesteruniversitypress.co.uk

Distributed in the United States exclusively by
Palgrave Macmillan, 175 Fifth Avenue,
New York, NY 10010, USA

Distributed in Canada exclusively by
UBC Press, University of British Columbia, 2029 West Mall,
Vancouver, BC, Canada V6T 1Z2

British Library Cataloguing-in-Publication Data is available

Library of Congress Cataloging-in-Publication Data is available

ISBN 978 0 7190 6879 9 paperback

First published by Manchester University Press in hardback 2005

This paperback edition first published 2009

Printed by Lightning Source

For
Ben Phipson
Vijay Keshav
Rosa Marshall Todd
Thomas and Sam

In memory
Mia Fabienne Nuttall-Mbembe
23–30 March 2004

Contents

Acknowledgements   ix

Introduction   1

1 Motherlands, mothers and nationalist sons: theorising the
   en-gendered nation   22

2 'The master's dance to the master's voice': revolutionary
   nationalism and women's representation in Ngugi wa Thiong'o   42

3 Of goddesses and stories: gender and a new politics in Achebe   54

4 The hero's story: the male leader's autobiography and the syntax
   of postcolonial nationalism   66

5 Stories of women and mothers: gender and nationalism in the
   early fiction of Flora Nwapa   88

6 Daughters of the house: the adolescent girl and the nation   106

7 Transfiguring: colonial body into postcolonial narrative   127

8 The nation as metaphor: Ben Okri, Chenjerai Hove, Dambudzo
   Marechera   140

9 East is east: where postcolonialism is neo-orientalist – the cases
   of Sarojini Naidu and Arundhati Roy   158

10 Tropes of yearning and dissent: the inflection of desire in Yvonne
   Vera and Tsitsi Dangarembga   172

11 Beside the west: postcolonial women writers in a transnational
   frame   187

12 Conclusion: defining the nation differently   207

   Select bibliography   223
   Index   235

Acknowledgements

I first wish to acknowledge with much gratitude the support of the A.H.R.B. Research Leave Scheme which gave me the time to complete the final part of the research towards, and a substantial part of the writing of, this book.

I am grateful to the Department of English and Media at the Nottingham Trent University for research leave support. I should like to thank my colleagues in the department, especially Alison Donnell, Patrick Williams, Tim Youngs and Nahem Yousaf of the Centre for Colonial and Postcolonial Studies, as well as Roberta Davari-Zanjani for her kind encouragement.

Many thanks to Susan Andrade, John Barnard, Shirley Chew, Lyn Innes, Hermione Lee, Susheila Nasta, Judie Newman, Benita Parry, Angela Smith, Rajeswari Sunder Rajan and Robert Young for support and inspiration, given in different contexts and capacities. I owe gratitude to Pal Ahluwalia, Rehana Ahmed, Derek Attridge, Bridget Bennett, Tim Brennan, Amit Chaudhuri, Rinka Chaudhuri, Laura Chrisman, Leela Gandhi, Philip Gehrens, Lucy Graham, Gareth Griffiths, Claudia Gualtieri, Liz Gunner, Lisa Hill, Graham Huggan, Neil Lazarus, Satish Keshav, Nazreena Markar, Gail Marshall, Achille Mbembe, Anne McClintock, John McLeod, Jo McDonagh, Jon Mee, David Mehnert, Bart Moore-Gilbert, Catherine Morley, Stuart Murray, Steph Newell, Sarah Nuttall, Rob Nixon, Ken Parker, Ranka Primorac, Terence Ranger, Helen Richman, Michael Roberts, Meg Samuelson, Kay Schaffer, Jon Stallworthy, Keya Tanguly, Alex Tickell, Helen Tiffin, Paula Teo, Wes Williams, Clair Wills, Naomi Wolf, and the other fellow writers, friends and scholars with whom I've been privileged to share ideas on gender and the nation – and other topics besides! – over the past several years.

Inexpressible thanks are owed to my family, Thomas, Sam and, above all, Steven, long-suffering endurer of late-night 'table-tapping' on the upper floor.

The journal articles and essays in books on which a group of the chapters here are based have been substantially revised, elaborated and, in certain cases, updated; however, I wish to express my thanks to the editors and publishers of the following:

'Motherlands, mothers and nationalist sons: representations of nationalism and women', *From Commonwealth to Postcolonial*, edited by Anna Rutherford. London: Dangaroo, 1992, pp. 229–47.

'Revolutionary nationalism and the representation of women in Ngugi wa Thiong'o', *Journal of Commonwealth Literature*, 26:1 (1991), 188–97.

'Of goddesses and stories: gender and a new politics in Achebe', *Chinua Achebe: A Celebration*, edited by Kirsten Holst Petersen and Anna Rutherford. Oxford: Heinemann, 1991, pp. 104–12.

'Stories of women and mothers', in *Motherlands: Black Women's Writing*, edited by Susheila Nasta. London: The Women's Press, 1991, pp. 3–23.

'Daughters of the house: the adolescent girl and the postcolonial nation', *Small Worlds: Transcultural Visions of Childhood*, edited by Rocio G. Davis and Rosalia Baena. Pamplona: University of Navarre Press, 2001, pp. 59–70.

'Transfiguring: colonial body into narrative', *Novel*, 26:3 (Spring 1993), 268–77.

'The nation as metaphor in post-colonial literature: Ben Okri and Chenjerai Hove', *English Studies in Transition*, edited by Robert Clark and Piero Boitani. London. Routledge, 1993, pp. 320–31.

'East is east and south is south: feminism and postcolonialism in Sarojini Naidu and Arundhati Roy', *Women: A Cultural Review*, 11:1/2 (2000), 61–70.

'Without the west: Indian and African women writers in the 1990s', *African Studies*, 58:2 (1999), 157–70. Reprinted in *English Studies in Africa*, 43:2 (2000).

'Tropes of yearning: the troping of desire in contemporary Zimbabwean women's writing', *Journal of Commonwealth Literature*, 38:2 (2003), 135–48.

Introduction

Nationalism can only ever be a crucial political agenda against oppression. All longings to the contrary, it cannot provide the absolute guarantee of identity. (Gayatri Spivak, *A Critique of Postcolonial Reason*)[1]

Say No, Black Woman
Say No,
When they give you a back seat
In the liberation wagon
Yes Black Woman
A Big No. (Gcina Mhlope, 'Say no')[2]

Girl at war

The beginning of this study of gender, nation and postcolonial narrative lies, appropriately, in story – a story about a 'girl', a girl at war.

The 'girl', Gladys, is the at first nameless young woman whom the narrator of Chinua Achebe's 1960s short story 'Girls at war' encounters at three representative moments during the years of the Biafra War.[3] Achebe has long been intrigued by the power granted women in myth (take Ani, Idemili), but what is at issue in the present story is not so much mythical presence as the 'girl' Gladys's nationally signifying condition. She is in effect on three different occasions and under three different guises a sign of the at-first-emergent and then declining nationalist times.

With 'Girls at war' Achebe expresses something of the exhaustion and disillusionment that was the aftermath of the 1967–70 Biafra conflict in Nigeria. In this protracted war, the secessionist, minoritarian nationalism of the Igbo East or Biafra that had brought Nigeria's triumphant, multi-ethnic nationalism of the anti-colonial era to crisis (and of which the writer, like the poet Christopher Okigbo, was a supporter), was painfully suppressed. In the short story three distinct phases in the worsening conflict are charted, each phase corresponding to a meeting between the narrator, Reginald Nwankwo, an official in the doomed new state's Ministry of Justice, and Gladys, the girl. As the narrator of the story, Reginald indexes each phase in the action relative to Gladys's various incarnations as a 'girl at war'. The term 'girl', with its compound implications of vulnerability, immaturity, helplessness and sexual provocativeness, is used throughout.

The first time the two meet, Gladys is off to join the militia and Reginald gives her a lift in his car. This takes place, it is said, in 'the first heady days of war, when thousands of young men *and sometimes women too* were coming forward burning with readiness to bear arms in defence of the exciting new nation' (*GW* 98, emphasis added). Reginald tells her that 'girls [are] not required in the militia' and instructs her to go home (*GW* 100). On their second meeting, he is again in his car, she on the side of the road, but as she is supervising a road block, she now gives the instructions. Reginald's irritation registers the extent to which this contravenes his expectations as a privileged government official and as a man. His feelings are somewhat mitigated, however, by the pleasure he takes in her appearance: her military look aside, she is 'a beautiful girl in a breasty blue jersey' (*GW* 99). He is even more impressed when she reveals her identity. 'Yes, you were the girl', says Reginald when he recognises her. As he drives off his preconceptions have been sufficiently shaken for him to acknowledge that 'the girls' in the national militia must now be taken seriously; they are no longer to be compared to children imitating their fathers' drilling exercises (*GW* 100). Significantly though, despite the potential subversion implicit in their new military work, 'their devotion' to the nation's cause, the time-honoured role of self-dedication, has redeemed them. The cause itself not only remains of the first importance, but also is elite-driven, firmly in the hands of those at the top. As he drives away, Reginald repeats to himself the words his new friend used to describe her activity: 'we are doing the work you asked us to do' (*GW* 100).

Reginald and 'the girl' meet for the third time 18 months later. The war is going badly; the once optimistic Biafra is crippled with defeat and mass starvation. Reginald has gone out for food supplies for his family, in 'search of relief', as he says (*GW* 101). On the way home relief comes in the form of his old friend the girl, once again hitch-hiking by the side of the road, once again in a different garb. The military look, Reginald observes with relief, has not lasted long: 'You were always beautiful of course, but now you are a beauty queen' (*GW* 103). In his eyes her new appearance secures her a measure of individuality; she is no longer merely an exponent of devoted national service. At last Reginald learns her name.

However, Reginald is not entirely comfortable with the way that Gladys has turned out. Taking note of her high-tinted wig and expensive shoes he concludes that these are smuggled goods: his friend has been corrupted, no doubt by an attack-trader dealing in looted goods. Once again the girl is not entirely in charge; she is susceptible to being manipulated. 'Too many girls were simply too easy these days', Reginald says to himself, 'War sickness, some called it' (*GW* 106). His friend's physical state, compounded by her alleged status as a pawn in an underground enterprise, becomes an emblem of the general state of the nation. Reginald himself recognises this: 'Gladys . . . was just a mirror reflecting a society that had gone completely rotten and maggoty at the centre' (*GW* 114).

The girl's 'rottenness', however, excites Reginald's desire. After she has '[yielded]' to him – another sign of her corruptibility – he offers to drive her to her home, hoping in this way to find out more about her. En route, having picked up another hitch-hiker, a disabled young soldier, they are caught in an air raid. Gladys runs back to help the soldier and the two of them are caught in the bombardment, immolated in one another's arms. This final image, significantly elaborated by the presence of the soldier bearing the wounds of his national service on his body, confirms Gladys's emblematic role. The moment of conflagration signifies the destruction of young Biafra, of brave, loyal soldiers and dutiful girls united in a hopeless and yet ennobling national struggle. Moreover, through her heroic act Gladys reasserts the integrity she appeared to have lost, but does so by becoming once again unambiguously feminine. Her death fixes her in the time-honoured attitude for women of self-sacrifice.

Indeed, across the course of the short story Gladys carries both the positive and the negative connotations of women's action in service of the postcolonial nation-in-formation – of national conflict as glorious, for a brief time, and then, more predictably, of double-dealing and civil strife as diseased and corrupting. The representation of the male soldier, introduced only at the point of glorious immolation, is more straightforward. If manipulable girls, crudely speaking, represent the state of the nation whatever its condition, male figures by contrast exemplify honest-to-goodness integrity and staunch national character.[4] This seems to be so not only because men command the action – driving the cars and carrying the guns – but also because they determine its meanings. The contrast pertains whether we look at the arena of postcolonial national politics – at national pageantry, presidential cavalcades, garlanded grandstands – or, as in this book *Stories of Women*, within the somewhat more secluded spaces of national literatures and the writing of the nation.

Gender, the nation and postcolonial narrative

As in the cross-section of a tree trunk that is nowhere unmarked by its grain – by that pattern expressing its history – so, too, is the nation informed throughout by its gendered history, by the normative masculinities and femininities that have shaped its growth over time. This concept, of the gendered configuration of the postcolonial nation, and, specifically, of the nation embodied *as* woman *by* male leaders, artists and writers, has demonstrated a remarkable charge in recent years, generating a large number of historical, literary and cultural studies. Joining this discussion, it is the contention of this book, too, that gendered, predominantly familial (patriarchal), forms have been invoked, paradoxically, to imagine postcolonial nations into being, and that, reciprocally, constructions of the nation in fiction and other discourses are differentially marked by masculine and feminine systems of value.

What then was the justification for adding yet another book to the expanding group? The answer comes in two parts. First, to a feminist critic it centres on the intriguing reappearance across time, and across nations, including anti-colonial nations, if with inevitable cultural modifications, of women as the *bearers* of national culture. This historical and 'transnational' reiteration is demonstrated in numerous fictional reflections and responses, from men and women writers (and, indeed, in my own continuing fascination with the trope). In this book I am therefore interested in questioning more closely, and in more cross-cultural detail than has been attempted up to this point, the political motivations for, and the possible feminist responses to, this apparent constant.

Yet, although women may be objectified by the nation, where the normative citizen is usually defined as male, there remains – and this would form the second part of my answer – the extraordinary *durability* of the nation-concept, *especially* in relation to liberation politics. Famously contradictory, nationalism can be deployed to reactionary and progressive ends; as a means to self-determination and social justice for an entire people, and a channel of their at once national and international consciousness, *and* as an oppressive formation run in the interests of an elite.[5] The nation has historically not only offered important ways of recovering self and reclaiming cultural integrity after colonial occupation, but has also remained an important ground for transforming political and economic conditions, forging identity and achieving social justice. Not only Janus-faced but protean, adaptative and affiliative rather than derivative, taking on different forms at the hands of different groups and classes, the nation continues to exert a hold on emergent geopolitical entities in quest of self-representation. Despite its 'en-gendering', its liberatory potential remains compelling, also to women. Therefore I was concerned to ask, in the later chapters of the book in particular, why this might be so, and how in an apparently transnational, globalised world, this appeal is expressed. These are questions that to date most discussions of nationalism as a patriarchal project have, as if by definition, tended to avoid.

It would be fair to say that my own critical work on iconic women and their nationalist creators, in particular 'Stories of women and mothers' and 'The master's dance' (expanded as chapters 5 and 3, respectively), played a role in the making of early 1990s gender-and-nation studies. This is demonstrated in their repeated citation, both overt and silent – in particular as regards the *interlocking* of national concepts and signifiers of femininity – in the influential work of critics such as Anne McClintock and Florence Stratton.[6] Crossing feminist critique and postcolonial debates with political theories of the nation, initial attempts (my own and others') to theorise the gender configurations of the postcolonial nation, brought feminist ideas into the heart of a field which was not particularly animated by women's issues *per se*. From such diverse and relatively modest beginnings, postcolonial studies of the woman-as-nation have since travelled widely in feminist circles, and in productive, cross-border ways. In view of this still-ramifying and, it should be said, still-contested interest, I feel it to be productive in this book to revisit and, variously, to elaborate, modify and consolidate my own thinking (and thus my own original essays) on the woman-nation topic. I also aim to do so within a more comparative, cross-cultural frame than I have attempted before, in order critically to reflect upon as well as to reflect the spread of gender-nation theory – as of the phenomenon of woman-as-nation. Taken together, these two interests form a synoptic justification for *Stories of Women*.

The case I wish to develop is, it is worth emphasising, a 'strong' one: not only that woman-as-sign buttresses national imagining, but that gender has been, to date, habitual and apparently intrinsic to national imagining. It is difficult, though not impossible, to conceive (of) the nation without the inscription of specific symbolic roles for male and female historical actors. 'The production of a unified, homogeneous entity such as [the nation] . . . hinges, to a large degree, on the determinate subject position of "woman" for its articulation', and it is this which has led to the entrenched but not irresolvable tension between nationalist and feminist agendas in many countries.[7] In short, national difference, like other forms of difference, is constituted through the medium of the sexual binary, using the figure of the woman as a primary vehicle.[8]

This claim is supported by another, which I share with Sangeeta Ray, Kumkum Sangari, Sudesh Vaid, and others, that *no* theory engaging fully with either (national) resistance or sociality at both micropolitical and macropolitical levels can adopt 'a gender-neutral method of inquiry'.[9] To theorise social relations and space in the absence of feminist theories of spatialisation and modernity is to lose 'a whole line of argument' central to such constructions, as Caren Kaplan emphasises by citing Doreen Massey.[10] Theories of the nation, and indeed of postcolonialism, like those of modernity in Massey's case, remain in this sense 'deeply invested' in their absences.

Yet if this argument respecting gender is one trajectory which *Stories of Women* traces, the second case it wishes to put, which is equally important, and, I would submit, equally generative, pertains to the allegedly compromised relationship of women to the postcolonial nation, given its marked gender differentials. On the face of it, progressive, self-assertive women appear caught in a dilemma, in that the ideology that promises self-expression, liberation and transformation through political action is characterised by their simultaneous marginalisation, and that nationalist resistance has often been resolved in a revivalist direction, reifying traditional gender differences. A number of the chapters in this book certainly take this line. In response to such gender weighting, as other chapters show, postcolonial women writers have questioned, cut across, upended or refused entirely the dominant if not dominatory narrative of the independent nation. They have placed their own subjectivities, sexualities, maternal duties, private stories and intimate pleasures in tension with conventional roles transmitted by national and other traditional narratives.

Yet it is also true, compellingly true, as Kumari Jayawardena urged in the 1980s, that in the twentieth century 'struggles for women's emancipation were an essential and integral part of national resistance movements' across the decolonising world.[11] Indeed, not only have women's political movements often borrowed from nationalist discourses of rights and identity formation (and vice versa),[12] but women nationalists specifically, where they have had the opportunity, have tended to develop the progressive dimensions of nationalism more profitably than their male counterparts. Whereas nationalist movements led by men, especially those of a nativist brand, have promoted cultural homogeneity and feminised traditions, women within such movements have tended to be more concerned with political egalitarianism founded on the recognition of diversity. As in Avtar Brah's reminder (the full version of which pays respects to both Lenin and Fanon): 'nationalist discourses construct and embody a variety of contradictory political and cultural tendencies'; therefore nationalism *can* operate powerfully as a force against oppression.[13]

With this in mind, *Stories of Women* asks whether, in the face of growing communalism on the one hand, and of the rise of economic, political and cultural transnationalism on the other, the nation may once again, or may continue to, provide channels for women's social and political transformation. If the nation may be said to remain a key actor in a globalised world and to lay important ground for political mobilisation against multinational corporations, might it then (still) offer women a platform from which to mount movements of resistance and self-representation? Does it give scope for a new or renewed purchase on public political life? Are women perhaps less ready than before to disavow the nation, despite its lasting gender biases? Transnational and multicultural discourses are after all as eager as nationalism to deploy the reductive concept-metaphor of woman, whereas only the nation, by contrast, specifically invites the woman as citizen to enter modernity and public space. Does the nation, in theory if not yet historically, provide a site of democratic belonging that embraces the domestic context, from which ethnocentrisms and fundamentalisms sometimes far more hostile to women's wellbeing may be questioned?

A study of the interrelationship of gender and nationalism which places itself, as does this book, within the ambit of postcolonial critique, has two important impacts on that body of critical discourse. For one, it usefully re-reminds postcolonial theory of the significance of the nation, as I will explain. For another, it persuasively introduces (and reintroduces) the constitutive reality of sexual difference to a critical practice that has till very recently, unless in passing, tended to overlook this formative legacy. In mainstream postcolonial studies, gender is still conventionally treated in a tokenistic way, or as subsidiary to the category of race. These two impacts correspond to the two major ironies or blind-spots of postcolonial theory which continue even today to compete for centre-stage. For, although the theory emerges from the political actions of the colonised involved in changing the conditions of their lives, great numbers of whom have been feminists and nationalists, postcolonial theorists have to date often neglected or peripheralised the legacies *both* of women's resistance *and* of nationalist struggles for self-determination.

In the 1980s Chandra Mohanty's essay 'Under western eyes' rightly gave warning about western feminism's proprietorial if not colonising approach to Third World women. This is a point to which I will return. Yet, as if sanctioned by this censure, but in fact loftily removed from it, male-authored postcolonial theory, however well-intentioned, has since then remained relatively untouched by any serious consideration of gender, and certainly not of the *engendered nation*, even though the nation has been widely dismissed as monolithic.[14] Similarly, while leading nationalist activists including Fanon have acknowledged the part played by women in national liberation struggles, the relative silence of the dominant postcolonial thinkers on the subject of nationalism, and of women's roles in nationalist movements, has, by contrast, been notable.

Following the work of Ernest Gellner, Étienne Balibar and Immanuel Wallerstein, and, most influentially, Benedict Anderson, the nation is widely conceptualised as a fabricated entity, even though it may be experienced as a community defined by certain 'real' attributes held in common: 'only imaginary communities are real', Balibar writes.[15] Far from being a biological or cultural given, a nation operates as a fiction uniting a people into a horizontally structured conglomerate into which they *imagine* themselves. As with the nation, so, too, for gender. Although experienced as natural, as a fundamental category of identity based on innate difference, gender as the construction of sexual orientation, too, is discursively organised, relationally derived, and culturally variable. Moreover, nationalism and gender have been deployed mutually to invoke and constitute one another (while at the same time being constituted, always inconstantly, frangibly, in relation to other categories of difference also).[16] Benedict Anderson himself once famously underlined the parallel: 'in the modern world everyone can, should, will "have" an identity, as

he or she "has" a gender'.[17] Yet, even if the most persuasive advocate of the
fictive nation thus openly recognised its base in male homosociality ('fraternity'), he was less quick to develop the question of what this meant for the
gender and sexual makeup of the imagined community. What were the reper-
cussions for women in their attempts to enter what Nadine Gordimer once
called the 'commonality' of a country?[18] He declined to be drawn.

It is a refusal or an overlooking, however, in which Anderson is not alone,
whether among theorists of the nation in general, or of postcolonial national
resistance in particular. Here it is helpful to cite a few examples, selected from
among many. Homi Bhabha's controversial though theoretically productive
suggestion that the homogenising 'pedagogies' of the prescriptive national
'master-discourse' are ceaselessly fractured by the performative interventions
of those on its margins, including women, is, despite this inclusion, undis-
turbed by gender.[19] For him, gender is effectively merely another sign of difference. Joe Cleary's *Literature, Partition and the Nation-State* cogently examines
minority divisions within nations, and the problem of conflicting claims to
self-determination where communities are territorially interspersed. Even so,
he erases in the course of his critique the widely recognised minority of
women.[20] Questioning Anderson's elite-based or 'top-down' theory of national
self-invention, he details the conflicting aspirations brought by class, ethnic,
regional and religious differences, yet seemingly overlooks gender. It is thus left
to Partha Chatterjee, when formulating his theory of apparently derivative yet
creatively adaptive Third World nationalisms some ten years or so before
Cleary, to point to gender as the operative means through which the nation distinguishes tradition from modernity. Although Chatterjee is exclusively interested in male proponents of anti-colonial nationalism (perhaps for obvious
historical reasons), his essays insightfully establish the female domestic sphere
as a storehouse of traditional attitudes (specifically for South Asia), one which
enables male nationalists to appropriate the forms of European modernity
while simultaneously conserving an apparent cultural authenticity.[21]

Differently from these thinkers, proponents and theorists of anti-colonial
nationalism, like Frantz Fanon and Nelson Mandela, have openly recognised
the important contribution of women to national struggles, and women's self-
transformation by way of that contribution. Yet even they, as chapter 4 on the
national leader's autobiography will also make clear, do not explore the full
implications of their gendered understanding of the nation and of anti-
colonial movements. Amilcar Cabral, independence leader of Guinea Bissau
and the Cape Verde Islands in the 1960s and early 1970s, for example, pays
noteworthy attention to the differential position of women as against men in
relation to the nation-state. Nonetheless, in his speeches and writing he views
the comrades and martyrs who stood at the head of the nationalist struggle as
normatively, if not exclusively, male: each comrade who has 'fallen under the

bullets of the . . . colonialists [is] identified . . . with all peace-loving men and freedom-loving men everywhere'.[22] On one occasion, during 'an informal talk with Black Americans' in 1972, Cabral acknowledges that his party has made important advances as regards the exclusion of women from power, thus honouring what he describes as the varying forms of recognition given to women among the cultures of his country. But as part of the same response he makes a straightforward further admission: 'We have (even myself) to combat ourselves on this problem [of the cultural marginalisation of women]'.[23] Significantly, the entire comment was made in answer to a question from the group of African Americans; he did not offer it of his own accord.

For Frantz Fanon, the leading theorist of nationalism as an unforgoable phase of opposition to the destructions of colonisation, the anti-colonial struggle is first and foremost always a struggle for 'man's liberation', a struggle waged by men against other men.[24] Such an assumption co-exists with Fanon's often remarkable insights for his time into the gendering and transgendering through which the colonial project is configured, and into how women's investment in anti-colonialism is therefore different from men's. Nationalism, he perceives in the trenchant essay 'Algeria Unveiled', as elsewhere, invokes men and women in contrasting ways, especially as, he writes, both the occupying *colons* and the (male) 'occupied' enlist women as signifiers of culture. Concomitantly, however, woman to Fanon becomes a subject of history *only* through her part in the national resistance. She is uniquely politicised by means of this involvement, and, moreover, politicised in an 'instinctive' way. In the fight for liberation, he revealingly writes, 'Algerian society . . . renewed itself and developed new values governing sexual relations'.[25] Women did not exercise a self-transforming agency in relation to these changes.

However, if gender poses difficulties for male theorists of the nation, how much more, comparatively speaking, has the nation, even Fanon's liberatory nation, become a troubling and troubled concept for many versions of postcolonial theory, in particular those privileging the heterogeneous (and rhetorically 'feminine') over the national and (allegedly) unitary. Developments in Eastern Europe, the former Soviet Union and southern Africa notwithstanding, the nation in the current 'globalised' world is widely and understandably regarded both by historians like Eric Hobsbawm and postcolonial theorists like Paul Gilroy, Deepak Chakrabarty, Achille Mbembe, and many others, as undermined or discredited. Consistently demonstrating elite-driven, appropriative, exclusionary and xenophobic tendencies often carried over from the colonial state, the post-independence nation is seen to have presided over kleptomaniacal surplus extraction, the formation of predatory cartels and contract cabals, and the immiseration of its people. It has fulfilled the predictions of the most pessimistic of its detractors as being 'one-eyed' and hate-filled, as, for example, in the work of self-consciously cosmopolitan writers such as James

Joyce, or, more recently, Salman Rushdie and Michael Ondaatje. As national GDPs widely attest, most Third World countries now are in real terms poorer than they were at independence (or at in-dependence, as a current pun has it). In the face of this evidence, Fanon's vision of the national project as an essential site of liberation struggle has been downgraded in importance relative to his apparently less obviously revolutionary analysis of colonial pathologies, as in *Black Skin, White Masks.*[26]

However, while strongly conditioned by the passing of the triumphal era of anti-colonial struggles, the predominantly metropolitan, postcolonial disaffection about the nation is, it should be acknowledged, equally a function of the (multi-)culturalist, counter-political turn in literary and cultural studies. In the wake of theories of globalisation that appear persuasively to describe de-centred, outsourced and networked conditions in the west, the emphasis is increasingly on the transnational movements of migrancy and diaspora (of floating upwards from history, in Rushdie's phrase, or 'being out of things'[27]). On the road towards this progressive dismissal of the monologic nation, Bhabha's paradigmatic 1990 essay 'DissemiNation', originally intended as a corrective to Benedict Anderson's by then authoritative account of 'the language of national collectiveness and cohesiveness', serves as a significant marker.[28] For Bhabha in this and other essays the discourse of those at the margins of national communities – immigrants, 'women', and so on – produces a performative doubleness that subversively unravels the centrality of the nation (as of the colony).

Against its emphasis on subversion, the ironic effect of Bhabha's work, and of the many imitations it generated, however, was to canonise the equation of the postcolonial with the migrant 'supplement' ('the postcolonial space is now "supplementary"'), demoting the nation as an object of postcolonially correct interest. Within many strands of postcolonial criticism it has thus gradually been forgotten that the nation may be more than a mere counter-force and mirror image to the colonial power it resists. To this it must be added that some of the responsibility for this forgetting can be laid at the feet, too, of feminist critiques of the (patriarchal, univocal) nation, if read superficially. I would want to contend, however, that the more insightful of these critiques have in fact had the reverse effect of *reconfirming* the liberatory potential of self-defining and/or nationalist discourses with respect to women's lives, even if this potential has to date rarely been fully realised. The nation, it is important to bear in mind, remains a place from which to resist the multiple ways in which colonialism distorts and disfigures a people's history.

The narrative of a nation imposes a meaningful chronology and continuity upon the anarchic flux which the coloniser ascribes to the native's past. This is by now a truism of postcolonial literary studies of the nation. Whether critics view the nation as grounded in a material facticity, or, from the other side of the spectrum, as *purely* a fictive 'invention', they tend to find overlapping interests in the area of the nation as conceived through the 'meaning generating institutions' of national literatures.[29] Narrative, like metaphor, can be said to have a discursive materiality; therefore the *story* of the nation permits the forging and testing of particular kinds of affiliation to a national community. Stories, as will be claimed many times in the course of this book, *embody* nations, inscribing a national destiny into time and injecting new life into its myths of the past.[30] In Chinua Achebe, for example, the repossession of a cultural inheritance requires an 'enabling story', to the extent indeed that *story* becomes for him virtually synonymous with words like *meaning* and *consciousness*.[31] From this it follows, as later chapters will show, that a departure from or break in such enabling, form-giving forms, especially where they become officially sanctioned and embedded, has the effect of disrupting, at times profitably, the coercive common destiny or shared cultural tradition that is invoked.

Perhaps the most influential, though also the most contested-against advocate of narrative as a 'process of [national] form-giving', of writing plot into history, is Fredric Jameson, in particular as he expresses his ideas in the widely cited, controversial essay 'Third-world literature in the era of multinational capitalism'.[32] Although Jameson is one of those prominent critical theorists whose work remains largely unperturbed by concerns of gender or the private sphere, his argument informs, indeed insists itself upon the present study, as upon the many readings of Third World writing which have, even so, strenuously sought to disavow his influence. The homogenising, transnationalising 'sweep' of Jameson's proposition regarding Third World writing needs of course to be carefully qualified, with respect to women's writing as to other cultural differences, as several critics have attempted in the wake of Aijaz Ahmad's initial excoriating critique.[33] (Feminist criticism has contended *contra* Jameson, for example, that women's texts focused on the family are not always necessarily intended as emblems of the body politic, although these texts may recognise at the same time that the family is part of that body politic, and may choose to symbolise it.[34]) Given the essay's influence, however, and that way in which it has become virtually paradigmatic in readings of writers ranging from Salman Rushdie and Shashi Tharoor, through Tsitsi Dangarembga and Ngugi wa Thiong'o, to Ian McEwan and Martin Amis, it is worth briefly looking at Jameson's original postulates more closely.

Jameson's 'sweeping hypothesis', as he himself calls it, posited as a countervailing force to the presumptuous criticism of the 'first-world' reader (and an over-aestheticised postmodernism), is encapsulated on a single page of the essay.[35] Here he writes that 'third-world texts, even those which are seemingly private and invested with a properly libidinal dynamic', are to be read as '*national allegories*'. '[T]he story of the private individual is *always* an allegory of the embattled situation of the public third-world culture and society' (emphasis added). By contrast, he further suggests, the First World text is not conscious of its nationalising designs in the same way. I would want to suggest against this, however, that many narratives preoccupied with the social and national imaginary can be understood as inscribing the nation, and that these nation-informing stories are by no means exclusive to the Third World. Indeed, many hail from the First World. If anything, this has become more evidently the case with the 1990s resurgence of nationalist preoccupations in the west and in the former Second World (think only of devolution in the UK).

Few would probably dispute the fact that nationalism remains a crucial force for liberation and justice *especially* in once-colonised countries. It is also true that the novels of these countries *in particular* will be concerned to configure the nation by way of organising (and often gendered) metaphors, if not strictly speaking as allegories in every case. For these elite-generated narratives, Jameson's thesis is almost a necessary hypothesis, as Neil Lazarus has argued; or, at least, a self-fulfilling prophecy.[36] Yet these metaphors and allegories are, I would say, discernible in most novels that collude with and condone processes of nationalist self-determination – such is the insight of Jameson's hypothesis. Take only such examples as Peter Carey's rewriting of Rushdie for Australia in *Illywhacker* (1985), Don de Lillo's *Underworld* (1997), which charts a 'half-century' in the 'soul' of American culture, and Ian McEwan's *Atonement*, a 2001 revisiting of the impact of the Second World War on British social identities. Texts such as these reflect back not only on Jameson's but also on Benedict Anderson's hypothesis, advanced some years prior to Jameson's, and without the same level of critical opposition, namely, that the modern novel is a key site where the nation is articulated.[37]

For obvious reasons, most notably that gender like the nation is composed by way of fictions, the concept of narrating the self represents a central area of *cross-over* between the study of *women's writing* and *postcolonial studies*. Although women writers tend perhaps to be especially concerned with those narratives that cannot be integrated into the grand teleological march of official history, they, too, deploy the genre to claim and configure national and other identities. By conveying women's complex give-and-take between public and private spaces, women writers use the novel as a powerful instrument with which to reshape national cultures in a way more hospitable to women's presence.[38]

At this point, however, invoking the broad category of 'women' in this apparently homogenising way, it is right that I bring myself up short, not before time, in order to offer a partial apologia by way of closing this section. A question that will unavoidably arise from the foregoing paragraphs is whether my references throughout this book to 'what women do' invite the charge of universalism – just as much indeed as does Jameson's sweeping 1986 gesture? Its progressive commitments notwithstanding, a feminist study such as this, written from within the western academy and seeming to pronounce upon the cultural productions of Third World women and men, inevitably runs the risk of 'collapsing' the world into the west.[39] Displacing subaltern interests, or so it might appear, a study of this kind can seem to become complicit with the 'rewriting and silencing' projects of patriarchy and imperialism. As Spivak cautions: 'a concern with women, *and* men, who have not been written in the *same* cultural inscription . . . cannot be mobilised in the same way as the investigation of gendering in one's own'.[40] Juliana Nfah-Abbenyi encapsulates a related, itself Spivakian, point when she observes that the 'spoken for' 'is no speaking subject'.[41]

Within feminism as within postcolonial studies the difficult question of *speaking for* resists satisfactory philosophical resolution, yet it may to some extent be politically negotiated. To begin with it must be emphatically stated that this book does not seek at any point to set up Third World woman as a *symbol* for the global struggles of 'women', or indeed for any struggle at all – unless self-elected. On the contrary. While giving non-western nationalist and women's texts a hearing, I have explicitly attempted to avoid lassoo-ing these texts into my own symbolic system or political programme. Against such a *commandement* approach, I recognise along with Françoise Lionnet, Caren Kaplan, Sangeeta Ray and others, that feminism must be viewed *both* as respect for the specificity of historical differences between women, *and*, even if aspirationally, as a relational, global process, that permits intersubjective exchange and cross-category comparatism. This is especially so in situations where the inequalities in power that impact on women's lives are contested.[42] The assertion of locale and particularity, which is often proffered as a countervailing force to globalising tendencies of feminism, can equally run the risk simply of interpreting the world in terms of the self, forgetting that cultures are fields of interrelationship that exist in dialogue. In contradistinction to this, a qualified, relational feminism that avoids prioritising any one axis of difference over any other should enable women to assert a politically effective even if always provisional consensus about issues in common to be addressed. Hence the comparative framework I have adopted for many of the chapters.

In short, a relational approach allows women, at least in principle, *both* to proclaim the specificity of their particular historical experience, *yet also* to affirm common interests and political transformations across cultural and national borders, as they act from a commitment to social justice for those constructed 'woman'. As Kadiatu Kanneh has described the 'Black feminism' of Ama Ata Aidoo's idiosyncratic novel *Our Sister Killjoy* (1977):

> The feminism of the text is, then, deliberately and inescapably placed within specific cultural locations, at the point of conflict between dominant and subordinate national identities. [It is] . . . both a re-evaluation of African femininity *in respect of African communities and men*, and a re-examination of racial and cultural differences *between women*. (emphasis added)[43]

My concomitant commitment is to 'read' and interrelate across boundaries, or as Lionnet urges, borrowing a line from Spivak (which might equally come from Emmanuel Levinas or Judith Butler): for feminism there is always a simultaneous other focus, 'not merely who am I? But who is the other woman?'[44] Feminism, Kumari Jayawardena usefully reminds us, has no ethnic identity. Even if they have in practice usually occupied secondary or minority positions, women – 'girls at war' – have always been part of democratic and revolutionary movements.[45]

Outline

In summary, *Stories of women* submits that literary texts – here especially novels and autobiographies – are central vehicles in the imaginative construction of new nations, and that gender plays a central, formative role in that construction. Postcolonial nationalist identities, iconographies and traditions are refracted through gender-tagged concepts of power, leadership, lineage and filiation, including, for instance, maternal images of nurturing and service. Developing these ideas, the book will consider how national father/son and mother figures were used in the independence era to imagine the nation into being. It will also look at how later generations of writers, both women and men, reworked those original form-giving symbols in order that they might bear the burden of their own experience. Taking a broadly cross-national approach tacking between West, East and southern Africa and South Asia in particular, *Stories of Women* balances comparative discussions informed by feminist and postcolonial theory, against situated readings of key emblematic texts. The comparative dimension is central to the book's conception, probing that tendency underlying many recent gender-nation studies to expound in general terms yet focus on only one particular region or nation – India, Africa or the Caribbean – by way of illustration.

As a structure *Stories of women* falls roughly into three (unmarked) parts, framed by the Introduction and the Conclusion, though there are numerous intertextual links connecting different chapters between and across these ostensible divides. First, chapters 1 to 4 group together to theorise and exemplify the gendered formation of the nation in text. Chapter 1, 'Motherlands, mothers and nationalist sons', examines why and how, overdetermined by colonial history, national structures in post-independent nations have conventionally been organised according to masculine patterns of authority, in particular the *family drama*, embodied in images like 'father of the nation', 'son of the soil'. Women, by contrast, are cast into the more passive roles/metaphors of motherland, Mother Africa, Bharat Mata. The next three chapters concerning, respectively, Ngugi's representation of women, the later writing of Achebe, and the male leader's autobiography in India and Africa, explore the textual inflections and intensifications of the national family plot. Of chief concern are the contradictions that lie at the heart of the nationalist project, essentially, that a liberatory mode of thought and organisation in practice produces discriminatory structures. So the elder statesmen of African literature, the Kenyan Ngugi and the Nigerian Achebe, set out in their later novels to construct historically redemptive roles for their central women characters – roles which turn out, however, to be as objectifying as the iconic mother roles of the past. Chapter 4, 'The hero's story', which looks at the independence autobiographies by national leaders such as Nehru and Mandela, Nkrumah and Kenyatta, further explores the self-imprisoning circularity involved in writing the nation as the male subject self. Where the story of the growth to self-consciousness of the independence leader presents as a synonym for the rise of the nation, and where that leader has historically been male, it follows that national-son figures become the inheritors of the nation's future. Some mention will be made of the self-representation of Sarojini Naidu as a political leader, whereas she appears in her westernised persona of ethereal poet in chapter 9.

Taking different generational and national perspectives, chapters 5 and 6, 'Stories of women and mothers' and 'Daughters of the house', form the conceptual hinge around which the book turns. They reprise the nation's symbolic legacy in relation to women, and then ask how post-independence women writers have addressed this legacy. First, what is the approach of women writers to the overdetermination of the nurturing 'motherland' myth, the symbolic co-ordinates and determinations of which appear inimical to women's investment in the postcolonial nation? And, second, how do they set about writing the erased or marginalised role of the daughter, indeed of the daughter-writer, into the male-authored national family script? How do they locate a (writerly and/or actual) national home? Even if preoccupied with the personal, interstitial and apparently microcosmic, these chapters suggest writers such as Flora Nwapa and Buchi Emecheta, as well as Christina Stead, Shashi Deshpande and Carol Shields, self-consciously work in resistance to the exclusions of the national family drama and establish alternative patterns of political affiliation.

The final five chapters connect through the medium of their concern with the *re-imagining* of community, nationality, subjectivity, sexuality or the native body, especially as a response to the agon of disillusionment of the neocolonised nation – or the *postcolony* in Achille Mbembe's now widely accepted phrase, discussed in chapter 7. Whereas the focus at the centre-point of the book was on postcolonial *women* as the 'spoken-for' of national traditions, chapters 7 and 8 act on the idea central to gender theory, namely, that the construction of one mode of sexual difference cannot be viewed in isolation from another. Gender cannot be seen as solely commensurate with 'woman'[46] – or, indeed, mother figures with nationalist self-projections, as was clear also from the discussion of the leader's autobiography.

Chapter 7, 'Transfiguring', which explores postcolonial retrieval of the figure of the native body in colonial discourse, unpicks the complex interconnections between colonialism, nationalism, hysteria, gender and sexuality. It concentrates in particular on postcolonial attempts – by Nuruddin Farah, Bessie Head and Michelle Cliff, among others – to recuperate or transfigure the native/colonised body by way of the 'talking cure' of narrative. Chapter 8, 'The nation as metaphor', investigates the self-interpellation and self-inscription of second-generation male writers as indifferently national subjects. Under a range of pressures from the global market to internal economic tensions and minoritarian divisions, the nation has increasingly been exposed as *destructive fiction* and experienced as trauma. The Zimbabwean writers Chenjerai Hove and Dambudzo Marechera, and the British-resident Nigerian novelist and poet Ben Okri, experiment with metaphor, nightmare and fetish as the signifiers of a national reality, as opposed to viewing the nation as literal truth. The postcolony here becomes phantasmagoria and malaise.

Chapter 9, 'East is east', on postcolonialism as neo-orientalist, continues the focus on the colonialist filiations underlying post-independence representations of the colonised body, especially the female body. A study of the *fin-de-siècle* construction of Sarojini Naidu as Indian female poet in the 1890s, and of the literary and publishing phenomenon of Arundhati Roy in the 1990s, explores how, in almost imperceptible ways, the past of colonial discourse repeats itself upon the present that is postcolonial criticism. Here, too, the reified female body is a central, governing emblem. By contrast, 'Tropes of yearning and dissent', chapter 10, extends the discussion of the interrelationship of gender and nation into an area rarely mentioned if not taboo in discourses both colonial and postcolonial, namely, the same-sex desire of women. By evoking women's unruly, erotic yearnings, the two prominent Zimbabwean writers Tsitsi Dangarembga and Yvonne Vera explore the libidinal energies that exceed, or leak out between the fractures of, the conservative postcolonial state.

Approaching from a different perspective the work of Vera and Arundhati Roy, the final chapter, 'Beside the west', returns to the question of how women writers, specifically of a younger generation, theorise and re-emblematise the nation in their work. Whereas some women writers choose to distance themselves from the nation as extraneous to their concerns, these two writers are representative of a subtly different approach. In the face of neocolonial disillusionment and the erasures of identity threatened by globalisation, they extend the 'revisionary scepticism' concerning the homogenising nation they share with their male counterparts,[47] yet strategically play off its different narratives – of patriliny and matriliny, of modernity and tradition – against one another. Avoiding the stance of spokesperson and the all-commanding epic voice, they reframe the male-defined co-ordinates of national selfhood in relation to other modes of situating identity, such as those of region, environment, belief and sexuality, without however refusing the nation altogether. They explore, in other words, the transformative instabilities of the nation viewed at once as narrative construct and as lived reality, intersecting different, contrapuntal discourses and practices. A reading of the Indian writer Manju Kapur's first two novels focusing on Partition and the Ayodhya crisis, decisive moments in the Indian national story, closes this study, developing further the idea of the redemptive nation as a countervailing space for women as against the threats posed by communalism.

Across in particular the latter half of *Stories of women* it is broadly contended therefore that writers, mainly women writers but also men, radically transform the conditions of national self-identification by viewing the nation not as a static but a relational space. The nation's value, they propose, comes not from a historically fixed, 'authentic' character but from an intersubjective exchange as to its meanings; not from stories *about* iconic women, but through interlinked stories *by* diverse women and men participants in the nation. The idea of the liberation of the soul of the oppressed that lies at the heart of anticolonial nationalism often retains its old power to convince, yet styles of nationalist belief are changing – have indeed had to change under the pressures of post-independence history. The nation-state remains entrenched as a bounding reality, but even so the concept of the nationalist fiction, *the nation as fiction*, provides diverse possibilities of self-conception for a people: not a single shining path of self-realisation, but any number of symbolic fictions, as many modes of redreaming as there are dreamers in a nation.

Notes

1 Gayatri Chakravorty Spivak, *A Critique of Postcolonial Reason: Toward a History of the Vanishing Present* (Cambridge MA: Harvard University Press, 1999), p. 188.

2 Quoted in Shamin Meer (ed.), *Women Speak: Reflections on our Struggles 1982–1997* (Cape Town: Kwela, 1998), pp. 44–5.

3 Chinua Achebe, 'Girls at war', in *Girls at War and Other Stories* [1972] (London: Heinemann, 1986), pp. 98–118. Page references will henceforth be cited in the text along with the abbreviation *GW*. As a suggestive contrast with Achebe's characterisations, see the discussion of literary representations of Biafra and of women's involvement in the conflict in the section on Buchi Emecheta in chapter 6, pp. 114–18.

4 Reginald's surrender to Gladys's charms does not form a moral issue in the story. As a highly placed government official, his improprieties may be significant, yet as an official and the narrator he represents normative male humanity and national citizenry. Masculine roles in national life are, as I will suggest, largely metonymic.

5 On national consciousness as 'universalising', and on the many paradoxes of liberatory nationalism, see Frantz Fanon, 'On national culture', *The Wretched of the Earth* [1961], trans. Constance Farrington (Harmondsworth: Penguin, 1985), pp. 166–99.

6 For attributed and unattributed citations, see Anne McClintock, *Imperial Leather: Race, Gender and Sexuality in the Colonial Contest* (London and New York: Routledge, 1995), pp. 354–5, but also p. 357; Sangeeta Ray, *En-gendering India: Woman and Nation in Colonial and Postcolonial Narratives* (Durham NC and London: Duke University Press, 2000), p. 129; Florence Stratton, *Contemporary African Literature and the Politics of Gender* (London and New York: Routledge, 1994), pp. 60, 162, 167, 168, but also p. 163.

7 See Ray, *En-gendering India*, p. 16.

8 Avtar Brah, *Cartographies of Diaspora: Contesting Identities* (London: Routledge, 1996), p. 156.

9 Kumkum Sangari and Sudesh Vaid, 'Introduction' to Kumkum Sangari and Sudesh Vaid (eds), *Recasting Women: Essays in Indian Colonial History* (New Brunswick: Rutgers University Press, 1990), pp. 2–3.

10 Caren Kaplan, *Questions of Travel: Postmodern Discourses of Displacement* (Durham NC: Duke University Press, 1996), pp. 152–6 in particular. See also Doreen Massey, *Space, Place and Gender* (Oxford: Polity, 1994).

11 Kumari Jayawardena, *Feminism and Nationalism in the Third World* (London: Zed Press, 1986), p. 8.

12 For a useful outline of the common ground between nationalism and feminism, see Anu Celly, 'The battle within and without: story as history, nation as woman', in Jasbir Jain and Avadesh Kumar Singh (eds), *Indian Feminisms* (New Delhi: Creative Books, 2001), pp. 196–206.

13 Brah, *Cartographies of Diaspora*, pp. 162–3.

14 Chandra Talpade Mohanty, 'Under western eyes: feminist scholarship and colonial discourses', *Feminist Review*, 30 (Autumn 1988), 65–88. With the term 'male-authored theory' I attempt to avoid singling out any particular critic for their gender-blindness, as, up until the publication of Robert Young's *Postcolonialism: A Very Short Introduction* (Oxford: Oxford University Press, 2003), the condition has been so widespread as to be well-nigh universal.

15 Ernest Gellner, *Nations and Nationalisms* (Oxford: Blackwell, 1983); Benedict Anderson, *Imagined Communities: Reflections on the Origin and Spread of Nationalisms* [1983], rev. edn (London: Verso, 1991); Étienne Balibar and Immanuel Wallerstein, *Race, Nation, Class: Ambiguous Identities*, trans. Chris Turner (London: Verso, 1991), p. 93.

16 On this mutual imbrication, see Andrew Parker, Mary Russo, Doris Sommer and Patricia Yaeger, 'Introduction' to Andrew Parker *et al.* (eds), *Nationalisms and Sexualities* (New York and London: Routledge, 1982), pp. 1–18. Marjorie Howes, *Yeats's Nations: Gender, Class, and Irishness* (Cambridge: Cambridge University Press, 1996), pp. 7–15, offers an illuminating account of the intimate embeddedness of gender and nationality, yet of their simultaneous fluidity of construction in relation to each other and to other categories of identity.

17 Anderson, *Imagined Communities*, p. 5.

18 Nadine Gordimer, *Writing and Being: The Charles Eliot Norton Lectures* (Cambridge MA: Harvard University Press, 1995), p. 132. For Gordimer, too, this commonality has historically been 'raced' rather than 'gendered'.

19 Homi Bhabha, 'DissemiNation: time, narrative and the margins of the modern nation', in Bhabha (ed.), *Nation and Narration* (London and New York: Routledge, 1990), pp. 297–302.

20 Joe Cleary, *Literature, Partition and the Nation-State: Culture and Conflict in Ireland, Israel and Palestine* (Cambridge: Cambridge University Press, 2002), for example, pp. 16–18. As a further case in point, a keynote 1990s collection on the subject of imagined communities, Gopal Balakrishnan (ed.), *Mapping the Nation* (London: Verso, 1996), includes only two women contributors in a list of more than ten – Sylvia Walby, 'Woman and nation', and Katherine Verdery, 'Whither "nation and "nationalism"?' Verdery sees the nation as past its peak due to globalisation, even if it is still accepted as a 'natural condition' for peoples; Walby bravely asserts that although women's struggles have local, national and international dimensions, gender and the nation need to be addressed in the context of one another, pp. 235–54. For other examples of postcolonial theorists 'untroubled' by or disengaged from gender, see Stratton, *Contemporary African Literature*, pp. 1–19; Ray, *En-gendering India*, pp. 4, 158–9; and chapter 1 in this book.

21 See Partha Chatterjee, in particular 'The nationalist resolution of the woman question', in Sangari and Vaid (eds), *Recasting Women*; and *The Nation and its Fragments: Colonial and Postcolonial Histories* (Princeton: Princeton University Press, 1994); but also *Nationalist Thought and the Colonial World – A Derivative Discourse?* (London: Zed Press, 1986).

22 Amilcar Cabral, 'Second address before the United Nations', *Return to the Source* (New York and London: Monthly Review Press, 1973), p. 19.

23 Cabral, 'Connecting the struggles: an informal talk with Black Americans', *Return to the Source*, pp. 85–6. For an alternative reading of this passage, see Laura Chrisman, 'Nationalism and postcolonial studies', in Neil Lazarus (ed.), *The Cambridge Companion to Postcolonial Literary Studies* (Cambridge: Cambridge University Press, 2004), pp. 183–98.

24 See, respectively, Frantz Fanon, *Black Skin, White Masks* [1952], trans. Charles Lam Markmann (London: Pluto, 1986), and *Towards the African Revolution*, trans. Haakon Chevalier (London: Penguin, 1967), p. 48, but any random sampling of pages will demonstrate the point. See also Robert Young, *Postcolonialism: An Historical Introduction* (Oxford: Blackwell, 2001), p. 274.

25 See Frantz Fanon, 'Algeria unveiled' and 'The Algerian family', *Studies in a Dying Colonialism* (London: Earthscan, 1989), pp. 35–67, and 109, respectively. On Fanon and gender, see the finely nuanced reading given by Madhu Dubey, 'The "true lie" of the nation: Fanon and feminism', *differences*, 10:2 (1998). See also McClintock, *Imperial Leather*, pp. 360–8; Bart Moore-Gilbert, 'Frantz Fanon: en-gendering nationalist discourse', *Women: A Cultural Review*, 7:2 (1996), 125–35; Kalpana Seshadri-Crooks, 'I am a master: terrorism, masculinity and political violence in Frantz Fanon', *Parallax*, 8:2 (2002), 84–98; Heather Zwicker, 'The nervous conditions of nation and gender', in Anne E. Willey and Jeanette Treiber (eds), *Negotiating the Postcolonial: Emerging Perspectives on Tsitsi Dangarembga* (Trenton, NJ: Africa World Press, 2002), pp. 3–23, an essay which discusses Dangarembga's gendered response to Fanon's 'gender-neutral' vision of the nation. For a commentary on

Fanon's nationalism as representing a socialist rather than merely a decolonising demand, see Neil Lazarus's chapter, 'Disavowing decolonisation', *Nationalism and Cultural Practice in the Postcolonial World* (Cambridge: Cambridge University Press, 1999), pp. 68–143.

26 See Lazarus, *Nationalism and Cultural Practice*, pp. 79–82.

27 Salman Rushdie, *Shame* (London: Cape, 1983), pp. 24, 63.

28 See Bhabha, 'DissemiNation', pp. 291–322; and also Rosemary Marangoly George's commentary in *The Politics of Home: Postcolonial Relocations and Twentieth-century Fiction* (Berkeley: University of California Press, 1996), pp. 186–8.

29 Cleary, *Literature, Partition and the Nation-State*, p. 57.

30 Richard Kearney, *On Stories* (London and New York: Routledge, 2002), p. 85.

31 Chinua Achebe, *Home and Exile* (Oxford and New York: Oxford University Press, 2000), p. 60, and see also p. 79. As the Old Man from Abazon observes in *Anthills of the Savannah* (London: Heinemann, 1987), p. 124, discussed in chapter 2: 'the story [continues] beyond the war and the warrior . . . it is the story that owns us and directs us'.

32 Fredric Jameson, 'Figural relativism', and 'Criticism and History', in *Situations of Theory: Essays 1971–1986*, vol. 1 (London and New York: Routledge, 1989), pp. 155, 127; and 'Third-World literature in the era of multinational capitalism', *Social Text*, 15 (1986), pp. 65–88. As Gayatri Spivak, *In Other Worlds: Essays in Cultural Politics* (London: Routledge, 1988), p. 85, similarly writes: the novel in general can thus be read as a '"nonexpository" theory of practice'.

33 See Aijaz Ahmad, 'Jameson's rhetoric of otherness and the "national allegory"', *In Theory: Classes, Nations, Literatures* (London and New York: Verso, 1992), pp. 95–122; first published in *Social Text* 19 (1987), pp. 3–26; and, for a convincing riposte to his riposte, see in particular, Neil Lazarus, 'Fredric Jameson on "third-world literature": a qualified defence', in Sean Home and Douglas Kellner (eds), *Fredric Jameson: A Critical Reader* (Basingstoke, Palgrave, 2004), pp. 42–61. I am grateful to Neil for an advance copy of this essay, given as a paper at the 'Connecting Cultures' colloquium, University of Kent, 15 March 2003. See also Laura Chrisman, *Postcolonial Contraventions: Cultural Readings of Race, Imperialism and Transnationalism* (Manchester: Manchester University Press, 2003), pp. 51–70.

34 See for example Susan Andrade, *The Nation Writ Small* (Durham, NC: Duke University Press, forthcoming). I am grateful to Susan Andrade for sending me drafts of her book chapters and for our continuing conversation on gender and the nation.

35 Jameson, 'Third-world literature in the era of multinational capitalism', p. 96; see also Lazarus, 'Fredric Jameson on "third-world literature"'.

36 On the Indian postcolonial novel in English as a nation metaphor, see also Amit Chaudhuri, 'Forms of renewal', *TLS*, 5262 (6 February 2004), 13.

37 Anderson, *Imagined Communities*, pp. 26–34.

38 Louise Yelin, *From the Margins of Empire: Christina Stead, Doris Lessing, Nadine Gordimer* (Ithaca and London: Cornell University Press, 1998), pp. 7–8; Stratton, *Contemporary African Literature*, p. 10.

39 Susie Tharu and K. Lalita, 'Introduction' to Tharu and Lalita (eds), *Women's*

Writing in India 600 B.C. to the Present, vol. 1 (New Delhi: Oxford University Press, 1991), p. 23.

40 Spivak, *A Critique of Postcolonial Reason*, p. 176.

41 Juliana Makuchi Nfah-Abbenyi, *Gender in African Women's Writing* (Bloomington: Indiana University Press, 1997), p. 5.

42 Françoise Lionnet, *Postcolonial Representations: Women, Literature, Identity* (Ithaca: Cornell University Press, 1995), in particular pp. 2–4. Lionnet's relational feminism also bears comparison with Avtar Brah's feminist 'politics of intersectionality'.

43 Kadiatu Kanneh, *African Identities: Race, Nation and Culture in Ethnography, Pan-Africanism and Black Literatures* (New York and London: Routledge, 1998), p. 154.

44 See Brah, *Cartographies of Diaspora*, p. 176; Gayatri Spivak, 'French feminism in an international frame', *Yale French Studies*, 62 (1981), 179. See also Teresa de Lauretis, 'Displacing hegemonic discourses: reflections on feminist theory in the 1980s', *Inscriptions*, 3–4 (1988), 136.

45 Jayawardena, *Feminism and Nationalism*, p. 4.

46 See Sara Suleri, 'Woman skin deep: feminism and the postcolonial condition', *Critical Inquiry*, 18:4 (Summer 1992), 756–69.

47 Jon Mee, 'After midnight: the Indian novel in English of the 80s and 90s', *Postcolonial Studies*, 1:1 (1998), pp. 127–41, in particular pp. 132 and 134.

1

Motherlands, mothers and nationalist sons: theorising the en-gendered nation

Woman is an infinite, untrodden territory of desire which at every stage of historical deterritorialisation, men in search of material for utopias have inundated with their desires. (Klaus Theweleit, *Male Fantasies*)[1]

Among postcolonial and feminist critics it is now widely accepted that the nationalist ideologies which informed, in particular, the first wave of independence movements and of postcolonial literatures from 1947, are cast in a gendered mould. Nationalism, which has been so fundamental to the decolonisation process around the world, bears a clear mark for gender, and this gender marking, rather than being referred to a monolithic or transhistorical concept of patriarchy, can be explained as a specific historical development of power defined by sexual difference. To put it more plainly, this book submits that, without this marking for gender, it is well-nigh impossible to conceive of the modern nation. Whether we look at its iconography, its administrative structures or its policies, the new postcolonial nation is historically a male-constructed space, narrated into modern self-consciousness by male leaders, activists and writers, in which women are more often than not cast as symbols or totems, as the bearers of tradition.

Stories of women explores the intricate, often paradigmatic negotiations between gender, sexuality and the post-independence nation which have marked postcolonial narratives, including novels by women, from the independence period up to the present day. The central concept informing the book, therefore, which this chapter will theorise, and the following chapters will further exemplify and expand, is that gender forms *the* formative dimension for the construction of nationhood, if in relation to varying contextual determinants across different regions and countries. This is a point which, with remarkable unanimity, leading male theorists of the nation such as Benedict Anderson, Eric Hobsbawm, and Anthony Smith have either ignored or failed to address, often choosing even so to define the nation, whether overtly or covertly, as normatively a male terrain, a masculine enterprise.

By contrast, since the mid-1990s there has been a virtual boom in gender-and-nation studies by women critics, including Susan Andrade, Nelufer de Mel, Marjorie Howes, Deniz Kandyoti, Anne McClintock, Sangeeta Ray, Rajeswari Sunder Rajan, Florence Stratton, Kumkum Sangari and myself. These critics have examined in close-up, if from different perspectives, and with respect to different constituencies (Africa, South Asia, Ireland, the Caribbean), 'the manipulation of gender politics in the exercise of national rule', the nation's 'sanctioned institutionalisation of gender difference' – the 'en-gendering' of the nation, in Ray's pithy phrase.[2] What, such critics ask, are the rationales and mechanisms through which the nation is almost invariably expressed as a male or male-led community in the Anglophone world, one which may, however, simultaneously be symbolised in the overarching figure of a woman: the woman-as-nation? How is it that, whether nationalism speaks the language of emptiness and desire, or of fulfilment and achievement of meaning, the codification of that meaning, of self and of those objects of desire, is gendered? Moreover, they contend that this gender weighting has historically tended to delimit nationalist identifications by women, although not universally so, and recently to a lesser extent, as my final chapters will suggest.

But first I want to epitomise these central ideas by considering two definitive novels, and relevant selected intertexts, in which the fortunes of embryonic nations are embodied in hero figures, comparable to how in Benedict Anderson or Ernest Gellner the nation is emblematised as a horizontal 'fraternity' or intellectual brotherhood.[3] Peter Abrahams's *A Wreath for Udomo* (1956) remarkably presages the trade-offs and compromises of Ghana's achievement of independence, Africa's first nation to be decolonised from Britain. Salman Rushdie's *Midnight's Children* (1981) retrospectively allegorises India's birth as a nation, a process already symbolically mediated by the political discourse of the 'tryst with destiny'.[4] Although they differ in multiple ways, the two novels have in common several paradigms of new nationality and the postcolonial nation founded on the imagery of national sons. To open the discussion with these two novels is in itself an anticipatory and symbolic gesture, in that Africa and India will comprise the two postcolonial 'constituencies' predominantly represented by this book.

Ranging across the wide terrain of African literature of the 1950s, 1960s and 1970s, the nationalist hero, often exiled or alienated from home (mother and heart(h)land), is cast as resilient and courageous (the soldier, the leader); idealistic or visionary (the poet); or resourceful, even omnicompetent (where women are absent from the arena of action, men must learn to 'do' for themselves). Michael Udomo in Peter Abrahams's *A Wreath for Udomo* is a representative case.[5] *A Wreath for Udomo* is a tale of exile from and return to Africa embodied in the activist Udomo's efforts to claim self-government for his nation and identity for his people, initially from the base of London. As the chief liberator he stands in the dominant position in the text; its positive terms (reason, assertiveness, resourcefulness, conviction) are confirmed in his character and action. He is also, unsurprisingly, vigorously masculine: he is the leader of '[o]ur young men [who] must ceaselessly prepare themselves for the fight'.

Contrasted with Udomo and highlighting his status as the one true national leader, are two centres of rival power, each in some way a negation or aberration of those characteristics and qualities which Udomo incarnates. On the one side are the members of the exiled elite (all male) who are at first suitably rational and freedom-loving, but who eventually fall from grace, turning to 'tribalism' and subverting Udomo's plans. On the other are 'the women', all of them either inconsequential or deviant. The single positive female symbol is that of Africa. It is only in an idealised form, purged of her materiality and her other-than-spiritual sexuality, that the feminine can be strong and single-minded. As her single upright and constant devotee, Udomo wins the right to be the follower and consort of Mother Africa and her most eloquent worshipper. On returning to Africa to claim power, he salutes the shoreline in tones of annunciation and adoration. Ardently identifying with sun/son imagery, Udomo claims agency and 'sonship' for himself: 'Mother Africa! Oh, Mother Africa, make me strong for the work that I must do. Don't forget me in the many you nurse. I would make you great. I would have the world respect you and your children. I would have the sun of freedom shine over you once more'.[6]

The sentiment of Udomo's cries, the yearning to cleave, champion and unite, recalls something of the longing and striving expressed in (the historically prior) Negritude poetry, once described as a 'vindication of the black *man's* humanity in the face of the white man's racism' (my emphasis).[7] The speaker in Negritude poetry is invariably male; the object of his desire female. Assuming the attitude of a supplicant and worshipper, the Negritude poet addresses himself to Africa, continent of his people, location of their historical memory, and conceived of in womanly form. Again, Africa is never so much Africa as when the landmass is incarnated as woman, as a manifestation of the people's (alleged and acclaimed) corporeality, mystery and sensuality. In Léopold Senghor's much-quoted poem 'Femme nue, femme noire', for instance, the woman is apostrophised as Beloved and as desirable body.[8] Her physical form is glorified, even fetishised: it is a body triumphantly corporeal, entirely body, and thus, in terms of the values endorsed by the poetry, a true embodiment of Africa. Yet, even if sexualised, her form is also maternal; she is the nurturing presence of the past: '*J'ai grandi à ton ombre; la douceur de tes mains bandait mes yeux*' ('In your shadow I have grown up; the gentleness of your hands was laid over my eyes').[9] Love for home and Africa is expressed simultaneously as sexual desire and as filial adoration – a yearning to cleave with a/the body of the land that is at once maternal lap and lapping flesh of the desired woman. The conjuncture is possible because the land of the poet's desire is both the place of his childhood dreams, associated with his mother, and the cherished object of his present need and future hope.

Camara Laye is not strictly speaking a Negritude writer, yet his terms of apostrophe in recalling Africa and the African woman, also produced in the 1950s, are similarly lyrical, even rhapsodic, and again bear comparison with those of Udomo. *L'Enfant Noir* (1953) (*The Dark Child* (1955)), which is roughly contemporaneous with *A Wreath for Udomo*, is the nostalgic autobio-graphical account of Laye's Cameroonian childhood and its hankering for the African heart(h)land is intensely mother-bonded.[10] Laye's mother is the still point – though far from voiceless – to which the increasingly more alienated child returns for sustenance. Echoing her centrality, the novel begins with a dedication which is also, as for Udomo, an invocation from an exiled son: a call to 'my mother', who is also Mother, a generic 'Black Woman, Woman of Africa', a muse of, simultaneously, nostalgic longing and belonging. In contrast to this mystic mother force, the male characters in Camara Laye's autobiogra-phy have specific jobs of work to do and a more localised power – the father is a goldsmith, the son an engineer-to-be. As the practical actors and authors of African life, males are the more normatively human.

If we are to believe Aijaz Ahmad's persuasive case concerning the canonisa-tion of writing preoccupied with national experience as 'Third World' litera-ture, Salman Rushdie is the definitive 'Third World' writer, not least because he is at the same time a leading proponent of postmodernist narrative form.[11] Rushdie himself repeatedly dramatises and literalises the understanding which forms the point of critical focus of this book: that 'legends make reality', 'homelands' are for a large part imaginary, and, to round off the syllogism, that the nation is as much a fictional construct as it is real.[12] The highly influential *Midnight's Children* and *Shame* (1983) thus do not hesitate to narrativise and allegorise the postcolonial histories of India and Pakistan, portraying these in terms of ironic epic and caricature, respectively.

Unsurprisingly for two such self-aware national allegories, both *Midnight's Children* and *Shame* are knitted together using the complicated, symbolically loaded lines of family trees, or the paradigm of the nation as family, which, cer-tainly in the case of *Shame*, reflects the monopolistic operation of nepotistic power. At the same time, in particular in the earlier novel, national history is played out in the life of a single protagonist, clearly identified as male, as a son figure: Saleem Sinai in *Midnight's Children*, and, in *Shame*, the more 'periph-eral hero', Omar Khayyam Shakil. The destinies of both characters match, or at least march in step with, the fortunes of their nation: as Saleem says, state and self are equated. The same could not be said of the dominant female characters. Their roles *vis-à-vis* the nation and the national family, by contrast, occupy an idealised or fabulistic sphere, one that is cast, even by the second-guessing, 'India-as-mother'-aware Rushdie, in essentialised, at times misogynistic terms.[13]

Midnight's Children is of course a novel teeming with plots, sub-plots and multiple minor heroes, not least the thousand other children of the independence hour, Saleem's virtual brothers and sisters. Even so, the relationship that provides the central axis for the novel's entire second half develops between the child of midnight, the hyper-symbolic Saleem – Hindu and Muslim, highborn yet plebian – and 'the Widow' of India, the Indira Gandhi surrogate. This Cruella De Vil monster, who significantly never appears in person, is determined to impose restraint upon India's 'teeming' through her rapacious agent and Saleem's rival, the castrator Shiva. Rushdie thus inflates and intentionally distorts the traditional equation of mother figure and nation, encapsulated in the novelist Bankim's nineteenth-century 'Bharat Mata' or 'Mataram' formulation. By short-circuiting history (the 1975 Emergency) and myth ('Mayashakti mothers' and destructive widows), the novel thus succeeds in setting up a malign (feminine) principle as the motor force governing the disintegration of the by-now-dysfunctional national family.[14] Along very similar lines, in *Shame*, the metaphysical quality of the nation's shame – all that has gone amiss in terms of the abuse of power – is embodied in the blushing, wordless, demented figure of Sufiya Zinobia, Omar Khayyam's at first virginal, then vampirish wife.[15] The deeply compromised representation of both characters, the Widow and 'Shame', demonstrates that Rushdie's national imaginary operates, even if cynically, as a specifically male construct, projected on to, yet ironically distanced from, archetypal embodiments of woman. As Nalini Natarajan comments in her reading of *Midnight's Children*, woman functions for Rushdie as a multifaceted sign in the imagining of national community – but, in particular, it could be added, in the imagining of failed, flawed or disjointed community.[16]

As these readings both suggest, it is virtually a literary and socio-political given that mother symbols cement national feeling, and that, worldwide, the cognate-metaphors of soil, earth, home and family buttress the process of making national claims, or invoking the modern nation into being. Constructing sexual difference is bound up with symbol-making and signifying practices, and in this regard the everyday vocabularies of the nation are no exception.

Consider, for example, the metaphors buried in the terms 'motherland' – and/or '-continent', '-country', '-tongue' – and the less frequently used 'fatherland'. Of immediate interest are the differing symbolic valencies of these terms, implying, like the literary examples above, that images of mothers and of men occupy different positions and levels in national iconographies and ideologies. Syntactically, the epithet 'father' cannot be used interchangeably with that of 'mother'; so, too, the meanings that collect around the mother metaphor when applied to lands, languages and other national entities are incommensurate with the idea of the father. The image of the mother invites connotations of origins – birth, hearth, home, roots, the umbilical cord – and rests upon the frequent, and some might say 'natural', identification of the mother with the beloved earth, the national territory and the first-spoken language, the national tongue. In contrast the term fatherland has conventionally lent itself to contexts perhaps more strenuously nationalistic, where the appeal is to *Bruderschaft*, filial duty, the bonds of fraternity and paternity.

As with figures of speech, so with narratives: literary tales, but also stories more broadly, replicate and inscribe gender roles in the nation. Indeed, narrative processes which tell the self into being may generally speaking be held to underpin the construction of identity, including national, class and sexual identity, as will be demonstrated many times in the course of this book. Any nationalist discourse demands the narrativistic invocation of birth and origins, historical continuity and synthetic closure – a demand that the novel, its fortunes closely tied to those of the emergent middle class, as to the nation's, has always been ready to meet.[17] The novel, as Simon Gikandi among others suggests, clears a space for the modern national community to narrate itself out of the traditional past[18] – typically, I would add, by way of its 'staging' of the iconic 'drama' of filial insurrection, generational conflict and eventual resolution. The postcolonial novel in particular, whether in Nigeria, India or Britain, allows for the rationalisation and validation of selected 'national' customs and traditions, including the embedding of talismans of fatherly power and motherly influence – those remnants of the past which are deemed still to have value. It is for this reason that the distinctive configurations of character in novels deployed in the service of nationalism may be adopted, as here, to derive paradigms for the nation's symbolisation of both masculine and feminine gender.

At a metatextual level, too, the novel operates as a powerful medium of nationalist self-articulation. It provides the writer with a space where nationalist traditions of 'sonship' or filial inheritance structuring the public sphere intersect with the vocabularies of patrimony and filiation which inform modern writing, from South Asia and Africa through to the Americas.[19] Establishing himself as at once an inheritor and a remaker of cultural traditions, the male nationalist writer both fashions his identity as a citizen of his modern nation-state and, setting himself against the European canon taught in university colleges across the colonised world, claims rights of literary paternity. In an oeuvre inaugurated by *Things Fall Apart* (1958) and *No Longer at Ease* (1960), Chinua Achebe, for example, simultaneously inscribes a formative narrative of the Igbo community, interrogates his father's legacy of

Christian conversion and Nigeria's post-independence history, and, in so doing, secures his status as a national writer.

It is of course true that, from the time of the late eighteenth-century revolutions, nationalism across the world developed alongside, indeed often as indistinguishable from, liberation movements in support of equal representation and in opposition to vertically organised authority. Nationalism, whether expressed as cultural self-representation or as the demand for political enfranchisement, makes its appeal, or professes to make its appeal, to all citizens equally: hence its worldwide attractiveness to feminists and reformers in quest of democratic rights. Whereas dynastic or colonial structures signify hierarchy, the controlling idea in nationalism is of a homogeneous, horizontally structured society: all are equally interpellated; all theoretically participate on the same terms.

In practice, however, and certainly in the operation of its iconographies and spectacles of power, nationalism operates as a masculine *family drama* (borrowing a term from Freud's 1909 work), based on, as will shortly be seen, gendered and unequal images of family roles.[20] In one of Cynthia Enloe's snappy formulations: '[women] have often been treated more as symbols than as active participants by nationalist movements organised to end colonialism and racism'.[21] Judith Butler sheds light on this central contradiction of nationalism in a 2000 essay on the paradoxes of universality, noting that feminist inheritors of Europe's age of revolutions demanded equal rights on two grounds: on the basis of their sexual difference, *and* as a logical extension of universal enfranchisement.[22] As things turned out, within the still-hegemonic, hierarchical and male-dominated state structures of the time, the second goal, the extension of male rights, proved more achievable or permissible than the recognition of the first, the rights of difference. The situation has persisted until the present day.

The symbolic economy or drama of nationalism would thus appear to be sharply delineated by gender, or, more precisely, by tropes that match up with prototypical categories of sexual difference. From this emerges the semiotic schema central to this study. Almost invariably, as *A Wreath for Udomo* in particular demonstrated, key national 'actors' are cast in conventionally masculine, typically 'alpha-male', roles: as a soldier, leader or representative of state, as an official artist or faithful citizen-hero – in most cases as a fraternal or otherwise as a fatherly figure. (It may be of course, as in chapter 4, that a national son grows into the role of father of the nation across the course of a narrative detailing his exploits, though he will continue to honour the nation or land as his mother.) By contrast, woman as equal participant in the *action* of the drama is noticeably absent. She is rarely assigned a role *alongside* that of the male actors, even, or perhaps especially, after the achievement of national independence. External to the 'serious' affairs of the national community, she assumes an emblematic status as a symbol of maternal self-sacrifice or of the nation's fierce, 'virginal' pride – if, that is, she is not excluded from the action entirely as an unknown subversive quantity and a threat.

Developing the schema further, I propose that male roles in the national family drama may be characterised as *metonymic*. As the author and subject of nationalism, the male is a part of the national community or contiguous with it; his place is alongside that of his brother citizens. Where he appears as a personification of the nation, he is often individualised – a John Bull, an Uncle Sam, a Saleem Sinai born alongside the other children of midnight (though in a pole position).[23] In contrast, the figure of the woman in the drama of national tropes is usually seen as generalised and generic (not to say generative also). Often set in relation to the figure of her nationalist son, her ample, childbearing, fully *representative* maternal form typically takes on the status of *metaphor*. Cast as originator or progenitress, a role authorised by her national sons, she herself, however, is positioned *outside* the central script of national self-emergence. In special cases, where, for example, she assumes the androgynous shape of a woman fighter, soldier or activist (as in the mature Parvati of *Midnight's Children*, Achebe's 'girl' Gladys, or Ngugi's Wariinga, as chapter 2 will describe), a woman character may be ranked together with her nationalist brothers. Yet, despite or indeed because of the cross-dressing, her singularity is totemic: it is at once a product of specialised conditions, and a means of reinforcing the *a priori* construct of the national subject as male.[24]

In general, then, the woman – and usually the mother – figure *stands for* the national territory and for certain national values: symbolically she is ranged above the men; in reality she is kept below them. If male filial figures experience the gravitational pull to the national ground, women constitute part of its gravid mass. As, for example, in the iconography of Hindu nationalism, in many forms of African nationalism, as also in Pan-Africanism, the elevated woman figure takes on massive, even continent-wide proportions. She is the Great Mother, Durga, Mama Afrika, embracing each and every one of her peoples in her generous arms. This *family romance*, in which the male leader, citizen-hero or writer addresses himself to his national mother (land, home) in tones variously deferential or reverential and gains her protection, repeatedly reproduces itself in the literature and history of national movements. At the same time, however, it is the case that right across the continent and the sub-continent women, subsisting as they may despite the bright myths of motherhood, make up the greater part of these territories' illiterate, oppressed and poor.

When viewed from the vantage point of the early twenty-first century, some of this may admittedly appear rather obvious and familiar. How long has it not been that the female form has been deployed as a repository of value in patriarchal societies? In the shape of Madeleine, Britannia, Liberty, Joan of Arc, Boudicca – or, more recently, of, say, Princess Diana, Indira Gandhi, Margaret

Thatcher – woman has served as the personification of national virtues and, sometimes, vices, even as ordinary women within nations have continued to occupy subordinate positions. Then again, it could be said that the dominance of mother images in nationalism is a natural outgrowth, an expression at a socio-political level of a respect for mothers built into social attitudes cross-culturally.[25] Therefore, in answer to the proposition that nationalism bears pronounced patriarchal features, it might simply be argued that this is only another expression of the worn if resilient figure of the father, a projection of male heterosexual desire, or the honouring of the mother writ large. As Maurice Godelier has aptly put it: 'It is not sexuality which haunts society, but society which haunts the body's sexuality. Sex-related differences between bodies are continually summoned as testimony to social relations and phenomena that have nothing to do with sexuality. Not only as testimony to, but also testimony for – in other words, as legitimation.'[26] Gender always already gives nationalism its legitimating symbols, its self-validating show.

On this point hangs a related objection, namely, that the symbolic baggage nationalism has inherited from older social formations should not be regarded as *necessarily* impinging on the ideology itself, or on the allocation of roles and power within the nation. As gender is usually 'implicated in the conception and construction of power', in Joan W. Scott's words, why make an issue of the nation's gender markings in particular? It is perhaps unrealistic to assume, as I may be construed as doing, that the artifice of the nation be free – or, given its assertions of equality, be relatively free – of such formative symbolic acts.[27]

To this the response must be that no matter how widely entrenched the symbols, nor yet how iconoclastic, recuperative or revolutionary the ideology – and its power against empire has indeed been important and immense – nationalism's vocabularies of self-representation do matter; fundamentally so. As I have emphasised, it is not merely the case that nationalism springs from masculinised iconographies, social memories and state structures (this would be the 'soft' argument for the nation as a gendered construct). It is also that, the nation's liberatory promises to the contrary, gender has become (though possibly need not be) its *formative medium*. Metaphors of self, place and history reveal not simply how national entities identify, but also how and why power relations in the nation are configured. As Florence Stratton writes in a commentary on Fredric Jameson's gender-blind theory of narrative as 'a socially symbolic act', the 'national allegory' which allegedly structures the Third World text is subtended and supported by the standard 'sexual allegory' that plays on the binary terms of male/female, good/evil.[28] The first allegory, in other words, is inconceivable without the second. If the structures of nations or nation-states are soldered onto the struts of gender hierarchies, and if the organisation of power in the nation is profoundly informed by those structures, how then is the nation to be imagined outside of gender?

This assertion is stronger than that which would refer only to the legitimating force of standard gender-specific tropes. The claim is instead is that nationalism articulates and consolidates itself through such tropes because it is ideologically imbricated in gender. The male-dominated family drama of most nationalisms embodies, justifies and *reproduces* the organisation of power within nationalist movements and in nation-states, and delimits the national participation of women. It is this androcentrism of the nation that co-exists comfortably with and indeed informs the dominant orientation to mother images. However, as a consequence of the persuasive representation of nations as collectivities of equals, questions concerning who occupies the position of subject and who of object are too infrequently asked of the national community. The codification of gendered power within nationalism, believed to be contingent and context-based, has till relatively recently been only superficially investigated.

It is important, however, to avoid seeming to attribute the 'genderedness' of nations to timeless truths or universal templates such as an unchanging and all-pervasive patriarchy. An argument of this kind would seek, for example, to attribute the close relationship between patriarchy and the nation to the tendency *innate* in both to favour unitary order and to suppress plurality.[29] As against such a reading, how might the male dominance of, in particular, established and successful nationalist movements be *historically* explained? Here the family connection becomes especially significant, as does the concept of national identity as constructed and incorporative, and as reproducible across different contexts.[30]

Nationalism, whether ideology or movement, is never *sui generis*: it relies on the formative structures which are immediately to hand, and across history these have tended to comprise the formations of the old dynastic state and the patriarchal family. In the capitalist societies of the late eighteenth and early nineteenth centuries, in Europe as in Latin America, as later in Europe's other colonised regions, the nation grew up in conjunction with the formation of the bourgeois family, characterised by its construction of the home as a private, feminine sphere.[31]

Putting it another way, nationalism, although it is an unmistakable development of a dynamic modernity, typically asserting rationalist objectives with regard to social organisation and political representation, is also classically 'Janus-faced'.[32] It legitimates itself via recourse to archaic rituals and time-honoured traditions – in short, to so-called organic social and cultural forms. It was relative to the private, hierarchical collectivity of the family, ostensibly a natural or given structure, that the horizontally organised nation found an ideal way to sanction its structures of power and to impose its boundaries. Existing, binary gender differences were repeated and reinforced within another dichotomy, of the feminine private as against the masculine public sphere, with the result that men defined national agency and apportioned the rights of citizenship by and between themselves.

Within the space of domesticity, as Anne McClintock among others has observed, the historical formation of gender was therefore successfully recast as women's externalised, static and a-historic relationship to power.[33] If men occupied the dimension of time – linear, future-directed, associated with change and progress – women presided over the static dimension of space – the past, tradition, nature. This development was particularly pronounced in the colonial context, as in Partha Chatterjee's now canonical explanation, deftly elaborated by Susie Tharu and K. Lalita.[34] Here a nationalist movement might adapt the political models of the west in the 'material' domain in order, contradictorily, to assert its freedom, yet reserve the 'spiritual', private domain of the family, a space so-called untainted by colonialism, to articulate a cultural nationalism that inflected those imported modes of thought.

The state should not, however, be left out of the picture of the modern nation's emergence. In a context where older forms of feudal and religious authority were disintegrating, state structures importantly found in nationalism a new means of representation and legitimation.[35] While nationalism endowed the middle classes with an ideology that insisted on wider, more democratic access to power, the inherited frameworks of the state at the same time provided an important means of establishing and maintaining their new political order. However, as these inherited formations and the capitalist economic system operated according to principles of gender-domination, in the state, as in the new workplaces, as also in the new middle-class home, lines of control emanated from the feared and/or revered figures of fathers.

Via these mutually reinforcing pathways, therefore, the new nation-state secured a controlling metaphor for its existence in the unitary and hierarchical structure of the patriarchal family. The family became at one and the same time an important vehicle of social organisation and a primary carrier of the gendered ideology of the middle class. As Alexis de Tocqueville wrote of post-revolutionary American society: 'every association, to be effective, must have a head, and the natural head of the conjugal association is the husband. . . . in the little society composed of man and wife, as in the great society of politics, the aim of democracy is to regulate and legitimate necessary power.'[36] A telling analogy to this appears in the 1980s African Charter on Human and People's Rights which, using the generic pronoun 'he' throughout, observes that 'the family shall be the natural unit and basis of society' (Article 18).[37] The step from embracing these figures of the male-headed national family and the feminine domestic space, to endorsing concepts of passive state-mothers, is a relatively easy one to take. Reproducing the 'natural', gendered division of the public as against the private sphere at a macropolitical level, the nation-state guarantees not only its own stability but also its reproduction over time.

The nation's *en-gendering* took on particularly acute forms in Europe's former colonies where the intersection of the male dominance prevailing within imposed and indigenous social structures meant that a *hyper-masculinity* became both the overdetermined legacy of colonial state power and a means of resistance to it.[38] As with colonial power, the most successful forms of national power worked through exploiting pre-existing power relations of hierarchy and subordination. So it was almost universally the case that the condition of woman under empire was deemed a key index of a people's level of 'civilisation'. Male-led imperialism effectively operated as a process whereby white men dominated native men by wresting away control over 'their' women in order to civilise them (the men), as, for example, in British India with legislation such as the banning of sati (1829) or the permitting of widow remarriage (1856). Far from being merely an outward manifestation of colonial rule, patriarchy, the articulation of imported with native forms, became its primary medium. In consequence, as chapter 5 describes at greater length, to male nationalists even more intensely than to colonials, 'woman', even or especially if vulnerable to co-optation, was set up as the redemptive carrier of the nation's cultural traditions and hence as the signifier to men of the community's integrity.[39] Women in the new postcolonial nations came to be subjected to a syncretic fusion of male rules, encoded as principles of law and enforced as cultural authenticity.

With national liberation essentially defined as male liberation – as resistance to colonial iconographies of native weakness – it was predictable that at independence the new national masters shifted smoothly into the halls and offices of power vacated by the male coloniser. These offices and other state formations, instruments of colonial rule imported from Europe, in any case remained in form and expression elitist, patrimonial and alienated from civil society. In this situation, were further legitimation of the state's power required, the family metaphor – local, familiar, embedding the a-political, domestic character of women – could again be put to official use. Despite claims of universal enfranchisement, power was confined to the authoritative positions that the trope made available, in particular, the role of 'father of the nation', a title assigned to national leaders from Gandhi through Kenyatta and Kaunda, to Michael Manley and Mandela. In a word, therefore, at independence an ideology privileging mother symbols did not in reality empower mothers; instead, the authority of national fathers and sons became the more deeply entrenched. Rather than extending a politics of self-assertion to women, postcolonial nations tended historically to re-enshrine male privileges even as nationalist men sought to regain control over the women who had become empowered during the struggle for independence.

In this context it is not surprising that the mother symbol has provided a powerful talisman for male-led pan-nationalist as well as national movements. 'She' stands as a figure both embodying and transcending national boundaries. 'Non-ethnic nationalisms', in Tom Nairn's definition, favour 'a personalised and totemic symbolism', in the case of Britain the monarchy, in Africa the image of Mama Afrika, in order to help arouse and crystallise supra- or transnational loyalties.[40] Here, once again, processes of compensatory representation are discernible. The identification of an entire continent – or in the case of India, subcontinent – as a mythical mother betrays clear affinities with iconic material adopted from Europe. Africa in popular colonial mythology was personified as a dark, alluring woman: Rider Haggard's She, Kurtz's African woman in Conrad. Woman, the unknown, dangerous and seductive other, habitually equates both with the 'East' and, as Freud pointed out, with 'the dark continent'.[41]

In sum, postcolonial independence across the world has manifested by and large as a take-over rather than a radical transformation of gendered power. For this reason the strong patriarchal presence built into nationalist ideologies and the nation-state has continued even in liberatory and revolutionary situations to dominate more or less unchallenged. Where anti-colonial nationalisms were marrying the symbolic legacies of at least two patriarchal systems, male elites, as in other spheres, remained manifestly in charge: they defined the shape and meaning of their new nationhood on behalf of 'their' people. Representations of the national territory that formed a part of colonial rhetoric were assimilated to local conventions of respect for the mother and the land. The nation as a body of people was imagined as a family arrangement in which the leaders had the authority of fathers and, in relation to the maternal national entity, adopted the position of sons.

The obvious conclusion to all this is that the unshackling of the colonised world by way of nationalism has tended to date to preclude a corresponding full emancipation for most women, including those of the middle class. In the iconographies of nation-states there have conventionally been few positive roles on offer to women that are not stereotypes and/or connected in some way to women's biological capacity for mothering. As regards women's day-to-day reality the situation is even bleaker. Notwithstanding the achievement of family and work rights by some women, as for example in Cuba, notwithstanding United Nations' efforts to raise awareness in this respect, the queenly status of mother icons only serves to point up by contrast the actual lowly status of women within most postcolonial nations. Instances of the nation-state mobilising against women appear right the way across the decolonised world, especially where Third World economic decline has produced crises in state power. Rarely if ever has military or political participation by women in the liberation movement translated into progressive gender politics.[42] Maria Mbilinyi outlines measures taken in Tanzania during the 1970s and 1980s to control the migration of women from the rural areas.[43] The Zimbabwean and Zambian states have since the 1980s undertaken regular campaigns against prostitution, baby-dumping, squatting and 'uncleanness' – ways of obtaining control not simply over unplanned urban settlement, but specifically, of disciplining women as urban dwellers.[44] Caribbean countries, too, have vigorously, even oppressively, heterosexualised the nation-state, in particular its sex industries, in order to mediate the pressures of globalisation.[45] Neocolonial India's collaboration with dam-building multinationals, as Arundhati Roy describes, put women, tribals and the rural poor in the direct firing line.[46]

Later chapters will address the questions that have been urging to speak themselves within the interstices of the foregoing propositions. That is, how are postcolonial women, specifically in this case women writers, to work their way around the patriarchal legacies embedded within nationalism, especially as postcolonial literature has been so deeply imbued with nationalist themes? In nations that are in fact less mother- than father(ed)-lands, where and how are women to find a voice, to position themselves as children or daughters of the nation? How do they interrupt the duologue of colonial master and national father? And how are male writers to respond to the nation once its fictive status as a natural given and a mother-surrogate is exposed?

I will suggest that the contradictory legacies of nationalism which have often denied women and other minorities a voice are to some extent addressed when these marginalised groups begin to claim access, even if circumspectly, to the public sphere. They go against the hegemonic line when they tell their own histories, re-place the unplaced space in the national drama with the concrete figures, bodies and voices of 'daughters'. Or, where, as in chapter 8, in the face of neocolonialism, they confront the implications of the nation as fiction, even as political nightmare. This assertion embeds an important premiss, which I share with Susan Andrade, that though they *appear* to deal more than do men in the domestic, the private, the 'small', women writers are always, even if implicitly or covertly, engaging the political.[47]

In order not to second-guess the readings that follow, I will at this point confine my comments on women writers' engagement with the national to a few observations on their fictionalisation of community. As intimated, the postcolonial novel has been dominated by historical and nationalist themes: in this respect, however, it provides a pre-eminent site for active reinterpretation and contestation by women involved in telling the story of their day-to-day lives. So we find that novelists such as the Nigerian Flora Nwapa, the Zimbabwean Tsitsi Dangarembga, or the Indian writer Manju Kapur situate their novels *alongside* the conventional narrative of a national, public history – the account, that is, of the deeds and exploits of nationalist males.[48] By concentrating on ordinary experience in a community of women, as later chapters will show in greater detail, these writers succeed in foregrounding women's presence in history and in claiming a moral and political validity for the parts they play. In the case of Nwapa, most prominently, this claim is reinforced by the assertive, conversational babble of her narrative style.

Nwapa's technique of sharing out narrative responsibility among a chorus of voices is also one employed by Bessie Head in her historical colloquy *Serowe: Village of the Rain Wind* (1981).[49] More formally than Nwapa, Head, who as a South African exile of many years' standing lacked a passport and an officially recognised nationality, engages with communal history, the experience of a Botswanan village suffering political and environmental change, yet consistently avoids the single perspective, the conventional 'national' line. In order to speak in others' tongues, or to allow those tongues to speak, Head gathers together the testimonies of village members, male and female. Multivocality becomes in her text a method and a formal principle – and a means of imagining community for herself. It is by commemorating voice and babble that a woman writer like Head begins to irrupt her presence as both participant and observer into the re-presented, idealised nation to which she aspires.

Notes

1 Klaus Theweleit, *Male Fantasies* (Minneapolis: University of Minnesota Press, 1987), p. 294.

2 Sangeeta Ray, *En-gendering India: Woman and Nation in Colonial and Postcolonial Narratives* (Durham NC and London: Duke University Press, 2000), p. 5.

3 See, for instance, Benedict Anderson, *Imagined Communities: Reflections on the Origin and Spread of Nationalisms* [1983], rev. edn (London: Verso, 1991), pp. 7 and 36, or Ernest Gellner's fabulistic characterisation of early European national formation as involving (male) labour migrants and iconic shepherd boys in *Nations and Nationalisms* (Oxford: Blackwell, 1983), pp. 58–62. See also the introduction to this book, pp. 7–8.

4 See Neil ten Kortenaar, '*Midnight's Children* and the allegory of history', *ARIEL: A Review of International English Literature*, 26:2 (1995), 41–62, on how the novel invites a provisional faith in the myth of the nation – one that it itself explodes.

5 Peter Abrahams, *A Wreath for Udomo* [1956] (London: Faber, 1979). See p. 15 for the quotation that follows.

6 Abrahams, *A Wreath for Udomo*, pp. 122–3. This bears comparison with Kamau Brathwaite's *Mother Poem* and *Sun Poems*, in which the mother is identified with the land, while the poet, the son of the 'i:land', draws on sun-god myths to present himself as the inheritor of that land, who will grant it i:dentity. See *Mother Poem* (Oxford: Oxford University Press, 1977); *Sun Poems* (Oxford: Oxford University Press, 1982).

7 Clive Wake, 'Invitation to dissent', review of Julio Finn's *Voices of Negritude*, *Third World Quarterly*, 11:1 (January 1989), 178.

8 Léopold S. Senghor, *Poèmes* (Paris: Editions du Seuil, 1973), pp. 12–15; and *Selected Poems*, trans. John Reed and Clive Wake (Oxford: Oxford University Press, 1964), pp. 16–17.

9 The same caring gesture is invoked in 'Nuit de Sine', and, sure enough, the Beloved, both desired and nurturing, is duly seen to comfort Senghor's poet.

10 Camara Laye, *The African Child*, trans. James Kirkup (London: Fontana, 1980). Camara is in fact the writer's surname, but he has always referred to himself as Camara Laye. The book was first translated in 1955 as *The Dark Child*.

11 Aijaz Ahmad, *In Theory: Classes, Nations, Literatures* (New York and London: Verso, 1992).

12 See, for example, Salman Rushdie, *Shame* (London: Cape, 1983), p. 29.

13 In the later novel *The Moor's Last Sigh* (London: Cape, 1995), p. 137, Rushdie concedes that 'Motherness . . . is a big idea in India, maybe our biggest: the land as mother, the mother as land, as the firm ground beneath our feet'. Even so, the emblematic protagonist of the novel is the powerful mother Aurora Zogoiby's son Moraes.

14 Salman Rushdie, *Midnight's Children* (London: Cape, 1981), p. 406. See also Rajeswari Sunder Rajan's analysis of how gender articulates with female political power – of Indira Gandhi in particular – in *Real and Imagined Women: Gender, Culture and Postcolonialism* (London and New York: Routledge, 1993), pp. 103–28.

15 See Ahmad, *In Theory*, p. 50.

16 Nalini Natarajan, 'Woman, nation, and narration in *Midnight's Children*', in Inderpal Grewal and Caren Kaplan (eds), *Scattered Hegemonies: Postmodernity and Transnational Feminist Practices* (Minneapolis: University of Minnesota Press, 1994), pp. 76–89. See also Meenakshi Mukherjee (ed.), *Rushdie's* Midnight's Children: *A Book of Readings* (Delhi: Pencraft International, 1999).

17 On the imbrication of the novel and the nation, see Ray, *En-Gendering India*, pp. 10–14; Steven Connor, *The English Novel in History, 1950–1995* (London and New York: Routledge, 1996).

18 See, for example, Simon Gikandi, *Reading Chinua Achebe* (London: James Currey, 1991).

19 In a variety of literary traditions, including several forms of African nationalism, writing has typically been characterised as a masculine activity, and the formation of a literary tradition as a struggle between 'author'-itative fathers and their sons. The theory of the anxiety of this influence (including the term 'sonship') is obviously adapted from Harold Bloom, *The Anxiety of Influence: A Theory of Poetry* (Oxford: Oxford University Press, 1973), and his cognate works. See also the canonical discussion of the 'legal fiction' of literary patrimony in Sandra M. Gilbert and Susan Gubar, *The Madwoman in the Attic* (Yale: Yale University Press, 1984); and chapter 5, p. 93.

20 Sigmund Freud, 'Family romances', *On Sexuality*, trans. James Strachey, rpt Penguin Freud Library, vol. 7 (Harmondsworth: Penguin, 1986), pp. 221–5. See also Jeffrey Moussaieff (ed.), *The Complete Letters of Sigmund Freud to Wilhelm Fliess, 1887–1904*, trans. Jeffrey Moussaieff (Cambridge MA: Harvard University Press, 1985), p. 56.

21 Cynthia Enloe, *Bananas, Beaches and Bases: Making Feminist Sense of International Politics* (1989; Berkeley: University of California Press, 2000), p. 42. As Valerie Smith, 'Gender and Afro-Americanist criticism', in Elaine Showalter (ed.), *Speaking of Gender* (London: Routledge, 1989), p. 60, has remarked of African American nationalism in the United States, the discourse of liberation and cultural assertion has tended controversially to '[enshrine] the possibilities of black male power'.

22 See Judith Butler, 'Restaging the universal', in Judith Butler, Ernesto Laclau, Slavoj Žižek, *Contingency, Hegemony, Universality* (London: Verso, 2000), in particular pp. 29–41.

23 The case of Nelson Mandela may be an exception in this regard. As a national father figure he is also considered as a generalised and elevated symbol of the new South Africa. To corroborate this fact, according to the *Guardian* (21 October 2002), p. 14, plans are underway to build a colossus of Mandela in the South African city of Port Elizabeth, based on the model of the Statue of Liberty. Towering 30 storeys high over the harbour, the statue, due for completion in 2006, will stand on a plinth housing a 'museum of freedom'.

24 See Ray, *En-gendering India*, pp. 23–50, for her discussion of the novelist Bankim's nationalist reification of woman as a naturalised category despite female character performances in male garb in his work (as in *Devi Chaudhurani*). Etienne Balibar and Achille Mbembe, too, have described the nation-state's and the colonial state's 'secret affinity' with family hierarchies.

25 Although the category 'mother' is named and conceived differently from culture to culture, no analysis should disregard such respect. In societies in southern and West Africa, in India north and south, in the Caribbean, and elsewhere, mothers are accorded significant social status, especially as they grow older. The name 'mother' may thus function as an honorific title, or a generic term of respect for an adult woman, as women accrue power in ways that exceed, though often depend upon, their reproductive capacity. The 1900s Bengali activist Sister Nivedita, for instance, was 'Mother' to her revolutionary acolytes, while Ramakrishna's mother was called 'ma' by his followers. See Elleke Boehmer, *Empire, the National and the Postcolonial: Resistance in Interaction, 1880–1920* (Oxford and New York: Oxford University Press, 2002), pp. 67–78, 115–17; Parama Roy, *Indian Traffic: Identities in Question in Colonial and Postcolonial India* (Berkeley: University of California Press, 1988). Kofi Awoonor, *The Breast of the Earth* (New York: Nok Publications International, 1975), pp. 99–100, describes the mother as the presiding 'inspirer' of the West African home and community: 'the most steadfast person in the homestead, but also the symbol of the eternal giver, the earth itself'. So, too, in the South African Mongane Serote's *Selected Poems*, ed. Mbulelo Mzamane (Johannesburg: Ad Donker, 1982), especially pp. 72–92, the mother image is the focus for his longing for Africa as place of authenticity – though the poet is concerned to tag his own identity as male. In Ingoapele Madingoane's *Africa My Beginning* (Johannesburg: Ravan Press, 1988), the dichotomies are starker: the mother is the comforting custodian of Africanness who serves to guarantee the 'manhood' of Africa's black men (pp. 4–5). See also Deborah Gaitskell and Elaine Unterhalter, 'Mothers of the nation: a comparative analysis', in Nira Yuval-Davis and Floya Anthias (eds), *Woman-Nation-State* (London: Macmillan 1989), p. 72. It is worth adding that, in societies where rates of urban and transnational migration for men are high, as they were in apartheid South Africa, and as they still are in Zimbabwe, women may practically speaking become the guardians of the land: they hold the earth in safekeeping.

26 Maurice Godelier, 'The origins of male domination', *New Left Review*, 127 (May–June 1981), 17. I am indebted to the Scott essay cited below for this reference.

27 Joan W. Scott, 'Gender: a useful category of historical analysis', *American Historical Review*, 91 (1986), 1069. See also Joan W. Scott, *Gender and the Politics of History* (New York: Columbia University Press, 1988).

28 Florence Stratton, *Contemporary African Literature and the Politics of Gender* (London and New York: Routledge, 1994), pp. 13–18.

29 Contrary to its principle of 'one, yet many', nationalism agrees with patriarchy – the claim might be – in promoting especially unitary or 'one-eyed' forms of consciousness: one birth and blood, one growth pattern, one future for all. Such an argument rests on the supposition that the masculine, like the national, favours rationality, homogeneity and unitary order. Nationalism did not therefore become gendered simply through transmission and association. The national instead is *intrinsically* monologic, as is the patriarchal – it is 'a world', to quote from Mikhail Bakhtin, 'of fathers and of founders of families'. Bakhtin has spoken influentially of the coincidence of nationalist unisonance and patriarchal motifs in 'epic' national art forms. See 'Epic and novel', in *The Dialogic Imagination*, ed. Michael Holquist, trans. Caryl Emerson and Michael Holquist (Austin: University of Texas, 1986), pp. 3–40.

30 My exposition concurs with Benedict Anderson's idea of the *serial* formation of nations to a certain extent. However, although Anderson would agree that the national idea is adaptable across cultural and temporal borderlines without *necessarily* being determined by any originary context, his concept of the 'homogenous empty time' of the nation is strongly identified with the onset of capitalism in the west. He is therefore forced to privilege the western modular nation over the post-colonial, and the metropolitan over the colonial context as a crucible for nationalism. By contrast, the colonial context, as in what follows, I regard as crucial. See Anderson's *The Spectre of Comparisons: Nationalism, Southeast Asia and the World* (London and New York: Verso, 1998).

31 See Philip Corrigan and Derek Sayer, *The Great Arch: English State Formation as Cultural Revolution* (Oxford: Blackwell, 1985), pp. 1–13, for their discussion of the familial affinities of nation-states.

32 Tom Nairn is the foremost exponent of the 'Janus' character of nations. See, for example, *The Break-up of Britain: Crisis and Neo-nationalism* (London: New Left Books, 1977), and the more recent essay, 'What nations are for', *London Review of Books* (8 September 1994), 6–7. See also Deniz Kandyoti, 'Identity and its discontents: women and the nation', *Millennium: Journal of International Studies*, 20:3 (1991), 431.

33 Anne McClintock, *Imperial Leather: Race, Gender and Sexuality in the Colonial Contest* (London and New York: Routledge, 1995), pp. 132–80.

34 See Partha Chatterjee, *Nationalist Thought and the Colonial World – A Derivative Discourse?* (London: Zed Press, 1986); and *The Nation and its Fragments Colonial and Postcolonial Histories* (New Delhi: Oxford University Press, 1993). On the cross-hatching of colonial and national patriarchies, see in particular Susie Tharu and K. Lalita, 'Reading against the Orientalist grain', in Susie Tharu and K. Lalita (eds), *Women's Writing in India 600: B.C. to the Present*, vol. 1 (New Delhi: Oxford University Press, 1991), pp. 41–64.

35 See Eric Hobsbawm, *Nations and Nationalism since 1780: Programme, Myth and Reality* (Cambridge: Cambridge University Press, 1990), on the ways in which states draw on nationalist sentiment to establish legitimacy where other socio-political bonds are in decline.

36 Alexis de Tocqueville, *Democracy in America*, ed. J. P. Mayer, trans. George Lawrence (New York: Doubleday, 1969), p. 601.

37 'The African Charter on Human and People's Rights', Appendix 1, *International Legal Materials*, 21 (1982), 61.

38 See Ashis Nandy's compelling thesis of the compensatory masculinity of anti-colonial nationalism in *The Intimate Enemy: The Loss and Recovery of Self under Colonialism* (New Delhi: Oxford University Press, 1983). For evidence of the intersection of colonial and indigenous patriarchies, a wide range of work might be cited. In relation to Africa see, for example: Christine Obbo, 'Sexuality and economic domination in Uganda', in Yuval-Davis and Anthias (eds), *Woman-Nation-State*; Omolara Ogundipe, 'African women, culture and another development', *Présence Africaine*, 141:1 (1987), 123–39; as well as Terence Ranger's discussion of the transference of kingly motifs in the colonial appointment of chiefs, 'The invention of tradition in colonial Africa', in Eric Hobsbawm and Terence Ranger (eds), *The Invention of Tradition* (Cambridge: Cambridge University Press, 1983), pp. 211–62. In relation to India see in particular Partha Chatterjee, cited in note 34, and also Inderpal Grewal, *Home and Harem: Nation, Gender, Empire and the Cultures of Travel* (London: Leicester University Press, 1996).

39 Enloe, *Bananas, Beaches and Bases*, p. 54.

40 Tom Nairn, *The Enchanted Glass: Britain and its Monarchy* (London: Radius, 1988), p. 11. The attractiveness of the overarching Mother Africa trope to Pan-Africanists as to African nationalists does not, however, imply a simplistic equation of Pan-Africanism with nationalism.

41 Freud, *On Sexuality*, p. 326.

42 See Amina Mama, 'Sheroes and villains: conceptualising colonial and contemporary violence against women in Africa', in M. Jacqui Alexander and Chandra T. Mohanty (eds), *Feminist Genealogies, Colonial Legacies, Democratic Futures* (New York and London: Routledge, 1997), pp. 46–62. Amina Mama points out that even a leader as gender-aware as Samora Machel of Mozambique reinforced the sexual division of labour by calling on women and not men to clean up Maputo's streets after liberation. See also Stephanie Urdang, *And Still They Dance: Women, War and the Struggle for Change in Mozambique* (New York: Monthly Review Press, 1989).

43 Maria Mbilinyi, 'Runaway wives in colonial Tanganika: forced labour and forced marriage in Rungwe District 1919–1961', *The International Journal for the Sociology of Law*, 16:1 (January 1988), 1–29.

44 Similarly, successive campaigns against indiscipline by different Nigerian governments have targeted women petty-traders as prime offenders. See Carolynne Dennis, 'Women and the state in Nigeria: the case of the federal military government 1984–85', in Haleh Afshar (ed.), *Women, State and Ideology: Studies from Africa and Asia* (London: Macmillan, 1987), pp. 13–27.

45 M. Jacqui Alexander, 'Erotic autonomy as a politics of decolonization', in Alexander and Mohanty (eds), *Feminist Genealogies*, pp. 63–100.

46 Arundhati Roy, *The Algebra of Infinite Justice* (London: Flamingo, 2002).

47 See Susan Z. Andrade, 'Rewriting history, motherhood and rebellion: naming an African women's literary tradition', *Research in African Literatures*, 21:1 (1990), 91–110; and her book *The Nation Writ Small* (Durham NC: Duke University Press, forthcoming).

48 Flora Nwapa, *Efuru* [1966] (London: Heinemann, 1987); *Idu* [1970] (London: Heinemann, 1987).

49 Bessie Head, *Serowe: Village of the Rain Wind* [1981] (London: Heinemann, 1986). See also Neil Lazarus, *Resistance in Postcolonial African Fiction* (New Haven, CN: Yale University Press, 1990), p. 211, where he writes that Head's small-scale agrarian politics 'stand opposed to the grand récit of national liberation struggle that constitutes the dominant narrative mode of political fiction in Africa'.

2

'The master's dance to the master's voice': revolutionary nationalism and women's representation in Ngugi wa Thiong'o

A writer needs people around him. . . . For me, in writing a novel, I love to hear the voices of the people . . . I need the vibrant voices of beautiful women: their touch, their sighs, their tears, their laughter. (Ngugi wa Thiong'o, *Detained*)[1]

With these affirmative words, the Kenyan writer Ngugi wa Thiong'o points to the strong position that women characters have held in his work over the years. It is a position virtually unique in Anglophone African literature. Not only is it the case that the internationally renowned African writers concentrating on themes of national self-assertion have by and large been male, but that in their work the emancipation of women has generally been rated as of secondary importance relative to the liberation of nations or of peoples. For this reason Ngugi's exertions to include women in his vision of a Kenya liberated from neocolonial domination merit recognition. Yet, at the same time, precisely because of the prominence of his achievement, the enduring masculinist cast of his ideas cannot be ignored. For it is by singling out female voices, by fixing women beneath the evaluative epithets 'vibrant' and 'beautiful', that Ngugi gives way to that tendency to objectify women which, even in the 1989 *Matigari*, qualifies his attempt to grant them a leading role in the revolutionary struggle for Kenyan liberation.[2]

The ambivalence in Ngugi's attitude towards women forms a significant, if not metonymic, part of a wider contradiction undercutting his populist nationalist programme for a new Kenya. Beginning with the writing of the epic-length *Petals of Blood* (1977), a project that extended across the early and mid-1970s, the time of his incarceration by the Kenyan state for alleged subversive practices, Ngugi came unequivocally to identify with the plight of the neocolonially betrayed Kenyan peasantry. His nationalism of the 1960s thus turned increasingly revolutionary and openly Marxist – an ideological trajectory to which *Matigari* still provides the high point. (A novel in Gikuyu, *Murogi wa Kigoogo*, slated for publication in 1999, has at the time of writing not yet appeared.) Whereas in the early novels the concept of the nation was identified with a leader figure, a Kenyatta-type patriarch, it is in the more recent work somewhat rigidly defined in terms of 'the people', led by 'patriots' and bound together by a shared history and cultural traditions. Liberation, however, is still seen to take place within the edifice of a Kenyan nation-state. For Ngugi it is through the formation of a truly national culture, through the reconstitution of the people's history language and identity, that oppressed groups are restored to themselves. If anything, it would seem, his revolutionary ideas have worked to consolidate and more precisely define his Kenyan nationalism.

To Ngugi, however – and here lies the contradiction – a revolutionary future is envisaged as involving participation in an ostensibly homogeneous culture centred in explicitly Gikuyu (as opposed to say Luo or Masai) myths and history.[3] Moreover, the nation is defined in unitary terms as an overarching people's nation in which other peoples as well as other sectors of society within Kenya would appear to occupy a secondary position. It is self-evident that this adherence to monolithic national definitions and concepts of national author-ity carries the negative potential of undermining Ngugi's proclaimed ideals for joyous populist expression and the people's (or peoples') self-realisation. The 'harmony in polyphony' of Kenyan cultures that he celebrates, in effect becomes a national unisonance that has worrying implications for some of his fondest aspirations.[4] On the nationalist level these would entail his project to champion the indigenous cultures and languages of Kenya and, as far as his commitment to social emancipation is concerned, his endeavour to give pre-eminence to the role of women in the national struggle. His compelling rhet-oric to the contrary, Ngugi in certain important areas gives his backing to the authoritarian and also patriarchal supports of the neocolonial regime he seeks to overthrow.

This tendency ironically becomes especially clear in his diligent efforts to include women in 'the people's' struggle. Investing his leading women charac-ters with the dignity of ages or with an almost bionic power, Ngugi has erected heroines of immense, if not impossible, stature: either great mothers of a future Kenya, or aggressive, gun-toting (effectively masculinised) revolution-aries. As he does at the start of *Detained: A Writer's Prison Diary* (1981), where he hails Wariinga, a central character in *Devil on the Cross* (1982), as his inspi-ration, his 'heroine of toil', he tends, in his more recent work in particular, to set up his women characters as icons.[5] They are allegorical figures represent-ing all that is resilient and strong in the Kenyan, implicitly Gikuyu, people. He thus seeks to identify the liberation of African women with his resistance to all forms of oppression. Yet, by maintaining relations of dominance in his por-trayal of revolutionary forces, he is pressed either to enlist his women charac-ters into the ranks of a male-ordered struggle, or to elevate women to the status of mascot at the head of the (male?) peasant and workers' march. Ngugi's neglect, both of the gendered and the structural nature of power, whether that power is held by national or by proletarian forces, ultimately works to inhibit his rousing call for a new dispensation in Kenya.

As suits the name he has made for himself as a revolutionary Kenyan writer, Ngugi has stimulated positive critical ratings by coming out in favour of the liberation of women in his non-fictional statements also.[6] As women are 'the most exploited and oppressed section of the entire working class', he will, he maintains, seek to create in his fiction 'a picture of a strong determined woman with a will to resist and to struggle' as an example for his audience.[7] He also makes frequent reference to the parts played by women like Mary Nyanjiru and Me Kitilili in resistance to Kenyan colonial oppression,[8] and to how women participated on equal terms with men in the dramatic experiments that he helped to organise at Kamiirithu in Kenya in 1977.[9]

It cannot escape notice, however, that Ngugi's gaze remains fixed on the 'most remarkable' historical figures (of men as well as women, it should be added).[10] His own protestations notwithstanding, he has increasingly sidelined the colourful crowds of *A Grain of Wheat* (1967) with their songs and ribald badinage in favour of single dominant personalities who stand as points of moral focus in his texts. Significant in this respect is his report 'Women in cultural work: the fate of Kamiirithu people's theatre in Kenya' (1983), in which the ostensible pro-woman stance is rather obviously grafted onto a fairly straightforward factual account of the experience.[11] Related inconsistencies fracture Ngugi's many indictments of the repressions and exclusions of colonial education. In *Decolonising the Mind* (1986), his study of colonial and national cultural practice, he chooses to overlook the ways in which women have been silenced by colonial and traditional power structures. Despite his professed delight at hearing women's voices (as entertainment on the side perhaps), he never mentions a woman writer, neither in his numerous inventories of canonical literary names nor in the lists of respected figures which he himself suggests for university curricula.[12]

It would seem that in Ngugi's view, as has been conventional across many postcolonial liberation movements, women's emancipation takes a second place to the national struggle against neocolonialism. The two struggles cannot be seen as mutually reinforcing. In accordance with a too-familiar formula, in order to ensure the liberation of Kenya from the grip of neocolonial powers, women are asked supportively to wait in the sidelines for the new social order as structured by men to emerge. Alternatively, they may usefully contribute to the struggle by fighting alongside 'their' men, but without distracting themselves or derailing the cause by manoeuvring for their own advantage after arms have been laid down. Yet, as histories of national liberation movements have shown, the establishment of a new order rarely if ever brings extended opportunities for women.[13] Traditional attitudes and roles prove resistant to change: patriarchal laws may be relaxed, or, in a crisis situation, adapted, but once the desired social transformation has been secured, political leadership tends to reimpose gendered structures with more or less the same severity as their former capitalist and/or colonial foes. Gender is in this respect the last redoubt of the radical activist. Considering his fervent commitment to liberation for all Kenya, Ngugi might have been expected to have in some way countered the sobering evidence of history. Yet apart from a glib didactic statement in *I Will Marry When I Want* (1982) regarding sex equality, an equality simply taken as understood by its spokesman Gicaamba,[14] Ngugi's most direct reference to social arrangements after the revolution is his 1981 blueprint for 'an education for a national patriotic culture'. 'Patriotic education' will produce individuals who are '*masters* of their natural and social environment', 'fully prepared in their twin struggle with nature and with *other men*' (emphasis added).[15] As the nation must be an association of producers who are also fighters, military training forms an important part of the programme. No provision is made for those who are the reproducers or nurturers of the nation.

In a 1982 interview for *Marxism Today* Ngugi makes his hierarchical ordering of values clear: though 'factors' of caste and race may contribute to social divisions he stresses that these must not be allowed to blur the 'basic' reality of class struggle (the 'gender factor' is completely omitted).[16] Ngugi could, it is true, justify his accentuating class in this way by contending that the imposition of colonial structures has aggravated existing patriarchal attitudes and, consequently, that the more immediate evil of (neo)colonialism must first be eradicated. Indeed, although he tends to see the coloniser as the chief oppressor, Ngugi has acknowledged the broadly 'reactionary' nature of traditional social norms.[17] And yet, confidently setting class above gender distinctions while still putting in a rhetorical claim for women's liberation, he does not pause to examine the overtly masculine premises of his economic arguments. He ceaselessly refers to the workers of Kenya, but he does not define precisely what he means by a worker. From his portrayal of those who work, however, it is clear that he views 'productive' labour as male-dominated: even in his utopian fiction, the workers, as opposed to the peasants, are male. Wariinga of *Devil on the Cross*, in becoming an engineer, is immediately a special case, a unique 'professional'. In her previous job as a secretary she was presumably not a 'worker'. These divisions can, perhaps, be defended on account of their correspondence to East African reality. In general terms, too, women's work spaces traditionally lie outside the field of so-called 'real' labour. Yet it is in his refusal to valorise in any way the activity of the marginal economic sector that Ngugi's disregard for the work of women becomes significant. In so far as most of Ngugi's women characters can be slotted into either one of two categories: of mothers, assumed to be non-workers, and of prostitutes, like Wanja of *Petals of Blood*, part of a lumpen-proletariat – both groups are automatically, and conveniently, sidelined. They are available either for over-valuation as the mascot heroines of national troops, as are reformed and conscientised prostitutes like Guthera in *Matigari*, or they are enlisted as the literal reproducers of those troops – support roles in an essentially male struggle.

Despite this, even in the face of such gender polarisation, we should pause to acknowledge that Ngugi's women characters do remain pioneers in the field of Anglophone African fiction written by men. In their strength of character, their spirit and self-reliance, they are undoubtedly unique. More often than not they demonstrate a firmer resolve and a deeper understanding than their male counterparts. Wanja is motivated by an energy and a conviction in the execution of her plans that even the revolutionary leader Karega in *Petals of Blood* cannot match. Wariinga blazing a trail of defiance through the final pages of *Devil on the Cross* must leave her vacillating beloved Gatuiria behind her. In *A Grain of Wheat*, *Petals of Blood* and *Matigari* the redemptive group of central characters is dominated by a single woman – linking them together, as in Mumbi's case in *A Grain of Wheat*, or forcing them apart, as does Wanja in her affairs with Munira and Karega.

Even so, it is clear that Mumbi and Wanja and perhaps even the daughterly figure of Guthera stand at the position of epicentre primarily on the strength of their *essentialised being* – in that they are women or, more precisely, biological females. Moreover, whether as lover, prostitute or potential childbearer, it is basically as sexual partner (or in Guthera's case, formerly sexualised body) that the male characters are drawn to them. Ngugi in effect fits his women characters into the thoroughly well-worn stereotypes of mother and of whore. In view of the prevalent biblical imagery in his work, we see woman defined either as Mother Mary, the long-suffering Mumbi, named for the mother of the Gikuyu, or as the prostitute Mary Magdalene, Wanja, who leads men, both the capitalists (Kimeria) and their opponents (Munira), into perdition. That remarkable magnetic power of Ngugi's women to which the critics David Cook and Michael Okenimkpe, among others, refer in glowing terms is simply another manifestation of the potent, nameless forces with which women as 'nature' or as 'wild' have traditionally been associated.[18]

It is interesting that with respect to his determination in the later novels to develop powerful women characters as counterparts to the strong hero figures he favours, in Ngugi's early work similar tendencies emerge in embryonic form. In particular, as the focus in the early novels is more on the remote past and the pristine origins of Gikuyu people, mother figures signify prominently. In the *Secret Lives* (1975) stories the mothers suffer and find fulfilment in so far as they can give expression to their maternal instincts and thus satisfy their husband's demands. Mwihaki of *Weep Not, Child* (1964), and Muthoni and the younger Nyambura of *The River Between* (1965), in their courage and endurance figure as Mumbis-in-the-making, and, like Mumbi, are consistently viewed only in their connection with men. Mwihaki, for example, gives Njoroge strength and support when he is wavering, yet the ideals she upholds are based on what he has taught her. Nyambura and Muthoni for their part passively represent the two sides of a conflict over female genital mutilation or 'circumcision' directed solely by men. At this stage of the writer's career, admittedly, these stereotypes were predictable: the younger Ngugi had not yet come out in support of sexual equality, let alone of class conflict. Yet it is for this very reason that the characterisation of women in the early novels provides a useful point of reference. Here Ngugi upholds a male-dominated order by establishing archetypal roles and patterns of relationships that will continue, albeit in transmuted form, into the later novels.

Characteristically, woman in the early novels is, if not silent super-heroine, then doomed to be equally silent victim. In *The River Between* Muthoni's excision wound (sign of her submission to a restrictive tradition) proves fatal, yet she dies in a beatific state. She believes she has been 'made beautiful in the tribe', that is to say, she has been glorified as a woman by submitting to the ancient laws of the elders, the fathers of the village.[19] In *A Grain of Wheat*, it is not merely the case that Njeri and Wambuku lay down their lives for the hero Kihika. As though to drive home the image of woman as victim, Ngugi also introduces the one account of a rape (of a white woman) in all the fiction about the 1950s Mau Mau conflict.[20] In the 1992 revised edition of the novel this incident is revealingly rewritten as the killing of the woman Dr Lynd's dog.

Moving to the later novels, in *Petals of Blood*, once again, a woman is used as victim. As a thriving madam, obviously equipped with an extremely long-suffering body and durable vagina, Wanja becomes a ready symbol for the ravaged state of Kenya.[21] Yet her courage and resourcefulness in turning her exploitation as a woman and as a member of the oppressed classes to her advantage is finally discredited. As Karega self-righteously makes explicit, thereby laying down male law, her struggle means very little because her method of resistance is simply to exploit in return. His final word is one of condemnation; no possibility of negotiation and certainly no expression of tenderness is permitted. And yet at times the only way in which Wanja was able to survive was 'to sell [herself] over and over again'.[22] Indeed, Ngugi allows her this; her immense resilience is recognised: but, in the last pages of the novel, the priority is given to the workers' struggle. The representative of the a-political lumpen-proletariat is discarded. Such a ranking of social values evidently rests on unquestioned assumptions regarding the submission of women to male demand. Here, as elsewhere, it would seem that female power is recognised only in those areas where it is ultimately subdued to male control. In the field of sexual relations, certainly, the willing submission of women is the order of the day. The texts are unabashedly frank: from *The River Between* to *Petals of Blood*, all descriptions of sexual encounters invariably and emphatically cast the man in the dominant position. The woman, whether she is the adoring Nyokabi, or the self-sufficient Wanja, is passive, openly subordinate, 'exhilaratingly weak' and, apart from the raped Dr Lynd, consistently transported by phallic power.[23]

As if to make amends, Ngugi in his more recent work introduces heroines who have made a decisive break with a former life of mothering and/or whoring in their commitment to a revolutionary cause. The figure of the old seer or 'Mother of men', Wambui of *A Grain of Wheat*, Nyakinyua of *Petals of Blood*, reappears as the ancient and noble Wangari of *Devil on the Cross*. Like her predecessors Wangari was involved in Mau Mau as a messenger and carrier of arms, but, unlike them, plays a more prominent role in the present-day action of the novel, finally being proclaimed as 'heroine of our nation'.[24] As for the younger women, the Woman and the woman fighter in the play *The Trial of Dedan Kimathi* (1976), Wariinga in *Devil on the Cross*, and Guthera in *Matigari*, if Ngugi's early heroines were forceful, then these women characters with their fortitude, resolve and resourcefulness are larger than life. As in the earlier novels, this stature is highlighted by their position as the lone representatives of their sex in a field of male characters. In contrast to those like Muturi the noble worker or Matigari the guerrilla, who, importantly, interact with one another as equals in carrying out specific tasks, the women, elevated on the basis of their being desirable or once-desirable objects, react *upon* rather than *with* their male associates.

With Wariinga certainly, perhaps even more so than with *Matigari*'s Guthera, Ngugi turns the heat up high. After her experience at the Devil's Feast, a satirical competition to choose the most successful capitalist thieves and robbers in the world, Wariinga finds a new purpose in life, the struggle for a more equitable social system, and changes accordingly. The reader is not allowed to miss a detail. Wariinga, we are told, new 'heroine of toil', simultaneously 'black beauty' and 'our engineering hero', has said '*goodbye* to being secretary', the flower in Boss Kihara's life, and has '[stormed] a man's citadel' (emphasis in text to denote use of an English word). She is not only a qualified engineer, a modest fourth in an all-male class, but a formidable practitioner of judo and karate who airily knocks down her opponents and, if they still offer resistance, produces a gun.[25] Yet, although she is said to engage enthusiastically in the struggle with nature that Ngugi has previously cast in terms of the male generic pronoun, she is reclaimed for womanhood; despite her hard labour in the workshop, she remains sexually attractive. The point is repeatedly emphasised: Wariinga's clothes are said to fit her like a skin; her beauty floors both her boyfriend and the Rich Old Man.[26] She is thus confirmed in her hyper-symbolic status. She is the exemplary female revolutionary, a fighter and 'still a woman', as perfect and untouchable as a holy image and made to order like her clothes.

Wariinga, it is fair to say, is put into the service of a basically didactic text. Just as the Woman's voice in *The Trial of Dedan Kimathi* sounds out, disembodied, enjoining the boy to 'become a man',[27] so Wariinga appears as an inspiration in a struggle that is still defined and operated by men. She is aggressive, fearless and single-minded; she will contribute her energies to changing society; but, though she gives up all else, she does not sacrifice her femaleness, her soft hair and comely shape: in her bag she carries both a phase-tester and a hand mirror.[28] And further, in order that there may be no mistake as to their crusading roles, both Wariinga and the Woman are granted the possession of a gun. Women, we realise, are not to be left out of any military-preparedness programme.

Yet, in bestowing upon his revolutionary heroines the quintessential emblem of phallic power in this way, Ngugi clearly betrays his masculine affiliations. Instead of preparing the way towards liberation by dismantling those structures and traditions that marginalise and oppress women, he disguises the rigid distinctions that such structures enforce when his women come dressed as men. Instead of questioning processes of objectification, he places a male weapon in the hands of his women characters and sets them on pedestals as glorified revolutionaries, inspiriting symbols for a male struggle. Women, that is, are made acceptable as national figures by becoming more like men. Male values come encased in female shape just as, in *The Trial of Dedan Kimathi*, guns come disguised as loaves of bread.[29]

Ngugi's most recent novel *Matigari* confirms these signifiers of normative patriotic identity. In this set-piece allegory, as Abdulrazak Gurnah has described it, the generic figure of the true Kenyan is the central character Matigari, the fighter, comrade and brother.[30] In other words, the margin of liberatory potential that Wariinga as a woman revolutionary earlier represented, is here overlooked. Where she flung off the final pages of *Devil on the Cross* brandishing her gun, Matigari walks into his eponymous tale carrying his AK 47 rifle, declaring his presence as at once an archetypal guerrilla fighter and popular patriotic leader.

Matigari's full name, meaning 'the patriots who survived the bullets', designates his symbolic status as the people's collective hero.[31] He has fought for the nation and has now come again to his homeland to guide and to save them. He is the people in ideal form: a 'little man' and yet a prophet. He speaks of the nation as his family, and the land as his house. Predictably, his mission is to lead his followers to become more like him – to become *matigari*. His characterisation thus confirms on every side the tenacity of time-honoured nationalist tropes: most obviously, those of the loyal nationalist as soldier, the patriot as patriarch, and of national fighters as a band of brothers; more generally, that of the national movement as a male-dominated family drama. It is under the persuasive influence of Matigari's paternal voice of authority that the woman Guthera is transformed from a life of prostitution into his helper, a fighter for the national cause. He saves her from her sin in the manner of a Christ, bidding her to 'Get up . . . Come, stand up, mother'.[32]

Although it is obviously heartfelt, Ngugi's interest in new images of women and women's power – I would submit – does not alter what is for him a more fundamental configuration of power, that involving national agency and authority. Guthera's role relative to Matigari is primarily one of support: she accompanies him courageously into his final moments, but it is he who leads. Like Wariinga, Guthera doubles up as a strong woman and a desirable object: her clothes fit her 'as though she was created in them'.[33] In the familial triad she forms with Matigari and Muriuki, the boy-supporter who survives the novel's final disaster, Guthera acting as both prostitute and surrogate mother can thus be seen as representative of all Kenyan womanhood. In relation to a character like Wanja she signifies an interesting new development in so far as she also appears to operate within the family triad as a postsexual *daughter* rather than as a mate to Matigari. Even so, the logic of family inheritance suggests that, unlike in *Devil on the Cross*, the child Muriuki (Wanja's baby grown-up?), and not the reformed woman, prefigures the free Kenyan citizen of the future. The true successor of Matigari can be neither a vulnerable mother nor a former prostitute. As Matigari, the people's hero, is a man and a fighter, and as he returns to his people so that his people in turn will become *matigari*, then the conclusion which seems inevitable is that Matigari can bequeath his AK 47 to no one other than a son.

To Ngugi, therefore, other interests give way before the 'higher social system of democracy and socialism' in a free Kenya.[34] Yet, even within his framework of values, the shells of the older systems, the skeletons of inherited structures and values, are not so easily discarded. A different statue may be erected in the town square, perhaps even a '(monument) / To our women', but it remains a monolith.[35] Ngugi of course acts alongside many others when he attacks the colossus of white western maledom, yet hesitates to dislodge the ramparts of its patriarchy. The difficulty lies not in his construct of the nation in itself but in the identification of national freedom with *male* freedom. The continent-wide adoption from earlier regimes of an unchanged patriarchal state has brought about, also in his writing, a continuing adherence to the concept of a centrally-based authority, an extensive apparatus of control administered from above (and by men). Within such structures the people's culture, whose vitality Ngugi so often proclaims, evidently cannot flourish on its own. Culture, he stresses, 'must prepare (its) recipients to change the world'.[36] Yet, as Mikhail Bakhtin, that famously ardent proponent of multivoicedness, once wrote, the 'consolidation' of any one dominant ideological system requires that: 'All . . . creative acts are conceived and perceived as possible expressions of a single consciousness, a single spirit . . . the spirit of a nation, the spirit of a people, the spirit of history'.[37]

In the name of national liberation, the people, the broad masses of Kenya and also the 'liberated' women, are expected to march in the forces and swell the one national chorus. The policies of the future remain official and bureaucratic, dominated by the interests of the patriarchal state before all else. The recuperation of the woman figure in cultural iconography becomes in effect a remaking of icons. Dissenting voices, decentring languages, are against the rules, and this despite the fact that in the 1998 *Penpoints, Gunpoints and Dreams* Ngugi defines art as that which resists state 'containment'. In his analysis of the failure of national liberation struggles, Benedict Anderson neatly encapsulates this resilience of the univocal order (and implicitly of the masculine presence securely lodged with it): 'Like the complex electrical-system in any large mansion when the owner has fled, the state awaits the new owner's hand at the switch to be very much its own brilliant self again'.[38] The overlord of old remains in charge; it is, in Ngugi's own words, still 'the master's dance to the master's voice'.[39]

Notes

1 Ngugi wa Thiong'o, *Detained: A Writer's Prison Diary* (London: Heinemann, 1981), pp. 8–9.

2 Ngugi wa Thiong'o, *Matigari* (London: Heinemann, 1989).

3 See Abdulrazak Gurnah, 'Transformative strategies in the fiction of Ngugi wa Thiong'o', in Abdulrazak Gurnah (ed.), *Essays on African Writing: A Re-evaluation*, vol. 1 (Oxford: Heinemann, 1993), p. 143. It is worth reading Ngugi's nationalism in connection with the important Gikuyu cultural text, Jomo Kenyatta's *Facing Mount Kenya: The Tribal Life of Gikuyu*, intro. B. Malinowski (London: Secker and Warburg, 1938).

4 Ngugi wa Thiong'o, *Devil on the Cross* (London: Heinemann, 1982), p. 60.

5 See Ngugi, *Detained*, p. 3. Ngugi began to write *Devil on the Cross*, his first novel in Gikuyu, during his period of detention in the 1970s.

6 As early as 1971, Eddah Gachukia commended Ngugi for correcting the negative image of women in African fiction. See Gachukia, 'The role of women in Ngugi's novels', *Busara*, 3:4 (1971), 30–1. In the 1980s David Cook and Michael Okenimkpe continued this trend by emphasising the vital role of women in Ngugi's novels: David Cook and Michael Okenimkpe, *Ngugi wa Thiong'o* (London: Heinemann, 1983), pp. 135–6. Charles Nama and Tobe Levin also find inspirational value in Ngugi's vision of women in revolt in: Charles A. Nama, 'Daughters of Moombi', and Tobe Levin, 'Scapegoats of culture and cult', both in Carole Boyce Davies and Anne Adams Graves (eds), *Ngambika: Studies of Women in African Literature* (Trenton, NJ: Africa World Press, 1986), pp. 139–49, and pp. 205–21, respectively. For a contrary view, see Gurnah, 'Transformative strategies', pp. 142–58; and Florence Stratton, *Contemporary African Literature and the Politics of Gender* (London and New York: Routledge, 1994), especially pp. 158–64. Gurnah discusses the consolidation of the authority of patriarchal figures, culminating in Matigari, in Ngugi's oeuvre. Stratton, in a reading engaged with an early version of the present chapter, neatly argues that Ngugi's attempted reversal of the sexual allegory

equates with an overdetermined othering: 'rather than rewriting nationalism, he rewrites [and masculinises] women'.

7 Ngugi, *Detained*, p. 10.

8 Ngugi, *Detained*, pp. 10–11, 46–8; *Barrel of a Pen* [1983] (London: Heinemann, 1986), p. 41, 55–6; *Decolonising the Mind: The Politics of Language in African Literature* (London: Heinemann, 1986), p. 102.

9 Ngugi, *Detained*, pp. 74–8; *Barrel of a Pen*, pp. 39–51; *Decolonising the Mind*, pp. 45, 54–6. Ngugi returns to the Kamiriithu project in *Penpoints, Gunpoints and Dreams: Towards a Critical Theory of the Arts and the State in Africa* (Oxford and New York: Oxford University Press, 1998), pp. 37–69.

10 Ngugi, *Detained*, p. 46.

11 Ngugi, *Barrel of a Pen*, pp. 39–51.

12 Ngugi, *Decolonising the Mind*, pp. 12, 18, 29, 70, 91, 99, 105.

13 See, for example, Miranda Davies (ed.), *Third World – Second Sex* (London: Zed Press, 1986); Sheila Rowbotham, *Women, Resistance and Revolution* (Harmondsworth: Penguin, 1972); and this book, pp. 34–5. With respect to a specific African liberation struggle, see: Josephine Nhongo-Simbanegavi, *For Better or Worse? Women and ZANLA in Zimbabwe's Liberation Struggle* (Harare: Weaver, 2000).

14 Ngugi wa Thiong'o and Ngugi wa Mirii, *I Will Marry When I Want* (London: Heinemann, 1982), pp. 104–5.

15 Ngugi, *Barrel of a Pen*, pp. 98–9.

16 Interview with Ngugi, *Marxism Today* (September 1982), 34.

17 Ngugi, *Detained*, p. 106.

18 See, among many other sources, Susan Griffin, *Women and Nature: The Roaring Inside Her* (London: Harper, 1975), and Shirley Ardener (ed.), *Perceiving Women* (London: Malaby, 1975).

19 Ngugi wa Thiong'o, *The River Between* [1965] (London: Heinemann, 1978), p. 44.

20 The observation regarding the uniqueness of this rape is David Maughan-Brown's in *Land, Freedom and Fiction: History and Ideology in Kenya* (London: Zed Press, 1985), pp. 252–5.

21 As, too, does the younger Wariinga. For an explicit analogy, see Ngugi, *Detained*, p. 59.

22 Ngugi wa Thiong'o, *Petals of Blood* [1977] (Cape Town: David Philip, 1982), pp. 325–7.

23 Ngugi wa Thiong'o, *A Grain of Wheat* [1967] (London: Heinemann, 1982), p. 45.

24 Ngugi, *A Grain of Wheat*, p. 70; and *Devil on the Cross*, p. 198, respectively.

25 All references are to Ngugi, *Devil on the Cross*, pp. 216–21.

26 Ngugi, *Devil on the Cross*, p. 217.

27 Ngugi wa Thiong'o, *The Trial of Dedan Kimathi* [1976] (London: Heinemann, 1985), pp. 22, 41, 43.

28 Ngugi, *Devil on the Cross*, p. 217.

29 Ngugi, *The Trial of Dedan Kimathi*, p. 43.

30 Gurnah, 'Transformative strategies', p. 155.

31 Ngugi, *Matigari*, p. 20.

32 Ngugi, *Matigari*, p. 32.
33 Ngugi, *Matigari*, p. 28.
34 Ngugi, *Barrel of a Pen*, p. 99.
35 Ngugi, *The Trial of Dedan Kimathi*, p. 73.
36 Ngugi, *Barrel of a Pen*, p. 99.
37 Mikhail Bakhtin, *Problems of Dostoevsky's Poetics*, ed. and trans. Caryl Emerson (Minneapolis: Minneapolis University Press, 1984), p. 82.
38 Benedict Anderson, *Imagined Communities: Reflections on the Origin and Spread of Nationalisms* [1983], rev. edn (London: Verso, 1991), p. 145.
39 Ngugi, *Petals of Blood*, p. 163.

3

Of goddesses and stories:
gender and a new politics in Achebe

The Almighty looking at his creation through the round undying eye of the Sun, saw and pondered and finally decided to send his daughter, Idemili, to bear witness to the moral nature of authority by wrapping around Power's rude waist a loincloth of peace and modesty. (Chinua Achebe, *Anthills of the Savannah*)[1]

Although he published the autobiographical meditation *Home and Exile* in 2002, Chinua Achebe's *Anthills of the Savannah* (1987) remains the culmination point of his achievement as a writer of fiction, as well as being an elaboration of his earlier novelistic interests. The novel is, as Ben Okri has remarked, Achebe's 'most complex and his wisest book to date'.[2] Dealing in coded terms with Nigeria's calcified power-elite, and the bankruptcy of its post-independence nepotistic politics, *Anthills of the Savannah* is in many respects a sequel to the penultimate novel *A Man of the People* (1966), which explored themes of political corruption and military takeover on the eve of Biafra.[3]

In the fifth and final novel Achebe's view of that elite and its position in the wider African context has become more uncompromising and – at least in theory – more attuned to gender and populist ideas. Unlike in the earlier text, the elite is no longer expected merely to engage in dramatic but gratuitous actions in defence of its political honour. Instead, the imperative is for it to revise its power base and its understanding of leadership, in so doing opening its doors to traditionally excluded groups. Achebe signals this change in his approach by admitting to the narrative representative members of 'the people' – taxi-drivers, a shop assistant, the urban poor and, towards the end, a market woman.

A degree of deliberate design would seem therefore to be animating the writer's new 'populist inclusiveness'.[4] The impression is reinforced by the over-determined development of the novel's two main heroes. The poet-journalist Ikem Osodi comes to realise the importance of establishing 'vital inner links with the poor and dispossessed . . . the bruised heart that throbs painfully at the core of the nation's being' (*AS* 141), while his friend Chris Oriko, carrying Ikem's light, works to forge contacts outside his elite group. The charge of deliberateness, however, should not disparage what is Achebe's obvious commitment to imagining a reformed national politics characterised by top-down inclusiveness and democratic participation, where the nation is restored as a common frame of reference.[5] Expressing at once mature disillusionment and extensively qualified fresh hope, his tentative new vision is manifested, too, in the strategic gender configurations of his central characters.

Opening on scenes of paranoid manoeuvre within a small, male elite determined to keep hold of power, the novel ends with the deaths of all three and a celebratory naming ritual involving three key female figures. The latter troika is made up of: Beatrice, Chris's old girlfriend, and a new priestess of the Igbo water-goddess Idemili; the pidgin-speaking Elewa, Ikem's lover; and Elewa's child by Ikem, called Amaechina, 'May-the-path-never-close' (*AS* 222). This life-affirming sisterhood, headed by the powerful Idemili 'taliswoman' (as I will elucidate), and reinforced by its affiliates from various classes, urban and rural, signifies a new conception of rulership, the beginning perhaps of a new era for Kangan, the Nigeria surrogate and nation-state in question. From the point of view of gender representation, the formation of this group certainly signals a new centring movement in Achebe's work, an attempt to revivify the nation as a unifying mythos by upgrading the position of women. The question is whether this shift indeed represents a thoroughgoing *revision* of ideas of power and leadership – in Ikem's terms, a 'new radicalism' – or whether it remains in the main emblematic. Is it rather a public enshrining of a canonised and perhaps stereotyped 'womanly' authority set up as a last resort in the face of a depraved political situation? Even with respect to a seemingly radical revision, the female gender in Achebe may continue to be a vehicle: woman is the ground of change or discursive displacement but not the subject of transformation. To determine to what extent this might be so, demands that Achebe's political vision in the novel be more closely scrutinised, in particular the conceptual language he employs to evoke that vision, his idea of the nation as integrative story.

Of the 'little clique' that found itself in a leadership position at Nigerian independence, Achebe has noted that it 'was not big enough . . . it had no perception of incorporating others'.[6] In *Anthills of the Savannah* Achebe has tried for incorporation – that is, he has attempted to stage a Gramscian 'top-down' or passive revolution, one that operates through the appropriation of popular elements by an elite. He has shifted authority out and away from the group that inherited state power in the 1960s, those first interpreters, in Wole Soyinka's phrase, of African nationalism. In so doing, he has called into question certain of the more inappropriate or destructive political conceptions that subtended the ruling ethos – the assumption of exclusiveness by the leadership, for example, and its unambiguous maleness. The challenge of his investigation depends heavily therefore on his portrayal of the new leaders, their style of politics and, in particular, on the viability of the class and gender constitution of the reformed ruling group.

In *The Trouble with Nigeria*, the pamphlet which Achebe wrote as an injunction to Nigeria just before the 1983 election scandal that ended in military takeover, light is shed on the political conception behind *Anthills of the Savannah*. 'The trouble with Nigeria', as Achebe cites the popular expression in that text, is, quite bluntly, the 'indiscipline' of its leaders, a national condition of 'lawlessness' and rampant selfishness.[7] The malaise is social, but its root cause and primary cure are to be found not in society at large, but in the nation's leadership. Leaders combine and so compound their lawlessness with influence and power: '[They] are, in the language of psychologists, role models. People look up to them and copy their actions. . . . Therefore if a leader lacks discipline the effect is apt to spread automatically down to his followers' (*TN* 31). The theory of the importance of strong and responsible leadership exercises Achebe throughout the pamphlet. Africa's national leaders have become its curse; they have succeeded in emptying the nation of its symbolic authority over a people. However, he also believes that the national leadership might even so be transformed into the postcolonial nation's salvation. Noteworthy in this diagnosis is his focus on character and role models, on the performative strategies of rule, in favour of class or neocolonial factors. Addressing Nigeria's elite as himself a self-conscious member of that group, Achebe is unambivalent in his view of leadership as the chief pivot of political and also of economic transformation. Although he believes that the advent of a new leader should be followed by a 'a radical programme of social and economic re-organisation or at least a well-conceived and consistent agenda of reform', he sees the first step in any process of change as being new rulership – in effect, the intervention of personality (*TN* 1).

In *The Trouble with Nigeria* Achebe upbraids a corrupt African elite; in *Anthills of the Savannah* he sets about deposing one. In the process, developing some of the concepts he introduces in the pamphlet, he begins to suggest what sort of leadership it is that might come in its place. Chris Oriko dies with the phrase 'the last green [bottle]' on his lips (*AS* 216, 231) – it is a cryptic reference to his own description of the increasingly more inward-looking and alienated rulers of the nation, Kangan. In a revelatory conversation with Ikem, Beatrice comments that, from the point of view of the three men trained for power at Lord Lugard College, '[t]he story of this country, as far as you are concerned, is the story of the three of you' – that is, of Sam, the present military Chief of State, Chris, his Commissioner for Information, and Ikem himself, the editor of the *National Gazette* (*AS* 66). During what will be the last days of his life, Chris comes to the same realisation: 'We? Who are we? The trinity who thought they owned Kangan as BB [Beatrice] once unkindly said? Three green bottles. One has accidentally fallen; one is tilting. Going, going, bang! Then we becomes I, becomes imperial We' (*AS* 191). As well as being a joke about Sam being left alone in power, the 'imperial We' reference also constitutes Chris's final comment on the obsession with power that, in different ways, motivated and so also undermined each member of the trinity.[8]

Ironically, however, after their demise, and despite efforts to incorporate and reform, a highly exclusive elite 'we' remains in place and in force. The small and still select group that coheres around Beatrice is to be the catalyst of the future. As Achebe remarks *à propos* of the novel, continuing his leadership thesis: 'the ultimate responsibility for getting us out of this bad patch is with the small group of people who, in one way or another, find themselves in positions of leadership'.[9] Within this group, the tendencies to nepotism and corruption that have compromised elite rule in the past will presumably be mitigated, at least in principle, by the advent of women's salubrious force. Yet their antici-pated beneficent influence does not eliminate other significant paradoxes. If woman is to be included in the new elite because she is uncorrupted by power, once included, how is she to retain that force for good? Is it because essential-ised woman is by definition a do-gooder? Putting this the other way about, if the faith in an alternative female rule depends on the stereotypical symbol or idea of woman as inspirer and spiritual guide, does that idea have much hope of practical application?

Paradoxes such as these emerge out of the uneasy co-existence in Achebe between two conceptions of national politics. On the one hand lies his politi-cal cynicism – not to say pessimism – which dominates the greater part of the novel, and to which Ikem gives chief expression. On the other hand is his apparent commitment to gender reform and to the redemptive power of myth and the homogenising national story, which comes into its own towards the end. As at once an exponent of the present politics and the herald of a future vision, Ikem gives us a clearer sense of these ambiguities.[10] In the incendiary speech to the university which is the immediate cause of his arrest and murder, Ikem resolutely rejects textbook revolutionary orthodoxies as presumptuously alien, and as being too theoretical within specific African or Kanganian con-texts (*AS* 158). The abstractions of such theories have permitted every sort of misinterpretation and licence on the part of their proponents. However, as he has already enjoined Beatrice, '[n]one of this is a valid excuse for political inac-tivity or apathy . . . the knowledge of it [is] the only protective inoculation we can have against false hopes' (*AS* 100).

Ikem's proposal, which recalls Achebe's own assertions in *The Trouble with Nigeria*, is to 're-form' [society] around . . . its core of reality' (100), that is, to develop its inner strengths and traditions, which in *Anthills of the Savannah* includes the conventionally respected power of womanhood. In typically metaphysical terms, Ikem wishes 'to connect his essence with earth and earth's people' (*AS* 140–1), yet is also aware of the classic dilemma of radical intellectuals, namely, that the knowledge and experience which constitute their power also isolate them.[11] Ironically, it is precisely his belief in indigenous sources of healing that tags his status as outsider, one who appreciates rituals as an intellectual and observer but does not live – or live through – them. The same paradoxically autochthonous custom marks Beatrice's position. Adherence to a redemptive vision does not transform her into a representative member of the earth's core: significantly, her status in the final ritual is that of specially elevated icon, not 'people's' goddess.

The point of resolution to which Ikem's ambivalent meditations lead is captured in Achebe's idea of incorporation, or broadening from the top – as opposed to, say, democratisation or widening from the base. As Achebe says, 'You have to broaden out so that when you are talking for the people, you are not only talking for a section or a group interest.'[12] Given his belief in an elite and therefore in hierarchy, the main possibility of reconciliation for Achebe lies in building and extending person-to-person connections across class, gender and political differences – and then to back these up with compelling stories. The intention is to maintain an elite leadership within a national framework, but to change its enunciative style: to develop social responsibility, a newly gendered image of power, not a little scepticism and a broader support base – in general to 'widen the scope' (*AS* 158). The leaders need to approach the 'owners' of the country in order to embrace and take into their bosom certain of their number. In keeping with the leitmotif of the novel, in the anthill that survives after the fires of the harmattan, Beatrice, seer and leader, inspirer of a select new group drawn from various social sectors, also serves as the queen who maintains the coherence of the colony. She may even represent the encapsulating anthill itself. As for Yeats's interlocking gyres, so important to Achebe as the signifier of his own anti-colonial practice, though things threaten to fall apart, though old vortices implode and collapse, centres – stable 'cores of reality' (elites, women as dispensers of succour) – are required if there is to be movement and change.

The question that remains unanswered, however, is how, following the broadening process, the non-sectional elite is to maintain its structural integrity and representativenesss, its invented identity as indigenous yet elevated cultural clique. It seems unlikely that the broadening process is always to be as conveniently *ad hoc* as is the formation of the group around Beatrice. How then to avoid the appearance of tokenism? Where are likely elite candidates – women, 'people' – to be found, and how will they be incorporated? How might an exclusive and reinvented water-goddess cult be transmitted to the masses? At this point, where questions of political identification and inclusion arise, Achebe as it were purposively intervenes in his narrative, transposing such difficulties into the finally irresolvable or numinous medium of the imaginary rather than trying for any sort of practical resolution. Just as oral story transmits the actions of the past into visions for the future, so *Anthills of the Savannah*, the African story in the form of a novel, carries its own vision of the future in appropriately figural terms. Achebe's transposition is in several ways quite openly an avoidance strategy, literally a displacement of the problem. In terms of the revolutionary or Marxist theory – 'orthodoxies of deliverance' (*AS* 99) – Ikem derides, the cop-out is patently obvious: existing economic and political structures remain firmly entrenched; class hierarchies (such as outlined in *The Trouble with Nigeria*) are endorsed; a soft-core, middle-class moralism is reinforced. From a gender perspective, by presenting the sisterhood's investiture as, in the main, metaphoric redemption, the danger is that woman's conventional position as inspirational symbol, the mentor who is never fully a political actor, becomes entrenched.

Achebe prepares for his caveat by eulogising the power and importance of myth and story-telling in the novel – in particular via the rhetoric of the Old Man from Abazon (*AS* 122–8), in the hymns and the poetic role of Ikem, and in the mythic apotheosis of Beatrice. For the present, the nation is to be redeemed metaphorically – and perhaps metaphysically – only: that is, by London-educated civil servants turning into Igbo priestesses, by syncretic ritual, and emblematic cross-class and cross-ethnic alliances. Achebe's general idea seems to be that, in the African context, where much metropolitan theory has already been uselessly imposed, political postulates, action plans and blueprints, even such as those set out in *The Trouble with Nigeria*, do not of themselves offer any hope of regeneration. Not by way of clichés from other histories and struggles, but in the figures of revivified gods and rituals drawn from its own local cultures, can the nation (whether Kangan or Nigeria) interpret present confusion and conceptualise a new future. Or, as Beatrice puts it, only with (implicitly homegrown) story is it possible to '[subvert] the very sounds and legends of daybreak to make straight my way' (*AS* 109).[13] This is related to Ikem's idea that humanity be remade around its own rich, inner resources; that, where 'times' will always 'come round again out of story-land' (*AS* 33), one should draw on history and story as it is and has been lived. The baby's name Amaechina significantly means 'May-the-path-never-close': tradition is cyclical, ongoing and constantly reinvented.

As the allusive, metaphoric images of a future dispensation give primary colour to the hope of *Anthills of the Savannah* – and to Achebe's own hope for the African nation – it is important to clarify the relation between symbolic transcendence and the presence of women that he attempts to forge. Key emblematic elements appear in Ikem's two dense prose poems, the 'Hymn to the Sun' (*AS* 30–3), and the meditation on Idemili's power (*AS* 102–5). In both, masculine images of power and agency are juxtaposed with 'feminine' evocations of peace and reconciliation: it is clear that dichotomous gender distinctions run deep. The final naming ceremony at Beatrice's flat dramatises and unifies some of these central symbolic meanings. It is now that Beatrice, prefiguration of a 'gynocentric' spiritual way, at last presents herself as the harbinger of a new order. From her initial act of pointing Ikem in the direction of his redeeming vision of woman (*AS* 96), through her being flippantly called a prophetess by Chris, we at last find Beatrice metamorphosed through her bereavement (though her suffering is stated not dramatised). She steps forwards as a priest-ess of Idemili, 'the unknown god [sic]' (*AS* 224). Simultaneously she also becomes the leader of the naming ceremony involving the baby Amaechina, replacing the traditional position of father or male family head (*AS* 222).

Whether the cross-reference is intentional or not, Achebe draws on the same redemptive (and ethnically specific) Igbo tradition of female devotion and worship as does Flora Nwapa in her 1966 novel *Efuru*.[14] That is to say, he adopts a well-established *woman's* tradition of exercising communal authority. With her moral gravitas, goddess-like carriage, and capacity for mediation and inspiration, Beatrice has recognisably become a daughter of the Idemili described in the myth earlier told by Ikem:

> In the beginning Power rampaged through our world, naked. So the Almighty looking at *his* creation through the round undying eye of the Sun, saw and pon-dered and finally decided to send his daughter, Idemili, to bear witness to the moral nature of authority by wrapping around Power's rude waist a loincloth of peace and modesty. (*AS* 102, emphasis added)

The incarnation of Idemili is a redemption of the present political situation, as it is of the neglect of the goddess in the past.[15] Attended by the pidgin-speaking child of the people Elewa, bearer of the seed of a poet, and a new child, a girl significantly carrying a male name – Beatrice's spiritual power as a blessed woman represents the fulfilment of Ikem's final vision of woman adopting a new and yet-to-be-imagined role. Woman in the final ceremony is in every respect the signifier of new hope (*AS* 98). In Achebe's own words, Beatrice and her entourage represent intrinsically compassionate women in their place 'in the forefront of history'.[16]

It cannot be denied that the potential of woman or women as celebrated at the end of *Anthills of the Savannah* represents a significant advance in the rep-resentation of women in the male-authored African novel (to the extent that such matters are teleological). It is most distinguished perhaps by Achebe's refusal to dictate exactly how that potential will be fulfilled. The novel clears a space for women to be themselves the prefiguring subjects of a new social and political vision. Yet at the same time, despite the efforts at rescheduling power, it is also true that the way in which Achebe privileges woman continues to bear familiar markings for gender, and that this to a certain extent compromises his

reimaged hope. Symptomatic of Achebe's difficulties is Elewa's transmogrifi-
cation as a woman of the people through conceiving Ikem's child (*AS* 184). As
part of the same symbolic logic, Amaechina's name – 'May-the-path-never-
close' – is part-translated as the 'Shining Path of Ikem' (*AS* 222). The implicit
idea of inheritance along a male line – of masculine influence as life-giving, and
of man as passing the rod of leadership on to woman – can of course be justified in terms of Achebe's belief in cyclical continuity: 'The remnant-shall-
return' (*AS* 222). Yet it equally signifies that maleness remains potently if also
laughably generative: as Beatrice discovers the day she dances with His
Excellency, 'the royal python' still stirs '[gigantically]' in the 'shrubbery' of
Idemili's shrine (*AS* 81).

Traditional gender-specific spheres of influence, too, appear to remain in
force. In their time-honoured way women in *Anthills of the Savannah*, especially the heroine who lacks 'book', wield power through sex and their bodies,
whereas man continues to control the word (Ikem's poetry) and also, we
presume, the world of politics. As in earlier nationalist writing, the artist, the
one who first defines the vision of the future and transmits the myths of the
people, is male.[17] Towards the end of the novel, it is true, a woman does decisively obtain control of vatic power. However, in that her transfiguration is,
almost by definition, couched in symbol, Beatrice remains confined within a
role that women have occupied many times before in the mythologies of
nations, states and polities; she incarnates the ideals and the desire of male
rulers and powerful spokesmen. It is made clear that she, too, will become a
writer in her own right, but her work will appear in the form of a memoir. It
will be very much *post hoc*, an after-shadow, concentrating on the exploits of
her powerful men friends. On a related point, to what extent is Beatrice's
induction into the cult of Idemili a specific development of a female 'spiritual'
stereotype, the inverse of the image of woman as unclean, or as body? As in
more traditional evocations of Mothers of Africa, or even of Mary Mother of
God, alternative woman in *Anthills of the Savannah* is represented as mystical,
in touch with the unknown, as mentor or genius of the (renewed) nation.

As problematic as the novel's networks of cross-gender filiation leading from
male leaders to female spiritual guides, are relationships within the group of
women. Here differences of class significantly complicate gender status, a
problem which connects with the question of the impossible constitution of
the ideal elite. In another representative scene, conflict arises during the crisis
period after Ikem's death when Agatha, Beatrice's maid, will not serve Elewa
because she is of her own class. In response Beatrice treats Agatha roughly,
pushing her aside to do the job herself. Achebe equips his heroine with a fair
amount of defensive rationalisation at this ungoddess-like behaviour. She is
exercised enough to repeat that Elewa's 'emergent consciousness' has acted
with transfiguring power, singling her out from the masses represented by

Agatha. It is this special 'almost godlike' touch which, in addition to being 'Ikem's girl', Beatrice concludes, has '[transformed] a half-literate . . . girl into an object of veneration', and someone she is able to befriend (*AS* 184).[18]

Beatrice makes quite clear that the complaining millions are to be saved, not by their own efforts, but by those with inner light – a capacity which further, mystically, separates the elite from the mass. Yet given this chasm of consciousness, or mystery of social redemption, how are the elite of enlightened humans – even if female – to interact with those in the masses, like Agatha, who do not have the gift of 'luminosity' (unless this is sympathetically transfused)? Conversely, with class barriers still in place, how are the masses to come into contact with those who have light? The apotheosis of the main women characters, impelled by the need to save the elite from itself, decisively brings the narrative back to the original problem of how to form an enlarged caucus, a problem now compounded by the reinforced distancing effect produced where symbolic women are (once again) canonised.

These difficulties are serious, especially as Achebe would want his novel, itself a restorative narrative, to give hints and guesses of a new, regenerative and 'regendered' order. That said, to criticise him for inconsistencies and moments of oversight is perhaps not to give sufficient regard, as he so emphatically does, to the redemptive art of narration and composition, and the metaphysics of that art. Where the problems of elite politics remain for the moment insoluble, symbol and story for him provide powerful, indeed crucial, means of thinking forwards. To borrow a phrase from Gayatri Spivak, a tale may become a '"non-expository" theory of practice';[19] in Fredric Jameson's terms, due to narrative, 'plot falls into history'.[20] 'What must a people do to appease an embittered history?' asks Beatrice. The answer is there in the eyes of her guests: they recognise in her act of articulation 'the return of utterance to the sceptical priest struck dumb for a season by the Almighty for presuming to set limits to his competence' (*AS* 220). It is in the radical adaptation of a mythical tradition and of indigenous oral resources that the new dispensation may be figured out.

In recent years Achebe's efforts to hone 'a new discursive space for a genuinely postcolonial [national and yet postnational] beginning', to quote from Simon Gikandi, has underscored his return to his Igbo roots.[21] In his sternly anti-colonial memoir *Home and Exile* (2000) he excavates further back in tradition for a genuinely *native* African state paradigm. Reading a national if premodern formation into Igbo precolonial society, he claims its internally co-operative conglomerate of villages and of market networks run by women, as radically egalitarian and as a possible model for present-day society.[22] If, as he strongly believes, 're-storying' people following colonial dispossession is an essential process, it is in this Igbo tradition of organising communal space, therefore, that a key 'enabling story' must lie.[23] At least in this text it would seem that Achebe, challenged by the imponderability of his vision of a new African state, has managed to find, albeit in a highly idealised form, the woman-friendly space that in *Anthills of the Savannah* he was still groping towards.

'Truth is beauty', Beatrice explains at the very end of the novel. It is the truth that lies in the final (if masculine) image of Chris withstanding his assailants like 'Kunene's Emperor Shaka' (*AS* 233); as well as the truth contained in the prominent image of the anthills holding their own truth of the past. Of course, implanted in the Keatsian 'truth [is] beauty' postulate is an inevitable suggestion of abstraction from real, material life: it is in keeping with this that Beatrice's new vocation, if we are to believe Flora Nwapa, demands retreat from the everyday. Yet Beatrice's statement is also a practical adaptation of the doctrine of aesthetic appreciation to a context, where, as Soyinka, too, has held, myth and ritual continue to thrive as living presences. They provide beauties of ceremony that may be redeemed for their lived reality or 'truth' as much as for their patterned form.[24]

Especially where, as in the quotidian reality of Third World military regimes or dictatorships, neither truth nor beauty is found in great abundance, Achebe appears to want to hold the two ideals in balance, the one intimating or anticipating the other:

> Man's best artifice to snare and hold the grandeur of divinity always crumbles in his hands, and the more ardently he strives the more paltry and incongruous the result. So it were better he did not try at all; far better to ritualise that incongruity and by involving the mystery of metaphor to hint at the most unattainable glory by its very opposite, the most mundane starkness – a mere stream, a tree, a stone, a mound of earth, a little clay bowl containing fingers of chalk. (*AS* 103)

So, just as a relatively ordinary woman may become, through her spiritual understanding, an example of a 'shining path' to her companions, in the same way an ordinary stick in the sand is transformed through ritual into a pillar of Idemili, the connection with 'earth and earth's people'. The real functions as an index to the beautiful. In this way, too, a random collection of individuals can come to represent the ritual passage into the future of a new Kangan. In 'serious' politics, symbols and supernatural signs such as these might seem superficial and, certainly from a gender point of view, compromising. Yet, where other options and modes of recompense are unsteady or have failed, symbols stand for points of intersection with, as Achebe would have it, the very present divine: as introjections of spirit; 'transactions' between the market-place, goddesses and the world (*AS* 102).

Notes

1 Chinua Achebe, *Anthills of the Savannah* (London: Heinemann, 1987), p. 102. References to *Anthills of the Savannah* will be included in the text along with the abbreviation *AS*.

2 Ben Okri, review of *Anthills of the Savannah*, *Observer* (20 September 1987), 9.

3 Chinua Achebe, *A Man of the People* (London: Heinemann, 1966).

4 Martin Turner, review, 'The story is our escort', *Wasafari*, 9 (Winter 88/99), 31–2, has commented that *Anthills* shows signs of a 'flirtation with *bien passant* ideology'. Odia Ofeimun, *Guardian* (Lagos, 20 November 1977), concurs, observing that Achebe has been learning from new trends in literature, and to some extent still shows himself to be a neophyte, the contemporary themes having been rather roughly assimilated into the novel's 'thin' plot structure.

5 See Simon Gikandi, *Reading Chinua Achebe* (London: James Currey, 1991), especially p. 138. Gikandi correctly reads the novel as an attempt to establish a multi-textured national narrative based in traditional communal morality, which will remind the disillusioned, post-independence nation of its optimistic, emancipatory beginnings.

6 Anna Rutherford, 'Interview with Achebe', *Kunapipi*, 9:2 (1987), 3.

7 Chinua Achebe, *The Trouble with Nigeria* (London: Heinemann, 1987), pp. 1, 27. References will henceforth be included in the text along with the abbreviation *TN*.

8 Neal Ascherson, 'Betrayal', *New York Review of Books* (3 March 1988), 4, comments: 'The three murders, senseless as they are, represent the departure of a generation that compromised its own enlightenment for the sake of power – even the power of bold opposition enjoyed by Ikem Osodi.'

9 Rutherford, 'Interview', p. 2.

10 On Achebe's endorsement of Ikem's views, and on his revisionist liberalism, see David Maughan-Brown, unpublished paper, '*Anthills of the Savannah*'s solution to *The Trouble with Nigeria*', ACLALS Triennial Conference, University of Kent, Canterbury, 29 August 1989, pp. 4–5.

11 As Ikem discovers in his second encounter with Braimoh, the taxi-driver. The ceaseless circlings of such cognitions about 'the people' are of course a measure of Achebe's political pessimism. See Ascherson, 'Betrayal', p. 3.

12 Rutherford, 'Interview', p. 3.

13 On interpreting the past 'creatively', see Rutherford, 'Interview', p. 4.

14 See Flora Nwapa, *Efuru* [1966] (London: Heinemann, 1987), and also *Idu* [1970] (London: Heinemann, 1987). Idemili is the equivalent of Nwapa's Woman of the Lake. See also Ifi Amadiume, *Male Daughters, Female Husbands: Gender and Sex in an African Society* (London: Zed Press, 1987), pp. 99–105; and chapter 5 in this book. It is noteworthy that Achebe draws on specifically Igbo symbols in a novel that takes Kanganian (Nigerian?) national unity as a political given.

15 Ikem's observation, that myth has been used to marginalise women (*AS* 98), is echoed by Achebe, both in the Rutherford interview, and in 'Achebe on editing', *WLWE*, 7:1 (Spring 1987), 1–5, especially p. 2.

16 Rutherford, 'Interview', p. 4.

17 Ifi Amadiume, 'Class and gender in *Anthills of the Savannah*', *PAL-Platform*, 1:1 (March 1989), 9, has suggestively pointed out that, although the Almighty in Achebe's (Ikem's) myth is male, she knows of 'no translation from Igbo which would render God a he and a man'. Moreover, Amadiume believes that Idemili in the Igbo pantheon is usually not given a father.

18 Bearing in mind the dichotomous characterisation of the 'girl'/militiawoman Gladys in Achebe's short story 'Girls at war' (see my introduction), the progression from 'girl' into sanctified object via a form of national service is revealing. See Chinua Achebe, *Girls at War and Other Stories* [1972] (London: Heinemann, 1986), pp. 103–23, as well as the reading of this story in chapter 1.

19 Gayatri Chakravorty Spivak, *In Other Worlds: Essays in Cultural Politics* (London and New York: Routledge, 1988), p. 85.

20 Fredric Jameson, *Situations of Theory: Essays 1971–1986*, vol. 1, *The Ideologies of Theory* (London: Routledge, 1988), p. 127.

21 Gikandi, *Reading Chinua Achebe*, pp. 147–8.

22 Chinua Achebe, *Home and Exile* (Oxford and New York: Oxford University Press, 2000), pp. 5–7.

23 Achebe, *Home and Exile*, pp. 79, 60

24 See also Rutherford, 'Interview', p. 4.

4

The hero's story:
the male leader's autobiography and the
syntax of postcolonial nationalism

I was literally carrying on my back the history, culture and heritage of my people.
(Nelson Mandela, *Long Walk to Freedom*)[1]

'In Quest of the Golden Fleece': the leader's autobiography as national genre

Narratives, as has already been seen in this book, give form to and legitimate
the process of postcolonial and national coming-into-being. Stories codify
national reality and space, and allow emergent national identities to be performed. By looking at a particularly definitive, *form-giving* or *in-forming* narrative genre, the independence leader's autobiography, the work of this chapter
is to show how the story of the growth to self-consciousness of the leader at
national independence often presents as a synonym for the rise of the nation.
In both Indian and African nationalist movements, the two points of focus in
this chapter, leaders' tales operate as inaugural symbolic texts shaping and justifying configurations of status and power in the postcolonial nation(-to-be),
including the interconnection of nationalist ideology and gender politics. Of
particular interest here will be the way in which the leader's autobiography
helps legitimate the gender specifics of the nation. Where the leader's individual selfhood is equated with the nation's collective identity, key nationalist
touchstones like pride and loyalty are represented as predominantly a matter
for men.

Benedict Anderson and Timothy Brennan have spoken of particular kinds
of texts, especially the novel, as tightly associated with the composition of
nationalist imaginings and movements.[2] The text which I would want to
assign a crucial place at the very point of inscription of the new nation, specifically the formerly colonised nation-at-independence, is the autobiography
of the chief or primary leader of the triumphant nationalist movement – often
also the president or prime minister of the new nation-state. Across African
postcolonial history, for example, the publication of the leader's autobiogra-

phy coincided closely with the moment of independence. The trend continued into the 1990s with the appearance of Nelson Mandela's *Long Walk to Freedom* in 1994, the year of South Africa's first multiparty elections. The 2003 publication of the authorised biography of Walter and Albertina Sisulu, African National Congress (ANC) struggle leaders alongside Mandela, was in all likelihood planned as an anticipatory ten-year anniversary marker of that historic year.[3]

The new nation that emerges after the incursions of colonisation, one based on borders and hierarchies drawn up in colonial times, in many ways constitutes an impoverished symbolic field, certainly when it comes to establishing that nation as a player in the modern world, even if also rooted in tradition. Within this field, the leader's life-story plays the important role of supplying the nation with a self-determining modern history, as I will suggest in a reading of Jawaharlal Nehru's *An Autobiography* (1936) and its partial sequel *The Discovery of India* (1946) as foundational nationalist texts and templates of the genre.[4] Yet in the same breath, even as it positions the leader at the historical summation point that is independence, the leader's autobiography also supplies defining images, drawn from the life, through which to understand the nation's emergence into subjecthood, and to justify its new arrangements of privilege and authority. As Declan Kiberd comments, though with specific reference to the visionary, form-giving impact of W. B. Yeats's poetry: 'In such a self-charged context, nation-building can be achieved by the simple expedient of writing one's autobiography: and the autobiography in [the nation] becomes, in effect, the autobiography of the nation'.[5]

A second key factor in addition to the struggle against colonialism to explain the importance of what I will call the national hero's autobiography, is that anti-colonial nationalist movements, like fledgling postcolonial nations, are typically distinguished by the existence of small, western-educated elite leaderships socially divided from the national mass. The autobiography of the (normatively) male leader therefore serves the useful purpose of writing the leadership *into* the nation. In other words, by dramatising and thus explaining the leader's self-description as nationalist, the life-narrative helps to validate his position and/or status. Self-inscription becomes nationalist self-realisation: composing the discrete, monadic entity, which is conventionally the objective of autobiography, involves incrementally knitting that entity into the national collective.[6] This aspect of the leader's life-story offers a special instance of the coercive effects that are wreaked upon the autobiographical subject by autobiography, as in Paul de Man's theory of the genre. In view of its conspicuous failure to achieve representational closure (in that past and narrating selves cannot coincide), de Man suggests that autobiography, which is necessarily a construction, instead reads itself back into the life in question: 'acquires a degree of representation productivity'.[7]

Looked at more closely, the leader's autobiography effectively sets in motion a process of reciprocal, even circular, legitimation. Nationalist values are enacted in the life-story of the leader, who is necessarily figured in that story as the pre-eminent, most trusty, typical or notable member of the nation. In turn, the achievement of national selfhood and independence acts to bestow pre-eminence upon him. (This applies, incidentally, not only to the subjects of personality cults, such as Kwame Nkrumah, but also to those protesting modesty and introversion, like Nehru.) In the life-story the leader's birth represents one of the modern origins of the new nation. His dedication and possible suffering in the national cause connect with the people's struggle while their pain and effort reciprocally amplify and explain his own. His route from provincial or rural obscurity and unselfconsciousness to the city, site of the achievement of modern nationalist self-awareness, traces the nation's own historical path or even, as the case may be, demographic profile. And, importantly, his self-positioning as male gives legitimating form to what is across the board the predominantly masculine image of the new national leadership. The fact that the 'shelf-life' of the postcolonial leader's autobiography in the public domain is usually relatively short, points up this overall constructedness as it does its occasional value: as the independent nation's history unfolds, so the context-governed 'representation productivity' of the autobiography rapidly grows obsolete. (Due to their iconic global status the life-stories of Nehru and Mandela are exceptions to this rule.)

Philip Dodd has observed that the point of closure of male autobiography is conventionally the subject's achievement of a vocation.[8] Emphasis in these texts is on the unfolding of a coherent self over time and on the singularity of the individual life.[9] In contrast, women's autobiographical writings, certainly in Britain and the United States, tend to show greater awareness of the gaps, uncertainties and fictions involved in the construction of identity. Models of the self are less individualistic, more relational and group-based, if also often alienated (given that autobiographical writing is itself seen as a masculine tradition).[10] The theme of accomplishment in these writings rarely dominates: self-disclosure and the recognition of achievement are usually linked to some higher cause, family role, public purpose or personal ideal.

Against these two trends, and bringing together features of both, the postcolonial leader's autobiography is distinguished by the linking of individual *with* national self-formation. Here it is essential at one and the same time to project an identifiable difference *against* the coloniser, *and* to configure a 'typical' national self, a *sameness*, to provide a model for the production of national citizens. As a leading spokesman for the African National Congress, Nelson Mandela is explicit concerning the heavily freighted symbolism of his walking into a white court of law wearing traditional Xhosa dress for his October 1962 trial: 'I was literally carrying on my back the history, culture and heritage of my people. That day, I felt myself to be the embodiment of African nationalism, the inheritor of Africa's difficult but noble past and her uncertain future.'[11] As Mandela's exemplary stress on embodiment and inheritance shows, the object of attention in the autobiography is at once the individual and the national past, where the leader's experience, character and physical presence are set up as metonymic of the national. The demand, too, is for an end-directed cohesion, for a steady convergence of individual and communal historical paths towards the specific culmination point of national unity and independence.

Most of the autobiographies explored in this chapter almost necessarily conclude with that moment of independence, or with its strong anticipation. The implication is clear: the leader's vocation is fully realised when the new nation is born. (Indeed, in that the publication of the autobiography is often timed to mark this event, market forces intervene in this area of postcolonial cultural production as in others, as discussed in chapter 9.) In these narratives the trajectory of the leader's life is allowed to merge with, and be subsumed in, the nation's, even as the leader is seen to carry the nation's political destiny upon his shoulders. This is formally demonstrated where the narrative closes with a statement of vision, intent or retrospection, as appears in its most pronounced form in *Awo* (1960), the autobiography of Obafemi Awolowo, leader of Action Group in Nigeria at the time of independence.[12] Across its latter half his life-narrative is almost completely paved over with debates about procedure and strategy, declarations of personal and nationalist belief quoted from contemporary documents and speeches, presumably mostly his own, and assessments of Nigeria's global political position. In Jawaharlal Nehru's *An Autobiography*, too, lengthy reflections on current debates and policy issues – the legacy of the Indian Civil Service, communalism on the sub-continent – are concentrated in the final third of the book. The preface to Albert Luthuli's autobiography *Let My People Go* (1962) glosses the close knit between autobiography, nationalist involvement and the leader's performance of his nationalist identification in this way: 'I regard my life as one among many, and my role in the resistance as one among many. If I have anything to say, it is not because of any particular distinction, but because I am identified with those who love South Africa.'[13]

Mandela's *Long Walk to Freedom*, which is in several ways a rewriting and consolidation of the forms of ideology of the earlier biographies, interestingly gives markedly more space to personal reminiscence, what are called 'family moments', than they do. There is, for example, the humorous and now revealing account of Mandela's attempt to give a 'headstrong' Winnie Mandela driving lessons. *Long Walk to Freedom* is of course the product of a more individualistic time, focused on the self, the personal and celebrity – a product that is moreover explicitly designed to appeal to an international audience. And in that Mandela's personal life, like Nehru's, was repeatedly taken over by political activity, including long periods of imprisonment, the need for some light relief is palpable. His autobiography is not required to be a policy document in the same way as were the 1960s life-stories. Yet, even so, the personal reflections continue to be offered mainly as interludes within the busier, more public, and inevitably more historically important story of Mandela the ANC leader. As he spells out:

> I have always believed that to be a freedom fighter one must suppress many of the personal feelings that make one feel like a separate individual rather than part of a mass movement. One is fighting for the liberation of millions of people, not the glory of one individual . . . [I]n the same way that a freedom fighter subordinates his own family to the family of the people, he must subordinate his own individual feelings to the movement.[14]

Aware of its status as public rhetoric, the leader's autobiography tends, therefore, to forswear personal testimony unless this can be justified politically, or may be presented in such a way as to provide points of identification for the new national citizenry.

The syntax of nationalist life-writing

It is possible to isolate out of the postcolonial leader's life-story-as-inaugural-history (in other words, as ideological form), a set of distinctive, interrelated tropes through which the new nation is conceived into being. In the second edition of his influential *Imagined Communities* (1991) Benedict Anderson speaks of nationalist imaginings in both colonial and independent postcolonial states as being organised according to a *symbolic grammar* generated and administered by the prevailing institutions of power, such as the museum.[15] Specifically, *grammar* to him signifies a bounded, rule-governed classificatory system, which can be flexibly repeated or serialised across different, often widely spaced contexts – contexts that then exist 'in parallel'. Anderson tends, however, to confine the term largely to the description of totalising grids, as in systems of racial codification, which may delimit its potential productivity. To extend that productivity in a different direction I propose in this chapter to apply *grammar* to the configuration of form-giving metaphors of national experience in *texts*, here in particular in autobiography.

In this case, therefore, the nationalist grammar would typically include the trope of the national *journey*, one common to several of the autobiographies I discuss. This journey takes several definitive forms: travel to the city or back to a hometown/roots, or the trek around the nation still lacking official and independent borders, or a 'journey' of discovery into the national past. It may also involve a time spent in the 'wilderness' – Europe, the city, a prison, often in another land or province, a time that is self-proving if sometimes trying, that may even reproduce in microcosm the history of national travail before independence. In the autobiography of the eastern Nigerian leader Nnamdi Azikiwe, called *My Odyssey*, a journey or pilgrimage figure is clearly signalled as a structuring motif: his sub-headings include, 'In Quest of the Golden Fleece', 'Safeguards and Pitfalls', 'The Pilgrim Returns Home'.[16]

Figures such as these do paradigmatic work on their own, yet in texts as symbolically weighted as early nationalist autobiographies they generally function relationally, not in free-floating form, justifying the use of the term grammar or even *syntax* on two counts. First, the tropes operate within the life-stories in an interactive, patterned or even rule-governed way, as will be seen. Second, they flexibly replicate *across* autobiographies from different geopolitical contexts, as well as *within* individual texts (such as in the rhythm of periods of incarceration, or trips to Europe, which governs Nehru's autobiography). The autobiographical syntax can therefore entail the configuration *as part of an interconnected, flexibly repeating sequence* of patterns (syntagmatic units) of individual/national development, in which key metaphors (paradigms) of the nation and the nationalist are then embedded.

To illustrate, almost without exception the autobiographies examined here begin with a *genealogy* setting out the leader's origins and socio-historical context. This serves as an opening 'clause' from which the syntax of the later life (in the form of, say, pilgrimage, conquest or some kind of overcoming) develops, as I will show. This same figure has, significantly, migrated into a form-giving national novel like Rushdie's *Midnight's Children* (1981), as well as Monica Ali's *Brick Lane* (2003) or Hari Kunzru's *The Impressionist* (2002), which begin with details of the hero/ine's birth, and with stories of immediate forbears. But the autobiographical grammar refers also to the *modes of address* the leader adopts, such as the non-specific collective first-person pronoun, which symptomatically resurfaces in autobiography after autobiography, in particular Mandela's, as well as to the *gender marking* built into the life-story (an appropriately grammatical function). Male autobiography, it perhaps goes without saying, will typically carry a masculine pronoun. Yet I would suggest that it is the seemingly self-evident, often invisibly *gendered syntax* of the leader's life-story that is worth highlighting among other features in so far as it helps inscribe and validate dominant gender roles in the postcolonial nation-state. So, for instance, the prominent form-giving tropes which structure the autobiography, such as the political journey or the educational quest, carry 'masculine' connotations of boldness, enterprise, single-mindedness, the pioneering spirit.

The second half of this chapter will look more closely at some of the salient features of nationalist autobiographical syntax in order to exemplify how the leader hero's story might have contributed to shaping new nationalist imaginings, including concepts of individuated, normatively masculine citizenship. Nehru's own inaugural work in this area will be examined for its distinctive tropes of the nation as multitude and as Bharat Mata, arranged within a narrative of 'mental development' or self-examination in which he repeatedly reflects on his inner 'conflict of ideas, desires and loyalties'.[17] In particular, Nehru's concept of nationalist thought as itself symbol-making will be investigated, especially in the light of his tendency to speak of India as Mother, and to view Gandhi as an embodiment of India. These images will be briefly compared with the nationalist ideas of Sarojini Naidu, the eminent Indian nationalist, poet and close colleague of both Nehru and Gandhi. Despite her interest in representing Indian women's interests, and despite Nehru's 'advanced' attitudes with respect to women, my suggestion will be that the progressive commitments of both were constrained by their traditional if nationalist ideas of the Indian woman.[18]

The section following the discussion of Nehru comprises a collage of diagnostic observations on autobiographical texts by a group of west and southern African nationalist leaders-at-independence, some of whom have already been introduced: Nnamdi Azikiwe and Obafemi Awolowo (Nigeria), Kwame Nkrumah (Ghana), Kenneth Kaunda (Zambia) and Albert Luthuli (South Africa).[19] These are combined with an authorised biography of Jomo Kenyatta (Kenya) that bears signs of being ghosted by the subject himself.[20] Most of the autobiographies were published within a decade of one another with Nkrumah's autobiography the first to appear, in 1957, and Azikiwe's, a long and retrospective account published in 1970, the last. The focus will rest in particular on the presence in these nationalist autobiographies of the structuring tropes of genealogy and ideological patriliny, of national mapping-by-travel, and of the exemplary nationalist hero.

Where appropriate the discussion will refer to Nelson Mandela's *Long Walk to Freedom* because, as anticipated, it participates in and highlights the patterns and preoccupations of the 1960s, the era of African independence. The 1960s also represent a key decade in Mandela's own life: his long imprisonment began in 1962, and the autobiography itself was undertaken as a reflection back on the events leading up to that fateful year. *Long Walk to Freedom* emphasises in particular the convergence between the individual life and the story of the coming-into-being of the nation, here specifically the story of anti-apartheid resistance. This convergence indeed confirms the convinced view of South Africans and non-South Africans alike that Mandela or Madiba ('old man', a customary term of respect) *is* in fact an incarnation of the nation. Despite – or perhaps because of – this close identification, Mandela's life-story noticeably lacks the strenuous tones of self-justification of the past, a shift due also to the nation-building and coalescing force of the long struggle against apartheid, and of the consolidating effects of the subject's own incarceration. Throughout, no matter how divided by apartheid, language or colonial history, the

South African nation is for Mandela a reality that he speaks of as unquestioningly serving and loving long before the watershed moment of 1994. This national *faith* is strongly reminiscent of Nehru's sense of India as spiritual force in *The Discovery of India*. Ironically, however, Mandela is the only leader examined here to have openly advocated militancy and the use of arms.

Questions will rightly be asked about the absence of women's texts. The absence, it should be clarified, was dictated not only by the normative maleness of independence discourse, but also, practically, by the fact that, as far as Africa is concerned, there were no women leaders of African nation-states or prominent nationalist movements at independence. (This is as opposed to iconic figureheads or spiritual leaders such as Nehanda in Zimbabwe.) Luisa Diogo, Prime Minister of Mozambique since 2003, is the first African woman to achieve political premiership. The African life-narratives, in short, could not be anything but gender-specific. With respect to India, although Sarojini Naidu became in 1947 the first Governor of the large Indian state of Uttar Pradesh, and played a prominent role as spokesperson for women in the independence movement, she did not write a formal autobiography, confining her thoughts and reminiscences rather to private letters. In fact, as with Nehru, in her comments on the nationalist movement she more or less takes for granted that masculinity, if 'soft' rather than tough, is normatively associated with the new nationalist leadership – and this despite her asseverations concerning the strength of traditional Indian femininity. Indira Gandhi, Nehru's daughter and to date India's only woman Prime Minister, did not preside at independence, although she did controversially identify with the nation as mother.[21] As for the belated postcolonial case of 1990s South Africa, as anti-apartheid resistance gave way to democratic elections the country witnessed the welcome publication of a number of life-stories and part-autobiographical narratives by women leaders or women prominent in their communities: Ellen Kuzwayo, Sindiwe Magona, Mamphela Ramphele. These narratives however, though they merit a fascinating study on their own, give predictable insights into the at-times-critical yet also broadly supportive relationship of South African women to the always male-led nationalist liberation movement, in which national freedom was prioritised over women's rights.[22]

Across the board, therefore, the leader's autobiography examined in this chapter has no reason to contest the masculine pronoun. In the act of writing his autobiography the male nationalist leader validates his role as the chief and representative son of the nation, and then – as he and the nation reach political maturity – as its father. He confirms, in other words, his pre-eminent, even dynastic, position in the national family drama.[23] From this it is already clear that, for the literate middle classes at least, the 'hero's' autobiography operates as an important vehicle in the articulation and authorisation of the dominant gender both of anti-colonial resistance and of nationalist self-imagining.

Significantly, though *Long Walk to Freedom* may have been published in 1994, it speaks of oppression in South Africa as the experience of 'the black man'. Mandela and his advisors chose for whatever strategic reason to keep hold of the central subject of 1960s Civil Rights discourse and of the 1970s Black Consciousness movement.

Jawaharlal Nehru: narratives of national destiny

Like Gandhi, Nehru did not see leadership in macho terms, often representing himself as vacillating, conflicted, uncertain, 'sensitive', 'weak' and 'introverted' in his political inclinations and personal tastes. In *An Autobiography* he bemusedly reports against himself a newspaper article in which his 'smileless', reflective public demeanour was compared to that of a 'Hindu widow'.[24] However, while he may thus have been exploiting as leader what Ashis Nandy, expounding his theory of the colonial psyche, describes as the androgynous 'Indian consciousness', Nehru in his relationship to India, 'the beautiful lady of our imaginations', always identifies specifically as male – as son and heir.[25] The 'Hindu widow' persona, he observes, had needs to take on more 'active' and 'aggressive' qualities.

In his preface to *An Autobiography*, in words that could also be applied to the more historical yet equally personal *The Discovery of India*, Nehru writes that the book represented an 'egotistical' process of 'self-questioning', yet was written with an explicitly Indian national readership in mind. The concept of the Indian nation as a united if diverse people, defined by a distinct yet numinous quality inhering in the many cultures of the subcontinent reaching from Cape Cormorin to the Khyber Pass, is, unsurprisingly, more clear-cut in *The Discovery of India* than in the earlier book. *An Autobiography* effectively records Nehru's process of self-interpellation as a modern Indian at once through the introspection of the prison cell, and through his political identification as a leader with the masses – a process which is then confirmed in the opening chapters of national self-affirmation of *The Discovery of India*. As his daughter Indira Gandhi was to write in her 1980 preface to the latter book, *An Autobiography* gives an 'insight into the making of the mind of new India'.

In both texts, however, Nehru is concerned to narrate how he, the 'coldblooded' only son of a prosperous Kashmiri family, prone to view the masses dispassionately (*A* 324, 374), learns to discover fellow feeling in their 'thousands of eyes' (*DI* 37, 61, 67). Via an incrementally unfolding syntax of self-identification extending across both books, he simultaneously transforms his holistic though materialist understanding of Indian freedom (political, economic and social) (*A* 137), into an appreciation, too, of the country's age-old 'special heritage' and 'depth of soul': the 'it' of India gradually becomes a 'we'. The country's 'continuity of cultural tradition' quickens in him increasingly more profound and characteristically nationalist feelings of reverence and respect (*DI* 36–7, 59):

> India was in my blood and there was much in her that instinctively thrilled me. And yet I approached her almost as an alien critic, full of dislike for the present as well as for many of the relics of the past that I saw. To some extent I came to her via the West, and looked at her as a friendly westerner might have done. I was eager and anxious to change her outlook and appearance and give her the garb of modernity. And yet doubts arose within me. Did I know India? . . . surely India could not have been what she undoubtedly was . . . if she had not possessed something very vital and enduring. (*DI* 50).

It is significant that although his appreciation of India's unifying vitality is described as a process of discovery, for which he deploys the suggestive metaphors of palimpsest and archaeological dig, the essential identity of India is at the same time something that must be struggled *towards*. It requires a 'thousand hand-written pages' to be fully comprehended (*DI* 35, 57, 59, 562).

Nehru is inspired by his sense of the nation as signified by an immemorial history and a vast multitude – all in all as an immense spiritual entity anthropomorphised against his better judgement as female (*DI* 59–61). Like his African counterparts, however, he is at the same time conscientious about identifying his *ideological genealogy* as a nationalist in strictly filial terms. These named personalities, he is concerned to emphasise, have shaped his core political mind. By contrast, his socialism, including his strong beliefs in industrial modernisation and central state planning, he attributes to internationalist contacts, many of them nameless, made in the Soviet Union and Europe, as in the League Against Imperialism (see *A* chapter 23). At base his *nationalist* filiation comprises two dominant influences: 'My Father and Gandhiji', to quote the title of chapter 18. Motilal Nehru, moderate, constitutional, initially Anglophilic, later a reformist nationalist, is the son's primary career mentor, and Gandhi, always identified as India's chief leader, stands as his foremost spiritual guide, if at times a frustrating one. Indeed, while Nehru is not as conscientious about plotting intricate networks of influence as are some of the African leaders, long chapters of the 1936 autobiography resemble an unresolved debate about the content of Indian nationalism with these two figures, especially Gandhi, '*the* master figure in India'.[26] Time and again, as Gandhi unpredictably takes decisions of which Nehru disapproves, such as proselytising for the 'non-political' issue of khadi, or fasting against untouchability in 1933, the younger man betrays uncertainty at his vast influence, and incomprehension at his 'intuitive', 'metaphysical' and potentially revivalist approach.

If viewed as unfolding across both *An Autobiography* and *My Discovery of India*, the grammar of Nehru's narrative as Indian Prime Minister-in-waiting describes an oscillating rhythm between binary states. This predominantly takes place between the introspective stasis of his nine terms of incarceration, and the otherwise ceaseless activity of political campaigning; but also between his Ahmedabad home and the rest of India, and, occasionally, between India and Europe.[27] Overall, the governing trope that brackets together these cyclical movements and imparts a sense of unilinear purpose to the whole, is, as elsewhere, that of *quest or discovery*, a quest that cumulatively traces out the shape of the subcontinent, as Kaunda's later will for Zambia (*DI* 61–4). Yet, unlike for the African leaders, for Nehru the object of his quest is not so much the achievement of national selfhood, as an understanding of the legendary quality of *maternal India*, as he finds out during his debate with himself concerning his residual yearning for faith (yet another oscillation). It is symbolically fitting, therefore, that while on 'national pilgrimage' Nehru meets crowds chanting 'Victory to Mother India'.

The image of India 'veiled' and mysteriously beckoning, at once evasive and enchanting, identified in camp terms as a 'hysteric' 'lady with a past' (*DI* 562–3), yet also as a symbol from popular legend, allows the westernised Nehru to gain conceptual hold of the nation's many paradoxes, its distinguishing indeterminacy. If, in general terms, the nationalist leader's mission is to configure a modern nationalist identity *and* to project an essential otherness distinct from the coloniser's culture, Nehru, beginning from the standpoint of a Europeanised modernity, chooses to prioritise the latter aim and does so in typically traditional terms. Bharat Mata or Durga was after all the female embodiment of India also for the Bengal Renaissance from the 1880s and for the 1905–8 Swadeshi movement.

Throughout his autobiography Nehru is strongly aware of the symbol-making power of nationalism; of that way in which national movements are constituted out of compelling images. Gandhi, for example, he writes, became by way of his identification with the peasant masses of India 'the idealised personification of those vast millions': 'Almost he was India' (*A* 253, 289, 403, 508). The 'National Flag', too, is a symbol to be honoured and treated with respect (*A* 333). Even the 'patron animals' of a nation, such as 'the lion and bulldog of England' or the cow of India, Nehru goes so far as to assert, have the power to mould national character (*A* 359). He will not have been unaware therefore of the potent symbolism of representing his 'discovery of India' as taking the shape of a quest for a beguiling if evasive woman. This is especially the case in so far as he heads up his quest narrative with an opening chapter recounting the death of his wife. His loss of Kamala, the implication seems to be, the 'Kamala who is no more' as the epigraph to *An Autobiography* describes her, has freed him to devote himself to the highly feminised 'thought of India . . . that possessed me' (*DI* 49).

Interestingly, the gendering of the nation and the national leader shifts subtly across the two texts in question. While in *An Autobiography* Nehru concentrates on positioning himself as a son in relation to his male mentors, in *The Discovery of India*, where Bharat Mata presides, he is not only cast as a child, but, recognisably, as a lover – a potential 'spouse', and future leader, of the feminised nation. In the opening chapter about his wife he describes how bazaar photographs depicted the two of them as an 'ideal couple', however far from the truth this may have been (*DI* 44). His political commitments and long periods in gaol, he confesses, imposed many constraints on his marriage. How much more important it then was to make a success of his symbolic relationship with this second idealised female presence, India itself, to whom he fittingly devotes the rest of *The Discovery of India*. Curiously, despite his open-handed support for 'women's right against the tyranny of men' (*A* 240), Nehru's image of the nation in the more 'feminine' second volume of his autobiography is narrowly gendered, even overdetermined as a kind of teasing siren.

Yet Nehru's pro-woman colleague Sarojini Naidu, too, though since 1914 the champion within Congress of 'women's struggle for freedom against man-made laws' (*A* 274), and an architect of the All India Women's Conference, consistently based her image of women's place in the nation upon highly traditional images of Indian womanhood.[28] It is helpful to be reminded of this – and, more generally, of the strong pull towards such gendered symbolism within nationalism – in relation to her colleague's apparent reliance upon stereotype. A supporter of 'Female Education', Naidu urged in speech after speech that women were central to the nation-building project in India, yet the women she had in mind, as she made clear, approximated to the devoted Savitri or Sati of myth. India in her nationalist poems and statements is always cast as Mother, statuesque and iconic. The country did not need a 'sex-focused' feminist movement, she often asserted, as Indian men and women needed but to revive these powerful ancient images 'to regain our lost inheritance'.[29] Predictably, therefore, Naidu's references to actual women in the nationalist movement are often instrumentalist: women are the 'sustainers' of leaders normatively defined as male.

Genealogy, patriliny: the African autobiographer as praise-singer

More prominently than in Nehru's case, one of the first moves generally made by the African leader-autobiographer in presenting as a model national subject is to position himself within a tightly woven *genealogical network*, that is, to claim pedigree. This takes the form either of drawing out a more or less conventional family tree (often of the 'begat . . . begat' variety), or a network of ideological inheritance plotting important precursors and mentors. In that the invocation of such connections is a widely observed device in traditional praise-singing in west and southern Africa, the leader could thus be said to turn himself, through the medium of the text, into his own modern praiser.[30] He simultaneously positions himself at the transformative point of intersection between his own past history, often rural and traditional, which the book narrates, and the story of the new, modern nation that the autobiography projects into a still virtual future. Throughout, his first-person pronoun is, as it were, at the point of becoming collective.

Albert Luthuli, the 1950s ANC leader and winner of South Africa's first Nobel Peace Prize, begins his life-tale in heroic style with a potted history of Kwazulu-Natal, the province of his birth. The history tracks back to the legendary rule of the great King Shaka and then moves forwards in time to merge into his own story. Nnamdi Azikiwe includes pages of an imposing network of familial contacts which, distinctly biblical in its detail and rhetoric, comes to a culminating point with his own birth. For Awolowo, father to his Yoruba Action Group party, genealogy has an almost prophetic and again dynastic relevance. He writes that 'the Oracle declared that I was the reincarnation of granny's own father': as a result his grandmother calls him father.[31]

Within the wider network of the national family, however, for a leader to claim his rightful place requires more than simple inheritance, or biological and parental connections. Not too long into their texts, most of the African autobiographers, more explicitly than Nehru, make efforts to name key role models, inspirational figures and personal heroes. The greater majority of these, other than their mothers, are male: in fact, in so far as mothers are 'family', and their naming as important influences customary, it can safely be said that *all* such ideological role models are male. In the boldly declarative *Zambia Shall Be Free* Kenneth Kaunda admits more than once to having been influenced by the Indian nationalist movement and the example of non-violence and self-help set by Gandhi.[32] Significantly, the inspiriting example of India's anti-colonial leaders carried force throughout Africa at this time. It was evidently the case that to cite India's successful deployment of passive resistance in a political climate that was becoming ever more militant and polarised was a powerful strategic move *vis-à-vis* the colonial (or in Mandela's case, internally colonial) power. Mandela as well as others in the ANC Youth League, he explains in *Long Walk to Freedom*, resolved in the late 1940s to embark on a programme of mass action 'along the lines of Gandhi's non-violent protests in India'. Kenyatta refers to Gandhi as a model (and is accordingly represented by the Kenyan writer Ngugi in *A Grain of Wheat* (1967) as an African counterpart to Gandhi). Nkrumah, too, whose autobiography is itself paradigmatic for the other African leaders' texts, justifies policy, such as his campaign of Positive Action, with reference to Gandhi.

The detailed enumeration of contacts and influences is perhaps most pronounced in Azikiwe's *My Odyssey*, though Nkrumah is also conscientious in mentioning important connections and big names. Both these leaders present highly individualised accounts, which accord with their role of self-made and to some extent self-appointed nationalist pioneer. Yet, even as they single themselves out by presenting a list of the men who have made their own lives fruitful, they are at the same time, significantly, situating themselves within a wider spiritual family of specifically black African or African-origin activists, leaders and politicians. Azikiwe claims as his contacts and mentors George Padmore, W. E. B. Du Bois, Simeon Bankole Wright, Dr Aggrey, Jomo Kenyatta and Nkrumah himself, while the 'mottos' and ideas of the Jamaican Marcus Garvey, he tells us, also 'captivated' him. Although of different ideological stripes and geographical locations, all those named are committed nationalists critical of colonisation. In a revealing conclusion to his mini-narrative of inter-connected influence, Azikiwe writes: 'I resolved to formulate my philosophy of life, so far as was practicable, towards the evangelisation of universal father-hood, universal brotherhood, and universal happiness'.[33] The ideological patriliny, or male line of nationalist influence, is to be repeated upon the future. Expanding a very similar, indeed form-giving network, Nkrumah in his *Autobiography* notes that he learned politics and African history from meeting people like Dr Aggrey and also Azikiwe, and, later, the West Indian radicals C. L. R. James and George Padmore.[34]

The constructedness of these accounts of influence may not be immediately apparent in that the writers are in many cases presumably describing actual meetings or contacts at a time characterised by intensive interaction among anti-colonial elites, and visits by African intellectuals to academic institutions in Europe and America. What is significant, however, is the way the meetings are literally placed to the fore in their texts, often to the exclusion of more per-sonal encounters. Especially where, as in West Africa, it was not possible to lay claim to a self-proving experience of resistance struggle or colonial incarcera-tion, the leaders are intent on presenting their credentials as public nationalist figures and as legitimate inheritors within their own particular black African lineage. (Awolowo and Azikiwe, it is also relevant to note, represented rival, ethnically divided political parties in Nigeria.) At the same time, the citation of masculine influence also underlines the specifically gendered, if not partheno-genetic, inception of their careers (and, therefore, life-stories). Biological mothers or grandmothers, and on a different level Mother Africa figures, briefly play nurturing roles, but their area of influence is restricted and chiefly symbolic. Once the hero's adult life gets underway they tend to fade out of the picture.

As far as wives are concerned, the textual space allotted to them, too, is limited. Especially in the 1960s autobiographies, but even in the case of the young Winnie Mandela, solicitously watched over by her husband during her first political protest, leaders' wives by and large inhabit a separate sphere of domestic, maternal, generally non-national activity.[35] His wife, Kaunda notes, is not able to identify fully with the all-important task of national self-making.

Although he respected her attempts at self-politicisation and involvement in protest marches, Nehru, too, pictures his (often physically ailing) wife Kamala in these contexts as taking on challenges too demanding for her.

Dedications to both wives and mothers admittedly appear as epigraphs to the leader-son's story, as happens in both the Luthuli and the Nkrumah auto-biographies, as well as in the Nehru.[36] Yet these same symbolically elevated wives and mothers, like women in general, are rarely invoked within the auto-biographical syntax as full subjects, despite the fact that women carried out important roles in nationalist struggles in Africa as in India, as both Mandela and Nehru do to an extent recognise. The ANC Women's League headed by Lilian Ngoyi, for example, played a key part in organising passive resistance to apartheid in the 1950s. Mandela's warm acknowledgement of this fact, however, does not penetrate through to the *form* of his work. For this reason the 2003 biography of Walter and Albertina Sisulu by their daughter-in-law Elinor Sisulu, which foregrounds the symbiosis of their political contribution, signifies an important new departure. For the rest, it is almost exclusively the case that father figures and brother-comrades pass on political inspiration and words of guidance to the new national leaders. The patrilineal genealogy that their interrelationships build undergirds the male dominance of the wider national family network. In this regard the characterisation of Azikiwe's mother is emblematic. *My Odyssey* pictures her as involved in a perpetual con-flict with his father over their son's education and plans. In a carefully staged episode, which explicitly alludes to the reconciliation scene with Volumnia in *Coriolanus*, it is his mother who goes to Ghana to persuade Zik to return home after he has stowed-away on a ship to the United States (via the Gold Coast) in pursuit of further education. She appears under an equivocal light: she is a determined and devoted emissary of the homeland, yet she also complicates and physically retards Zik's plans. By contrast it is the father who is seen sending him off to America with his unqualified blessing and the message to 'sail in quest of the golden fleece of knowledge that is guarded by the dragon of ignorance . . . as Jason did'.[37]

From the beginning of the diachronic process of leaderly self-realisation, therefore, the influence of the father or of fathers is paramount. For Nkrumah in particular, women are irrelevant to the 'real' work of preparing for national power. His anxiety over the distracting influence of women is unambiguous, at times puritanical if not openly misogynistic: 'if I allowed a woman to play too important a part in my life I would gradually lose sight of my goal'.[38] Significantly, these words mark the Ghanaian leader, no doubt unconsciously, as the product of a colonial and mission education in which, as is well docu-mented, western structures of male dominance reinforced traditional patriar-chal hierarchies. As in India, colonial schools and colleges across the African continent concentrated mainly or in the first instance on the manly education of boys. It was predictable then not only that political elites at the time of independence were almost exclusively male, but that they would have conceived of nation-making as a strenuously male exercise from which female company would be a distraction.

Mandela's 1950s and 1960s networks of mentors and friends, too, are made up of men only – predictably once again, as the ANC leadership was itself exclusively male at this time. So it is revealing and prophetic that when Winnie Mandela offers her husband stoic support on the night before his secret departure on a 1962 African trip, handing over a suitcase she has packed, she is described in positive terms as behaving 'as much like a soldier as a wife'. The term of praise, 'soldier', is clearly intended to give her womanly, supporting role a masculine edge of authority and self-control. In other words, only when the woman's contribution is wholeheartedly, if not self-sacrificially, identified with the mission represented by her husband (and/or if she cross-dresses), is it spoken of in a way that approximates her role to that of a man.

National journeying

In his autobiography the *spatial movements* of the nationalist leader as bearer of his movement's vision and ideals, too, help to give imaginative outline to the new nation. As in the case of Nehru, the grammar of his travels, a progression or circulation through significant symbolic 'stations' or moments that may repeat several times across his narrative, meshes his life-story into the geographical space occupied by the nation.

Most protagonists in the African leader-autobiographies chart a progressive journey away from the rural village to the city (often followed by further moves to a foreign metropolis). Prevalent also in African novels of the period (as in Achebe's *No Longer at Ease* (1960) or Soyinka's *The Interpreters* (1965)), the journey is particularly significant for linking together two conventionally opposed sites within a single-stranded narrative of national coming-into-being. The reader sees the hero succeed in both rural and urban spaces; both are shown to hold national significance. This is perhaps especially important in nations where not only national boundaries but also legislation governing the distribution of land and migration to the city were by and large the creations of the European colonial process.

Kaunda's *Zambia Shall Be Free* probably offers the most elaborated example of the national hero's city-oriented pilgrimage as authorising the transformation of colonial space into national terrain. (The autobiography was interestingly one of the first five books published in the Heinemann African Writers Series, along with Achebe's *Things Fall Apart* (1958).) Kaunda's 'life' begins by mapping a journey leading from his rural village to Lusaka, the capital around which the new Zambia will organise itself. He then, significantly, spends time in white-ruled Southern Rhodesia, hostile, oppositional, non-national land, where not surprisingly he is badly treated, goes hungry, and is made to feel like a stranger and prodigal son. Thereafter, in the course of many political missions and campaigns, he tracks his way around his 'own' land, plotting different routes between the city and the villages, and between villages in both mining and agricultural areas, discovering in so doing, as he says, 'myself and my people'.[39] Almost literally mapping the shape of Zambia as he goes, Kaunda validates that space as national, investing it with his attention, time and experience, including various symbolically loaded encounters with lions (as possible emblems of British power). Applying the syntactic terminology introduced earlier, the *diachronic* progression of journeying eventually produces the spatial *paradigm* of the national map. The achievement is crucial given that Zambia, formerly part of the Rhodesian Federation, did not exist as a discrete, bounded geopolitical entity before its independence.

Operating underground as the so-called 'Black Pimpernel' prior to his long imprisonment by the apartheid state, Mandela in the 1960s, too, travelled the length and breadth of his nation on a journey again styled as a process of getting in touch. His activity of 'moving through townships in different parts of the country' was obviously aimed at introducing and defending the ANC's still controversial decision to abandon its policy of non-violence. But it also traced the lineaments of a wished-for democratic South Africa, the nation embracing different classes, racial groups and regions that Mandela was seeking to bring into being, especially in so far as this 'country' was in fact coterminous with the apartheid state. In his narrative he is therefore concerned to enumerate a wide variety of encounters and the different kinds of role-play he practised en route, such as, 'I was with Muslims in the Cape, with sugar workers in Natal, with factory workers in Port Elizabeth'. And: 'I stayed in a doctor's house in Johannesburg, sleeping in the servant's quarters at night, and working in the doctor's study during the day . . . I lived in a hostel and posed as an agricultural demonstrator'.[40] He effectively performs the diversity of the nation-to-be.

A particularly interesting feature of Mandela's underground journey in its later stages is that, on a far wider scale than Kaunda's, it expanded on to an international, specifically Pan-African, stage. In February 1962 Mandela secretly left South Africa on a 'mission' to establish contact with what would become the Organisation of African Unity (OAU) at their conference in Addis Ababa, and also to raise political and economic support for the ANC's new military campaign. Following time spent in Ethiopia, which he regards as the immemorial seat of true Africanness and African resistance, the journey he describes embraces several capitals of the continent's newly emergent nations, meetings with its important leaders, and a trip to view the treasures of ancient Egypt in Cairo.[41] Mandela thus raises his travels into a romantic, mythic dimension, setting classic symbols of African nationhood within a continent-wide, Pan-African frame. In a process of simultaneous reinforcement, his mission establishes him as an African leader recognised by much of Africa, even as he at the same time achieves recognition as a specifically South African statesman in waiting.

The hero as model

From Nkrumah through to Azikiwe a key element that exemplifies the operation of the nationalist autobiographical syntax appears at those moments in the narrative where the leader-autobiographer uses his own experience as a model or object lesson. As in Mandela's account of entering court in a traditional *kaross*, the leader offers episodes from his own life-story as a parable for the new nation, as an illustration of national policy, or as directed towards a specific goal, in particular national self-formation (so confirming yet again his symbolic status). The individual story of national emergence is repeatedly made to throw up signifiers of the national good. This typicality is incidentally something that the self-doubting Nehru forswears in *An Autobiography*, yet must willy-nilly succumb to simply by writing his story.

As a lad of 14, Azikiwe tells us, he derived a moral from his job of carrying 'burnt bricks' at school: 'man should make some sacrifice for the welfare of his fellows'.[42] Early on in *Zambia Shall Be Free* Kaunda constructs himself forthrightly as the bearer of the parable of his own life. He notes that a boyhood beating taught him the value of non-violence, and working for his school money he learned the importance of self-help. He also points out that he and his nationalist friends invested in watches in order to be on time for political meetings.[43] The careful noting of this detail establishes it as a particularly instructive moment, one that works simultaneously as self-validation. Entering into and learning to manage the homogeneous, measured time of the modern nation, as described by Anderson, the friends mark themselves out as leaders who merit a following, and as exemplary modern citizens of an independent Zambia. The greater influence of the Christian mission school in Africa than in India may offer another reason, in addition to Nehru's self-doubt, for explaining why this tendency to generate improving tales from the individual life is not in evidence in the same way in the Indian leader's autobiographical writing.

As well as its didactic force, the leader's embodiment of the best of the nation has other political uses, such as that of helping to elide ethnic or tribal boundaries. By encouraging identification with the leader as model citizen, the autobiography places emphasis on oneness, on national unity and masculinity, in favour of a 'feminine' plurality that might encourage disunity. Leader-as-model examples also serve the purpose of grounding the personal history in the present and giving it immediate relevance to a national audience: it is in the here and now that the model must be actuated, that the new nation waits to realise itself.

A special case of the exemplary life occurs when, as intimated, the autobiographer embeds in his text documents he has authored, that have played some part in the nationalist cause. The autobiography consolidates its authority by a kind of self-doubling, by backing itself up with reference to important or exemplary texts its 'hero' himself would have had a hand in producing. The trend towards such 'thick' documentation begins with the Nkrumah autobiography. By the time of Zik's account it is *de rigueur*: in parts his life-story comprises more citation than narrative. In Nkrumah references to formative events are interleaved with quotations from his political writings and illustrative official documentation (the pamphlet 'Towards Colonial Freedom', his 1948 Removal Order, the six-point programme for the Convention People's Party).[44] Mandela's autobiography from time to time, too, draws on excerpts from letters to the press, ANC leaflets and his own 'political testament' as read out in court.[45] This feature of the nationalist grammar appears to gain in intensity with serial repetition, emphasising over and again that the individual life is crosshatched with national history. Textually the effect is to enact the leader's complete involvement in national concerns.

Their deployment of a nationalist grammar thus illustrates how postcolonial male leaders use autobiography to confirm their pre-eminent, form-giving and even dynastic position in the national family drama. In sum, the leader's iconic dominance as alpha male in the nationalist tale demonstrates a powerful way in which normative masculinity in the new nation is inscribed. Especially as national transformation is conventionally associated with maleness, in particular with a dominant brand of maleness, with virility and potency,[46] the national leader-hero masterfully aligns his lifeline with that of the new nation and claims for himself the part of true son and servant to the national mother. Even as the nation's history is made to converge with his own, the son progresses in the national genealogy to the position of father: his story tells how helped sire a nation.

Notes

1 Nelson Mandela, *Long Walk to Freedom* (London: Abacus, 1995).
2 Benedict Anderson, *Imagined Communities: Reflections on the Origins and Spread of Nationalisms* [1983], rev. edn (London: Verso, 1991); Timothy Brennan, *Salman Rushdie and the Third World* (London: Macmillan, 1989).
3 Elinor Sisulu, *Walter and Albertina Sisulu: In Our Lifetime*, foreword by Nelson Mandela (London: Abacus, 2003). The writer Richard Stengel, Mandela writes in his Acknowledgements, 'collaborated . . . in the creation of [his autobiography]'.

4 Jawaharlal Nehru, *An Autobiography* [1936], rev. edn (London: The Bodley Head, 1942); and *The Discovery of India* [1946] (New Delhi: Oxford University Press, 2002). See the biographies of Nehru: Judith Brown, *Nehru: A Political Life* (New Haven CN: Yale University Press, 2003) and Stanley Wolpert, *A Tryst with Destiny* (Oxford: Oxford University Press, 1996). See also Neelam Srivastava, 'Secularism in Salman Rushdie and Vikram Seth: history, nation, language', unpublished D Phil thesis, University of Oxford, 2003.

5 Declan Kiberd, *Imagining Ireland* (London: Cape, 1995), pp. 118–19.

6 James Olney, *Metaphors of Self: The Meaning of Autobiography* (Princeton NJ: Princeton University Press, 1972) is the canonical account of autobiography as self-realisation – self-realisation both as the object and as the means of the representation. See also Mark Quigley, 'Modernity's edge: speaking silence on the Blasket Islands', *Interventions*, 5.3 (2003), 382–406.

7 Paul de Man, 'Autobiography as de-facement', *MLN*, 94.5 (1979), 919–30; Quigley, 'Modernity's edge', pp. 400–1.

8 Philip Dodd (ed.), 'Introduction', *Modern Selves: Essays on Modern British and American Autobiography* (London: Frank Cass, 1986), p. 5.

9 See the essays collected in James Olney (ed.), *Autobiography: Essays Theoretical and Critical* (Princeton: Princeton University Press, 1980). See also Laura Marcus, *Auto/biographical Discourses: Theory, Criticism, Practice* (Manchester: Manchester University Press, 1994).

10 Shari Benstock, 'Authorising the autobiographical', and Susan Stanford Friedman, 'Women's autobiographical selves: theory and practice', both in Shari Benstock (ed.), *The Private Self: Theory and Practice of Women's Autobiographical Writings* (Durham NC and London: University of North Carolina Press, 1988), pp. 10–33 and 34–62, respectively; Alison Donnell and Pauline Polkey (eds), *Representing Lives: Women and Autobiography* (Basingstoke: Macmillan, 2000); Carolyn Heilbrun, 'Women's autobiographical writings: new forms', in Philip Dodd (ed.), *Modern Selves*, pp. 15–16; Françoise Lionnet, *Autobiographical Voices: Race, Gender, Self-portraiture* (Ithaca and London: Cornell University Press, 1989); Sidonie Smith and Julia Watson (eds), *De/colonising the Subject: The Politics of Gender in Women's Autobiography* (Minneapolis: University of Minnesota Press, 1998).

11 Mandela, *Long Walk to Freedom*, p. 385.

12 Obafemi Awolowo, *Awo: The Autobiography of Chief Obafemi Awolowo* (Cambridge: Cambridge University Press, 1960).

13 Albert Luthuli, *Let My People Go: An Autobiography* [1962] (London: Collins, 1987), p. 15.

14 Mandela, *Long Walk to Freedom*, pp. 267–8.

15 Anderson, *Imagined Communities*, pp. 163–85. Anderson intriguingly ends the revised edition with the acknowledgement that nations like individuals need 'biographies', within which narratives significant individual's lives may be read symbolically. He does not, however, develop the idea. See pp. 204–6.

16 Nnamdi Azikiwe, *My Odyssey: An Autobiography* (London: Hurst, 1970).

17 Nehru, *An Autobiography*, p. 207.

18 This section will supply a counterpoint therefore to the discussion of the young Naidu as 'Oriental' poet in chapter 9.

19 In addition to those texts already referenced: Kenneth Kaunda, *Zambia Shall Be Free* (London: Heinemann, 1962); Kwame Nkrumah, *Autobiography of Kwame Nkrumah* (1957; London: Panaf Books, 1973).

20 Jomo Kenyatta, *Suffering without Bitterness: The Story of the Founding of the Kenyan Nation* (Nairobi: East Africa Publishing House, 1968).

21 See Rajeswari Sunder Rajan's discussion of Indira Gandhi as a case study for her feminist analysis of women's political power in *Real and Imagined Women: Gender, Culture and Postcolonialism* (London and New York: Routledge, 1993), pp. 103–28.

22 See for example: Ellen Kuzwayo, *Call Me Woman* (Johannesburg: Ravan Press, 1985); Sindiwe Magona, *To My Children's Children* (Cape Town: David Philip, 1990); Mamphela Ramphele, *A Bed Called Home: Life in the Migrant Labour Hostels in Cape Town* (Cape Town: David Philip, 1993), and *Across Boundaries: The Journey of a South African Woman Leader* (New York: Feminist Press, 1997).

23 For discussion of how the nation is conceptualised as a family drama, see chapters 1 and 5.

24 Nehru, *An Autobiography*, p. 207. In this particular section references will be cited in the text together with the abbreviation *A*. Page references to *The Discovery of India* will be cited together with the abbreviation *DI*.

25 See Ashis Nandy, 'Woman versus womanliness in India', *At the Edge of Psychology* (New Delhi: Oxford University Press, 1982), p. 42; and *An Autobiography*, p. 431.

26 Nehru, *An Autobiography*, pp. 375–6, 573. For his internal debates with Gandhi, see, for example, chapter 15 'Doubt and Conflict'; chapter 61 'Desolation'; chapter 62 'Paradoxes'.

27 Nehru was incidentally imprisoned by the colonial authorities more *frequently* than Mandela, though the African leader's final prison term was of course far longer than any of Nehru's.

28 See Hari Banerjee, *Sarojini Naidu: The Traditional Feminist* (Calcutta: K. P. Bagchi and Co., 1998); Makarand Paranjape (ed.), *Sarojini Naidu: Selected Letters 1890s to 1940s* (New Delhi: Kali for Women, 1996). See also the forthcoming biography by Amrita Bhalla.

29 Banerjee, *Sarojini Naidu*, p. 24.

30 On the different traditions of praising involved in Yoruba *oriki* and Zulu *izibongi*, see, for example: Karin Barber and P. F. de Moraes Farias (eds), *Discourse and its Disguises: The Interpretation of African Oral Texts* (Birmingham: University of Birmingham, 1989); Ruth Finnegan, *Oral Literature in Africa* (Oxford: Oxford University Press, 1970); Liz Gunner and Mafika Gwala (eds), *Musho!: Zulu Popular Praises* (Johannesburg: Witwatersrand University Press, 1994); Leroy Vail and Landeg White, *Power and the Praise Poem* (London: James Currey, 1991).

31 Awolowo, *Awo*, pp. 13–15.

32 Kaunda, *Zambia Shall Be Free*, pp. 6, 9–10. For the following references, see Mandela, *Long Walk to Freedom*, p. 130; Nkrumah, *Autobiography*, p. 92.

33 Azikiwe, *My Odyssey*, p. 35.

34 Nkrumah, *Autobiography*, pp. 12, 18–19, 36–7 and 41, respectively.

35 Mandela, *Long Walk to Freedom*, pp. 257–60.

36 Luthuli's epigraph dedication, for example, reads: 'To Mother Africa, so long in fetters . . . And to two noble women of Africa: . . . my mother, and . . . my wife'.

37 Azikiwe, *My Odyssey*, pp. 60–1, 72.

38 Nkrumah, *Autobiography*, p. 34.

39 Kaunda, *Zambia Shall Be Free*, pp. 31–2, 114

40 Mandela, *Long Walk to Freedom*, pp. 316 and 330.

41 The references are to Mandela, *Long Walk to Freedom*, pp. 342–65.

42 Azikiwe, *My Odyssey*, p. 28.

43 Kaunda, *Zambia Shall Be Free*, p. 6, 9–10, 45, respectively.

44 Nkrumah, *Autobiography*, pp. 37–9, 66, 82–3.

45 Of the many other examples that might be quoted, see Azikiwe, *My Odyssey*, pp. 48, 56, 184; Kenyatta, *Suffering without Bitterness*, pp. v, 35–8, 76–7.

46 See Jean Franco, *Plotting Women: Gender and Representation in Mexico* (London: Verso, 1989).

5

Stories of women and mothers: gender and nationalism in the early fiction of Flora Nwapa

When the baby was five days old, Ajanupu told her sister that it was time to put alligator pepper in her mouth so that her tongue will be free. If this was not done, Ajanupu said, the baby might be deaf and dumb. So early the next morning, some alligator pepper was brought and Ajanupu chewed it very well and then put it under the tongue of the baby. The baby yelled and yelled. She was quickly breast-fed, and she stopped crying.

'Ajanupu, my daughter will talk like you. I am afraid she will be very talkative.' Efuru's mother-in-law teased her sister.

'That is all right. Aren't you lucky that I am near to put alligator pepper in her mouth? Who wants to be quiet these days? Don't you know that if you don't lick your mouth the harmattan will lick it for you. You stay there and talk of being quiet these days.' (Flora Nwapa, *Efuru*)[1]

She is there at the beginning of the lives of individuals and of nations. In nationalist and pan-nationalist mythologies and, more recently, too, in the matriarchal yearnings of historically dispossessed women seeking their own place in tradition and history, mother figures cradle their children in comforting and capacious laps. Symptomatically, in the period before and immediately after Nelson Mandela's release from prison in 1990, his then wife and at the time celebrated consort Winnie Mandela (now Madizikela-Mandela) was given the laudatory title 'Mother of the Nation'.

Elsewhere, as has been seen, mother figures bulk large in nationalist imaginings. By way of a cross-national encapsulation of what has been seen so far, the Caribbean poet and historian Kamau Brathwaite has addressed his home island of Barbados as 'mother', the matrix of this connection with the past, the source of meaning and identity.[2] In his writings on India, such as his *An Autobiography* (1936) and *The Discovery of India* (1946), as the previous chapter showed, Jawaharlal Nehru idealises and feminises India as an age-old, at once distant and exacting yet nurturing maternal presence.[3] Mehboob Khan's much-discussed 1957 film *Mother India* definitively represents India as heroic mother. The Somalian Nuruddin Farah has commented that referring to a nation as a father- (rather than as a mother-) land is to him an absurd idea.[4] Many post-independence male writers from across Africa – Camara Laye, Kofi Awoonor and Wole Soyinka among them – speaking from various historical and regional perspectives, have seen the image writ larger, within a pannationalist framework: Africa, the entire continent, whole and full-bellied, is both the beloved land and mother. In 1988, when making a call to Africans to stand together on the basis not of colour but of Africanness, Jesse Jackson adopted this grand trope, urging that African people everywhere 'identify with Africa as . . . mother continent'. His conviction was that 'the blood that unites us is stronger than the water that divides us', a politically motivated metaphor knitting together images of common womb and origin, and of shared birth ground.[5]

Although they perhaps hold different sentiments and ideals in this regard, the figure of the common national mother is, significantly, one to which post-independence women writing from Africa and India have also paid their respects. Buchi Emecheta, the London-based, Nigerian-origin novelist, for example, once expressed the opinion that 'the white female intellectual may still have to come to the womb of Mother Africa to re-learn how to be a woman'.[6] For the Zimbabwean poet and former guerrilla fighter Freedom Nyamubaya, writing in the 1980s, to speak of the Zimbabwean nation is to speak of the motherland. To her the concepts knit together so tightly that she bestows upon the concept of freedom the same honorific title: 'mother freedom'.[7] Despite her acerbic criticisms of the postcolonial Indian nation, the Indian activist writer Arundhati Roy in her polemical essays follows Nehru in so far as she, too, addresses her country as (a wronged yet still noble) 'she'.[8] Indira Gandhi, Nehru's daughter, herself infamously elaborated on the woman = nation equation with her slogan 'India is Indira'. Speaking from an African American perspective the poet and activist Aneb Kgotsile observes: 'Mother Africa is of great importance . . . Through our study of African history the motherland was unearthed to us and we reclaimed Africa'.[9] In her schematic novel *The Temple of My Familiar* (1989), Alice Walker sings threnodies over the destruction of the ancient matriarchal worship of Africa: history in Walker's representation achieves meaning in so far as her characters become either avatars or acolytes of the composite, omni-benevolent 'Africa/Mother/ Goddess'.[10]

But to what sort of mother image is it that women writers appeal when they speak in this way? Is their gaze fixed longingly on the same object as their male counterparts? Does the icon represent for them a simple reversal within the vocabulary of a male-dominated nationalism, and, if so, what does this reversal mean for their own strategies of self-retrieval via the mother image? Do nationalist vocabularies not implicate women in certain paradoxes of identity and affiliation? How, straightforwardly put, are they to legitimate themselves in national terms when the legitimating symbolic traditions of the nation tend to admit them as stereotypes, not as full citizens? In theory, and rhetorically, anti-colonial, nationalist movements made provision for the self-representation of women, yet did women's roles within the post-independence nation-state in practice have an equivalent status to those of men? Such questions point to the main concern of this chapter, which will explore how an investment in a typically masculine nationalist imaginary impacts on women's politics of self-realisation and on their involvement in the modern nation-state. Thereafter, in a reading of Flora Nwapa's early fiction, suggestions will be made as to what an alternative symbolisation of women's identity and language might entail.

In a nutshell, the dilemma is that where male nationalists have claimed, won and ruled the motherland, as has generally been the case across the post-independence world, this same motherland may not signify 'home' or 'source' to women, or does so in significantly different ways. Registering an acute dis-comfort with the male glorification of African women as national and conti-nental mothers, Mariama Bâ once wrote: 'We women no longer accept the nostalgic praise to the African mother whom, in his anxiety, man confuses with Mother Africa'.[11] The South African nationalist and woman of letters Lauretta Ngcobo analyses this seemingly hypocritical idealisation in terms of the tradi-tional and (apparently) transcultural split of 'real' as against ideal women. 'Africa holds two contradictory views of woman', she writes, 'the idealised, if not the idolised mother, and the female reality of woman as wife'.[12] In post-independence India, as Rajeswari Sunder Rajan observes, women in positions of political authority have been conceptualised predominantly in stereotypical 'good mother-bad mother' terms.[13] (This widely prevalent tendency is, inci-dentally, as Sunder Rajan recognises, exacerbated across the world by the rela-tive lack of an adequate gender theory of political power for women.)

As is clear from this sampling, to Third World women as well as to histori-cally dispossessed women in the west, issues of at once identification with, yet exclusion from, a nationalist tradition of masculinised self-assertion speak with particular urgency. Women encounter the strong need to resist the com-pounded oppressions of colonialism, gender, race, class, sexuality, etc., and find at the same time that tactics of self-representation are often usefully adopted from the more established and yet compromising nationalist politics of their male counterparts. Indeed, as Kumari Jayawardena has shown, anti-imperial, nationalist struggles in many parts of the world historically gave birth to (usually middle-class) feminist movements.[14] Yet, even so, the exclusions imposed on women by the independent nation, especially by those nationalist brothers concerned to police cultural authenticity and purity after colonialism, mean that many postcolonial women have, as the so-called bearers of cultural tradition, been denied their entitlements as modern citizens. Some women might therefore continue rightly to feel, along with Virginia Woolf in her famous anti-patriarchal pacifist manifesto *Three Guineas* (1938), 'in fact, as a woman, I have no country. As a woman I want no country'.[15] Because men have drawn up, defined and directed national boundaries and national affairs, as Woolf suggests, women cannot legitimately lay claim either to a national territory or to their own national mythology, history or theory of power. The lap of the Mother Nation may not be as soft and capacious for women as it is for men.

As has already been demonstrated in this book, despite its professed ideals nationalism does not address all individuals equally: significant distinctions and discriminations are made along gendered (as also class, racial, regional and other) lines. Such distinctions are not merely superficial. On the contrary, as in the chapter on Ngugi, nationalism, whether as ideology or as political movement, configures and consolidates itself through a variety of deeply embedded gender-specific structures. The idea of nationhood bears a masculine identity although some national ideals may wear a feminine face. Such gender tags are clearly illustrated, for example, in the iconographies the nation cherishes. In the literature, rhetoric and pageantry of nations, as in nationalist politics and political structures, it is a male figure who is traditionally cast as the author and subject of the nation – as faithful soldier, citizen-hero and statesman. In the national family drama that has the achievement of selfhood as its denouement, it is he who is the chief actor and hero. The mother figure in this drama may be his mentor, fetish or talisman, but advice and example are taken from a heritage – an affiliative line, as Edward Said puts it – of father figures.[16]

In short, typically therefore, the male role in the nationalist scenario may be characterised, as throughout this book, as metonymic. Male figures are brothers and equals, or fathers and sons and thus rivals; but in both cases their roles are specific, either horizontally positioned, or in some way contiguous with one another. The female, in contrast, as was seen in the case of the national leader's autobiography, puts in an appearance chiefly in a metaphoric or symbolic role. She is the strength or virtue of the nation incarnate, its fecund first matriarch – but it is a role that vertically elevates and so excludes her from the sphere of public national life. Figures of mothers of the nation are everywhere emblazoned, therefore, but the presence of women in the nation has in many cases been officially marginalised and ignored. In the representative case of nationalist Ireland, for example, a rhetoric of martyrdom, as in the build-up to the 1916 Easter Rising, encouraged son-sacrifice to the Mother, variously identified as Land, Nation and Church.[17]

In most post-independence nations, given the male presence rooted in the colonial state and, formerly, in indigenous patriarchal structures, it was predictable that a gender bias would persist within (neo)colonial nationalist parties, movements and other organisations well beyond the time of 'freedom'.

Whether in literature, in law or in daily life, the national subject was in most cases implicitly or explicitly designated male. Despite the promises of independence, women were by and large left out of full national participation on an equal footing with men. Even where women fought for freedom alongside men, as in Algeria or Zimbabwe, national consciousness was authored and authorised by male leaders, Frantz Fanon's insightful reading of the Algerian struggle notwithstanding. Women ex-combatants were soon made to feel where they stood 'as women'. Mother Africa, Mother India, may have been declared free, but the mothers of India and Africa remained manifestly second-class citizens.

Little resistance to such processes of patrimonial derivation could be expected from within the ranks of the newly empowered. In the manichean allegory that typified the colonial power struggle, dominant 'true' power – that of the coloniser – had been characterised as rational, disciplined, assertive, masculine, whereas inertia, weakness, deviance, the disorderly, had been represented as feminine.[18] In that nationalists were committed to rebuilding their shattered self-esteem, to 'selving', images signifying autonomy, force, will – and by implication, masculinity – were avidly promoted.[19] So the new rulers might proclaim themselves as a rising strength, as self-determining, as powerful – and also as patriarchal and/or as one another's brothers. Seeking to step out of inherited allegorical roles, they would strive to avoid as far as possible 'negative' – that is, feminine – attributes. At the level of national iconography, it is true, colonial images of the land as invincible protectress or progenitress (Africa as Woman, as She; India as Mother) might be assimilated to local conventions of respect for the earth, domestic traditions and/or mothers. This ensured that national leaders granted some form of compensatory iconic recognition to the 'mothers of the nation' while simultaneously vouching for the cultural integrity of the whole national entity. Observe once again, however, that it is the 'sons' who are the authors of meaning: whether of 'tradition', or of present social realities; whether of their own self-image as national representatives or of the women they would presume to represent. Underlying gendered values remain intact.[20]

The glad achievement of national selfhood therefore presented women with a conundrum. Such selving, with its emphasis on the male personality, effectively only confirmed in them a lack of self, their difference from national wholeness or essence. This difference, this alienation, represented, and still represents, an especially serious issue for the nationalisms of the south or Third World. For where, in nationalist rhetoric as in the official discourse of the state, masculine identity is normative, and where the female is often chiefly addressed as an idealised *carrier* of nationalist sons, woman as such lacks a valued or marked position. At least until very recently, nationalism has tended not to interpellate women as, in the first instance, *nationals*. The weighty presences of national mothers have overshadowed and disguised the actual absences of women in public national life.

This then means that a woman seeking to claim a place or an identity in most fields of national activity faces multiple perils of self-contradiction. Literature as a medium of self-expression offers a representative case. Within African nationalism, for instance, especially that of the immediate pre- and post-independence periods, writing provided the middle classes with an important source of national myth-making and dreaming. For a writer to be a nationalist, was to be that much more a worthy writer, as well as that much more self-assertively male – in relation to which equation the figure of woman was habitually regarded as the vehicle or medium of male creativity, as for example in Wole Soyinka's work. The circle of mutually reinforcing identities shut – and still shuts – women out.

A woman might choose to crack this ring of identity by attempting to repossess matriarchal myths. For some women the reclaimed myth of an age-old, long-suffering 'Afrika' – Walker's Africa/Goddess/Mother presiding over the '500, 000 years' of human history covered by *The Temple of My Familiar* – has continued to hold out much promise of communion and liberation. The South African dramatist Gcina Mhlope, for example, has expressed her loyalty to this mythical maternal entity, speaking of the 'Women of my country' as 'Mother Africa's loved daughters'.[21] Motherhood remains closely linked to the configuration of African, Caribbean and South Asian women's identities in many of the sociocultural contexts they inhabit.[22] Yet the problematic facing mother-oriented women is whether and how such apparently redemptive symbols might be separated from those which continue to shore up a system of gender-tagged national authority. After all, the idealisation and possible fetishisation of mother figures bears an uncanny resemblance to the monolithic aspects of male-centred nationalism, just as to the romanticisation of conquered land under colonialism. Subscribing to the unitary icon may therefore threaten to defeat women's objectives of affirming their own particular mode of being.

Given that men have to a large extent monopolised the field of nationalist identity and self-image, women have in many cases sought to evolve other strategies of selving – less unitary, more dispersed and multifarious, more alive to the contradictions involved in the process of self-making. The challenge is not only that the patriarchal roots and sources that inform nationalist images must be in some way confronted. It is also that it is necessary to explore forms of women's self-representation that would counterpoise the inherited symbolic languages of gender as well as the grand stories of the nation. In this, despite influential national traditions of male authorship, writing – experimental, exploratory, nuanced, ironic – holds out fruitful possibilities of redress. Fredric Jameson, speaking here as a Marxist, not as a 'Third World' critic, has referred to such redress as the 'restoration of an essentially dialogical . . . horizon'.[23]

In the case of Africa, for instance, it is the case that, if literature in the past has constituted something of a nationalist and masculinist preserve, then,

simply by writing, women directly confront and face down the male prerogative. In writing, as many postcolonial women critics have by now recognised,
women express their own reality, unsettle male-focused (and other exclusionary) narratives, and so question received notions of national character and
experience. But writing is more than this, too. To write is not only to speak for
one's place in the world. It is also to *make* one's own place and narrative, to tell
the story of oneself, to create an identity. It is in effect to deploy what in another
context might be called a typical nationalist strategy. As Simon Gikandi once
put it: 'To write is to claim a text of one's own; textuality is an instrument of
territorial possession . . . narrative is crucial to our discovery of selfhood'.[24]

This idea of self-creation through narrative intersects with the Kristevan
concept of excess in writing. Julia Kristeva observes, à propos of Barthes's criticism, that writing is transformative, operating through the displacement of
what is already signified, bringing forth the not-yet-imagined and the transgressive.[25] Indebted to Bakhtin, yet concentrating on women's expression in
particular, Kristeva maintains that language – the symbolic order, syntactic
completion – is threatened by the irruption of the heterogeneous, the disorderly, the semiotic, that which lies outside language though is finally only conceivable within it. Such irruption, which for Kristeva constitutes the poetic,
comes about, among other methods, through a process aptly demonstrated by
Flora Nwapa, that is, 'transposition', the shift between literary and linguistic
media that creates possibilities for polysemy. Through writing, through claiming a text – and a narrative territory – women sign into and at the same time
subvert a nationalist narrative that has excluded them as negativity, as corporeal and unclean, or as impossibly idealised.

Possibilities for the disruption and/or transformation of a masculine nationalist text can therefore be seen to operate in two main ways in women's writing:
the *textual* and the (broadly) *temporal/territorial*. The first occurs through the
medium of the text, in the substance of the writing, and involves *interrupting*
the language of official nationalist discourse and literature with a women's
vocality. Nationhood is so bound up in textuality, in 'definitive' histories and
official languages and mythologies, that to compose a substantially different
kind of text, using vernacular, non-literary and phatic forms that are part of
people's everyday experience, is already to challenge normative discourses of
nationhood – even where, as in Rushdie's *Midnight's Children* (1981), that discourse announces itself as always-already multivoiced. Moreover, as this suggests, these different forms of composition manifest, crucially, *within* the
poetics of the text, as nuance, emphasis and ironic juxtaposition – disruption is
not expressed merely at the level of externalised, 'protest' writing.

Yet, because national identity rests on received images of national history
and topography, the second method of transformation is as important. It
involves *changing the subjects* that have dominated the nationalist text – and

therefore questioning the centrality of the male-defined nation as *the* key historical player in the post-independence period. Where women tell the story of their own experience, they map their own geographical perspectives, scry their own history and so, necessarily, contest official representations of a nationalist reality. They implicitly – and in some cases explicitly – challenge the nation's definition of itself through territorial claims, through the reclamation of the past and the canonisation of heroes. At the same time they also lever the icons of heroes and national mothers from their dominant positions as mascots and symbols of the quintessential national experience.

Both these methods obviously correspond closely to techniques of literary subversion in which women writers have long been engaged. Yet where post-colonial literary narratives since the 1950s have centrally depended on nationalist ideas and themes – and so on gendered interpretations of social reality – such transgressive methods have particular relevance and impact.

The second part of this chapter will demonstrate how such techniques work in practice in a discussion of two early novels by the leading African woman novelist Flora Nwapa, *Efuru* (1966) and *Idu* (1970). Published during the first decade of Nigerian independence, a time featuring robust and cocksure, if also embattled, nationalisms, Nwapa's novels represent the first narrative appearance from a woman on the broader Anglophone African literary stage. This in itself was a significant voicing, yet added to this was Nwapa's specific focus on women's community and colloquy in Igbo culture.

Flora Nwapa

Like Elechi Amadi or Nkem Nwankwo, her male counterparts of the first post-independence decade, Flora Nwapa wrote 'after Achebe', both chronologically and in terms of literary influence.[26] Like Amadi's, like Achebe's, Nwapa's narratives remember and recreate the Igbo village past in the colonial period. Period generalisations, however, tend to obscure the significant differences that exist between Nwapa and her male cohorts. Most obviously, Nwapa's fictions are situated outside traditional, male-centred narrative history. She chooses to engage neither with the manly adventures and public displays of patriarchal authority described by other writers from her community (emblematised in Achebe's Okonkwo), nor with the stylistic conventions of their accounts. Instead she concentrates, and at length, on what was apparently incidental or simply contextual to male action – domestic matters, the politics of intimacy, the grubby reality and drudgery of maternal experience. Nwapa's gender focus has demarcated an area of communal life that was elsewhere, in texts by male writers, forgotten, elided or ignored.

In both *Efuru* and *Idu*, Nwapa's interest is in the routines and rituals of everyday life specifically within women's compounds.[27] Women press into her narratives as speakers, decision-makers, brokers of opinion and market prices, and unofficial jurors in their communities. But Nwapa's specific intervention as a writer goes beyond her interest in women subjects. What also distinguishes her work from that of her counterparts in the 'Igbo school' are the ways in which she has used choric language to dramatise and empower her representations. In this way she creates the effect of a women's verbal presence within her text, while at the same time bringing home her subject matter by evoking the vocality of women's everyday existence.

Nwapa's narrative style, in particular her reliance on conversational techniques, drew a certain amount of negative criticism from an early generation of post-independence critics.[28] It was deemed to be 'sociological', 'claustrophobic' and generally limited. The apparent lack of conventional novelistic complexity in *Efuru* and *Idu*, I would argue, however, far from being a deficiency, instead clears the space for the elaboration of another kind of narrative entirely – a highly verbalised, collective women's biography, 'transsubjective, anonymous', transgressive.[29] This narrative method bears comparison with the African American writer Zora Neale Hurston's recreation of porch-side comment and of gossip on the road.[30]

The critics Florence Stratton and Susan Andrade have productively read *Efuru* as engaged in intertextual dialogue with, respectively, Achebe's *Things Fall Apart* (1958), and with Buchi Emecheta's fiction.[31] The precise, women-centred contribution represented by Nwapa's early work can perhaps be most effectively demonstrated, however, when set in dual contrast with, on the one hand, a contemporaneous historical narrative by Elechi Amadi and, on the other, Ifi Amadiume's anthropological account of women's roles in a Nigerian Igbo community. In his novel *The Great Ponds*, written in 1969, Elechi Amadi depicts Igbo villages as controlled by the forces of war, rumour and disease.[32] Over war and rumour, it becomes clear, men hold undisputed sway; of disease, the gods decide, but they, like the village leaders, are all male.[33] As in Achebe's *Things Fall Apart*, the story focuses on the male trials of strength and endurance exacted during times of community crisis, and, as with Achebe, *The Great Ponds* is not uncritical of the social values which may contribute to and exacerbate such crisis. (The hardships suffered by the village, for instance, call into question the ethical soundness of the male leaders' counsel and policies of governance.) Yet, unlike in Achebe, no locus of value is suggested which might form the rallying point of a new order: the male characters represent different types and gradations of manliness, but their actual position of authority is not called into question. It is consistent with the terms laid down by the novel that the women in the community form a completely marginal and passive group. Their existence is affirmed by the male subjects – they are desired, taken in marriage, captured as booty in male wars. From the point of view of the male hut in the compound, they are respected in so far as they fulfil their maternal function. For the rest, they are ignored.

Superficially, this arrangement would seem hardly to differ from conventional gender divisions of power and cultural space in the West African novel. Upon closer scrutiny, however, it appears that in Amadi the gender separation is perhaps even more pronounced. The physical distance of the gender groups and their extreme social and political non-equivalence, as well as the marginalisation of all feminine values, suggest that the groups may well be independently produced and regulated. It is this view of a society *radically* split by gender that allows Amadi in *The Great Ponds* to represent the male side of Igbo life as though it were not only normative and authoritative, but self-sufficient and entire.

Yet, the writer's individual bias aside, it does not necessarily follow that this sort of exclusivity signifies a lack of power or self-determination on the part of women. It may equally be the case that the distance between the genders signifies and makes possible autonomy and social validity for women. The women have jurisdiction over an area of social life which, though separate, is only *apparently* marginal: women conduct the business of their lives convinced of the coherence and importance of their activity.

Contrary to appearances, the representations of writers such as Amadi and Achebe, rather than defining the whole compass of the Igbo world, describe only one section of it. That another, independent sphere of social existence exists is intimated only once, and then very briefly, in the Amadi text. It does, however, represent a significant break in the narrative when, in confrontational tones reminiscent of some of Nwapa's speakers, a senior wife, though nameless, comments on the folly of the current protracted war and its goals:

> Why can't men take advice? . . . They think they are wise but they are as foolish as a baby in arms. Look at all the suffering of the past month. What good will that pond [the site of contention] do us?[34]

Ifi Amadiume offers a corroborative perspective on the self-reliance of Igbo women, and on one of the chief conditions of that self-reliance – what might be called the mutual exclusivity of Igbo gender groups. In her study *Male Daughters, Female Husbands*, she shows that women obtain a great deal of power in Igbo – and specifically Nnobi – society from the separation of gender and sex roles.[35] Amadiume does not always deal satisfactorily with the continuing predominance of *de facto* patriarchal authority in the community – and the status commanded by the roles of son and husband. Yet she does present evidence not simply for the existence of a clearly demarcated women's 'sphere' (which, however, says relatively little), but also for the independence and self-coherence of women's lives within that sphere. She indicates that in precolonial times political and economic roles, as well as compound space and village ground, were divided according to conventional sex dualities, with family units being matri-centric. She argues, however, that these socially constructed dualities were mediated by the cross-gender roles available to women. Women were thus granted a range of powers with the appeal to Idemili, the water goddess, as offering the highest sanction of their authority.

It is this autonomous, self-validating women's world delineated by Amadiume that Nwapa embodies in *Efuru* and *Idu*. She extends the boundaries of the West African novel to include the women's side of the compound, a domain of village life which writers like Amadi neglected for reasons not of patriarchal lack of interest alone, but also perhaps of ignorance.[36] She decisively refracts the women's presence into her text through creating the conceit of women representing themselves in voice. Dialogue dominates in both novels, especially in *Idu*, as numbers of partly curious, partly phatic and frequently anonymous women's voices meet, interact with and 'call upon' or interpellate one another. This vocality, rambling and seemingly unstoppable, pulls against the confinements of the women's lives – their market rivalries, their anxieties about husbands, families and children. If, therefore, as Nwapa portrays it (though rarely overtly), male values in the society remain normative, women's talk can be interpreted not only as a way of life but as a mode of self-making.[37]

It is a fact of course that the impression of the fullness and autonomy of women's lives Nwapa creates is qualified by the acquiescence on the part of the women characters in patriarchal views and values. Yet, at the same time, in their discourse, even as they speak, not only do the village women share their woes and confirm female bonds, they also translate their lives into a medium which they control. The reader is made privy to the women representing and, in effect, recreating their lives in dialogue. (Moreover, by concentrating on their need to please their husbands, and on problems of barrenness, their conversation reflects upon, objectifies, and so in some sense 'ring-fences', the social restrictions they experience.) The narrative result is that most of the (non-discursive) action in *Idu* and *Efuru* happens off-stage, and is more or less incidental to the 'spoken' text. Nwapa's writing is a decisive vindication of the congenital fault of garrulousness often attributed to 'the sex' (for example, in *The Great Ponds*, 23, 42, 25).[38] As Idu bemusedly observes: 'You know women's conversation never ends' (*I* 97).

How does this mode of verbal self-representation work in practice? *Efuru* and *Idu* unfold as conversations; both are loosely chronological, often digressive, and markedly lacking in the temporal frameworks of conventional narrative. *Efuru* begins at the time that the heroine marries Adizua without parental consent: 'one moonlit night' they make plans; the next Nkwo (market) day she moves to his house (*E* 7). With this information in hand the gossipmongers can have their say and, sure enough, by the second page of the novel speculations are afoot regarding Efuru's movements. These form the first soundings of that hum of conjecture that will run throughout the novel, commenting on the heroine's fortunes, her barrenness, her second marriage, her second barrenness. Against the background of this flow, market days, trade seasons, other moonlit nights, gestation periods, come and go with their accustomed regularity, but have significance in the conversational narrative largely as arbitrary starting points for new fragments of chatter. In *Idu* the verbal presence of the community would seem to be even more pervasive. Of the novel's 22 chapters, 14 including the first begin in mid-dialogue, and then usually in relation to events mentioned in some earlier conversation, the dialogue thus propagating itself across the pages of the novel.

The social setting Nwapa has chosen for her novels enables this self-generating orality. In each, the women occupy a self-enclosed, stable domestic domain: custom and environment are known to all the speakers, and few characters are unfamiliar. Where these may be physically gestured at or taken as understood, reference to external objects or to habitual activity is elided or abbreviated. From the non-Igbo reader's point of view, this is emphasised when in both novels Igbo words and concepts are left unexplained and cannot always be elucidated by context: *ganashi, obo, nsala* soup. The names for other referents are roughly transliterated: *a black stuff* (*E* 14), *the white disease* (*E* 48), *the small cough* (*I* 35). Within the village, the meanings of such phrases do not require elucidation. The insularity of the community is also suggested by the frequent repetitiveness of the conversation: comments are echoed, opinions reiterated, events retold. At times an anonymous speaker is brought into the conversation without any kind of formal introduction. The point of talking is often simply the interaction, confirming contact, and not an exchange of information. Or, as Uzoechi in *Idu* says: 'Sometimes, after discussing something, I like to come back to it and talk it over again' (*I* 29).

So much is action a function of what is spoken that, especially in *Idu*, 'plot' developments, such as they are, take place off-stage as the conversation passes. At one point in *Idu*, for example, Adiewere and Idu discuss 'their' troublesome new wife and think of sending her away; within a few pages it is announced that she has left for another man's house (*I* 49–50, 56). In chapter 13 of *Efuru*, Eneberi, Efuru's husband, expresses an interest in taking a new wife; in the next chapter, in the course of a chat between his mother and her friends, we learn that she has a new daughter-in-law (*E* 195). A particular state of affairs may thus change into its opposite within a few pages, in the course of a few fragments of dialogue: here Idu observes that the market is bad, there that it is good (*I* 45 and 47, 121 and 131). With dialogue constituting the main action, narrated or conversational time predominates over chronological time. Gossips summarise changes that have taken place over a span of years while also running through the community's opinion of these changes. One of the clearest examples of this occurs in *Efuru* when the heroine hears of her husband's desertion through overhearing gossip at the market (*E* 54–5, and also 208–9). The women's community lives through this propagation of its voices, this telling of its stories. Even more so than their oral versatility, it is probably the sheer reiterative quality of the women's speech which impresses itself most upon the ear/eye – the ceaseless resumption of old complaints, the untiring return to familiar formulae, the echoic corroborative phrases (*I* 199, for example). In this respect the talk can be seen as self-reflexive: its repetitiveness forcefully communicates the unremitting routine of women's lives, the round of birthing, surviving and death.

Though Nwapa's dialogic approach (in the precise sense of the term) appears as the dominant feature of her narrative, its prominence should not detract from that important aspect of her writing which in fact enables the vocality of her style – her focus on women's affairs. Nwapa's women characters in *Efuru* and *Idu* represent themselves in voice, yet their spirit of pride and self-reliance is manifested also in the relative diversity of their quotidian activity.[39]

Both novels document in some detail women's customs, business preoccupations and worries: certain sections, in particular the chapter on childbirth in *Efuru* (chapter 2), read as if they were extracts from an almanac of women's simples. By creating a sense of the fullness of Igbo women's lives in the colonial period, Nwapa begins to chart out the neglected, rural, gender dimension in the grand narrative of historical nationalist literature told by male writers. She questions, if mostly implicitly, the gender-bound space–time co-ordinates of that narrative. More specifically even than this, however, she delivers her riposte to a male-dominated nationalist tradition and its iconography of womanhood by making available for her women characters roles and symbols of identity which diverge from the mother stereotype. Her women characters are concerned about bearing children and being good mothers, yet their lives are not defined solely by their maternal function. Especially in *Efuru*, Nwapa delineates the 'clearly expressed female principle' in Igbo life where 'fecundity [is] important, not entire'.[40]

Efuru opens with the heroine marrying without parental consent, defiant and unafraid. Later, when her husband proves unworthy, she leaves, as defiant. Though her action is more problematic, *Idu* ends with the heroine willing her own death so as to join her husband. She decides that the relationship provided by the marriage was more important to her than children. Both heroines are admittedly exceptional figures, yet it is important to note that they are not unique. Characters like the older woman Ajanupu in *Efuru* and the resolute Ojiugo in *Idu* exemplify comparable qualities of decisiveness, outspokenness and self-sufficiency.

In Igbo society, as Amadiume shows, it is in trade as much as in marriage and childbirth that women obtain power. Accordingly, putting into practice Nwapa's lifelong concern with economic independence for women, both novels focus on marketing as the chief dynamic of women's lives and the means whereby they obtain status (*I* 29; *E* 125). Attracted to the lure of a good reputation, women like

Efuru and Idu structure their lives around market days and keep a vigilant eye on profit. In this way, as well as through sheer audacity and hard labour, they develop the trading prowess for which the community respects them. Two important qualifications should perhaps be made here. One, that the economic abilities shown by Nwapa's women characters could be seen as compromised in her later writing where, in a capitalist, post-independence cash system, marketing heroines turn exploitative and conspicuously consumerist.[41] And two, that while women command power through economic means, the patriarchal status quo is never challenged, even in matters of trade (for example, *E* 140–1).

It is primarily when women take on spiritual power, and therefore, according to convention, discard their sex roles, that they are able to enter a sphere where male authority has little effect. Nwapa's Woman of the Lake deity in *Idu* and especially *Efuru* bears a strong resemblance to the water goddess Idemili described by Amadiume. In Amadiume's account, women wield considerable power as the worshippers and representatives of this water spirit, also referred to as the Great Woman: ritual elites are based on her worship; successful market women are seen to be blessed by her.[42] So too, in Nwapa, Uhamiri, the Woman of the Lake, is held in high regard, as are her followers. Although it may be her last resort as a barren wife, when Efuru is chosen at the end of the novel to represent the deity, this comes as a recognition of her status in the community and her success as a market woman. As infertility is a necessary condition of the goddess's chosen followers, Uhamiri's intercession gives Efuru's childlessness new, positive meaning – in a sense, makes it fruitful.

Where Amadi recognised only male deities, Nwapa in effect puts the community's shrines in order, setting the female goddess back in her rightful place. This readjustment reflects on what I have suggested is a powerful effect of her writing: that of counterbalancing in her use of language and in characterisation a postcolonial literary patriarchy and a matrifocal nationalism. In the crucial decade of the 1960s, Nwapa in *Idu* and *Efuru* re-angled the perspective laid down in male writing, showing where and in what ways women wield verbal and actual power. If nationalism is typically embodied in patriarchal formations and fraternal bonding, and involves the apparent exclusion of women from public life, then Nwapa, in choosing not to engage with 'big' national themes, in commenting on colonial history from the sidelines, dealt with that exclusion in two main ways. First, she effectively reproduced it – by situating her narratives in another place entirely; and then she converted that occlusion into a richness. By allowing a women's discourse apparently to articulate itself in her writing, she elaborates the text of Igbo national experience. Yet, even more importantly than this perhaps, she also uncovers the practical, *lived* reality of motherhood. She digs into the muddy, grainy underside of nationalism's privileged icon without undermining the importance of the institution of motherhood in West African culture. The mothers of Africa,

Nwapa shows, also have voices, anger, rival aspirations, their own lives to live. They are as much the worthy subjects of a communal history as are their nationalist sons.

Notes

1 Flora Nwapa, *Efuru* [1966] (London: Heinemann, 1987), p. 33.

2 (Edward) Kamau Brathwaite, *Mother Poem* (Oxford: Oxford University Press, 1977). *Mother Poem* forms a trilogy with *Sun Poems* (1982) and *X/Self* (1986), also published by Oxford University Press.

3 Jawaharlal Nehru, *An Autobiography* [1936], rev. edn (London: The Bodley Head, 1942), and *The Discovery of India* [1946] (New Delhi: Oxford University Press, 2002).

4 Nuruddin Farah, 'A combining of gifts: an interview', *Third World Quarterly*, 113 (July 1989), 180.

5 Cited in *West Africa*, 3729 (16–22 January 1989), 59–60.

6 Buchi Emecheta, *New Society* (4 September 1984), cited in Kathleen McCluskie and C. L. Innes, 'Women in African literature', *Wasafiri*, 8 (January 1988), 4.

7 Freedom T. V. Nyamubaya, *On the Road Again* (Harare: Zimbabwe Publishing House, 1986), pp. 3–4, 10–11.

8 See Arundhati Roy, *The Algebra of Infinite Justice* (London: Flamingo, 2002), throughout.

9 Cited in *West Africa*, 3721 (12–18 December 1988), 2324. The African American critic, Barbara Christian, too, has injected nationalist sentiments into her interpretation of images of African American and African motherhood in Alice Walker and Buchi Emecheta. Stressing the importance of the institution of African motherhood for cultural regeneration she observes: 'Motherhood provides an insight into the preciousness, the value of life, which is the cornerstone of the value of freedom'. See Barbara Christian, *Black Feminist Criticism: Perspectives on Black Women Writers* (Oxford: Pergamon Press, 1987), p. 247.

10 Alice Walker, *The Temple of My Familiar* (London: The Women's Press, 1989). The quotation is from p. 63, but the remythologising occurs throughout.

11 Cited in Mineke Schipper (ed.), *Unheard Words*, trans. Barbara Potter Fasting (London: Allison and Busby, 1985), p. 50.

12 Lauretta Ngcobo, 'The African woman writer', in Kirsten Holst Petersen and Anna Rutherford (eds), *A Double Colonization: Colonial and Postcolonial Women's Writing* (Aarhus: Dangaroo, 1986), p. 81.

13 Rajeswari Sunder Rajan, *Real and Imagined Women: Gender, Culture and Postcolonialism* (London and New York: Routledge, 1993).

14 Kumari Jayawardena, *Feminism and Nationalism in the Third World* (London: Zed Press, 1986).

15 Virginia Woolf, *Three Guineas* [1938] (London: Hogarth Press, 1986), p. 125.

16 For Said's concept of modernism's affiliative relations, as opposed to filiative or cross-generational familial links, see 'Introduction: secular criticism', *The World, the Text and the Critic* (London: Faber, 1984), pp. 1–30.

17 See David Cairns and Shaun Richards, *Writing Ireland: Colonialism, Nationalism and Culture* (Manchester: Manchester University Press, 1988); Marjorie Howes, *Yeats's Nations: Gender, Class, and Irishness* (Cambridge: Cambridge University Press, 1996); Richard Kearney, *Myth and Motherland* (Belfast: Field Day Theatre Company, 1984); Clair Wills, *Improprieties: Politics and Sexuality in Northern Irish Poetry* (Oxford: Clarendon Press, 1993).

18 See Abdul JanMohamed's reading of the Fanonist (and Sartrean) concept of the manichean in 'The economy of the Manichean allegory: the function of racial difference in colonialist literature', in Henry Louis Gates Jr. (ed.), *'Race', Writing and Difference* (Chicago: University of Chicago Press, 1986), pp. 78–106; and also in his *Manichean Aesthetics* (Amherst, MA: University of Massachusetts Press, 1983).

19 Consider, for example, the now canonical characterisation of the alienated, self-hating colonised in Frantz Fanon, *Black Skin, White Masks* [1952], trans. C. L. Markmann (London: Pluto Press, 1970), or Jean-Paul Sartre, *Black Orpheus* [1948], trans. S. W. Allen (Paris: Présence Africaine, 1976). On Indian effeminisation and the countering force of 'hyper-masculinity' under empire, see Ashis Nandy's groundbreaking *The Intimate Enemy: Loss and Recovery of Self under Colonialism* (New Delhi: Oxford University Press, 1983); and Mrinalini Sinha, *Colonial Masculinity: The 'Manly Englishman' and the 'Effeminate Bengali' in the Late Nineteenth Century* (Manchester: Manchester University Press, 1995).

20 To modify slightly Simone de Beauvoir's words in *The Second Sex* [1949], trans. H. M. Parshley (Harmondsworth: Penguin, 1979), p. 175: 'Representation of the [nation], like the [nation] itself, is the work of men; they describe it from their own point of view, which they confuse with absolute truth'.

21 Gcina Mhlope, 'We are at war', in Susan Brown (ed.), *LIP from South African Women* (Johannesburg: Ravan, 1983), pp. 159–60.

22 See Juliana Makuchi Nfah-Abbenyi, *Gender in African Women's Writing* (Bloomington: Indiana University Press, 1997), p. 35; Filomena Steady (ed.), *The Black Woman Cross-Culturally* (Cambridge, MA: Schenkman, 1981), p. 29. While the present study acknowledges the importance of motherhood and of mother figures to African and South Asian women, it also wishes to consider women writers' concerns with identities configured in contradistinction to the institution of motherhood.

23 Fredric Jameson, *The Political Unconscious: Narrative as a Socially Symbolic Act* (London: Methuen, 1981), p. 87.

24 Simon Gikandi made this point as early as 'The politics and poetics of national formation: recent African writing', *ACLALS Triennial Conference* paper, University of Kent, Canterbury, 24–31 August 1989, pp. 1–20, and has interestingly elaborated it in his work since, as, for example, in *Reading Chinua Achebe* (London: James Currey, 1991). See also Richard Kearney, *On Stories* (London: Routledge, 2002).

25 Julia Kristeva, *Desire in Language*, trans. Léon S. Roudiez (Oxford: Blackwell, 1987), in particular the essay, 'How does one speak to literature?', pp. 92–123.

26 See Bernth Lindfors, 'Introduction', in Bernth Lindfors and C. L. Innes (eds), *Critical Perspectives on Chinua Achebe* (London: Heinemann, 1979), pp. 5–6, for

further comment on the 'School of Achebe'. Nwapa has been referred to, for example, as one of 'the sons of Achebe'.

27 Flora Nwapa, *Efuru*, and *Idu* [1970] (London: Heinemann, 1987). Page references will henceforth be cited in the text, along with the abbreviations *E* and *I*, respectively.

28 For critical discussion of Nwapa's narrative strategies see: James Booth, *Writers and Politics in Nigeria* (London: Hodder and Stoughton, 1981), pp. 80–1; Eldred D. Jones, 'Locale and universe', *Journal of Commonwealth Literature*, 3 (1967), 127–31; Adeola A. James, '*Idu*, Flora Nwapa,' *ALT*, 5 (1971), 150–3; Eustace Palmer, 'Elechi Amadi, *The Concubine* and Flora Nwapa, *Efuru*', *African Literature Today*, 1 (1969), 56–8; Kirsten Holst Petersen, 'Unpopular opinions: some African woman writers', in Holst Petersen and Rutherford, *A Double Colonization*, pp. 112–13; Oladele Taiwo, *Female Novelists of Modern Africa* (London: Macmillan, 1984), p. 47.

29 See Kristeva, *Desire in Language*, pp. 104–6. Nwapa's facility in creating the effect of conversation in text has been noted by other critics, including Lloyd Brown, *Women Writers in Black Africa* (Westport, CN: Greenwood, 1981), pp. 122–57, and, although he is patronising, Ernest N. Emenyonu, 'Who does Flora Nwapa write for?' *ALT*, 7 (1975), 28–33. Nwapa is on record for having said that the genesis of her writing could be traced to conversations overheard in her mother's sewing shop. See Jane Bryce-Okunlola, 'Motherhood as a metaphor for creativity', in Susheila Nasta (ed.), *Motherlands: Black Women's Writing* (London: The Women's Press, 1991), p. 204.

30 Zora Neale Hurston, *Their Eyes Were Watching God* (London: Virago, 1987).

31 See Florence Stratton, *Contemporary African Literature and the Politics of Gender* (London and New York: Routledge, 1994), pp. 80–107; Susan Z. Andrade, 'Rewriting history, motherhood and rebellion: naming an African women's literary tradition', *Research in African Literatures*, 21:1 (1990), 91–110.

32 Elechi Amadi, *The Great Ponds* [1969] (London: Heinemann, 1982).

33 The deity of earth and fertility who in Achebe's *Things Fall Apart* is female, is male in Amadi's pantheon. Then again, Achebe in this novel masculinises the water goddess.

34 Amadi, *The Great Ponds*, p. 72. Relatedly, Carole Boyce Davies, 'Motherhood in the works of male and female Igbo writers', in Carole Boyce Davies and Anne Adams Graves (eds), *Ngambika: Studies of Women in African Literature* (Trenton, NJ: Africa World Press, 1986), pp. 241–56, finds in the Chielo-Ezinma episode in *Things Fall Apart* the traces of a 'suppressed larger story'.

35 Ifi Amadiume, *Male Daughters, Female Husbands: Gender and Sex in an African Society* (London: Zed, 1987), in particular pp. 38–40, 52–3, 59–62, 64–7, 86, 111–14. As her later *Afrikan Matriarchal Foundations: The Igbo Case* (London: Karnak, 1987) also argues, Amadiume's thesis is that Nnobi – and Igbo – society, originally matriarchal, was invaded by a patriarchal people. Femaleness has therefore come to carry a stigma.

36 On women's separate spaces, especially in West African culture, see Shirley Ardener (ed.), *Defining Females: The Nature of Women in Society* (London: Croom Helm, 1978), and *Women and Space: Ground Rules and Social Maps* (London: Croom Helm, 1981).

37 For instance, Nwapa's central women characters submit to the rule of callow husbands and to the 'circumcision' knife, and, in every case, take responsibility for their
barrenness. See *Efuru*, pp. 53, 55, 63; *Idu*, p. 91. In her critical reading of the novels,
Femi Nzegwu makes the different, if related, observation that the centrality of the
institution of motherhood to Igbo social ordering is never questioned in Nwapa.
Gender relations, she argues, existed in a situation of complementarity in African
society before colonisation, and Nwapa is concerned to recognise this. See Femi
Nzegwu, *Love, Motherhood and the African Heritage: The Legacy of Flora Nwapa*
(Dakar: African Renaissance, 2001), for example pp. 43–4.

38 The practice of (always non-specialist) women *oriki* performers (or praise singers)
in Yoruba culture offers a correlate for this mode of verbal self-representation by
women. As the *oriki* medium is highly rule-bound, and is traditionally performed
by men, women manipulate it in such a way as to make their mark upon it, to insert
themselves within it. In particular, they use to their advantage the fragmentary or
disjunctive nature of the appellations they inherit. See Karin Barber, 'Interpreting
oriki as history and as literature', in Karin Barber and P. F. de Moraes Farias (eds),
Discourse and its Disguises: The Interpretation of African Oral Texts (Birmingham:
University of Birmingham, 1989), pp. 13–23; Karin Barber, *I Could Speak Until
Tomorrow: Oriki, Women and the Past in a Yoruba Town* (Edinburgh: Edinburgh
University Press, 1991). Nwapa's women speakers may not be professional oral
artists, yet their verbal sufficiency bears comparison with that of the *oriki* artists.
They, too, subscribe to patriarchal injunction, but at the same time succeed in rep-
resenting and indeed promoting themselves through their use of language. In most
cases this may happen through their sheer loquacity, yet like the *oriki* artists, they
make inherited forms their own.

39 Amadiume's anthropological study *Male Daughters, Female Husbands* can be read
as suggesting that Nwapa could have gone even further in representing the range of
roles, activities and social positions available to women. In the event, her representations may have been constrained by the values she herself acquired as part of a
Christian colonial education.

40 Davies and Graves (eds), *Ngambika*, pp. 243, 249; Amadiume, *Male Daughters*, p.
29.

41 The calculating materialism dramatised in the later stories belongs to an urban
context where the restraining forces of village values and commentary are no longer
available. The cut-throat individualism of a heroine such as Amaka in *One Is
Enough* (Enugu: Tana, 1981), directly counters the collaborative choric harmonies
of village community. Similar heroines people the pages of Nwapa's short story collections, *This is Lagos and Other Stories* (Enugu: Tana, 1986), and *Wives at War and
Other Stories* (Enugu: Tana, 1984). Of this urban shift Nwapa observes: 'My heroines have changed because of the change in circumstances'. See Adeola James, 'Flora
Nwapa', in *In Their Own Voices: African Women Writers Talk* (London: James
Currey, 1990), p. 115.

42 Amadiume, *Male Daughters*, pp. 42, 53–5, 102–3.

6

Daughters of the house:
the adolescent girl and the nation

till I have been delivered I will deliver no one
(Olive Schreiner, *The Story of an African Farm*)[1]

In relation to the national son, the self-defining inheritor of the post-independence era and the protagonist of the nation-shaping narrative, the female child is a – if not *the* – non-subject within the national family romance. Revealingly, if paradoxically, given that her self-determination has been in principle achieved, the daughter figure within the framework of the postcolonial narrative that inscribes the new nation is, if not subordinate, peripheral and quiet, then virtually invisible.

The pre-eminent status of national sons, and the overshadowed position of their sisters, is exemplified in postcolonial fiction from the 1950s and into the 1990s by writers as diverse as George Lamming, Sam Selvon, V. S. Naipaul, Alex La Guma, Salman Rushdie, Shashi Tharoor and Romesh Gunesekera. A nuclear family fronted by a male heir is emblematically carved onto Gikonyo's stool, a gift of marital reconciliation presented at the end of Ngugi's *A Grain of Wheat* (1967). By contrast, the daughter of the new nation in male-authored texts is predominantly pictured, as ever, as homebound and tradition-bound. She inhabits either private spaces or the peripheries of public, national space. As in the case of the veiled Jamila, Saleem Sinai's sister in Rushdie's *Midnight's Children* (1981), the daughter's fate encapsulates the negative destiny of the nation whenever early national promises are betrayed: she is in this sense, as befits her status, a lesser or secondary national 'mother', a subsidiary figurehead.[2]

Postcolonial women writers have, however, confronted the symbolic inheritance that is the peripheral figure of the postcolonial national daughter, whether child or adolescent, either as a part of, or in addition to, adopting the writerly resistance strategies outlined in the previous chapter. Their engagement with women's national identity therefore emerges not only in the manifest content of their work, but also, for example, in their preoccupation with rewriting authoritative cultural texts. Instead of resuscitating and resituating the fetishised tropes of motherlands, some women writers have chosen to revise the family dramas that structure national narratives, including the male *Bildungsroman* and nationalist autobiography, by focusing on the roles and character of daughters. In particular, they have explored the daughter's relationship to her immediate, father-led family, and to the patrilineal community of which it is a microcosm. They have dramatised her negotiated bid for selfhood and status within what might be called the national house, that is, within the inherited and correlated structures of both family and nation-state.

This chapter will address how three very different postcolonial women writers, each one a 'daughter', if lost or prodigal, to one or other nation, have written themselves into the national family script, or redrafted the daughter's relationship to the national father. The novels in question are: the expatriate Australian Christina Stead's *The Man Who Loved Children* (1940), a realist narrative of qualified daughterly rebellion set in North America; the Nigerian-born London writer Buchi Emecheta's *Destination Biafra* (1982), a journalistic tale which intervenes in a history of civil (hence fraternal) conflict in order to foreground the role of a woman go-between; and the American-born Canadian Carol Shields's *Unless* (2002), a mother's story in which a daughter's silence is presented as protest.[3] The chapter will concentrate in particular on the daughter's position in the three novels relative to the family, tradition or community, where these structures are in each case figured as analogous to or integrated with the nation. I will thus approach the narratives as gender and nationalist theories-in-text – as texts which attempt to work out the daughterly possibilities within the social and national frameworks they inscribe. The writers of course speak for widely divergent postcolonial constituencies – a heterogeneity that must be recognised. Yet, despite their varying determinations, all three are distinguished by their preoccupation with daughterhood, broadly interpreted, and with the young woman's position in relation to wider, national society, and this if nothing else justifies netting them together within a comparative reading.

Towards setting up the comparative frame, the gender roles inscribed within what I earlier called the national family drama can be further elaborated by drawing on Olive Schreiner's *The Story of an African Farm* (1883) as an interpretative paradigm, which I will do at two points, here and later on. Schreiner's novel's temporal co-ordinates usefully give historical expansion to the triangulated group of Stead, Emecheta and Shields, while her nineteenth-century context counterbalances and complements the mid- and late twentieth-century, and early twenty-first-century perspectives of the other texts, respectively. Together, the four texts create a type of cross-connected intertextual matrix.

In *The Story of an African Farm* the South African settler-writer Olive Schreiner self-consciously establishes the figure of the child as at once 'primitive' *and* as the social pariah of the colonial world represented by the microcosm of the South African Karoo farm. The child in this sense operates within the narrative as a synecdoche for the native, where black Africans are represented largely as simple-minded and inarticulate, if also as perceptive. All three children are orphans: it is as if they have sprung fully formed from the arid soil of the farm. In the voice of the girl protagonist Lyndall, Schreiner draws an explicit analogy between 'the progress and development of one individual and of a whole [colonial] nation', in that the struggles for selfhood of the one equate with the other's writ large (*SAF* 182). However, Lyndall adds, speaking to Waldo her closest friend on the farm, this analogy applies more to a boy like him than to herself. Lyndall's own energies as a woman-in-the-making, she observes at length, must be directed to self-adornment rather than to the progress of a nation.

As is laid out in some detail in this book, the script of national coming-into-being that orchestrates postcolonial independence interpellates young men and women differently, as Schreiner perceives. Engaged in the difficult process of giving birth to itself, the emergent nation plays out a family drama in which colonial and/or native-nationalist fathers bequeath power, not without a struggle, to their male heirs. (In Schreiner's colony, however, the parental generation is either absent or morally deficient.) In most texts the national heir is typically a leader, soldier, prophet, pedagogue or writer, or a combination of these: in all cases he is engaged in definitively shaping the new community (Waldo the carpenter is an artist and also, as we find out, an amateur engineer).[4] First-generation post-independence male writers certainly energetically involve themselves in the process of engendering inspirational national stories out of the stuff of their own lives. By contrast, young women, the daughters of the nation, have generally not been in a position to shape the nation by means of their own self-generated narratives. Even if they escape the symbolic burdens of the national mother, they traditionally remain the objects or recipients of national definitions, not their originators.

And yet, although the stories of national daughters are rarely regarded as authoritative in the same way as are those of their brothers, they are as *writers* more advantageously positioned to intervene in the national drama than is the iconic mother. Their intervention is *double-edged* for, by articulating their own struggles for selfhood, as does Lyndall, they not only address their traditional muteness and/or marginality in the national script, but also, in so doing, rewrite their role within it. Writing becomes their vehicle of agency. By *writing themselves* as children and citizens of the nation, they rework by virtue of who they are the confining structures of the national family to encompass alternative gender identities. Moreover, they break out of the synchronic/symbolic and into the temporal dimension of the nation-in-formation – into its 'homogeneous time', in Benedict Anderson's phrase – which their fathers and brothers had earlier claimed.

The national impact of daughterly intervention possibly explains why it is that a large number of first- and second-generation postcolonial women writers have taken up family narratives in order to examine girl children's relations with their parents or parent surrogates. Margaret Atwood, Anita Desai, Bessie Head, Nadine Gordimer, Jamaica Kincaid, Manju Kapur, among others, confront what it is to be engendered, and gendered, by the patriarchal family, community or nation-state. For them, as for Louie in *The Man Who Loved Children* for example, writing itself becomes the expression of a troubled will-to-identity through which the female child imagines herself into autonomous being, abandoning the dependent, derivative position of the traditional daughter. Here, then, is another difficulty which women writers as national daughters must explore. The duties and responsibilities of daughterhood must be remade in order to produce texts that diverge persuasively from the male-authored script of national self-formation. Although Rosa Burger in Nadine Gordimer's *Burger's Daughter* (1979), for instance, tries to free herself from parental bonds in bold and creative ways, she cannot escape the ethical claims her father's political past places upon her. As Lynda E. Boose and Betty S. Flowers suggest in their study *Daughters and Fathers*, daughter texts must be determinedly self-authoring to 'produce texts that confirm independent separation from the father's authority'.[5]

At this point it should of course be acknowledged that such considerations apply to most texts that deal with daughters' relations to parental authority. It is after all the underrated, downgraded or subordinate position of the daughter within cultural scripts that conditions her status in national texts also. As Boose and Flowers write:

> Of all the binary sets through which we familiarly consider family relationships, the mother–daughter and father–daughter pairs have received the least attention, a hierarchy of value that isolates the daughter as the most absent member within the [social and cultural] discourse of the family institution.[6]

While this situation has been redressed to some extent by western feminist attention to the mother–daughter relationship, the father–daughter dyad continues to represent an area of neglect. In western literature and in literatures influenced by the west, the latter relationship, which this chapter recasts as the nation–daughter relationship, has been transmitted and understood through a number of influential, mutually reinforcing dyadic paradigms – Zeus and Athena, God and Eve, Prospero and Miranda. Each one of these firmly inscribes the father's power, and the daughter's non-presence or non-assertion anywhere outside the dyad.

To grant the Eve/Miranda figure a will-to-identity that extends beyond the definitive paradigm is fundamentally disruptive, therefore, not only of the dyad, but also of scripts of cultural and national authority more generally.[7] Tradition and authority are heavily invested against making any change. For the daughter, benefit and protection are exclusively to be obtained by deferring to the father. This is again in marked contrast to the restorative son figure who, in relation to the nation, has the power to rewrite the colonial past. Indeed, as I will show, the would-be rebellious Miranda characters occupying centre-stage in both Stead and Emecheta, or seeking moral authority in Shields, achieve only a qualified, uncertain or compromised success despite their efforts to break free from the cultural legacies that buttress their fathers' authority.

'Undelivered' daughter: Schreiner's Lyndall

Schreiner's *The Story of an African Farm* interprets the Karoo homestead as a figure for colonial society, as Ruth First and Ann Scott among others have noted.[8] In relation to the ridiculous but by no means inconsiderable figure of the farm-owner Tant' Sannie, the children, the child of nature Waldo and the two girls, the submissive Em and the rebellious Lyndall, are positioned as subordinate, exploited, voiceless. They all discover that it is necessary to leave the farm in order to come into their own in some small way as independent agents.

Contrasted with Waldo, the girl-child Lyndall is pictured within the repressive structure of the farmstead not only as the figure of the colonised, for this would include Waldo also, but, explicitly, as the powerless colonial daughter. She is subject to and inhabits, yet in no sense is able to inherit, the traditions and legacies of the farm. Anxious to leave its strictures behind her, to educate herself (*SAF* 77), and to resist women's traditional role as mother (*SAF* 167), she is uncertain, however, to what end her efforts should be directed, what position she might fill. Aware of lacking formal power in the wider colonial world, she feels, as she tells Waldo, 'branded' and cursed in that she is a woman (*SAF* 171).[9] Significantly, she also describes herself as undelivered of herself, as lacking the agency to deliver, to be delivered of. Looking forward to a time when 'woman's life is filled with earnest, independent labour', when self-fulfilment, which she calls 'sudden sweetness', will be 'not sought for, but found', she comments: 'I will do nothing good for myself, nothing for the world, till someone wakes me. I am asleep, swathed, shut up in self; till I have been delivered I will deliver no one' (*SAF* 179).

It is a predictable outcome of her hyperbolic representativeness that Lyndall dies as a result of childbirth and her baby does not live. As both a woman locked into domesticity and as the daughter of a derivative, stagnated society (which does not yet identify nationally and would be racially divided if it did), she literally cannot deliver herself of anything. The daughter enclosed within the sterile, alienated colonial family here represents an unshaped and unshaping, unrealisable potential.

Yet it is not only Lyndall and her baby who are dead by the end of the novel. To this extent the novel demonstrates, especially in its silences, its not saying, that the cultural script of the deferential colony, while it stultifies daughters, also withholds narratives of self-making from its native sons. In its final scene Waldo, too, dies, though unlike Lyndall he returns to the farm before his death. Their deaths thus have different valencies. If Lyndall's refusal to endure represents a protest which, however limited, the farmstead cannot countenance and must exclude, Waldo's death in the bosom of the farm suggests that the reproduction of the society itself has become untenable. The colonial/adult world in which vindictive white men are dominant is a sterile place. It defeats aspirations, repels idealism; it offers no alternative sources of identification, no escape routes from the child's social alienation. The child in this novel, to adapt from a reading by Jo-Ann Wallace, is forced to remain mere raw human capital, primitive, untapped, not fully developed, by analogy of course with 'unimproved' and 'unevolved' colonised people. [10]

Rereading the canonical script: Stead's Louie

The Man Who Loved Children by Christina Stead appeared just prior to the independence era, yet it far-sightedly participates in a number of postcolonial preoccupations, most notably in this context the idea of the child within the family as embodying an exploited, unformed potential that signifies the colonised also. From its opening pages the novel unfolds a disturbing family drama in which the eldest daughter Louie, the focaliser, seesaws between her allegiance to her father Sam Pollit, based on her respect for his knowledge and authority, and her attachment to her abjected stepmother Henny, founded on the gender loyalty. Accompanying this unsteadiness, the novel's underlying national identifications are subtly split – divided between, on the one hand, the United States with its Civil War scars, where the novel is set, and whose national icons the text investigates, and, on the other hand, Stead's native Australia, which provides a strong narrative undertow. As the only one of Sam's six children to grow up lacking her biological mother, who died in her infancy, Louie is at once freer to define herself but the more a victim of her 'Uncle Sam' father's 'czar-like' whims and edicts.

Swarming and boisterous, yet stifled by their father's absolute command – shaped to his will, governed by his work schemes, made to contribute to the family economy – the children of Sam Pollit, 'the Great White Father', in several ways equate with the classic subaltern, the wretched of the earth (*MLC* 105). Exploited and harshly disciplined, they form, it could be said, the underclass of the parental state (see, for example, *MLC* 337–9). [11] At home Sam is the self-confessed absolute ruler, the 'Monomaniac' in Louie's words, who sees his children as extensions of his own nature ('You are myself'). Unsurprisingly, the women in the family bear the brunt of this tyranny. While he seeks to mould his sons in his image, he imposes culturally subservient roles upon his daughters and subjects his recalcitrant wife to relentless verbal and financial persecution. Moreover, as the narrative takes pains to signal, Sam's patriarchal power over his family connects vitally with his broader political ideology, as expressed in his professional ambitions as a naturalist. To Sam the world, like the home, is an arena in which to actualise authoritarian, eugenicist beliefs: there is little in his view to distinguish the two spheres.

The interconnection becomes explicit on Sam's Smithsonian Field Expedition to Malaya where, like a true orientalist, his objective is to classify, organise and produce the country as a scientific object for US consumption. At this point in the novel the 'displaced' Australian-born Stead, who wrote *The Man Who Loved Children* in America, intriguingly maps her antipodean landscape and colonial experience on to the politically and mythically invested co-ordinates of Washington DC, where the Pollits' two family homes are located.[12] In Malaya, in a series of darkly ironic scenes that tell strongly against him, an excited yet climactically overwhelmed, sweating Sam shares with his native colleagues his two central eugenicist fantasies. First, there is his concept of 'the One Great Nation' (or 'internation') of the future, a globalised, US-dominated empire based on his own principle of unequal, international brotherhood. Second, he outlines a fantasy of fathering a family of many-coloured babies, unmistakably a seedbed and prototype for that same Great Nation (*MLC* 235–9, 247, 311, 380: the family-nation analogy is thus carefully established). In Judith Kegan Gardiner's description: '[the] father's domestic narcissism [is identified] with the capitalist patriarchy that dominates the ["childlike"] undeveloped world [sic]'.[13] The two exist in symbiotic relationship. As this implies, child, especially daughterly, rebellion in Sam's world signifies the ultimate – the most difficult, costly and disruptive – project of liberation, breaking open the tightly packed equations of domestic, national and international/imperial power.

The rebellious Louie is, crucially, a writer, and it is through her different forms of writing – journals, poems, doodles, drama – that she struggles to inscribe a selfhood which is also a potential citizenship of a new political future. In a classic anti-colonial and feminist move, she appropriates the role model of male literary genius (*MLC* 163), as well as her beloved writers' canonical works, and manipulates them to articulate her own resistance. Rejecting the constraints of womanhood by claiming the privileges of men, she seeks to recast the 'obscene drama', as she calls it, of her family's life (*MLC* 337). She writes a coded diary, which her snooping father cannot read, stages her play *Herpes Rom*, probably her moment of greatest triumph within the family circle, and dedicates a sonnet cycle to her admired school teacher Miss Aiden, thereby disrupting traditional patterns of male literary filiation. The message this 'natural [outlaw] of womanhood' signals to her uncomprehending father is clear: 'I am triumphant, I am king' (*MLC* 351).

Louie's play *Tragos: Herpes Rom* (*Tragedy: The Snake Man*), written in a 'pseudo-classical gibberish' which baffles her father, whose birthday present it is, rewrites Shelley's *The Cenci* but also bears the imprint of *Genesis* and John Milton's *Paradise Lost*.[14] By means of the play, in which a daughter is strangled, literally stifled, by her serpent father, Louie shockingly exposes and rejects her father's rule, enacting her deeply subversive wish to 'hunt [him] out like the daughters of King Lear' (*MLC* 408). Not long after this she contributes more practically to heightening the family drama by acting as a knowing if finally helpless accomplice in her stepmother Henny's suicide. But the primary medium of her quarrel with her father is her play, whose language and patricidal urges defeat his understanding, reducing him, the would-be all-knowing patriarch, to a 'stupor of amazement' (*MLC* 407).

The sense of recalcitrant autonomy Louie develops through her writing eventually enables her to leave home, her destination her mother's homeground, Harpers Ferry, a key site of John Brown's resistance to slavery. The child who was once disturbed by being called 'a norphan' (*MLC* 199), now enacts her fantasy of being parented, or so she hopes, by relative strangers (*MLC* 373). In contrast with Lyndall's sense of being undelivered of herself in Schreiner's novel, Stead's iconic daughter rejects her father's demand that she mother her motherless siblings, choosing rather, as she announces, to be her own mother: to engender her own future (*MLC* 511, 521).

The last scene of the novel sees Louie leaving on what she romantically if vaguely styles her 'walk around the world', yet what the substance of her new life might be is something that is left unresolved (*MLC* 523). Most of her writing up to this point has remained strongly derivative even in its resistance; indeed she has on occasion self-defensively demonstrated complicity with her father's hatred of femininity. It is unclear therefore whether her attempt to inscribe her protest by rewriting the canonical masculine texts of Europe and America has given her enough independence of spirit to forge out on her own for very long. As for the alternative offered by Harpers Ferry, here, too, a repressive, highly puritanical, patriarchal regime prevails. Louie was tellingly not made welcome on a previous visit.

At the close of *The Story of an African Farm* Lyndall is dead. At the end of *The Man Who Loved Children* Louie the chief rebel, the eldest daughter of the American (and colonial Australian) white nation, is lustily alive, convinced of her new powers to resist and thrive. Yet what her 'daughterly declaration of independence' might consist in, what social or creative alternative it offers, is effectively as ambivalent and foreclosed as it is in Lyndall's world.[15] Although she had no use for the feminist label as a writer, Stead with this novel demonstrates an awareness that gender identity significantly complicates already uncertain national identifications (where, for example, America overlays Australia). Louie is finally unable to negotiate a role for herself *outside* the filiative, patrilineal networks that configure the nation. Without the means to enlist into a new community, the implication is that the daughter's inscription of a role in the national story forces her to take a pathway away from familiar political frameworks, towards a realm where, as for Stead, as for Buchi Emecheta, national affiliations are doubled and complicated.

Being it all: Emecheta's Debbie

Like Christina Stead, Buchi Emecheta's national identifications are ambivalent, yet she, too, attempts to write a daughterly role into an unsettled national script. A novelist concerned at once with expatriate Africans in Britain and with changing conditions for women in West Africa, Emecheta's struggle to locate herself within the once-colonial metropolis while simultaneously maintaining links with her homeland has informed much of her work. In no other novel, however, is she as centrally preoccupied with the role of the *daughter* of the nation, and with the nation's heterogeneous makeup, as she is in her 1982 novel of civil war, *Destination Biafra*.[16]

In her historical novels, such as the acclaimed *The Joys of Motherhood* (1979), and in fantasies such as *The Rape of Shavi* (1983), Emecheta's approach, like Flora Nwapa's, is to recast African social space as inhabited by women over time and to define the postcolonial nation from their perspective. Indeed, in the autobiographical *Head Above Water* (1986) she self-consciously situates herself as a 'new [woman] of the new Africa', more assertive, more complex (she claims) than her mothers, but still connected with the past, and situated within a family lineage of female storytellers.[17] As with Stead and Schreiner, therefore, Emecheta's method might be characterised as broadly 'temporal/territorial' according to the definitions set out in the previous chapter, but also as (auto)biographical, in so far as her heroines play out episodes from her family's matrilineal history. In most of the West African novels, keynote experiences in the lives of African women across the twentieth century – in-group slavery, the 'double yoke' of the educated woman in Africa, the contradictory 'joys' of motherhood – are transformed into the organising leitmotifs of her narratives. In order to raise female subjects into twentieth-century Igbo/Ibibio history, she extracts a lexis of significant metaphors or defining images from those subjects' lives – images which in each case arise specifically from their day-to-day reality.

Emecheta's West African work can therefore be read as a more or less chronological collection of themed essays on the condition of eastern Nigerian women across the past 80-odd years.[18] Rewriting the past in order to 'write home', her work offers a gender-aware commentary on Achebe's epochal oeuvre *and* runs in intertextual parallel with Nwapa's endeavour.[19] Emecheta, it could be said, has openly constructed herself as a literary *daughter* or younger sister to Nwapa. Although there may be some ground to the criticism that her heroines are confined to their biological and sex roles (where *Destination Biafra* arguably escapes this charge),[20] her entire corpus is energised by the enabling, can-do assertiveness which Igbo culture approves in market women.

Emecheta's commitment to historical intervention and national reinvention is vividly demonstrated in her novel of the 1967–70 Biafra War, *Destination Biafra*.[21] The war having been widely represented in narratives by male writers, she sets out to fictionalise the painful history of national division from a woman's point of view. Where Nwapa's war novella *Never Again* (1975) portrays the part played specifically by Biafran wives and market women in the war, Emecheta goes a stage further by dealing in more representative detail, and in an openly assertive way, with the subject of women's roles in national life during wartime.[22] In particular she is interested in how the experience of a young, unmarried woman, Debbie Ogedemgbe, a self-consciously patriotic daughter of a federated Nigeria, both refracts the broad scene of the war and eventually, even if with limited success, redefines the nation. Of course, as Emecheta would have known from the start, the Biafra material was not particularly tractable for her purposes. Unlike the Algerian or Zimbabwean wars of liberation, the conflict did not put female combatants in the frontline (although women did serve in militias, as Achebe's *Girls at War* acknowledges). Her solution is to aim at the very heart of the male-dominated narrative of the war. Boldly reading Biafra's history with a woman-centred focus, she invents an idealised heroine, a 'dream woman' who identifies with a reunited Nigeria, who is a member of no dominant ethnic group, and who is placed, improbably but also uncompromisingly, in the thick of the fratricidal conflict-mongering of the time.[23]

Destination Biafra's fairly even-handed reconstruction outlines the build-up to hostilities from 1959, just prior to Nigerian independence, telescopes the colonial and neocolonial causes of the conflict, and describes in some detail the key battles. The reported action, which relies heavily on journalistic summary, enumerates atrocities on both sides. Significantly, Emecheta is in this narrative of civil war loyal to the idea of Nigeria as a national entity, in this respect endorsing Wole Soyinka's to-her-inspirational nationalist commitment in his memoir of the war, *The Man Died* (1972). Within the linear narrative frame, it is the Oxford-educated, middle-class Debbie's story that knits the history together. Her mission of national rescue is closely bound up with a personal pilgrimage of self-discovery: the conjunction is important.

Where Biafra threw into stark relief the contradictions of a unitary nationalism defined by inherited colonial borders, Emecheta attempts to reconcile

some of the nation's divisions in the person and role of her resilient heroine. It
is Debbie's symbolic mission to travel from Federal Nigeria into Biafra as an
emissary of peace for Saka Momoh's Federal government (Momoh being the
equivalent of the historical Yakubu Gowon). She is asked to persuade the Biafra
leader Chijioke Abosi (the Lt Colonel Ojukwu surrogate), who is a former
friend of hers, to sue for reconciliation. He will be tempted, it is hoped, by
Debbie's 'feminine charms' (*DB* 123). As this implies, Emecheta's attitude to
nationalism and its impact on women, specifically their sexuality, is not free of
ambivalence. By contrast, towards the end of the novel, Uzoma Madako, one
of the women with whom Debbie is travelling across the war-torn country,
makes the following comment on the marked divergence between the hopes of
peace, and the present harsh reality of war and its implications for women: 'A
few years ago it was "Independence, freedom for you, freedom for me". We
[women] were always in the background. Now that freedom has turned into
freedom to kill each other, and our men have left us to bury them and bring up
their children (*DB* 214).' From Uzoma's point of view, nationalist politics as
run by men make up a harsh tale of internecine conflict and betrayed hope in
which women have a place only at the beginning and end points of birth and
death. On the road Debbie sees soldiers horrifically rape and murder a pregnant woman, another of her travelling companions (*DB* 136). Even if uninten-
tionally, the massed historical detail of the novel sharpens the overall
impression of a meaningless recurrence of violent conflict – a conflict waged
by brutalised troops, directed by an alienated leadership, and masterminded by
foreign powers.

As a figure counterbalancing the bleak national situation, Debbie
Ogedemgbe anticipates another form of national being: more integrated,
inclusive and tolerant, but equally self-assertive, neither pre-1967 Nigeria, nor
post-1967 Biafra. Like Stead's Louie she carries a burden of generalised hope
for the future. Appropriately, therefore, rather than continuing to act as a
soldier in the Federal forces, Debbie becomes in the course of the novel a peacemaker. She begins her mission to Biafra as the representative of a small elite,
yet learns in the course of her journey to identify with the masses of women in
flight that she encounters, on the grounds of their suffering together as women.
Having tried and failed to participate in the 'men's war' by joining the army –
defying her mother by '[doing] something more than child breeding' (*DB* 45)
– she performs at the last the volte-face of volunteering to care for war orphans.
Her task will be to reconcile maternal values with her nationalist aspirations.
Far from being the token female representative of the national status quo, as
her Federal bosses see her, she comes to stand for an egalitarian, if traditionally defined nationalism. Marie Umeh reflects the idealism that went into the
creation of the character when she observes that Debbie 'is symbolic of Nigeria
in search of its rightful place in world history'.[24]

As this implies, Emecheta ultimately endorses Nigerian nationalism as a viable political belief for her country, even if she is wary of its flawed incarnations in ethnic violence, government corruption and gender-based oppression.[25] In her foreword to the novel she emphasises the non-sectarian aspects of Debbie's public identity: Debbie identifies and is identified as 'neither Ibo nor Yoruba nor Hausa, but simply a Nigerian'. As such she is the sign of a better nation, 'the [non-tribal] Nigeria I would like to see' (*DB* vii–viii). For Emecheta, therefore, the first conditions of Nigerianness – a concept that is taken as both self-evident and possible – are non-partisanship and interethnicity. Hence her often expressed attachment to her border town of Ibuza, a community which was attacked by both sides in the war and thus experienced to its fullest extent its cruel absurdity.

However, a novel which charts the excesses of a nationalism gone awry acknowledges, too, that the concept of Nigerianness can for the present only be theoretical, and, given Debbie's class status, may even be something of a bourgeois fantasy, a 'dream'. In a symbolic scene following her capture by Federal troops, Debbie declares: 'I am not on anyone's side. I am on the side of Nigeria. I want Nigeria to be one as we have always been' (*DB* 175). She adopts the familiar rhetoric of national independence struggles, recognisable for its concern to implant a 'true Nigeria' dating from precolonial times. Yet this is an isolated and embattled declaration, one which is immediately contradicted by Debbie's captor, the Hausa officer Salihu Lawal, who mocks her idealism with the comment: 'You are wrong, young lady from England. Nigeria has not always been one'. Privately Debbie concedes that 'Nigeria was only one nation as a result of administrative balkanisation by the British and French powers' – yet she does not have much time to pursue this line of thought (*DB* 175). Lawal drags her away and rapes her, only to back off in disgust soon after when Debbie informs him that she was earlier gang-raped by her fellow soldiers, Nigerians from the south of the country. Here Emecheta opens an important axis within the complex of intersections between gender and nationalism, acknowledging that women's subordinate status in relation to the nation has historically had, as one of its more violent consequences, rape. Debbie takes on in this scene the problematic role of victim of a type of institutionalised sexual assault, becoming the literal vehicle or channel for a mingling of ethnicities.[26]

Lawal's comment on an impracticable united Nigerianness, emphasised by his violent gesture of aversion, is left suspended over the rest of the text, exposing the implications for women when national affiliation is configured through discriminatory, gendered distinctions. If Debbie's status as other to the Nigerian national entity was at first signalled by her English education, foreign perspective and elite position (not forgetting also her Irish ascendancy boyfriend, Alan Grey), her distance from the nationalist mainstream is now further confirmed by the officer's rejection. She is punished for her visibility, her agency, her involvement in the thick of things, by brutally being made to serve as a site of male bonding. By the same token, in an instance of painful irony on Emecheta's part, her ordeal demonstrates that, as before, it is chiefly as *body* that woman plays a part in national experience. Nationalist politics remain divisive and oppressive: Debbie is doubly rejected, both for having mixed with northern and southern Nigerians and, as a female body, for having acted as the conduit for that mixing. As Abosi says when rejecting her peace mission (effectively a bid to be recognised as a national subject): 'You are not a man' (*DB* 239).

The ideal of an integrated, egalitarian Nigerianness therefore remains remote. As an ideal it is espoused by Debbie alone, and her status as at once self-proclaimed 'daughter of Nigeria' (*DB* 258), and as cultural and class outsider, exposes the idealism. She operates on both sides in a civil war, but without double-dealing; on every front she attempts to resist the barbarities of men, as well as the exploitation of neocolonialists, yet also magnanimously refrains from judging those who harm and insult her. In her attempt to lay claim to national subjecthood for Debbie as a woman, Emecheta falls back on the *exorbitant trope* of the bionic woman as national fighter familiar from revisionist nationalist texts by writers such as Ngugi.[27] In such tropes the gender of the fighter is intended on one level to signify a new national ideology, yet at another level, especially in the hands of a woman writer, there is the concession that this '[super]woman of Africa' is an almost entirely illusory and self-contradictory figure (*DB* 245). The reader is revealingly told that Debbie, the would-be defiant daughter of Nigeria, must still learn 'to back' a baby (*DB* 188). She cannot yet give expression to – cannot deliver – a practically viable Nigerianness that accommodates women in other than maternal roles.[28]

Static goodness: Shields's Norah

Just as Buchi Emecheta takes up and expands her compatriot Flora Nwapa's legacy with respect to privileging women, the Canadian Carol Shields develops her powerful peer Margaret Atwood's focus on the lives of Canadian women. As against this commonality, however, Shields's last novel *Unless* (2002) marks a number of differences in relation to the other daughterly texts discussed in this chapter.

As an American-born writer who moved to Canada as a young woman, Shields's national co-ordinates may seem, at least potentially, as unsteady as Stead's or Emecheta's. Yet, despite her occasional forays into the United States in, for example, *The Stone Diaries* and *Unless*, her fiction is securely located in a Canadian landscape and social world. *Unless* is exemplary in this regard, mapping the day-to-day life of Reta Winters, a well-off, middle-aged writer, mother and doctor's wife living in southern Ontario, who rejoices in a happy marriage, a respected career, and a supportive and undemanding group of women friends (*U* 43). Hers is a multicultural political context in which women's self-determination is legislated for and socially accepted. The repressions and exclusions of Schreiner's and Stead's colonial worlds, or the destructive divisions of Emecheta's war-torn Nigeria, are not part of this picture.

And yet, even so, far more acutely and plangently than in the other narratives, this is a novel about the pain of misunderstanding and exclusion still suffered by women on a day-to-day basis – a pain which, the novel tries to claim, connects women in the west with women worldwide. As its troubled, trochaic title suggests, *Unless* is Shields's lament for a women's power which, regardless of a long struggle and some hard-won successes, is in the twenty-first century still largely unachieved – a power moreover which not only continues elusive but is likely to remain so (*U* 99–100, 224, 313–14). Women, in her opinion, have not so far been in a position to formulate fully and explicitly what their social and political authority might entail. She therefore shares with the Indian Shashi Deshpande, a writer of similarly 'quiet' narratives, although located in a significantly different cultural context, the assumption that the balance of favour in the world remains tilted to the disadvantage of women.[29] Unless conditions change, Reta's angry letters to various male pundits and opinion-makers across the course of the novel contend, women's unease in the world, their out-of-jointness, is likely to continue (see, for example, *U* 136–7). Whereas men are allowed to be serious and get things done, women, if they are permitted to succeed, must do so without appearing threatening, by using charm (*U* 28–35). As this suggests, Shields is a writer, as Margaret Atwood acknowledges, who in the course of her writing career worked her way ever more deeply into feminism.[30]

In *Unless* the vehicle of women's historical pain is Reta's 19-year-old daughter Norah, who one day without explanation (before the beginning of the narrated action), opts out of life – her university degree and relationship – to sit on a street corner holding a cardboard sign inexplicably announcing 'GOODNESS'. This is the source of the 'great unhappiness' in Reta's life, which has changed the balance of how she views the world, and women's place in it (*U* 1). The novel becomes the narrative of Reta's attempt to comprehend and to some extent come to terms with her daughter's act, to try, even if necessarily imperfectly, to comprehend it via a series of essay-like chapters ostensibly about the contingencies of her own life. *Unless* in other words is a mother's story of a daughter who, up to the point that she takes to the street, is dedicatedly and sensitively parented. In this respect, too, the novel diverges from the tales of orphans and half-orphans told from the daughter's perspective that I have explored so far.

In feminist rewritings, as in this chapter, the subjectivity of mothers (including the much symbolised national mother) is to a large degree displaced in order to foreground the subjectivity of daughters. In contrast, Shields in *Unless* endorses the call issued by feminist critics such as Brenda Daly and Maureen Reddy to consider revisioning motherhood not as a biologically inscribed and conferred role, but as a choice, one which involves evoking the mother's inter-subjectivity with the child.[31] As Shields writes, 'a memoir must have a mother somewhere in its folds': which is also to say, however, that the writer must reconcile with her identity as a daughter (*U* 319). It is telling in this regard that the writer-narrator Reta begins her career as the translator of a respected bisexual, francophone feminist philosopher, Danielle Westerman, a literary mother figure. Thereafter, even as she herself branches into fiction, she continues with the intimate task of representing Westerman's thoughts and sentences, 'accommodating' her *partis pris* in the ongoing translation of her memoirs (*U* 63, 101).

Yet even if *Unless* takes the mother's part, it is the sign of the daughter which is placed within a national if not transnational (or cross-cultural) dimension. As is only gradually revealed in the course of Reta's at once troubled and curiously serene narrative, Norah was prompted to take her cryptic protestation of goodness to the streets following an unsuccessful attempt to assist 'a Muslim woman [who] set herself on fire in Toronto' (*U* 41). Reta and her friends, who mention the self-immolation in conversation, initially see the event as the symptom of a more widespread springtime depression that might be affecting Norah also, but otherwise as disconnected from the young woman. In an alternative explanation, Westerman, the novel's de Beauvoir surrogate, concludes early on that Norah is acting out the traditional passivity and exclusion of women, which is in fact presciently close to the truth (*U* 104).

As the novel builds its case for Norah's diagnosis (*U* 136), Reta and her circle have a discussion based on the assumption that goodness (in contradistinction to 'greatness', a male preserve) involves exercising ethical responsibility towards an other. In particular, being 'on the path to goodness' equates with re-presenting and attempting to alleviate another woman's predicament (*U* 12, 115–18). However – here the political implications of 'goodness' become disturbed – the three examples of women in need which the friends give all refer to Third World, in fact 'other' women – from Mozambique, a 'Muslim' country and Nigeria, respectively. The second woman, though they do not know it, is the one Norah tried to help. In this case of a Muslim 'sati', the protest by self-immolation carried out by a woman in a burka, the friends remark only that an unspecified 'woman', assumed to be white Canadian, came to her aid and tried to beat out the flames with her hands. It is the burns on their daughter's wrists and a CCTV videotape that eventually reveal to her parents that this woman was Norah. The reader is led to believe that the shock of this act, in effect the pain of spontaneous, cross-cultural empathy, drove her out on to her Toronto pavement in 'an ellipsis of mourning' (*U* 309). The sign she holds can therefore be interpreted less as a claim of goodness for herself, than as an ironic label of the (in)significance of her act, a confession to the impossibility of translating the other body-in-pain.

However, by the end of the novel, once her daughter is restored to her, Reta's narrative loses interest in the ethical and political questions that Norah's impassive resistance, if that is what it is, poses. The moral axis around which the plot turns is thus left both politically and morally ambivalent – an ambivalence that poses significant problems in a text that earnestly professes its feminism. It is therefore as well to examine further the implications of Norah's intervention as both a cross-cultural and as a gender-marked gesture.[32]

To begin with, the sheer unreadability of Norah's sign, even to her parents, her lover and her sisters, suggests that within the nation, even the social democratic Canadian nation, the scope does *not* exist for a cross-cultural or transnational solidarity between women to be successfully realised. Perhaps the implication is even stronger than this: 'daughter citizens' lack a platform in the nation from which to express collectivity and make their voices heard. Just as in Norah's university essay Madame Bovary is deemed ousted from the moral centre of Flaubert's novel, the figure of the young woman is displaced from the moral centre of the nation. This much Reta would probably concede. Lacking the official sanction to convey a message Norah becomes 'all perch, she and her silent tongue and burnt hands' (*U* 310). She reaches out to the unnamed Muslim woman in her mysterious victimhood, to become herself a victim: it is a Levinasian act of conceding the absolute demand of the other that is, however, in this case both misdirected and misinterpreted.

Several other mixed messages and tangled 'chains of semiosis' further confuse the signifiers of 'good' and 'woman' which Norah bears, albeit that the novel appears only partially aware of them.[33] Significantly, while staging her (im)passive protest, she is described using a vocabulary more immediately associated with an Indian, specifically Hindu, socioreligious context (a language of being 'on the path', for example), yet which in her situation is mystified and thus emptied of its political content. Not only the means of the protest but its object, too – the veiled woman in flames – crosses several signs of Third World female victimhood (sati, the veil) in such a way that the wrong that the woman may herself have been resisting is lost to view.

In the absence of any indication of what the Muslim woman's cause might have been, Norah's act of positioning herself as object in her place, no matter how empathetic her identification, replicates the appropriative moves characteristic of historical colonialism, as well as of certain forms of western feminism. The western feminist's typical reading of the Third World woman as the victim of native patriarchy, as analysed by Chandra Mohanty and others, is generally followed by an attempt benevolently to intervene on her behalf.[34] To this Shields importantly adds a second level of intervention, Norah's replication of the victim's position in her retreat to an ascetic yet public protest, in which she keeps her own wounds hidden and surrenders agency by deploying an obscurantist language of gesture. In this she is presumably intended to be representing the marginalisation of women everywhere, yet as her mother consistently speaks for her, it is impossible to know for sure (*U* 197, 227). Norah carries a name allusive of Ibsen's great feminist nay-sayer, but she is finally allowed only the word 'Yes' to affirm a question of her mother's. Norah's protest, in Danielle Westerman's words, is an inversion rather than a subversion, 'a retreat from society' behind the figure of the burned, veiled woman that 'borders on the catatonic' (*U* 218). As if by way of a justification of this position, Reta explains towards the end of her daughter's story that the world is divided into those who command power, men, and: 'all of us who fall into the *uncoded otherness* in which the power to assert ourselves and claim our lives has been displaced by a compulsion to shut down our bodies and seal our mouths and be as nothing (*U* 270, emphasis added).

The three or, with Schreiner's paradigmatic text, four writers discussed above in their different ways demonstrate that 'having a gender' has an unavoidable impact on having a nationality or cultural identity.[35] At each point on the intertextual matrix a daughter figure explores women's tangential relationships to national and social structures, and the difficulty of writing a self-authorising identity, while also, in so doing, at once repeating and yet revising those difficulties. Schreiner and Stead, Emecheta and Shields, reveal that, when it comes to national family dramas, the symbolic dice are weighed against women's self-representation. Although, as Rajeswari Sunder Rajan and other feminist critics have argued, it is in 'the process of the creation of selfhood that self-cognition occurs, and an identity is taken on', identities within the nation are at the same time communally authorised.[36] As is indicated by the ersatz, perfectly made-to-measure quality of Emecheta's idealised war heroine, on the public national stage the daughter's identity, even if self-validated, *also* requires public recognition and respect.

Ultimately none of the daughterly options offered by the three postcolonial texts *on their own* suggest how women's subjectivity might be refashioned in such a way as to produce equal participation on the national stage as well as publicly endorsed self-assertion. The point of still-virtual resolution may lie in a negotiated mediation between three options: neither a rewriting of masculine myths of authority alone, nor the fabrication of female icons and spaces, nor even gestures of universal solidarity made on the basis of shared oppression, but something of all three. The prerogative of daughter-citizens may be to activate what Homi Bhabha has referred to as the performative strategies of nationhood (even if his reading is not particularly attentive to gender).[37] In writing a nation, he suggests, pedagogical or ideological imperatives, the normative categories of national authority (gender images, race), are creatively resisted by the invention or *performance* of new identities. In at least one of its incarnations nationalism, regenerative, protean, endlessly malleable, in fact stimulates and encourages such self-deliverance.

Notes

1 Olive Schreiner, *The Story of an African Farm* [1883] (London: Virago, 1989). Page references to this edition will henceforth be included in the text along with the abbreviation *SAF*.

2 See the discussion of Salman Rushdie's *Midnight's Children* in chapter 1.

3 Christina Stead, *The Man Who Loved Children* [1940] (Harmondsworth: Penguin, 1974); Buchi Emecheta, *Destination Biafra* (London: Fontana, 1982); Carol Shields, *Unless* (London: Fourth Estate, 2002). Henceforth page references to these editions will be included in the text with the abbreviations *MWLC*, *DB* and *U*, respectively.

4 See chapter 3 on Achebe's *Anthills of the Savannah*, and also C. L. Innes, *Woman and Nation in Irish Literature and Society: 1880–1935* (Hemel Hempstead: Harvester Wheatsheaf, 1993), especially pp. 9–42, which examines the relationship between the feminised nation and the poet-son.

5 Lynda E. Boose and Betty S. Flowers (eds), 'Introduction', *Daughters and Fathers* (Baltimore: Johns Hopkins University Press, 1989), p. 11.

6 Boose and Flowers (eds), *Daughters and Fathers*, p. 2.

7 On the cultural legacy of the Miranda figure, and the position of the daughter in the colonial script, see Laura E. Donaldson, *Decolonizing Fictions: Race, Gender, and Empire-building* (London and New York: Routledge, 1992), pp. 1, 16–17.

8 Ruth First and Ann Scott, *Olive Schreiner: A Biography* (London: The Women's Press, 1989), pp. 92–8. See also Doris Lessing, 'Introduction', to Schreiner's *The Story of an African Farm* (London: Century Hutchinson, 1968), pp. vi–xxv; and Anne McClintock's highly identified reading of Schreiner in *Imperial Leather: Race, Gender and Sexuality in the Colonial Contest* (London and New York: Routledge, 1995), pp. 258–95.

9 A condition exacerbated by her property-less status.

10 Jo-Ann Wallace, 'De-scribing *The Water Babies*: the child in post-colonial theory', in Chris Tiffin and Alan Lawson (eds), *De-scribing Empire* (London: Routledge, 1994), pp. 171–84.

11 See David Lloyd's discussion of Antonio Gramsci and recalcitrant subalternity in *Anomalous States: Irish Writing and the Post-colonial Moment* (Dublin: Lilliput Press, 1993), pp. 126–8.

12 On Stead's national displacement as a writer, see Lorna Sage, *Women in the House of Fiction* (London and New York: Routledge, 1992), pp. 37, 46.

13 Judith Kegan Gardiner, 'The daughter of *The Man Who Loved Children*', in Boose and Flowers (eds), *Daughters and Fathers*, pp. 384–99, especially pp. 384 and 389. See also Louise Yelin's excellent, layered reading of the perils of national identification in the novel, *From the Margins of Empire: Stead, Lessing and Gordimer* (New

York: Cornell University Press, 1998), pp. 17–37. I am indebted to discussions with Paula Teo about Stead's novel.

14 Shelley's *The Cenci* (1819) dramatises the story of Beatrice Cenci executed for the 1599 murder of her father.

15 See Yelin, *From the Margins of Empire*, p. 31.

16 In 'Lagos provides a warm welcome', *West Africa* (19–25 January 1981), 110, Emecheta speaks of England as a place that, though not 'the country of my birth', provided her with 'comparative peace of mind to carry on with my creative work'. In Adeola James (ed.), 'Buchi Emecheta', *In Their Own Voices: African Women Writers Talk* (London: James Currey, 1990), pp. 34–45, Emecheta expresses self-satisfaction at being a writer living in England and working in the English language, and, as it were reciprocally, voices her disapprobation regarding contemporary Nigerian social conventions.

17 Buchi Emecheta, *Head Above Water* (London: Fontana, 1986), pp. 7–17. The question 'why are women as they are?' Emecheta observes, lies at the centre of her fiction. In accordance with her aversion to full-blown 'western' feminism, however, Emecheta urges that writing itself is sexless. See James, 'Buchi Emecheta', pp. 42, 40; Buchi Emecheta, 'Feminism with a small "f"!', in Kirsten Holst Petersen (ed.), *Criticism and Ideology* (Uppsala: SIAS, 1988), pp. 173–85. On the ambivalences of her position as a woman writer, see Cynthia Ward, 'What they told Buchi Emecheta: oral subjectivity and the joys of otherhood', *PMLA*, 105:1 (January 1990), 83–97. In the chronological line-up of her works, Emecheta has moved from autobiographical accounts of her life in London (*In the Ditch* (1972), *Second-class Citizen* (1974)), out to the Africa of her youthful memories and her foremothers' stories, and then via historical and futuristic fantasy (*Destination Biafra* (1982), *The Rape of Shavi* (1983)), back to the synoptic autobiography of *Head Above Water*. Her more recent work returns to the experience of second-generation black women in Britain, as in *Gwendoline* (London: Collins, 1989).

18 *The Slave Girl* (1977), for example, concerns the 1920s and 1930s in rural and urbanising mid-eastern Nigeria; *The Joys of Motherhood* (London: Heinemann, 1979) explores World War II and the immediate post-war period in Lagos, *The Bride Price* (1978) the 1950s, *Naira Power* (n.d.) the oil-boom period, and *Double Yoke* (1982) the academic sexploitation issue of the 1980s.

19 See Bernth Lindfors, 'The palm oil with which Achebe's words are eaten', in Bernth Lindfors and C. L. Innes (eds), *Critical Perspectives on Chinua Achebe* (London: Heinemann, 1979), pp. 47–8. Emecheta's intertextual dialogue with Nwapa extends further than the call-and-response structure between *Efuru* and *The Joys of Motherhood*. See Juliana Makuchi Nfah-Abbenyi, *Gender in African Women's Writing* (Bloomington: Indiana University Press, 1997), p. 35.

20 See Davidson Umeh and Marie Umeh, 'An interview with Buchi Emecheta', *Ba Shiru*, 12:2 (April 1987), 19–25; Emecheta, 'Feminism with a small 'f'!', pp. 175–81; and Nfah-Abbenyi, *Gender in African Women's Writing*, p. 41.

21 The Biafra War broke out when, following Igbo massacres in northern Nigeria, oil-rich Igboland in the east of the still newly independent Nigeria attempted to secede from the republic, which then declared war. The war claimed 2.5 million lives.

22 See Flora Nwapa, *Never Again* [1975] (Enugu: Tana, 1986). The body of Biafra War fiction is growing. Marie Umeh, 'The poetics of thwarted sensibility', in R. Vanamadi *et al.* (eds), *Critical Theory and African Literature, Calabar Studies in African Literature*, vol. 3 (Ibadan: Heinemann, 1987), pp. 194–206, mentions war fiction by three other women writers: Catherine Acholonu, *Into the Heart of Biafra*; Terisa Meninu, *The Last Card*; Leslie Ofoegbu, *Blow the Fire*. Male war writers include Chinua Achebe (in *Girls at War* (1972)), Wole Soyinka (in autobiography), Cyprian Ekwensi, Chukwuemeka Ike, Eddie Iroh, Festus Iyayi and Ken Saro-Wiwa. Marie Umeh commends the credibility and topicality of Emecheta's account.

23 See Emecheta, *Head Above Water*, p. 1. Debbie is neither Hausa, Ibo, nor Yoruba, but Itsekiri. She is also, though at different times, both a soldier and a peacemaker. In this chapter the allusions to the nation as a fraternity split by civil war ironically recall Benedict Anderson's description of the nation as a brotherhood, as discussed in the introduction.

24 Umeh, 'The poetics of thwarted sensibility', p. 203.

25 Speaking of her return to Nigeria in 1981 after a long absence of 18 years, Emecheta in 'Going home: Calibar, contrasts and complaints', *West Africa* (12–18 January 1981), 72, describes herself as susceptible to feelings of national loyalty. However, she indicates these sentiments would come more easily to her in a new-look Nigeria, one less corrupt, parochial and 'indisciplined': 'Somehow amidst the chaos I felt uplifted because to me the new National Anthem with the drums in the background is more the Nigeria I would like to see'.

26 See Rajeswari Sunder Rajan, 'Life after rape', in *Real and Imagined Women: Gender, Culture and Postcolonialism* (London and New York: Routledge, 1993), pp. 62–83.

27 See Florence Stratton, *African Literature and the Politics of Gender* (London and New York: Routledge, 1994), p. 124. My reading of Emecheta at this point is indebted to discussions with Nazreena Markar.

28 Even so, Buchi Emecheta brings up for discussion, if in passing, the implications for a daughter's hard-won autonomy when she becomes a mother.

29 Shashi Deshpande's *Collected Stories*, vol. 1, ed. Amrita Bhalla (New Delhi: Penguin India, 2003), are in this sense exemplary.

30 Margaret Atwood, 'To the light house', *Guardian Review* (26 July 2003), 28.

31 Brenda O. Daly and Maureen T. Reddy (eds), *Narrating Mothers: Theorizing Maternal Subjectivities* (Knoxville: University of Tennessee Press, 1991).

32 It is curious that none of the early reviews of the novel, to my knowledge, pick up on the problematic semiotics of the veiled woman who is helped by a westerner because she has set herself alight. For Elaine Showalter, *London Review of Books*, 24.13 (July 2002), 13, this 'political twist does not displace the fundamental debates about women's art and its reception'. Rachel Cusk, *The New Statesman*, 131.4585 (29 April 2002), 47, hints that Reta's 'surrender' to family can be viewed metaphorically as an act of self-immolation. In both cases the Third World woman implicitly becomes a vehicle to represent the condition of the western woman. On the veil, see Alison Donnell (ed.), *Interventions, Special Topic, The Veil: Postcolonialism and the Politics of Dress*, 1:4 (1999).

33 See Gayatri Spivak's discussion, crucial in this context, of the 'sati' as object of

knowledge, in 'Can the subaltern speak', in Patrick Williams and Laura Chrisman (eds), *Colonial Discourse and Post-colonial Theory* (Hemel Hempstead: Harvester Wheatsheaf, 1993), 66–111; revised in Spivak's *A Critique of Postcolonial Reason: Toward a History of the Vanishing Present* (Cambridge, MA: Harvard University Press, 1999), pp. 227–49. See also Rajeswari Sunder Rajan's arguments concerning the reconstruction of female subjectivity on the basis of pain and therefore victim-hood in *Real and Imagined Women*, pp. 15–39.

34 Sunder Rajan, *Real and Imagined Women*, pp. 34–5.

35 Yelin, *From the Margins of Empire*, p. 7.

36 Sunder Rajan, *Real and Imagined Women*, p. 143.

37 Homi Bhabha, 'DissemiNation: time, narrative and the margins of the modern nation', in Bhabha (ed.), *Nation and Narration* (London and New York: Routledge, 1990), pp. 297–302.

7

Transfiguring:
colonial body into postcolonial narrative

> to get me out of the belly of my patriarchal mother . . . [distance] my eye from
> her enough so as to see her in a different way, not fragmented into her metaphoric
> parts. Crossing through the symbol while I am writing. An exercise in decondi-
> tioning that allows me to acknowledge my own legitimacy. The means whereby
> every woman tries to exist; to be illegitimate no more. (Nicole Brossard, *These
> Our Mothers*)[1]

The silenced and wounded body of the colonised is a pervasive figure in colonial and postcolonial discourses, although its valencies obviously shift with the
transition from colonial into postcolonial history. In the postcolonial process
of rewriting, certainly, the trope of the dumb, oppressed body undergoes significant translations or transfigurations, which this chapter will examine in
closer detail. In *Maru* (1971), a novelistic indictment of intra-black racism, the
South African writer Bessie Head stakes out a number of epigraphic moments
with which to begin the discussion.

Maru recounts the tale of a woman who learns to paint – to *figure* – and in
so doing undergoes significant changes of status and position in her society:
from having no place or recognition she becomes a figure in the community.[2]
This character, Margaret Cadmore, is marginalised on a number of counts: she
is a woman, an orphan and above all a Marsarwa (more commonly known by
the derogatory term 'Bushman'). Her experience exemplifies what Head
understood as the hierarchies of prejudice that can operate within communities, including those which are themselves prejudiced against.[3]

Margaret Cadmore's mother having died at the time of her birth, she is
brought up by a white woman, by and for whom she is named. This woman,
the first Margaret Cadmore, is inspired to adopt the child when, during a visit
to a hospital and following an idiosyncratic habit, she sketches the dead mother
of the child. She is thus confronted by the incontrovertible evidence of the
woman's humanity, something which contrasts starkly with the prejudice
expressed by the wider Botswanan community for the Marsarwa. In an

unusual chain of impacted replications, Margaret Cadmore, the adoptive
mother, reproduces an image of the biological mother, while also, in her act of
adoption, claiming and 'reproducing' the child. She projects her values and her
vision upon the child: 'environment everything, heredity nothing' is the creed
she lives by (*Maru*, 13).

Lowest of the low, the negation of the negated, the daughter Margaret
Cadmore is granted selfhood in so far as she is *re*-produced as image, not unlike
her mother; in so far as she is filled full of another's subjectivity. This logic of
replication is halted and reversed only when the second Margaret, the
Marsarwa, takes charge of the process of replication, and, by beginning to
paint, produces her own images. She effects a split between image and self,
body/heredity and subjectivity. Some of the first subjects she paints are, significantly, the women of the community, whom she observes involved in 'ordinary
common happenings' (*Maru*, 107).

As a corollary to this process, at the same time as Margaret is developing her
art, her closest friend, Dikeledi, in many ways her double, becomes pregnant.
'Reproduction' at both levels, of image and of child, is in relation to *Maru*
neither simple replication nor fulfilment, the achievement of wholeness. It is
rather a separation, the creation of difference, the possibility of new meaning
– in particular, the possibility of creating a new narrative of self, a self-authored
tale of the everyday. Woman as sign of the extreme other, the definitive subaltern, becomes a sign-writer in her own right.[4] The second Margaret follows
with her pencil the 'carved wounds' experience has left around the eyes and
mouth of her friend: 'her portraits and sketches [trace the] unfolding of the
soul' (*Maru*, 108).

The figured begins to figure by figuring the other – itself. How might this
concept, this narrative of transfiguration, or indeed self-transfiguration, be
more closely related to the question of colonial and postcolonial bodily representation? Here I want to introduce the partial analogy for symbolisation
under colonial conditions offered by the Freudian condition of hysteria (the
'partiality' will become clearer in a moment). I will take up the analogy once
again when considering postcolonial self-articulation, applying it more
directly under the specific aspect of the talking cure.

According to Freud, a key symptom of hysteria is the tendency to take metaphor literally or anatomically, as described by or inscribed on the body.[5]
Putting it another way, the hysteric expresses her condition through convert-
ing 'mind' to 'body', translating her fears and repressions into a language of
body images. As Mary Jacobus in her own adaptation of Freud's theory points
out: 'As hysteria produces symptoms, so symptoms produce stories. The body
of the hysteric becomes her text', and hence the text of the analyst.[6] Physical
disorders are seen to enact the psychological distresses of the hysteric: most
famously Anna O.'s phantom pregnancy is interpreted as unconfessed desire.

In colonial representation, exclusion, suppression and relegation can often be seen as literally *embodied*. From the point of view of the coloniser specifically, fears and curiosities, sublimated fascinations with the strange or 'the primitive', are expressed in concrete physical and anatomical images. The seductive and/or repulsive qualities of the wild or other, as well as its punishment and expulsion from the community, are figured on the body, and as (fleshly, corporeal, often speechless) body. To rehearse some of the well-known binary tropes of postcolonial discourse, as opposed to the coloniser (white man, centre of intellection, of control), the other is cast as carnal, untamed, instinctual, raw, and therefore also open to mastery, available for use, for husbandry, for numbering, branding, cataloguing, possession, penetration. Images of the body of the other are conventionally conflated with those of the land, unexplored land too being seen as amorphous, wild, seductive, dark, open to possession. Differently from the psychoanalytical scenario therefore, agency in this case belongs to the colonial/analyst, not to the colonised/patient (hence the only partial analogy).

Examples of such embodiment are fully present in the texts of the European explorers and travellers who prepared the ground for colonisation. Examples could be taken from as far back as the early colonisation of the Americas, but in relation to Head's continent of Africa, Mungo Park in his journal narrative of 'opening up' the Niger River sees the African women in the towns he comes across specifically as sexual bodies. Indeed, he describes with some relish the physical enticements they have to offer.[7] As regards the 'Orient', the explorer Richard Burton demonstrates in his notorious accounts of his travels a specular fascination with the impressive 'venereal requirements and reproductive powers' of the 'Oriental' female compared to those of the male, as well as with the genital size and sexual prowess of African men.[8] He quite explicitly exhibits the other as sexual body. In early nineteenth-century exhibitions of Saartjie Baartman, the 'Hottentot Venus' – like Margaret Cadmore, a Southern African extreme other – the fleshly, 'animal' black was represented to the eyes of Europe as a single female body. It was evidence as concrete as it was possible to obtain of the implacable physicality of the other woman.[9]

Under colonialism such representations of course offered crucial self-justifications of the imperial project. What is body and instinctual is by definition dumb and inarticulate. As it does not (itself) signify, or signify coherently, it may be freely or 'legitimately' occupied, scrutinised, analysed, resignified. The representation carries complete authority; the other cannot gainsay it. The body of the other can represent only its own physicality, its own strangeness – although that quality of inhering strangeness is again exclusively defined by Europe.

In a concrete illustration of this phenomenon, in a 1770s description by Captain James Cook of the 'Indians' – in fact, Maoris – of New Zealand, the ultimate sign of their difference or weirdness is taken as their 'tattowing' – the marks scored upon their bodies. After having made observations in his journal of the physical stature and habits of the Maoris, and then of their alleged cannibalistic practices, Cook comes round to giving an account of their bodily lines and contours, in effect their tattoos. Decoration is converted into inscription; description becomes meticulous inspection. The Maoris have of course marked *themselves*, yet the Europeans here interpose themselves in the process, assuming agency and retracing these markings in their text. To offer a sample:

> they have marks impressed by a method unknown to us, of a very extraordinary kind: they are furrows of about a line deep, and a line broad, such as appear upon the bark of a tree which has been cut through after a year's growth; the edges of these furrows are afterwards indented by the same method, and being perfectly black, they make a most frightful appearance.[10]

The body of the Maori is seen as signifying its black difference. The other is body as sign, itself signed, furrowed and impressed, made to advertise its own unknownness and savagery.

Yet colonial enterprise did not stop at the inscription of the marked silenced body. It could, and in many cases did, go further and deeper, become closer, intrusive, a wounding, a violation. The enslaved or indentured body was often an engraved body, a bloodied form. Its mutilation denotes one of the more extreme forms of colonial marking and subjection. The difficulty here is that to speak of such bloody realities by way of literary representation can appear to distance and to sanitise them. Yet at the same time – and this must be the justification however meagre of commentaries such as these – to describe the colonial situation in this way is also to obtain some form of theoretical purchase on at once the importance and the near impossibility of self-articulation as resistance to colonisation. (By 'self-articulation' I intend a back-reference to the second Margaret Cadmore's self-reproduction in the form of signs.)

J. M. Coetzee's novel *Foe* (1986), correctly described by Gayatri Spivak as a 'didactic aid' staging the 'undecidability' of the margin, comments on the legacy of colonial figuring by representing the silence of the colonised body as, fittingly, a dumb, ravaged mouth.[11] In this narrative, a rewriting of aspects of Daniel Defoe's novels, *Robinson Crusoe* (1719) and *Roxana* (1724), Friday the representative of the enslaved 'wholly other' is a figure literally silenced, made dumb like Philomel in the myth, his tongue plucked out. Cut, mute, disabled, Friday is locked in a silence that begs to be read as symbolic yet which, as the narrative unfolds, consistently – and rightly – sabotages signification, refuses to mean within the coloniser's language. Struck dumb at some point in time that cannot be told and is unknowable, Friday remains outside European time, outside white signification, a cipher without an apparent historical point of reference, a character lacking definable character. As Susan Barton the chief narrator, or female Defoe, puts it: 'The story of Friday's tongue is a story unable to be told, or unable to be told by me. That is to say, many stories can be told of Friday's tongue, but the true story is buried within Friday, who is mute. The true story will not be heard till by art we have found a means of giving voice to Friday' (*Foe* 118).

The forms of expression available to Friday are either silent or repetitive. He dances, whirling round and round (*Foe* 92); he plays one tune on the flute, one combination of notes (*Foe* 95). At a point towards the end of the novel, after painstaking writing lessons from Susan, he manages one letter, one character, which he writes over and over on a slate. The character is the exact opposite to 'I': it is 'o', the empty set, the empty mouth, the same figure as he traces in the turning dance, in the recurring tune. His writing effectively means nothing and yet it is (presumably) full of all the figuration he can muster. For the one silenced, the language of the master remains closed: signification can mean no more than signalling one's silence. Recalling the condition of the hysteric, Friday scarred, marked, excluded, remarked upon, has as his sole mode of expression a body language (rather than his body itself). Muted by his oppressors, Friday's dumb mutilation has now become its own sign: 'the home of Friday is not a place of words' (*Foe* 157).

Friday blots Foe's (or Defoe's, or Susan's) 'I' of autobiographical narrative with his own zero, his open empty mouth; he crosses the 'I' with a nought – but a nought can also be read as a full circle. Till the unspoken is spoken, the character Foe observes, we cannot come to the heart of the story (*Foe* 140). What he fails to realise, however, is that the unspoken themselves must speak this heart, and that their first sign, as with Friday, must be negation, the refusal to mean within the oppressor's symbolic system. The refusal represents a crucial taking of initiative. Friday's display of non-linguistic signs can be seen as his art, at once the denial of meaning and the intimation of another story. His inability to speak signals what Susan Barton and Foe cannot speak, yet his incapacity, his empty mouth, signifies potential plenitude as much as negation, 'silence, perhaps, or a roar, like the roar of a seashell held to the ear' (*Foe* 142).

Silence as negation – or as a fantasised potential, a not-yet-articulated fullness of speech. This is perhaps one of the key distinguishing features of the postcolonial: the acting out of paradox, the conversion of imposed dumbness into self-expression, the self-representation by the *colonial body* of its scars, its *history*. As confirmation of this, in postcolonial nationalist narratives of the last number of decades, images of the scrutinised, scored subject body have become the focus of attempts at symbolic reversal and transfiguration. Representing its own silence, the colonised body speaks; uttering its wounds, it strives to negate its muted condition.

This is ideally speaking a process not of reclamation only, but, importantly, of self-articulation, reconstitution through speaking one's condition, as with the hysteric. The unspoken time with which the native body is loaded, with which it may be marked, is converted into language, often into autobiography, at once a fabricated story of the self and a self-recuperation. Signifying, the once-silent, apparently timeless subject body places itself within a syntax of history. Yet, it is helpful to remember, in practice the situation is not as all-embracing or as liberating as this description might suggest. Social exclusions dictate that *not all* colonised bodies get the chance – or an equal chance – to represent themselves. Indeed as Elaine Scarry has influentially argued, pain is a radically incommunicable experience, and the body in pain an absolute other which is rarely if ever brought into representation.[12] This notion is counterbalanced, however, by the assertion of the universality of the experience of suffering, undivided by difference, as in Rajeswari Sunder Rajan's reading of Scarry. Even so, discourses of post-independence nationalism and racial solidarity inevitably impose their own definitions of normative pain; certain dominant recuperative selves stand in place of others. There are consequently those among the once-colonised for whom the silences of history have not ended.

Considering, however, the ungainsayable self-representation of *some* colonised, the earlier analogy of the hysteric may be extended. If colonial iconography figured repression upon the colonised body, then postcolonial nationalist writing can be seen to equate with the hysteric's talking cure. As with the hysteric, reminiscence, the retelling of the past, brings release from that past. The object body, the formerly unspoken, exposed and denuded figure, is clothed with words; the subjected becomes the subject of its/their own narrative. The spokespersons and writers among those who were denied representation, by articulating their condition, experience themselves as figuring rather than as figures. They exhume the dead metaphors of their repressed condition, 'disembody the text [of the past] and discover what the picture covers'.[13] Such transfiguration, because it involves self-representation, implies self-division, which is a condition of narrative. It unfolds in, and is structured by, time – a further definitive condition of narrative. Transfiguration, in effect, becomes the recuperation of the body through the medium of time-bound, self-reproducing narrative.

Yet, at least in its initial stages, the body in this narrative of nationalist recuperation remains a significant term. The tendency is first to locate and consolidate self-identity on the site of the whole, restored, healed body – whether the physical body or the national body, the body of the land. Like the hysteric, the early nationalist seeks completion, a seamlessness of subjectivity (or of history, of the nation-state). So the reversal of the sign of the colonised does not in the first instance necessarily imply an erasure or a scoring out of the native body image. The female body form, for example, that most fetishised and silent of body symbols, as has been seen, figures prominently in early nationalist/postcolonial representations. National wholeness, fusion with the maternal and national body-land, suggests a hoped-for plenitude, a totality with which to subsume the denial that was colonised experience.

Under nationalism, the female body signifies achieved desire, ideal made flesh, rather than repressed fascination or neurosis. Yet, as under colonialism, the invocation of the body rests upon the assumption of predominantly mas-culine – and upper or middle-class – authority and historical agency. Inevitably, given that postcolonial discourses of self-determination have a con-siderable investment in concepts of self-making and of retrieving history, the gender and class specifics of such nationalist imaginings are often either endured or overlooked. The widely celebrated attempt to upturn the master–slave dialectic of colonial discourse reinforces the tendency. If the most grievous colonial violations were those inflicted upon the utterly objectified body, that of the subjected motherland, or of the dumb subaltern, nationalist texts invoke this body as the ultimate signifier of sacrifice endured.

So it remains the case that, as in other symbolic systems, femininity in nationalism 'is experienced as a space that . . . carries connotations of the depths of night (God being space and light), while masculinity is conceived of in terms of time [national history and myth]'.[14] As Nuruddin Farah graphically demonstrates in his (now tragically prescient) novel of Somali identity *Maps* (1986), within the symbolic make-up of the male nationalist, pride of place is held by a great mother ideal, a multimammia figure.[15] The hero Askar's entry into manhood coincides with his discovery of himself as national son to Mother Somalia:

> something which began with the pain of a rite had ended in the joy of a greater self-discovery, one in which he held on to the milky breast of a common mother that belonged to him as much as anyone else. A generous mother, a many-breasted mother, a many-nippled mother, a mother who gave plenty of herself and demanded loyalty of one, loyalty to an ideal, allegiance to an idea, the notion of a nationhood – no more, and no less. (*Maps* 96)

Askar seeks fusion with the illiterate mother-as-body yet can do so only by objectifying it. In this predicament a central contradiction of postcolonial nationalist narrative is epitomised. Self-articulating narrative cannot deliver what it promises: a completely united and unifying history, an absolute iden-tification with the national body. To conceptualise that fusion demands, in practice, self-division. To transfigure body into narrative, to escape from being a mere figure in another's text, is to effect a break in the self. The talking cure, too, was predicated upon self-estrangement. Reminiscence is at once the retrieval and redemption, and the effective alienation, of the past.

Paradoxically, then, to tell a self-constituting tale implies the acceptance of the narrative (and deconstructive) conditions of temporality and lack. Such a paradox becomes perhaps most evident and extreme in those situations where early post-independent nationalisms have been compromised, and transform into travesties of national unity, parodies of egalitarian ideals, where, in the emptying of national meaning, 'signifiers are prized loose from any signified'.[16] No longer is the absolute consummation that the reconstitution of the motherland and the subjected body represented seen either as possible or as completely desirable. Too many have been left out of the process; too many bodies have as a result been discarded and abused.

As writers such as Amitav Ghosh, Salman Rushdie, Dambudzo Marechera and Ben Okri, among others, suggest, national wholeness has in many postcolonial contexts turned out to be little more than a dream or a folly; and national identity rarely anything but partial and split. The nation is in such cases regarded not so much as an ideal, an essential and necessary good, than as a necessarily imaginary composition, or even compulsion, as chapter 8 discusses at greater length. It is the product, constantly in flux, of a history of risks and chances and sudden reversals, rather than the outcome of a smooth historical flow from a determinate origin to a predetermined, preferably glorious future. The writers dramatise the intractability of postcolonial self-representation within the political and aesthetic languages of the colonial west. Indeed, from the point of view of Third World artists who are not part of an elite of any description, the nation itself, whether perceived as real or imaginary, may well appear as an irrelevance or a luxury. As Kwame Appiah has pointed out, to such artists one national cell of structural adjustment or neoliberal management will seem as good or as bad as another.[17]

And where a unified national narrative begins to fragment, so, too, does the iconography of the body. Where national histories are revealed as stochastic, divided, painful, where origins are obscure, the body, too, is exposed as fissured, reduced, violated. In Ben Okri's *The Famished Road* (1991), a dream-allegory of Nigeria's reiterative post-independence history, the symbolic spirit-child's Dad is repeatedly beaten almost to death and his body torn and severely bruised in a series of boxing bouts with ever more fearsome otherworldly opponents.[18] As is also demonstrated in Farah's *Maps*, an ironic consequence of the single-minded effort at nationalist self-determination may be increasing divisiveness and a recurring process of self-doubling and self-defeat. In *Maps* Askar is an orphan boy born in the Kallafo area of the Ogaden: his father was a dissident Somali nationalist and his foster mother Misra is a woman of Ethiopian, specifically Oromo, origin. Askar's bond with Misra represents a more visceral reality than his theoretical Somaliness, yet across the narrative her 'foreign body' is repeatedly gouged, maimed and dismembered, her plight clearly figuring that of internally riven Somalia itself. As the nation projects itself upon divided and controversial maps, and assumptions of national integrity are repeatedly called into question, the mother body in the novel, putatively the symbol of national wholeness, consistently signals absence and pain. Askar's own self is divided: he is male yet menstruates.

By definition, the process of establishing national identity involves an attempt to gather together the self in language, usually by way of narrative, by way of that which at once alienates and yet connects. At the end of his cycle of tortures, Dad in *The Famished Road* gives a visionary speech intimating spiritual and political reconstitution located somewhere in a dream-like future. In *Maps*, identity lies in self-inscription, literally the inscription of the body. As Askar grows to manhood, which in his case also means coming into his own as a male nationalist, he marks himself as textual or 'texted' body. (In a dream he revealingly wanders through a landscape full of people 'tattooed with their identities' (*Maps* 42–3).) As the existence of his narrative itself testifies, he tells his own story. But he also effectively inscribes himself – he writes the words of the Koran into his flesh; he draws the (to him) true map of a fully united Somalia on his skin. His inscribed, mapped body figures and makes concrete the figurative in nationalism. Bodily inscription here, self-imposed, signifies not so much subjection (being subsumed into another's body of knowledge), but self-realisation.

If Askar's tale were to be taken as a metafiction for the strategies of self-representation in postcolonial narrative, then such strategies – writing the body, splicing the self – seem to take two main forms, which are not mutually exclusive. The first is the *literalisation* (or defamiliarisation) of the accepted status of the body as sign, in particular of the national body as woman/mother. The second is *figuration* or *transfiguration*, the translation of such metaphors into an other, self-directed if often self-doubting system of signs, usually one that is diachronic, that attempts through writing its own temporality to come to some kind of historical terms. As part of this process, scars, lines of wounds, the body text, may be retraced and objectified as actual violations, as lived silencings, as in the case of Okri's Dad.

The representational strategies which group under the headings of literalisation and figuration are predictably diverse, yet generally involve a self-conscious or self-reflexive rewriting of the already inscribed colonised body. The body is exposed as colonial fact and artefact, as overproduced, written upon. Devices such as mimicry or, more accurately, a kind of excessive self-replication, are used to indicate the weightiness and oppressiveness of the body's status as sign. The body complex as a palimpsest of different symbolic layers – land, mother, scored flesh – is disclosed, opened out and ultimately divided up into multiple constituent narratives of bodily/national investment. Symbol is expanded into plot, or plots; history in the epic sense of the tale of a nation is reduced to (auto)biography, anecdote, stories of growing up (as in *Maps* and *The Famished Road*). Icon, that is to say, is transformed into individual or communal narrative, less lofty than national epic, certainly not as coherent, not as authoritative. Character (as in symbol, cipher) is transfigured into character (as in the subject of the story). The inscribed body – woman, oppressed – inscribes itself.

In Askar's case in *Maps*, where the originary land/mother is absent, divided and alienated, a foreign body, that of Misra, because it signifies familiarity and a local, specific loyalty, becomes the more dear and desirable (and also, as Askar grows older, the more repressed). The mother, even if adoptive, the nation, even if divided, signify a joyous plenitude of physical feeling and deferred desire (therefore, *literalisation*). However, in the space of lack opened up by Askar's process of maturing, as he grows further away from Misra, alternative symbolic rallying points are located: here the alternative strategy of *figuration* comes into its own. His life reads a tale of self-constitution, and the novel becomes a correlative to that narrative, a fictive supplement, an answer to 'the fictive riddle asking a factual puzzle': on which national side does he belong? (*Maps* 65) Often speaking in the second person, Askar objectifies himself in story. His reliance on story constantly reminds us that selfhood – individual, communal or national – is not fixed or *sui generis* but invented, protean, adaptable (*Maps* 216–17). Askar's identity is made up out of symbols often without explicit national reference, acquired at random, extracted from dream-memory (*Maps* 42–6). Unattended and orphaned at birth, self-inventing and self-doubting, he becomes the literal embodiment of a tragically divided Somali nationhood.

I will end by looking at self- and body representation in the Jamaican Michelle Cliff's *No Telephone to Heaven* (1987), a novel which boldly illustrates the overlapping strategies of literalisation and trans/figuration.[19] As Françoise Lionnet has noticed, Cliff's interweaving of official and forgotten histories powerfully asserts the 'liberating potential of counter-narratives'.[20] The following commentary is offered therefore as a way of focusing and to some extent summarising the central issues of this chapter.

No Telephone to Heaven is structured around a guerrilla incident that took place in Jamaica in the early 1980s. The narrative of this incident is intersected with the personal histories, often truncated, of the main actors involved. In the course of this many-layered account, tracked across three key geographic regions (the Caribbean, North America and Europe), Cliff maps on to her novel an inventory of Jamaican/Caribbean colonial experience. The narrative is strung across episodes blatantly paradigmatic of colonial violations and delusions: sentences bulge out at certain points to offer lists of synonyms for postcolonial afflictions and pathologies.

For Cliff, colonial and, perhaps even more so, post-independence signification involves the ceaseless, self-reinforcing replication of the signs of power and colonial presence, or latterly, the mere simulacra of such a presence. First World brand-names dissociated from their original products are 'quoted' in incongruous contexts: they are hand-outs without useful contents, past their sell-by date. Dingle, the Kingston slum, is described as a 'town of structures made by women and children. Structures made from packing crates which once housed Vauxhalls, Morris Minors, Renaults, Kelvinators, Frigidaires, Maytag washer-dryers' (*NTH* 31). The experience is one of: 'Depression. Downpression. Oppression. Recession. Intercession. Commission. Omission. Missionaries' (*NTH* 17). From the point of view of those Jamaicans who remain unfree and poor, postcolonial history denies both conflict and continuity, cancelling that which is not itself: 'Like a mule working a cane cutter – [going] round and round' (*NTH* 169). 'So lickle movement in this place. The place of their people's labour. From this place. Then only back and forth, back and forth, over and again, over and again – for centuries' (*NTH* 16). Circularity, synonymity, like the replication of the metropolis in myriad tourist resorts on its periphery, figures the influence and primacy of the centre. That which is different, not like itself in every part, is dismissed as trivial, marginal and unnatural.

As the divide or pivot in his/her name suggests, the character Harry/Harriet is one such 'unnatural' creature, 'one that nature did not claim' (*NTH* 21): 'Not just sun, but sun and moon' (*NTH* 128). His/her identity is indeterminate, divided. Her/his body, a literal symbol of colonial violation, has been split – he was raped as a *bwai* by a British army officer. The rape forms one of the text's highly self-conscious metaphors for colonial violence figured on the body (an instance of literalisation). Yet Cliff is vigilant about the potential glibness of these symbols. Harry/Harriet, recognising this danger, refuses to reify the rape as symbol, asserting instead the value of what happened as a formative experience, and a way of identifying with others:

> Darling, I know it is hard to listen to all of this; it is hard to tell. I have been tempted in my life to think *symbol* – that what he did to me is but a symbol for what they did to all of us, always bearing in mind that some of us, many of us, also do it to each other. But that's not right. I only suffered what my mother suffered – no more, no less. Not symbols, not allegory, not something in a story or a dialogue by Plato. (*NTH* 130)

But Harry/Harriet refuses not simply the subjection to symbol, the split body. S/he also seeks to alienate and reverse the process that entails that subjection, the signifying practices of colonial othering. Not quite female, s/he yet chooses to be female, which on the colonial periphery is conventionally to be triply oppressed. Yet through a process of transsexual transformation, 'H/H' makes of this femaleness an audacious diversity, a constantly changing and therefore unlawful difference. His/her various, necessarily imperfect acts of copying produce slippage, a shift away from symmetry and sameness, and the absolute two-term division of self and other, male and female. The body of the other, already 'denatured', is multiply refigured. For H/H gender differences cut both ways: s/he parodically performs as a male ballet-dancer, s/he works as a female nurse, and in a notable act of double disguise, plays, while in female dress, at being a cartoonic 'Prince Badnigga' to a gullible American tourist.

In the case of Clare Savage, H/H's close friend and the central protagonist, self-splitting, less in evidence, is as significant – in fact, it is her story. Clare's body, almost white, suggests near colour purity from the point of view of the Jamaican national elite. Yet, in conflict with her own upbringing, she identifies with that in herself which is dark, 'impure'. She has been taught 'to quell one side, honey,' but finds it 'amazing how the other side persists' (*NTH* 152). As with H/H, the desire to be different is mediated by the intrusion of the body, again figured as the target of colonial history, though with her the resolution is in a different direction, giving neither one, nor two. When she becomes pregnant by her lover, a black Vietnam war veteran, she finds that his war experience brings the likelihood of genetic abnormality. As he points out, the child will be less a body than a 'disharmony of parts' (*NTH* 156). Their own bodies in spite of themselves enact the distortions of their historical inheritance and the end result of the experience is to tamp Clare's womb. She miscarries and is told she will no longer be able to bear children. Yet this bodily wounding, this apparent lack, ultimately acts to return her to her past and to the land, the two intersecting in her grandmother's abandoned property, where she sets up house. Her individual development becomes a trope for national transfiguration. Instead of a preoccupation with ravaged symbols, instead of reproducing the denatured body of colonial suffering, she makes history, she turns to narrative, both by connecting with her familial past, and, at the last, by committing the self-sacrifice that is involved in her guerrilla insurrection.

Notes

1 Nicole Brossard, *These Our Mothers: Or the Disintegrating Chapter*, trans. B. Godard (Toronto: Coach House, 1983), p. 16.

2 Bessie Head, *Maru* [1971] (London: Heinemann, 1987).

3 Head observes: 'if the white man thought Africans were a low, filthy nation, Africans in Southern Africa could still smile – at least, they were not Bushmen . . . Of all things that are said of oppressed people, the worst things are said and done to the Bushmen' (Head, *Maru*, p. 11). Page references to *Maru* will henceforth be cited in the text along with the title *Maru*.

4 On extreme otherness or the 'wholly other', see Gayatri Spivak, 'The Rani of Sirmur: an essay in reading the archives', *History and Theory*, 24:3 (1985), 247–72, as well as her reading of Coetzee's *Foe*, also cited below. The latter appears in its most recent form in *A Critique of Postcolonial Reason: Toward a History of the Vanishing Present* (Cambridge, MA: Harvard University Press, 1999), pp. 169–97.

5 I refer here to the theory of hysteria first analysed by Freud but for the purposes of this chapter usefully adapted as a paradigm of reading by Mary Jacobus. See Mary

Jacobus, 'Readings in hysteria', in *Reading Woman: Essays in Feminist Criticism* (New York: Columbia University Press, 1986), pp. 195–274.

6 Jacobus, *Reading Woman*, p. 197.

7 Mungo Park, *Travels in the Interior of Africa* (London: The Folio Society, 1984).

8 Richard Burton, *Love, War and Fancy: The Customs and Manners of the East from Writings on the 'Arabian Nights'*, ed. Kenneth Walker (London: Kimber, 1964), pp. 154, 156. On Burton's orientalism, see also Rana Kabbani, *Europe's Myths of the Orient* (London: Macmillan, 1986).

9 See Sander Gilman, 'Black bodies, white bodies', in Henry Louis Gates Jr. (ed.), *'Race', Writing and Difference* (Chicago: University of Chicago Press, 1986), pp. 223–61. Saartjie Baartman's remains, it is worth knowing, were finally repatriated from France to South Africa in 2002.

10 John Barrow (ed.), *Cook's Voyages of Discovery* (London: A. C. Black, 1925), pp. 104–5.

11 J. M. Coetzee, *Foe* (Harmondsworth: Penguin, 1986). Page references will henceforth be cited in the text together with the title *Foe*. See also Spivak, *A Critique of Postcolonial Reason*, pp. 169–97, in particular pp. 174–5, 181–2, 189–90. Spivak reads the novel, too, as enacting 'the impossible politics of overdetermination' in a situation where, as for Susan Barton, one is both author and mother: a depressing reading for any woman who would seek to combine these roles.

12 Elaine Scarry, *The Body in Pain: The Making and Unmaking of the World* (Oxford and New York: Oxford University Press, 1985). For Rajeswari Sunder Rajan's reading, see *Real and Imagined Women: Gender, Culture and Postcolonialism* (London and New York: Routledge, 1993), pp. 15–39.

13 Jacobus, *Reading Woman*, p. 217.

14 Luce Irigaray, 'Sexual difference,' in Toril Moi (ed.), *French Feminist Thought* (Oxford: Blackwell, 1988), p. 120.

15 Nuruddin Farah, *Maps* (London: Picador, 1986).

16 Jean Franco, 'The nation as imagined community', in H. Aram Veeser (ed.), *The New Historicism* (London: Routledge, 1989), p. 205. On the second, cynical, 'postnativist' stage in African writing, see Kwame Anthony Appiah, 'Is the post- in postmodernism the post- in postcolonial?' *Critical Inquiry*, 17:2 (1991), 336–57.

17 Appiah, 'Is the post- in postmodernism', p. 353.

18 Ben Okri, *The Famished Road* (London: Cape, 1991). The spirit child or *abiku* is one who repeatedly dies and returns to the world (as does the *ogbanje* child in Achebe), thus signifying in Okri's work truncated cycles of growth.

19 Michelle Cliff, *No Telephone to Heaven* (London: Minerva, 1987). An earlier form of the novel centred on the young Clare was published as *Abeng* in North America in 1984. Page references will be cited in the text along with the abbreviation *NTH*.

20 Françoise Lionnet, *Postcolonial Representations: Women, Literature, Identity* (Ithaca: Cornell University Press, 1995), p. 20.

8

The nation as metaphor:
Ben Okri, Chenjerai Hove,
Dambudzo Marechera

metaphors are the public history of nations (with apologies to Balzac). (Timothy Brennan, 'The National Longing for Form')[1]

Unreal nation

The first, post-1945 phase of anti-colonial nationalism in Africa, as in other colonised regions, was distinguished by *literal* belief structures: a strong, teleological faith in the actual existence of the nation as 'people', and the sense that history essentially unfolded as a process of that nation's coming-into-being. There was a belief, too, in Africa as in South Asia, as in the Caribbean, that the distinctive forms of modernity, in this case in particular the sovereign state, could be incorporated, indigenised, repatriated.[2] These may seem at face value rather obvious statements to make about nationalism, which broadly demands some form of belief in the national entity, and acts of loyalty expressed towards it. Yet the obviousness here is part of the point. In post-independence Africa, as in other former colonies, the nation as a group defined by particular observable traits and/or a distinctive, ascertainable history, was for some time believed to have a geopolitical, historical and even spiritual existence. Crucially, it was also seen to provide a means through which identities detached from European stereotypes, and distinctive, local (in this case African) modernities might be generated.

However, in the decades since independence, as the coherence of the nation – whether as geophysical space, symbolic leadership or unitary people – has been questioned in various ways, especially perhaps in Africa, national self-awareness in fiction, if not the concept of the nation itself, has undergone significant shifts and revisions. In consequence, as was intimated in the previous chapter, writers acting out of both disillusionment and cynicism have come round to concentrating on the imaginative as opposed to the actual status of the nation. The *constructedness* of the nation is now engaged as an issue and, in certain more recent writings, as a source of invention. Writers investigate metaphor, symbol, dream and fetish as signifiers of a national reality or as constituents of a sense of national being, rather than the nation as literal truth. Under a range of pressures – political dislocations and violence, economic trauma, geographical and cultural displacements, other forms of national schizophrenia – the *made up* nature of nationhood has emerged into greater prominence. And so, as the split between nationalist fantasy and nation-state reality has been teased open, the emphases have heftily shifted in the once-grand tale, as recorded in leaders' autobiographies, of African national coming-into-being.

Mid- to late 1980s narratives from a range of writers – Achebe, Farah, Ben Okri, Chenjerai Hove and Dambudzo Marechera, among others (including the early 1980s writing of Bessie Head) – attest that it is the nation's story *as story*, and as nightmare, that forms the focus of attention. Writers are now preoccupied with the at-once-liberating-yet-appalling possibility of there being no there *there*. The fact that women have long been aware of the metaphorisation of their social realities may explain why more men than women writers have been involved in exploring the nation as metaphor in this new phase. The open secret is that the formulation of a national eschatology and identity depends not so much on an 'actual' national history of national coming-into-being as on fictions of the nation – fictions ostentatiously, even obscenely, crafted, exuberantly dreamed up; on nations represented in and as story.

Within such narratives, as this chapter will explore in relation to Okri, Hove and Marechera in particular, symbols no longer figure merely as the signs of nationhood, but are understood as substantively representative and constitutive of national belief, if not of the nation itself. The nation is a space in which the people and the state entity *collude* in generating and exchanging the significations of power, while narrative at once reflects on, and participates in, this process. Instead of codifying the new national reality, as did Achebe, Soyinka and Ngugi from the 1950s, the African novel now explores that codification as process; it situates itself on the *performative* rather than the *pedagogical* axis of nation-state existence.[3]

The seemingly hallucinogenic, disjunctive writing of the Nigerian-born British writer Ben Okri can be taken as iconic of this shift in preoccupation from the material to the mythic, animist, and even surrealist dimensions of national reality. That said, it is important to concede that on Okri's part this shift at the same time entails a formal and epistemological engagement with traditional Yoruba myth-systems, and an intertextual convention of writing about the bush established by D. O. Fagunwa, Amos Tutuola and, later, Wole Soyinka.[4] Okri's two collections of short stories, *Incidents at the Shrine* (1986) and *Stars of the New Curfew* (1988), and his cyclical novel *The Famished Road* (1991), the first in a trilogy completed in 1998, dramatise the elaborate, nightmarish displays that are part of quotidian existence in the African postcolonial nation.[5] His landscapes, in particular the road walked by the *abiku* or spirit child in *The Famished Road*, are extravagantly 'tropographic', charged with portents. A path can be a mysterious script of dream signals, a palimpsest of signs from other spiritual planes, each as palpable and 'real' to the *abiku* Azaro as any other. Okri maps the otherworldly spaces of the neocolonial city, its compounds and out-skirts, as a phantasmic or occult phase of alienated social being resembling that which Fanon describes in *The Wretched of the Earth* with reference to the pre-national, colonial period.[6] As magical excursions relentlessly rupture his narra-tives, and as daimons, symbols and other mystical occurrences irrationally, even profligately, exhibit themselves, not only the nation as such but the violent and seductive dream of the nation is revealed as a key reagent, if not malign motive force, in recent neocolonial history.

Okri favours invention – what he calls *dreaming* – over convention or tradi-tion both in the composition of his fiction and in understanding the world.[7] Breaking a dominant trend in African writing, his concern is to avoid handing down normative images of African national reality derived from the oral tradi-tion or from the nationalist realist style of the early decades of independence. In contrast both to the colonial writing which placed Africa as signifier of the exotic and the forbidden, and to early nationalist writing which sought to reverse colo-nial stereotypes, Okri's worlds have absorbed the extremes of the exotic and the real. In his tales syncretic display is inescapable: frenetic heterogeneity, surreal-ist confusion, these make up the world. His fiction participates actively in what Harry Garuba and others have discussed as 're-traditionalisation' processes in post-independence Africa, whereby traditional cultural forms, such as ancestor worship, are used to incorporate and interpret the signs and objects of the modern world.[8] Moreover, according to Garuba, such 're-emergences' may be probed as manifestations of an 'animist unconscious', in relation to which abstract states of mind manifest in concrete forms. Such a characterisation would certainly apply to aspects of Okri's work up to 1991. His work since has arguably become more imbued with a New Age-type spiritualism.

Where dreaming or an animist consciousness saturates reality, one conse-quence may be the evacuation of public political spheres as spaces of resistance, as will be seen. Yet in Okri the combination of a collective, escapist madness with the peculiarly cynical quality of the destruction inflicted on people by 'the powers that be', can at the same time produce a mordantly cutting, if also dis-affected political commentary. Okri's urban slum society is at the extremity of its illusions, including those of national independence. It has been tricked, deceived, betrayed: quack chemists stock 'curved syringes' and bogus medi-cines; elections by definition involve 'political fevers and riggings'; city god-fathers spray counterfeit money at crowds of supporters; wars of divided national identity create irrational enmities.[9] The present moment is shown to be the outcome of a long political history of cruelty and irrationality, both colonial and neocolonial, into which the people have been drawn as accomplices. The nation, too, is deeply imbricated in the overriding logic of exploitation and deception. This is in effect *post*-post-independence fiction that does not pretend to invoke a higher political meaning or truth – indeed it cannot hope to. Nation-state politics – the political rivalry of the Parties of the Rich and the Poor in *The Famished Road*, for example – is presented as one more symbolic display among others, all of them ironic, surreal, absurd.

Postcolony

The nation in Okri, therefore, to the extent that it is in fact recognised either as ideal or as political entity, is a phantasmagoria comprising demonstrations of random cruelty and pomp, and fetishes of abusive power and bizarre magic. Even so, as his stories and novels repeatedly make clear, such phantasms are to be understood as part of *lived* existence and thus as 'real', not as escapist mystifications: the spiritual frames of existence have the same status of believability as the material world. The nation, in other words, is not represented *by* unreality so much as that it *is* (un)reality. This literalisation of the metaphoric in Okri coincides interestingly (and, as regards the future of the nation-state for Africa's intellectuals, revealingly) with the philosopher Achille Mbembe's suggestive, if pessimistic, postmodern characterisation of the African *postcolony*.[10] Mbembe sees the postcolonial nation as defined by its excessive symbolisation of arbitrary authority – in fact as saturated with such symbolisation but also as emptied of its 'nationness' (due to the people's lack of citizenship). The postcolony forms a 'regime of unreality' and violence, an entire obscene cosmology, from which there is no exit route. Within this regime power has 'fallen' from the hands of those supposed to be exercising it, creating 'a situation of extreme material scarcity, uncertainty, and inertia' in which the state begins to wither away.[11]

To explicate this historical sclerosis Mbembe turns to the structures of colonial sovereignty, which he names *commandement*, structures distinguished by the arbitrary deployment of a self-legitimating violence. However, whereas the colonial state imposed its unconditional power to achieve certain levels of economic productivity, the postcolony, which might also be called the *unreal nation*, has failed to replace colonial structures with workable economic and political systems of regulation and order.[12] In their stead have grown up 'state entities' within which unconditional power has become fully socialised, the 'cement' of the authoritarian regime. Although the early postcolonial state did initially collaborate in creative ways with indigenous social ties and traditional economic bases, like market networks, these prodigal, prebendal, at times parasitic structures eventually proved inflexible to global economic pressures. In

consequence, in Mbembe's view, economies in the postcolony are often operative only within small, transnationalised, highly predatory enclaves. Moreover,
the perpetuation of traditional elite structures has produced an unprecedented
level of privatisation, including of the security forces, resulting in the further
generalisation throughout the society of armed violence.

Arbitrary power in the postcolony thus converts itself into a common reality,
structuring all social meanings, in which the obscene and scatological (the
Bakhtinian grotesque) operate not merely as parodies of power but are intrinsic to the system, deployed as part of the spectacle of authority. In this situation the binary oppositions of domination and resistance (as in Okri) melt
away: the state is characterised by relations of disturbing conviviality between
the ruler and the ruled. 'Those who laugh . . . are simply bearing witness, often
unconsciously, that the grotesque is not more foreign to officialdom than the
common man is impervious to the charms of majesty'.[13] The ruled *at once*
domesticate the fetishes of state power *and* ridicule them. At this point
Mbembe's ideas exhibit a contradiction in the fact that his dominated are
simultaneously as zombified as the dominant, their allies, yet (due to the unsta-
ble pluralism of the society) able to splinter and morph their identities and
negotiate different social spaces seemingly as agents. It is for this reason that
unexpected coups and overthrows do occur.[14] However, with respect to the
postcolonial nation in Africa represented by the writers discussed here, he
accurately characterises how the ruler's power, constantly on show, theatrical,
gross, extravagant, rabidly phallocratic, impels the participation of the ruled.
That this participation is expressed mainly as derision is a backhanded
acknowledgement that the state's power is incontestable – an acknowledgement that then allows the postcolonial subject to ridicule it all the more. The
fetishes of state power, which are all-pervasive, are also revealed as a sham.

Although for Mbembe the nation has strictly speaking bankrupted itself out
of existence because of the *commandement*, his reading of the postcolony
relates productively to writers' understanding of the nation as constituted in
metaphor, and lived as unreality. As in the work of the younger, mid- and late
1980s generation, the nation becomes a densely textured mix of symbolic narratives and collective fantasies, some of them necessary illusions, others
knowing deceptions. A nation's history, such as it is, they imply, can be best
explained as the performance, often grotesquely flawed, of mythic and fabular
tales. This writing therefore bears witness to crises in national confidence
running across Africa, the perception that nationalism as the modus operandi
of governments has been used to legitimate abuses of power and absurd displays of megalomania, with consequences both tragic and banal. In terms that
are different from yet related to Mbembe's, the situation is one in which
nationalism is detached from its associations with honour, unity, lofty
purpose, belonging. National identity becomes less an ideal than a dilemma,

an agon or a burlesque.[15] As Jean Franco has commented of like developments in Latin American writing, in such a world, nationalist truths will inevitably come to be perceived as empty metaphors or as jokes.[16]

It is relevant to add here that the political scepticism of writers and the breakdown in their national commitment has of course been affected by their experiences of internal and/or external exile, the often uninvited condition of national truancy which has become pervasive among Third World elites. Fleeing political repression or economic deprivation, encountering experiences of estrangement as migrants in the metropole, writers in exile have become perhaps the most prominent and vocal interrogators of nationalist doctrine. Okri, for instance, came to Britain in 1978 on a scholarship from Nigeria, where he has lived ever since. Marechera, for his part, spent the years 1974 to 1982 in Britain initially as a student in Oxford, then, following his 'sending down', attempting to make it as a writer within the lower depths of squatter communes and prison. Chenjerai Hove escaped Robert Mugabe's increasingly autocratic Zimbabwe in 2002 in order to live in exile in France. As these and other writers reconstruct lost 'imaginary homelands' in their fiction, or remember back to their own compromised national pasts, they vividly experience the uncertainty and provisionality, indeed the fictionality, of national realities.[17] Reconstructing a national consciousness in writing, they are in an ideal position to demonstrate the writerliness of that consciousness.

It is a writerliness which operates fruitfully at both the diachronic and synchronic axes of narrative. On the one hand (though these processes are not mutually exclusive), writers exploit the structural analogies between *nations* and *narrations*: the preoccupation with origins, the maintenance of continuity over time, the synthesis of difference into a unified whole.[18] To expatiate on the title of Homi Bhabha's edited collection *Nation and Narration*, where the 'real-life' political nation fails to provide meaningful codes of identity, writers turn instead to narrative structures in order to locate the signifying forms with which to give shape to an 'unreal' social life. On the other hand, as was seen in earlier chapters, writers self-reflexively elaborate on the figurality or quasi-religious symbolic logic that has long been embedded in nationalism.[19] The icons which were definitively associated with particular national entities – metaphors of wholeness, unity and the purity of its origins, images of the gendered national body, or of the harmonious consort of the national community – are now recognised for what they are, as literary conceits rather than national truths. What is more, the supposed national reality is no longer seen as naturally generating the symbols – flags and figureheads – that will signify and define its character. Instead, invented symbolic structures – fictions *and* narrative figures – are adopted and reshaped as the primary *embodiments* of an illusory nationhood. So, in *Anthills of the Savannah* (1987), for example, Chinua Achebe cryptically but insightfully pointed to the conglomerations of metaphor which make up a postcolonial national reality. In Nuruddin Farah's novel *Maps* (1986), as more cynically in Okri, dream and vision were used to develop new morphologies for imaging a damaged polity.

By way of a provisional summary, whereas in the immediate post-independence period writers assume that story helps to constitute nationhood, or forms the cultural wealth of the nation, more recently they audaciously imply that it is in story and metaphor that nationhood is *chiefly* defined. The novel in the postcolony simultaneously participates in and denounces the regime of unreality. This need not necessarily mean, however, that national beliefs are jettisoned completely. Especially if writers exist in a condition of exile, even if internal exile, they use the critical distance of narrative to dena-turalise or 'de-doxify' the neocolonial system of truth (where 'doxa' represents received public opinion).[20] In this regard the practice of the African and South Asian writers discussed in this book departs interestingly from that of contemporary novelists in, for example, postcolonial Australia. As in Peter Carey's *Illywhacker* (1985) or Murray Bail's *Eucalyptus* (1998), national signifiers, no matter how self-reflexive and postmodernly arch, are deployed in sizeable numbers not merely to signify but effectively to overdetermine the surrounding national reality. The real world status and significance of the national hold good. These two iconic Australian novels teem with recognisably national metonyms – fakes, liar figures and a farm filled with eucalyptus – all of which ultimately refer back to the master signified, Australia.

Nation as metaphor: Hove and Marechera

In his novella *Bones* (1988), the Zimbabwean writer Chenjerai Hove has given close ear to the so-called 'divinity' present in, and traduced by, everyday nation-state existence.[21] In *Bones* a mother Marita, a worker on a white farm, travels to the city on a quest for her guerrilla son, and is killed, presumed murdered by agents of the state. Her prospective daughter-in-law Janifa mourns her, is raped and becomes mad. When at the end of the novel Marita's son finally returns (though he may be merely an apparition in Janifa's distressed mind), Janifa rejects him. In contrast with the brute reality described by these social relations, which occur both before and after the always implicit moment of Zimbabwean independence, it is evident that collective memory based in the oral tradition, and enacted in the multivoiced narrative structure, alone retains a redemptive power for the community.

Written a decade after the time in which it is set, Hove's short novel can be read as an oblique and wistful retrospective comment on the hierarchical, alienated state that passes for independent Zimbabwe. The city, a predatory, male space, is represented as the seat of government and is remote from the people. Ancestral voices alone, represented chiefly by the voice of the spirit-medium

Nehanda, signify a hoped-for national unity, yet the novel's highly symbolic, temporally static writing may at the same time point to the possible dangers of an over-idealised formation of the nation on the basis *primarily* of communal traditions. In this sense the romanticised complex metaphor of the ancestors' bones, welcoming their return to the dispossessed land yet oddly unable to envisage their inclusion in everyday village life, provides an ironic index to the alienation of ordinary people from state hegemonies. With the benefit of hindsight the metaphor could even be seen as a sideways comment on the cynical deployment of land redistribution programmes in Zimbabwe.

To tell his tale of nationalist conflict and compromise, revival and return, Hove uses a chorus of different voices, traditional and contemporary, rural and urban, named and unnamed. This polyphonic form allows him to range across a set of different conceptual and metaphoric structures in an attempt to typify proto-national being from the point of view of the village. In the course of this search, the trope of the ancestors' returning bones, which embraces some of the dualities of the recent national experience, yet develops out of oral legend, is set up as a definitive emblem of the Zimbabwe-to-be. As Hove has said, his aim in *Bones* was to force English, a language of abstraction, to 'tell a story in imagery', as does his native Shona, even though his apparent imitation of the latter language is highly impressionistic.[22] At the same time, I would want to suggest, his use of the complex bones symbol, however nostalgic its construction, can be taken as an organising metatextual figure (at once critical and collusive) for the representation of the national community in – and as – metaphor.

In a pivotal section at the centre of *Bones*, a litany on the events of 1897, the time of Rhodesian land alienation and the first *chimurenga* or war of resistance, the bones of the ancestors are seen 'falling like feathers' (*B* 47). Yet, despite the advent of the big guns and the wasting diseases brought by the white man, the bones are urged to rise again from the battlefield that is the nation-in-formation. Figures of mats, clouds, tongues of fire, sky, insects, tightly connected with Shona oral motifs, are made to overlap and cross over as the bones are transfigured into redeeming armies:

> I saw many bones spread like rough mats on large plains and on the hills. Bones spread like rough mats on the banks of the rivers and in the water. But the fish would not eat them. Rising bones. They spoke in many languages which I understood all. Tongues full of fire, not ashes. Clouds of bones rose from the scenes of many battles and engulfed the skies like many rain birds coming to greet the season. There were so many bones I could not count them. So many they made the sky rain tears. Some I did not see where they were buried, but they leapt into the sky like a swarm of locusts, with such power that they broke the branches of the sky where they rested in their long journey to places I did not know. Right across the land of rivers that flooded all the time, they heaved on the chest of the land until they formed one huge flood which trampled on the toes of armed strangers. (*B* 49)

The 'songs of the endless bones' signify a heritage of struggle and a directive for the future, yet, despite their weight of history and authority, the songs are also recognised as constituted out of words that are 'weak . . . Very weak. They fly in the wind like feathers. Feathers falling from a bird high up in the clouds' (*B* 59). The words are the weightless birds of a history that has till recently been misplaced and partially forgotten. Bones and words are linked by the metaphor of feathers: both are light, perhaps frail. Both, however, as the residues of history, connect across the generations. In an interesting reversal of the idea of the postcolony as predominantly phallocratic, as is explored in this book, in Hove, whereas the bones are sexless (although the fighters are male), words and images in the oral tradition are the domain of women. As Caroline Rooney has recognised, by charting the opposition of state to family, *Bones* pays respect to those who have been written out of official history, in particular peasant women.[23]

With the ancestral bones figure, therefore, Hove impacts collective and already interconnected symbols from oral tradition to find a suitable paradigm for the nation's shared and fractured history. A highly pictorial, customary language seemingly transliterated from vernacular sources and including the voices of spirits, allows him to inflect the act of imagining that history towards what could be called the communal symbolic. With the fading memory of the event and the dying of the fighters, we are told, the village community transposes the struggle into song. The fighters who visit the villages 'always had new things to say' and '[i]f they had nothing to say, they had something to sing. If they had nothing to sing, they had something to dance' (*B* 73). Without shared song and image, the notion of a national historical struggle would be obscure, or in Marita the old woman's appropriately metaphorical words: 'If the birds and insects refused to sing, what would the forest be?' (*B* 75).

Old wisdom and new knowledge, war involvements both collaborative and oppositional, communings between past and present, living and dead: a broad range of experience in *Bones* is conceived and anticipated in metaphor, and remembered and commemorated in the same way. History is at once lived and told by way of proverb and parable; it is experienced and received as already symbolic, already mythic, and in this case it is *not* unreal. In that the characters hold double roles as representative historical actors and as interpreters of that history, they make (compose, create) their history even as they are making (living) it. Images from the oral tradition are continually adapted and reinterpreted to construct a contemporary historical and yet parabolic account. The *mhondoro* Nehanda herself speaks at one point in the place of Marita. Natural imagery, too, presumably drawn from collective rural experience, is used to evoke ideas of historical displacement and replacement: 'when leaves fall, they are doing so, so that other new leaves may come, leaves of the same pattern, the same smell, but on different nodes' (*B* 88).[24] '[R]oots drink from the rotten leaves and feed the inside of the tree again so that new leaves can sprout' (*B* 97). Names, too, are a conduit for history: 'a name tells many stories, many paths that have been walked with bare feet' (*B* 105).

Given that *Bones* narrates the highly polarised late war situation from the point of view of a rural community, the freedom fighters are not directly present, yet their influence is palpable everywhere. It is an influence again transmitted by way of legend and symbol. National *imaginings* in this context are nothing new. The fighters are seen as demonic and yet as saviours, as fearful monsters recalled from grandparents' tales of 'long-toothed ogres' (*B* 39–40, 59). They are fantastic characters, more spirit than human, representing threat and promise: 'do they not say a terrorist eats people without roasting them?' (*B* 4). And, again:

> my sister, have you heard the stories people were spreading about the children when they came back? Some said their shoes pointed the other way when they are going one way. Some said their bodies were so strong the bullets of the soldiers did not go through their skins. All sorts of things like the one about how the fighters disappeared when the soldiers came. They said all the women became heavy with children, so when the soldiers came, they would not beat up pregnant women. After they left all the women just passed some air and there the fighters were. (*B* 69–70)

Through the medium of such proverbial and mythical figures, the narrative develops incrementally, circularly, imagining communal history by way of recursive metaphors of survival, restoration and revival, and looking forward to an alternative, more heterogeneous and inclusive national consciousness. Simultaneously, with each recurrence, the key metaphors in the narrative underscore its circular unfolding and are mutually reinforced. Their pervasiveness in the text and the thickness of their significance demonstrate the inconceivability of narrating a nation's history without such tools. With the benefit of hindsight, however, they also betray that, in a neocolonial situation where ruled and ruler collude in a regime of almost legendary violence, metaphor, even from an apparently static peasant tradition, may be manipulated, deformed and corrupted, used to signify death rather than rebirth. In Mbembe's words, 'the debris of the ritual acts of the past . . . intertwined . . . form the postcolonial dramaturgy'.[25] It is noteworthy that towards the end of the novel the vision of the returning bones of the dead is once again, chillingly, repeated, in a way that does not suggest rebirth:

> dreams of rains, bones and footsteps falling from the height of a cliff, scattering to the earth while the boys in the field whistle and shout as if they have seen a vulture tearing away the flesh of a carcase. Bones in flower-like flames of skeletons spread all over the place like a battlefield strewn with corpses of the freshly killed. (*B* 107)

In contrast with his compatriot Chenjerai Hove, the writing of Dambudzo Marechera, sometimes dubbed the African Kafka, is cynical, streetwise, absurdist, and determinedly experimental and cosmopolitan. For these reasons, even two decades on from his death at the age of 35 in 1987, his reputation remains controversial. Although his language is often highly wrought and allusive, he has no interest in bending metaphor in service of the nation, however illusory the nation is imagined to be. Marechera, who like Hove grew up in a country 'sick with the Rhodesian crisis', was set on avoiding what he called the 'ghetto daemon' of his mother-tongue Shona for his art, and disparaged a Hove-like resuscitation of oral resources.[26] Misrepresented as aspiring to write 'white', he was, however, as concerned as is Hove with the internal lives of 'unsung', ordinary Africans, even if these were interpreted mainly as versions of himself.[27] To evoke these lives he 'brutalised', as he said, the 'racist', 'male' English language, with which he paradoxically felt comfortable, into bearing the burden of his 'normal condition', grinding childhood poverty in Rusape township, and the later miseries of homelessness in Europe and in urban Zimbabwe.[28] Even his work produced in England is presciently imbued with disgust not only at the social prejudices of Europe and its colonial sidekick, Rhodesia, but at the violence and exploitation of post-1980 Zimbabwe, its dog-eat-dog *danses macabre.*

Marechera published two books during the time he spent in England, *The House of Hunger* (1978) and *Black Sunlight* (1980), that reflect largely on the internal conflicts he experienced from early childhood, the dilemmas of 'colonised consciousness', and his alienated situation as a black 'colonial' artist claiming international precursors.[29] This reading will, however, concentrate on *Mindblast* (1984), a collection of three short plays, a nightmarish sequence, poems and a fragment of autobiography, which, against many odds, not least its perceived 'difficulty', was the first book he published after his return home.[30] Although the collection is mainly preoccupied with a nihilistic or modernist concern to 'blast' social and aesthetic norms, its fragmentary structure allows Marechera to engage directly at certain points with the condition of newly post-independent Zimbabwe.

It is clear from as early as *The House of Hunger* that Marechera's work, much of it contradictory and internally tortured, is torn at base by two now overlapping, now divergent debates. Both press in upon *Mindblast* also. First, there is his existentialist concept of himself as an artist in quest of his own particular truth, distorting reality in order to fit that truth, and resisting the claims of state, language or belief. Second, despite the fact that he wrote self-consciously as an African, there is his quarrel with the conventional idea of the African writer as a socially responsible realist, especially with the 'committed' form this took in the new Zimbabwe, as elsewhere (*M* 52). It was Marechera's powerful contention that after Fanon, and after European modernism, African writers could not avoid relaying the distorted and distorting shapes of the psyche in their art, of translating the world whether postcolonial or metropolitan as nauseating horror. He described this process as a confrontation with the skeleton in one's own cupboard, that is, oneself. 'I don't know whether the writer can offer the emerging nation anything,' he wrote, 'there must always be a healthy tension between a writer and his nation'.[31] When Marechera returned to his home country after nearly a decade abroad it was to find that *Black Sunlight* had been (temporarily) banned on the grounds of obscenity. Therefore, although he had once seen writing as a way of fighting for freedom, a type of guerrilla action, he now became prone to seeing the new nation, like the old, as a travesty and a prison, darkened by disillusionment. 'I have no ear for slogans . . . I run when it's A LUTA [CONTINUA] time'.[32]

In Marechera's clear-sighted, if not prophetic view, the postcolonial state depends for its existence on arbitrary violence and an economics of rabid extraction – in other words, Mbembe's *commandement*. As the playlets in *Mindblast* in particular make clear, Zimbabwe is no exception in this regard. Echoing Ngugi, the first African writer he encountered, Marechera observes: 'The black inheritors had not changed [the capital city] – just the name' (*M* 51). From this he concludes that all revolutions must inevitably lead to the 'alienation' of artists, as the artist's compulsion is to expose the true nature of the state (*M* 58). Framing rhetorical questions that could well stand as an epigraph to the entire *Mindblast* collection, Alfie, the Marechera surrogate in the playlet *Blitzkrieg*, asks, 'Ah, Zimbabwe, what are you doing to me? Zimbabwe, what am I doing to you?' (*M* 37) The words form part of a soliloquy, yet Alfie is in reality addressing himself to the toilet. As this backhandedly implies, the artist's work of exposure is both repellent and imperative. The postcolony or neocolonial nation has embedded itself in recuperative, Negritude-style illusions even while simultaneously compromising its principles of socialist redistribution by retaining colonial and capitalist hierarchies constructed on similar lines to those in, for instance, apartheid South Africa (*M* 26, 29–42).[33]

Whereas, as was seen earlier, Hove and Okri are especially concerned to investigate the make-up of the nation's regime of unreality, to dissect how the postcolony both embellishes and literalises communal symbols, it is Marechera's intention to strip such camouflaging figures away. He lays bare the general lack of symbolic proportion for what it is, while at the same time representing his many alter-egos as themselves victims of 'phantoms' or as living, breathing nightmares, demonstrating how pervasive these in fact are (*M* 54–5).[34] As in the *Grimknife* sequence (*M* 43–72), institutionalised violence obliterates the boundaries between the private and the public. The citizen is merely s/he who does what s/he is told by the powers that be, who mouths 'patriotism, loyalty and responsibility' (*M* 45, 54). Brute authority is stamped upon the suffering body and the grotesque is everywhere naturalised. In the play *Blitzkrieg* the white businessman-politician Drake intones with deeply res-onant irony: 'I cannot afford to forget the dreams of the great, for in them are the secrets of a nation's destiny' (*M* 33). The 'great' are, however, 'African mutants in transition' (*M* 97).

That said, it is important that Marechera does not in fact repudiate the *ideal* of the independent nation. On the contrary, he uses the nation as a space of potential in which to 'weave [his] own descriptions of reality into the available fantasy we call the world', as is clear from the journal extract in *Mindblast* written during a period of sleeping rough in Harare's Cecil Square (*M* 119–59). At the same time, in terms of its practical application in postcolonial Zimbabwe, the nation is experienced as an unending charade, an excessive and inescapable performance, and, from the artist's point of view, as psychological *agon*: 'Fatrich, thinpoor – Power's gravy over the same rotting carcass' (*M* 76). Especially in Marechera's *Mindblast* poems, external urban reality takes on a quality of random accumulation, in which everything bears the same commercial valency, while also seeming distorted, denatured. Nothing is more prominent or signifi-cant than anything else, other than the artist's utterance perhaps, rushing out in a 'ghoulish mixture' of 'blood-clotting vomit' (*M* 72; see also 'The bar-stool edible worm' and 'The footnote to Hamlet', *M* 96–7). Marechera's Zimbabwe, classically pictured as a prostitute, is generally to be found 'in beerhalls and she-beens . . . selling the last bits and pieces of her soured vision' (*M* 106–7).

Conclusion: postcolonial nightmare

If Marechera's disengagement from the nation is marked by disillusionment, cynicism is the keynote of Okri's post-/national phantasmagoria. The Nigerian writer could indeed be read as *dramatising* in his fiction Mbembe's theory of the postcolony. (The *vice versa* case, too, applies.) As in Mbembe's depiction, the fantastical aspects of lived existence in the postcolony can in Okri appear completely to detach characters' experience from the dimensions of a recognis-ably real world, although in a way that Okri, unlike Mbembe, might contend has spiritual plausibility. This chapter will end with a more detailed discussion of Okri's early dystopian work, as it is in these texts, perhaps more intensively so than in the work of his contemporaries, that the unavoidable metaphoric-ity of national (and, to him, all other) being is enacted.

In Okri, more pessimistically than in Hove, and in language more ornately figural than Marechera's, the predominant political atmosphere is one either of horrified amazement, such as is expressed in *The Famished Road*, or of the befuddled resignation of the protagonist in the title story 'Stars of the new curfew'.[35] In his bleak if colourful worlds, where those who proclaim integrity are the most corrupt of all, the plain, almost proverbial truths of nationalism – the idea of history as embodying the integrity of a people, the willingness of that people to come together as one – are exposed as nonsense. In the story 'The city of red dust', Okri uncovers the destitution suffered by Nigeria's burgeoning urban underclass, a destitution intimately and outrageously bound up with the wealth and power of the governing elite with which it is juxtaposed. The close juxtaposition of the Party of the Rich and the Party of the Poor in *The Famished Road* similarly points to the disastrous parasitism which marks contemporary politics. The pathology of contemporary national society, it seems, is not to be comprehended except partially, under the flickering light of magical vision and through the medium of gnomic narrative.

As Okri represents it, the life of the Nigerian urban underclass is a cut-throat game of chance and multiple risk-taking generated by superstitions and rival cult wisdoms to the difficult end of surviving chaos. The only enduring truth of this society seems to be the inevitability of recurring defeat and dogged endurance. The stakes in the game of survival are, unsurprisingly, extremely high. Arthur in 'Stars of the new curfew', for example, is a small-time charlatan and seller of quack medicines. His cures are designed to inhibit disease and chaos merely by creating more problems and aggravating social disorder (*SNC* 87–8, 89). Blood, the fluid of life, when donated, becomes one of the few ways for the unemployed and poor to obtain a regular source of income, yet donation in effect only impoverishes them further. The Dad figure in *The Famished Road*, too, is described as driving himself beyond all conceivable human limits, carrying leaden cement bags in order to make a living, and later, pitting himself against ever larger and more supernaturally powerful boxing opponents.

When in 'Stars of the new curfew' the mountebank Arthur's boss invents a new potion, an aphrodisiac panacea or 'Power-Drug', it is billed as salving all the 'afflictions of the poor' (*SNC* 98), as being a national cure-all, a kit to national salvation. The logo on the package is an index to the drug's illusionary promise. It features the triad of an African nuclear family: a strong-arm wrestler as patriarchal figure, the 'generalised face of a beautiful African woman', and a child. The narrative has grown wise to nationalist fantasies, the hollow symbol of the cohesive male-led national family, to grand illusions packaged as national cures. Significantly, when Arthur is involved in a bus accident while selling 'Power-Drug', a 'nationalist' on board, a Rastafarian who denounces the betrayal of African independence, is exposed as a fraud – his dreadlocks are false. This moment registers the depth of Okri's cynicism: nothing is so real as state-led and -abetted deception, nothing so true as the delusion that exposes it, or the dream that provides a means of escape.

Hungry for sacrifices, lying in wait on the good, the bad and the unsuspecting, the predatory road of Okri's novel *The Famished Road* ramifies crazily through a chaotic and mystically charged reality, implicating the destinies of multitudes, unravelling and reweaving their dreams.[36] Not merely a path of life, or the way of the poor, it is the spaghetti junction of various planes of being, of dead, unborn and living, of spirits and ancestors. The road multiplies, reproduces itself, subdivides: it pullulates with mangled disproportionate bodies, mythical apparitions reminiscent of the stories of Amos Tutuola, manifestations of a world out of joint, of mysterious, inexorable corruptions. The spirit-child Azaro, a strangely knowing, second-sighted narrator who 'does time' on the road, retains the insights and the longings of the spirit realm and yet has chosen 'the liberty of limitations' by deciding to live in the human world (*FR* 487). Even so, as he is constantly tempted to give way to spirit beckonings and return to the state of being unborn, his road seems to have built into it a repeating loop, a break in the logic of reality into which he occasionally falls. There, he experiences the other fantastical dimensions of the road, its magical ramifications and expansions that are oddly both separate and yet in many ways indistinguishable from the distortions of the human world.[37]

One of the prominent personalities in *The Famished Road* is an eccentric photographer whose work exposes the odd juxtapositions and ugly poverty of family life in Azaro's compound: 'We all looked like celebrating refugees. We were cramped, and hungry, and our smiles were fixed. The room appeared to be constructed out of garbage and together we seemed a people who had never known happiness' (*FR* 91). The photographer's image-making activities, which plot unsuspected and even visionary correspondences in the midst of confusion, can be taken as an index of the work of the writers examined in this chapter, in particular in national contexts where images seem more real than reality. As I have tried to show, it is probably true to say of the postcolonial worlds evoked by Okri, Hove and even Marechera that, far from metaphors merely connoting reality, reality is perceived as always already an iconic display. If due to different impulses, ranging from the traditional through the magical to the modernist, human perception makes up a tissue of metaphors thickly embossed with dream-images. Moreover, as these different writers have demonstrated, this is taken as more or less the usual state of things. Daily life is full of bizarre conjunctures: stars that become words or gods or bones; white men with silver eyelashes who have the same otherworldly status as fetishes wearing dark glasses, four-headed beggars, spirits shrouded in sunflower flames holding blue mirrors over their heads (*FR* 456–7).

In the early years of independence, fiction, variously identified as historical or realistic, was deployed and shaped in the service of national politics. Now, increasingly, there has been a shift from realistic fact into self-reflexively symbolic fiction. Writers consciously render the troubled spirit or inner chaos of the nation in and as metaphor. Literary symbols – the compound bones metaphor in *Bones*, the mind blasted by contradictory images in Marechera, Okri's road – signify, in particular, emergent nations already fatally mired in delusion. While not discarding allegiance to the concept of the nation as such or indeed to their narrative craft, these writers query the nation's profligate fictiveness, especially in situations where such effects are used at once to cover up and to propagate violence and corruption. In the face of the already constructed identity of the nation, symbolic narrative appears to offer a literary elite one of two possibilities. Either there is aesthetic redemption against the odds, as in Achebe and possibly in Hove, where narrative's shape-giving power is raised to a higher symbolic level in order to resuscitate the nation; or, as in Marechera and Okri, there is the dismantling of delusion through the effects of nightmarish de-formation. As if holding up a distorting mirror, the novelist in the latter situation reflects back and exaggerates the state's own distorted self-imaginings.

Notes

1 See Timothy Brennan, 'The national longing for form', in Homi Bhabha (ed.), *Nation and Narration* (London and New York: Routledge, 1990), p. 64.

2 Partha Chatterjee, *Nationalist Thought and the Colonial World – A Derivative Discourse?* (London: Zed Press, 1986).

3 For his explication of these terms, see Homi Bhabha, 'DissemiNation: time, narrative and the margins of the modern nation', in Bhabha (ed.), *Nation and Narration*, pp. 297–302; as well as pp. 122–3 in this book.

4 In the work of these writers, as defined by Ato Quayson in his reading of Tutuola, Soyinka and Okri, a 'will-to-identity' is expressed in mythic rather than in realist terms. See Ato Quayson, *Strategic Transformations in Nigerian Writing* (Oxford: James Currey, 1997), p. 158. See also Christopher Warnes, 'Magical realism and the cultural politics of the postcolonial novel', unpublished PhD thesis, University of Cambridge, 2003.

5 The second title in the trilogy based on the adventures of the *abiku* Azaro, is *Songs of Enchantment* (London: Jonathan Cape, 1993), the third, *Infinite Riches* (London: Phoenix House, 1998). Neither of the second two novels is as technically accomplished as *The Famished Road,* certainly not with respect to the framing of Azaro's alternative planes of being as *at once* fantastical and real. For an alternative interpretation of Okri as a questing spiritual romantic, see Robert Fraser, *Ben Okri* (Tavistock, Devon: Northcote House, 1992).

6 Frantz Fanon, *The Wretched of the Earth* [1961], trans. Constance Farringdon (Harmondsworth: Penguin, 1985), pp. 43–5.

7 See Ben Okri, 'Redreaming the world: an essay for Chinua Achebe', *Guardian* (9 August 1990), 23.

8 Harry Garuba, 'Explorations in animist materialism', *Public Culture*, 15:2 (Spring 2003), pp. 261–86.

9 Ben Okri, *Incidents at the Shrine* (London: Fontana, 1986), pp. 55, 107, 1–22.

10 Achille Mbembe, *On the Postcolony*, trans. A. M. Berrett *et al.* (Berkeley: University of California Press, 2001). See also his essay, 'Necropolitics', *Public Culture*, 15:1 (Winter 2003), 11–40.

11 See Mbembe, *On the Postcolony*, pp. 24, 57, 108.

12 Mbembe, *On the Postcolony*, pp. 31–2.

13 Mbembe, *On the Postcolony*, p. 110.
14 For critical commentary on Mbembe's postcolony, see Richard Werbner and Terence Ranger (eds), *Postcolonial Identities in Africa* (London: Zed Press, 1996).
15 As is well described in Fanon, *The Wretched of the Earth*, pp. 119–65.
16 Jean Franco, 'The nation as imagined community', in H. Aram Veeser (ed.) *The New Historicism* (London: Routledge, 1989), pp. 205–6.
17 Salman Rushdie, *Imaginary Homelands* (London: Granta, 1991), pp. 11–14.
18 See Steven Connor's succinct summary of these analogies in *The English Novel in History, 1950–1995* (London and New York: Routledge, 1996), p. 44. On the fictional aspects of national construction, see also the introduction, pp. 10–11.
19 As Regis Debray, Benedict Anderson and Timothy Brennan, among others, have pointed out, nationalism carries a strong symbolic or ritualistic dimension and relies on religious modes of thought. These would include the idea of an apocalyptic or momentous birth, and beliefs in national redemption and in history as the act of manifestation of a chosen people. See Benedict Anderson, *Imagined Communities: Reflections the Origin and Spread of Nationalisms* [1983] rev. edn (London: Verso, 1991); Timothy Brennan, *Salman Rushdie and the Third World: Myths of the Nation* (London: Macmillan, 1989).
20 See Linda Hutcheon, *The Politics of Postmodernism*, rev. edn (London and New York: Routledge, 2002), pp. 2–3.
21 Chenjerai Hove, *Bones* (Oxford: Heinemann, 1988). Page references will henceforth be quoted in the text together with the abbreviation *B*. For the reference to 'the divinity that controls remotely but diligently the transactions of the market-place that is [the] world', see Chinua Achebe, *Anthills of the Savannah* (London: Heinemann, 1987), p. 102.
22 Hove quoted in Carita Backstrom, 'In search of psychological worlds: on Yvonne Vera's and Chenjerai Hove's portrayal of women', in Maria E. Baaz and Mai Palmberg (eds), *Same and Other: Negotiating African Identity in Cultural Production* (Stockholm: Nordiska Afrikainstitutet, 2001), p. 91. On Hove's intertextuality with Shona oral forms, see Dan Wylie, 'Language-thieves', *English in Africa*, 18:2 (1991), 39–62.
23 Caroline Rooney, 'Re-possessions: inheritance and independence in Hove's *Bones* and Dangarembga's *Nervous Conditions*', in Abdulrazak Gurnah (ed.), *Essays on African Writing: A Re-evaluation*, vol. 2 (Oxford: Heinemann, 1995), pp. 119–43.
24 Such displacement should in theory unsettle the forbidding logic of historical recrimination and recurrence, of evil paid back by evil: 'To fight on is all right, but a good fighter knows when to postpone the fight for another day' (*B* 102).
25 Mbembe, *On the Postcolony*, p. 123. I am grateful to Ranka Primorac for discussion about the static chronotopes of peasant life in Hove's work.
26 Dambudzo Marechera, 'Thought-tracks in the snow', in *The House of Hunger* [1978] (Oxford: Heinemann, 1989), p. 144.
27 Dambudzo Marechera, *The Black Insider*, ed. Flora Veit-Wild (Harare: Baobab Books, 1990), p. 109.
28 'Dambudzo Marechera interviews himself', in Flora Veit-Wild and Ernst Schade (eds), *Dambudzo Marechera 1952–1987* (Harare: Baobab Books, 1988), pp. 7–8.

Biographical accounts of Marechera may also be found in: Robert Fraser, *Ben Okri: Towards the Invisible City* (Tavistock, Devon: Northcote House, 2002), pp. 45–7; Flora Veit-Wild, 'Introduction' in Marechera, *The Black Insider*, pp. 5–22. For his internal struggles with language, see also *The House of Hunger*, pp. 30–1. For a discussion of Marechera's work as self-critically autobiographical, see: Melissa Levin and Laurice Taitz, 'Fictional autobiographies/autobiographical fictions', *Journal of Commonwealth Literature*, 32:1 (1997), pp. 103–15.

29 For an insightful account of Marechera as a spokesman for colonised disenchantment, see Abdulrazak Gurnah, '"The mid-point of the scream": the writing of Dambudzo Marechera', in Gurnah (ed.), *Essays*, pp. 100–18.

30 Dambudzo Marechera, *Mindblast* [1984] (Harare: The College Press, 1989). Page references will henceforth be cited in the text along with the abbreviation *M*.

31 Marechera, 'Beneath reality there is always fantasy', in Veit-Wild and Schade (eds), *Dambudzo Marechera*, pp. 10–11. See also p. 19.

32 Marechera, 'Beneath reality', p. 30. And see *M* 62.

33 See also, for example, *The Black Insider*, pp. 80–1.

34 And see Mbembe, *On the Postcolony*, p. 119.

35 Ben Okri, *Stars of the New Curfew* (London: Secker and Warburg, 1988), pp. 25–79, 81–144. Page references will henceforth be cited in the text together with the abbreviation *SNC*.

36 Ben Okri, *The Famished Road* (London: Cape, 1991). Page references will henceforth be quoted in the text together with the abbreviation *FR*.

37 The road in these guises joins up with the road of Wole Soyinka's play of that exact name, *The Road* (1965). Its god is Ogun, the god of road accidents, destruction and transitions, the deity who governs in Soyinka's words 'the dark continuum of transition where occurs the inter-transmutation of essence-ideal and materiality'. See Wole Soyinka, *The Road*, in *Collected Plays I* (Oxford: Oxford University Press, 1973); and *Myth, Literature and the African World* (Cambridge: Cambridge University Press, 1976), pp. 26–7.

9

East is east:
where postcolonialism is
neo-orientalist – the cases of
Sarojini Naidu and Arundhati Roy

Oh, East is East and West is West, and never the twain shall meet. (Rudyard
Kipling, 'The Ballad of East and West', 1892)[1]

This chapter, which considers the continuing exoticisation of the other woman
that is involved in the postcolonial privileging of her voice, begins with a symptomatic account of the remarkable critical reception in 1890s London of
Sarojini Naidu (1876–1949), the Indian woman poet or 'little Indian princess',
later Gandhi's right-hand woman.[2]

Born in Hyderabad into a prominent intellectual Bengali family, the
Chattopadhyays or Chatterjees, Sarojini Naidu as a girl showed an extraordinary precocity in writing poetry, mainly in imitation of British Romantic
writers: her ambition was to be 'a Keats for India'.[3] At 15 she was sent to
England, to King's College, London, and then Girton in Cambridge, both to
continue her education, and – her parents' explicit desire – to separate her from
the man who was anyway to be her future husband; as a non-Brahmin he was
deemed unsuitable as a marriage partner. In 1892, the year of Kipling's 'The
Ballad of East and West' which gives this chapter its epigraph, the remarkable
facility of Naidu's poetry, collected in *Songs* (1895), her first book, came to the
attention of the foremost English critics of the day, in particular Edmund
Gosse and Arthur Symons. Edmund Gosse was later to give an account of his
encounter with this 'most brilliant', 'most original' work and of its outcome,
an equally remarkable mimicry in reverse, which he would encourage:

By some accident . . . Sarojini was introduced to our house at an early date after
her arrival in London, and she soon became one of the most welcome and intimate of our guests. It was natural that one so impetuous and so sympathetic
should not long conceal from her hosts the fact that she was writing copiously in
verse – in English verse. I entreated to be allowed to see what she had composed,
and a bundle of MSS. was slipped into my hand. I hastened to examine it as soon
as I was alone, but now there followed a disappointment, and with it an embar-

rassment ... The verses which Sarojini had entrusted to me were skilful in form, correct in grammar and blameless in sentiment, but they had the disadvantage of being totally without individuality. They were Western in feeling and in imagery; they were founded on reminiscences of Tennyson and Shelley; I am not sure that they did not even breathe an atmosphere of Christian resignation ... this was the note of the mockingbird with a vengeance.[4]

Disappointed, Gosse then took it upon himself, as he goes on to recount, to give Sarojini some fatherly advice: she should make herself over again, reconstitute herself as 'a genuine Indian poet of the Deccan', not 'a clever machine-made imitator of the English classics':

I ventured to speak to her sincerely. I advised the consignment of all that she had written, in the falsely English vein, to the waste-paper basket. I implored her to consider that from a young Indian of extreme sensibility, who had mastered not merely the language but the prosody of the West, what we wished to receive was ... some revelation of the heart of India, some sincere penetrating analysis of native passion, of the principles of antique religion and of such mysterious intimations as stirred the soul of the East long before the West had begun to dream that it had a soul.[5]

Confronted with this 'sincere' request – in effect a demand from the authoritative 'we' of western literary opinion, sanctioned by the promise of its still qualified praise – Sarojini did indeed 'docilely', in Gosse's words, strive to shed the trappings of her Romantic masquerade. The new literary daughter of the west (note the fatherly solicitousness implied by Gosse's first name terms), would 'write no more about robins and skylarks, in a landscape of our Midland counties, with the village bells somewhere in the distance'. She instead began to produce, no doubt to a great extent without cynicism, a very different type of pastiche, yet one which was ironically, and again symptomatically, another imitation of a western invention. In effect she was to recreate once more the 'tone of the mockingbird with a vengeance', though reverberating from a different vantage point. This would be not the west as the east due to its colonial education in the English classics believed it was to be seen, but the east as shaped by the west, represented by an eastern woman writing from the perspective of the west. In her second and third collections, *The Golden Threshold* (1905), and *The Bird of Time: Songs of Life, Death and the Spring* (1912), as Gosse goes on to write, Naidu no longer concealed 'the exclusively Indian source of her inspiration'.[6] Addressing herself to 'emotions which are tropical and primitive', she now became, through her western make-over, 'fully' native: 'she springs from the very soil of India'. Combining technical skill learned outside 'the magic circle' of the Orient with inside knowledge, her poems, as Gosse says, will be found 'as luminous in lighting up the dark places of the East as any contribution of savant or historian'.[7] In her own words from a January

1905 letter to Gosse, she now worked to 'add my little exotic flower to the glorious garland of English verse'.[8]

The bizarre and disturbing force of Naidu's ventriloquism is a fascinating instance of the double-voiced as well as doubled colonial mimicry of a European aesthetic. It is amply demonstrated, for example, in the decorative and fatalistic effects, and exotic details of spice and veil and *champak* threaded through *The Bird of Time* collection. Her complicated mimicry is worth an extended study in itself, and is probably only fully heard in juxtaposition, when her poetry is read side-by-side with an awareness of her career as a nationalist activist, her involvement in passive resistance and her rhetoric urging a 'battle' for India (see chapter 4).[9] This rhetoric increased in force and focus across the 1910s till, with the coming of civil disobedience in the early 1920s, her poetic voice, disabled perhaps by its bad faith or split identification, fell completely away. What I am interested in here, however, is not so much Naidu's response as such, as the orientalising and implicitly coercive terms of Gosse's critical appreciation. These terms were echoed in the praise she received from other European admirers, including Yeats, and the influential symbolist critic Arthur Symons, who appreciated in particular the sinuous sensualisms not only of her work, but of her physical presence clad in 'clinging dresses of Eastern silk'. As Symons rather barefacedly wrote: 'Through that soul I seemed to touch and take hold upon the East'.[10] For him, Naidu's prose as well as poetry appeared as sensation embodied, vehemently sincere, 'un-English, Oriental' in feeling even though English in structure.

Symons's vocabulary of appreciation is evidently overheated and to our ears perhaps excessive, but not, when read alongside Gosse, untypical. Indeed, theirs are terms, I want to suggest, which repeat themselves across the twentieth century, and up to the present time, in western readings of foreign, especially perhaps Indian, writing. It is possible to find in recent criticism of postcolonial work a configuration of cultural differences between west and east, or north and south – between 'village bells' and bazaar cries – that remains not entirely dissimilar from that with which Gosse and Symons were working.[11] In sometimes imperceptible ways, the past of colonial discourse seems to reiterate itself within the present that is postcolonial criticism.[12] Despite postcolonialism's anti-colonial agenda, and its intersection with other liberatory theories such as feminism and minority discourses, forms of the criticism, as I will demonstrate, appear to have inherited still unexamined categories of the past, and to be repeating, certainly in their journalistic manifestations, its objectifications of otherness. These objectifications manifest in particularly acute ways traditional concepts of the other woman. Therefore, if the phenomenon under investigation here bears evidence of the postcolonialist commodification of non-western cultures also discussed by Graham Huggan in *The Postcolonial Exotic*, it testifies at the same time to the entrenched, gendered inflections of such processes, where the woman becomes the epitome of the ethnic, the exotic.[13]

At this point I want to engage in an exercise of juxtaposition – to keep the phrases and images used in the appreciation of Naidu's work in mind, and turn to look at the 1990s critical reception of an Indian woman writer, one hundred years on from the time of Gosse's ardent appreciation of Naidu, this English but 'un-English Oriental'. The writer is Arundhati Roy, much-hyped and hailed as the long-awaited female Rushdie even before winning the 1997 Booker prize for her best-selling first novel, *The God of Small Things* (1997), a publication well-timed for the fiftieth anniversary of Indian independence.[14]

In the paragraphs that follow, I should immediately say, I want to set to one side the criticism of Roy's writing as lushly overwritten, overwhelmed by its poetic effects – though it is important to signal that such criticism certainly does exist.[15] My penultimate chapter will attempt to discuss Roy's aesthetic and politics more on their own terms. Instead I want to focus on the elements that were repeatedly accentuated in the critical promotion of Roy in the west. First, most prominently, there was her being female in a group of predominantly male younger Indian novelists (Vikram Chandra, Upamanyu Chatterjee, Amit Chaudhuri, Amitav Ghosh, Vikram Seth, Shashi Tharoor, Ardashir Vakil, many of whom are usually seen as standing in some sort of relationship to Salman Rushdie).[16] Related to this was her intensely feminine, ineffably photogenic, elfin beauty.[17] Another marked-out feature of her experience was her cross-caste, hybrid background (which is to an extent reflected in the central drama of the novel, the love affair between Ammu, the single mother of twins, and the Paravan Velutha). Added to this complex of promotional features there was also the 'overwhelmed' response of some of the first British readers of *The God of Small Things*, especially that of David Godwin her agent.[18] Avoiding any significant mention of the novel's appeal to certain western cultural forms – the worldwide 1960s popularity of Elvis Presley, for example, or the influential representation of India in Merchant Ivory films – this powerful effect was critically accounted for by reference to the novel's 'exuberant', 'shape-shifting narrative'.[19] Its remarkable 'linguistic inventiveness' and 'original' use of English were further regarded as of a piece with these protean acrobatics. Still in terms of the critical publicity, the work's verbal intricacy was seen as strikingly contrasted with its disturbing subject matter: the 'intimate and revealing portrait of the caste-system', especially the focus on the 'forbidden' sexual touch of the (almost godlike) Untouchable, and on the horrific punishment which follows it.[20] And as if this were not enough, the novel almost impossibly heightens the *ne plus ultra* of its cross-caste theme with its representation of child molestation and incest between twins. In some reviews, the layerings of contrasting extreme experiences, of national turmoil and personal suffering, of physical wounding and linguistic artistry, of pain accented by play, and play hollowing out pain, were considered to be even further elaborated by the narrative's cultural and political interleavings. The novel was seen to stage the particular mingling of Hindu ritual, especially Kathakali performance, Marxist activism and Christian proselytising that typified social life in Kerala in and around 1969.

An unmissable feature emerging out of the juxtaposition of the 1890s and 1990s moments of reception of these two Indian women writers is that certain critical elements have resonated down the century, from the time of the acclaim for Naidu to the present day.[21] Most prominent among these elements is the conflation of biography, female body and writing, which characterises the terms through which the works of both Naidu and Roy are perceived. Noteworthy, though not always typical, is also the singling out of a slight, feminine body shape as somehow corresponding to stylistic whimsicality, or specifically, Indian stylistic whimsicality, or as worth mentioning in relation to it. The decorated, sinuous and again 'feminine' writings of both poet and novelist are generally regarded as being appropriate to their eastern subject matter, including caste restrictions, but also as interacting evocatively with the distresses that they describe. Her 'lyric energy', Gosse writes of Naidu, has an intensity imparted by the sorrow implicit in her subject matter, and present in her life (presumably, the circumstances of her marriage)[22] – the words could be a paraphrase of comments made about Roy whose bohemian lifestyle allegedly masks fascinating personal secrets.

The first thing to remark about these to me intriguing parallels is that there is of course very little that is new about a woman writer being either censured or praised, and, either way, objectified, on the basis primarily of her gender (reinforced by race or ethnic) identity. What is especially striking about the parallel instances of Naidu and Roy, however, is how the several interconnections converge in the notions, on the one hand, of lyric complexity and emotional intensity, and, on the other, of singular femaleness. In the case of Naidu, this convergence is also explicitly tied in with her being oriental, and her explicitly orientalised poetry. For Gosse she is the foremost Indian poet in English because her 'technical skill' illuminates her authentically 'tropical and primitive' emotion, that 'magic circle' of India present in her verse. To this sultry, delicate magic her femaleness is appropriately connected. The Orient with its perfumes and ardent sensations is for Gosse and Symons classically conceptualised as feminine (although, as chapter 4 showed, to Naidu herself the 'oriental female' signified loyalty and strength of character). But Naidu's femininity also labels her as a creature apart. As a *woman* poet of the Deccan she stands out as almost entirely unique, as a special witness. In her imitativeness she is in some sense safely inimitable: there will be few more like her to intervene in western aesthetic perceptions of the east.

In Roy's case, in the so-called postcolonial 1990s/2000s, the western projection of an eastern identity on to an Indian writer appears to be less in evidence.

Yet, arguably, both in the attention paid to her ornate linguistic effects, and in the acceptance of her excesses (reflected in the book's success), there is a tacit understanding that this style in some way suits, while also contrasting productively and provocatively with, her Indian subject matter. The deft verbal play is set against the brutal ravages of caste prejudice, seen by westerners since at least the 1700s as an essentially oriental problem. Involved with this acceptance is also that excitement over Roy's unique position as the 'first' girl among the 'new boys'. In Roy's situation as in Naidu's, therefore, the critical interest in verbal effects, and the general responsiveness to their emotional, indeed 'tropical', intensity, are significantly inflected and perhaps also intensified by their being women writers, which is related to their writing *as women*, from familial, allegedly personal and domestic perspectives. (Here we might think, for example, of Naidu's somewhat stage-managed concern with purdah and child marriage, and Roy's with female frustrations in the domestic context, and with the status of the single mother in southern Indian society.)

Given that Naidu's poetry was seen to require a more oriental slant, and that the Orient of her verse was conceived in feminine terms, I now want to ask whether, in the postcolonial perception of Roy, a similar conflation has not taken place. It is a conflation which, I would suggest, bears characteristic signs of a gender-marked, even nationalist mode of thinking – one for which single, so-called typical images are held to mark an entire community. In relation to Roy this mode might most succinctly be described as new or neo-orientalist, as against the fact that Roy herself emphasises that the India she writes about is not extraordinary but ordinary.[23] Does the critical perception of Roy in western critical circles, in other words, not approvingly intersect her harrowing themes and verbal extravagance with her Indian/oriental and feminine identity (with comparatively little regard for the regional complexities of 1969 Kerala with which the novel is so intensely concerned)?

One response to this might be that an appreciation of Roy or of other Indian writers which lays a positive accent on the feminine qualities of the writing could justly be viewed as an inversion of conventional gendered values. In my view, however, any such inversion by a postcolonial text must be considered in the particular cultural and political context of its production and reception. The construction of a contemporary Indian literary femininity as at once typical and symbolic shines a searching light on the stereotyped ways in which the west continues to read the east, setting it up as a lasting emblem for its fascination with difference. From this a number of related questions emerge. Does the underlying characterisation of the oriental feminine in some postcolonial critiques (of which the critical reception of Roy is symptomatic), not leave embedded entrenched differences between an exotic and impassioned east and a consuming west, interested in yet distancing itself from that east's enticements and intensities? And does this characterisation not reinforce the ways in which the west has always scrutinised and objectified the other, whether the east in the case of India, or the south more generally? Aren't there elements of this criticism that create a profound sense of *déja vu*? Have Indian writers not been feted and exceptionalised in this way before, at the height of Empire, and feted in very similar terms?

Expanding these questions, the neo-orientalist tendency I want to underline is a critical inclination to regard as more culturally alive, interestingly authentic and intensively 'postcolonial' than other kinds of international writing, the extravagant realism and exuberant word-play associated with certain Indian writers, including Salman Rushdie and Arundhati Roy.[24] A criticism has developed that replicates inherited categories of colonial difference – in particular the objectification of otherness memorably described by Edward Said in *Orientalism*. Yet again India is transmitted as multiple, extreme, scented, sensual, transgressive (obligingly complying with western concepts of itself), *and* as quintessentially feminine. It is an objectification that perhaps becomes particularly noticeable and worth questioning when a woman writer is involved. In this criticism we see locked together traditional characterisations of the eternal feminine and the eternal oriental – an interconnection that produces an equally traditional, gendered notion of orientalist typicality that has shifted, as it were, from racial character to text, and to writer's biography. To overstate the matter in order to make the point: the writing that is deemed most interesting and typical seems to be a writing that is perfumed, decorated, sinuous, sensuous, plural, unruly – most intensely and appropriately so when produced by a woman. Overdetermined in all its strangeness, abstracted from its local context, stereotyped and restereotyped, the exotic attraction of the once-colonised appears to have been imported into postcolonial criticism, and, in the process, to have been commodified and made safe for a western readership.

The critical interest in a still feminised Orient – an 'Indo-chic', to quote Padmini Mongia, or indeed an Indo-chick – leads on smoothly to the preoccupation of the last portion of this chapter. Here I consider in broader terms the neo-orientalist underpinnings of postcolonial literary criticism from the west, based in part on its location in the neoimperialist centre, and complicatedly manifested in the increasing prominence accorded Third World women writers.[25] Colonial modes of seeing and knowing were notoriously articulated through gendered metaphors of possession, penetration, and so on. It is therefore important for postcolonial critics to ask whether the current privileging of women writers as more fully, authentically or differently representing their alterity than others, can be taken as they would want to take it – as a justified privileging, an affirmative writing other-wise? Or do western critics in the process of such attention-giving risk deploying native women, as before, to signify, to catachretise, that which is most exotic, intriguing and strange about once-colonised cultures?[26] Does the gendered primitive remain, though in a magic realist or postmodernised guise, the bearer of the west's exotic interests and subversive desires? In this regard it is worth being reminded that *The God of Small Things* tells a heated tale of multiply forbidden desire. Exquisitely narrated from a feminine point of view, it is a tale which takes place against the luxuriant tropical backcloth of south India, a relocated, velvety black and only semi-ironic 'heart of darkness' (*GST* 1, 52, 125, 204, 267).

In attempting to foreground the neocolonial and gender biases of some versions of postcolonial criticism, I am, I should belatedly stress, having to bracket the complicities and nuances of tone through which Roy's prose, as well as Naidu's writing, subversively confuses and throws sand in western eyes. In paragraph after paragraph of Roy's dense experimental narrative we see the English language – the language bequeathed by the British coloniser, as she has recognised – expanded, distorted, excavated, disconcerted. There is to my mind no question about the energy and oppositionality of this writing. But what *is* up for scrutiny are the evaluative vocabularies and critical techniques which, in the academy, and in the critical columns often supplied from the academy, are used to represent, for instance, Roy's work. Can these become correspondingly oppositional, self-critical and sensitive to creative ambivalence? Can they participate in a critical postcolonialism rather than a globalised 'postcoloniality'[27] without falling into the trap of objectifying difference?

In exploring the theoretical and institutional determinants of this situation further, we have to recognise how the mostly enabling currency of Homi Bhabha's theories of hybridity, or Bakhtin on polyphony, have caused postcolonial literary subversions and multiplicity to become almost too expected as being always already there. These allegedly subversive features are in consequence seen as almost self-sufficient in their displacement from, and confounding of, a Eurocentric history. In a postmodern context of shattered temporalities and rejected essences, it has now become customary to view migrant or Third World texts as having the potential to undercut or reverse the west's foundational concepts, primarily on the basis of the writer's syncretic or migrant vantage point. This trend is exacerbated by the redemptive story of ethical progress which postcolonial criticism in the western liberal academy and in publishing circles tells itself: it represents itself as advanced, advancing and democratising because voices from the margins are being given a hearing. So a female Indian writer wins the prestigious prize which Rushdie first claimed for India not so long ago, establishing if there were any remaining doubt in the matter, the cultural striking back of the once-peripheral.[28] In short, wherever western-origin postcolonial critical attention touches down, in east or south, there is a tendency for mixing and multivocality, a feminine polymorphousness, to reproduce itself whatever the historical or cultural location (and for plainer, less adorned, realist writers to be sidelined). The impression

that results is of an energetic if bewildering babble of novelistic voices which
can be best organised, it seems, simply by burying it under the title 'postcolonialism'. India in effect remains the teeming spectacle of the Grand Trunk Road
in Kipling's *Kim* (1901), viewed god-like from on high. As Aijaz Ahmad puts it
in a typically strenuous essay, 'the whole of the "Third World"'... singularized
into an oppositionality, [is] idealized as the site, simultaneously, of alterity and
authenticity' – and, I would add, of femininity.[29]

With this scenario in mind it is significant, as Arif Dirlik has also observed,
that postcolonialism has emerged at a time when transnational capital continues to generate stark economic and power imbalances between different parts
of the world – a time when globalisation has produced a neocolonial depen-
dency of the chaotic, helpless 'rest' on the rational/ised, masculine west.[30] I do
not want to go as far as Dirlik in suggesting a *knowing* complicity between postcolonial studies and global neocolonialism. I also do not wish to argue that
postcolonial studies in some sense consciously does the ideological work of a
global free market, in which cultural diversity is restlessly de-contextualised
and commodified.[31] Yet it does seem to me that postcolonial criticism *is* related
to, and representative of, the continuing dominance of the formerly imperial
metropolis. The dominance is indicated by such factors as the persistence of a
(neo-)orientalist rhetoric, the location of critics, the subsequent direction of
the postcolonial gaze at already 'othered' cultures, and, till recently, the relative
neglect of transnational capitalism as a subject for discussion and critique. It
is precisely because of this emphasis on the textual over the contextual that
postcolonialism can in certain respects come to resemble both a camouflage
for a still-powerful centre, and a subterfuge: an 'opportunistic [adjustment] by
the centre of power to accommodate changes of power without loss of authority'.[32]

To put it yet another way, postcolonial criticism has landed in terrain which
under another aspect it knows all too well. Here is the familiar city – the appropriative metropolis; over there, beyond the city walls, are jungles, dangerous
rivers, elephants and other exotic phenomena, the other against which the
imperial city defines itself, and which it tirelessly monitors and seeks to control
in order to maintain its ascendancy.[33] The difference now is that certain individuals and texts from out there, promoted by their class position or other
elitist structures, have been admitted to the city the better to ensure the effi-
ciency of its monitoring.

The question must then be, are there ways of cutting through this neocolonial and still masculinist bind in order to give the very real vitality and oppositionality of postcolonial literatures their due regard? It is evidently true that
no cultural or academic interest in reversed values or subversive texts will of
itself reverse hierarchies in the world, especially where these postcolonial interests themselves work within hierarchies which still exclude east and south. Yet

a criticism that remains continually vigilant about the neo-orientalist and feminising aspects of its own interpretative terms, and of its neocolonial context, will go some distance towards at least confronting if not challenging those hierarchies. In order to effect this vigilance it may be necessary to set up *contextualising temporalities*, histories or background stories that would reveal, for example, the many social, political and linguistic determinants that have shaped, and continue to shape, what we now call postcolonial hybridity. Roy's extravagant play with English, her 'compactness and intensity', does not simply float free of her time: it is in all likelihood politically motivated, as chapter 11 will show.[34] Women living out the contingencies of their lives break mythic moulds, even a mould as resilient as that of the eternal, oriental other. Alongside this, and at least as important, postcolonial readings also demand a sensitivity to agency, including once again women's agency, and an effort to relate interpretative practices to cultural knowledge. What, for instance, is the relationship of *The God of Small Things* to a vernacular tradition of Kathakali with its open-ended structures of narration? On related lines, Gayatri Spivak has usefully warned that any postcolonial reading must be approached as a continuously self-critical, contextualising and intensively 'inter-literary' rather than a conventionally 'comparative' exercise.[35]

To circle round to where I began, it is imperative to remember that resistances emerge in texts just as much as they do in contexts: the point is to keep both in play – in play against one another so that neither lapses into prescribed Eurocentric moves. Through a restless layering and contortion of accepted meanings, postcolonial fictions, plays and poems, whether in English or in other languages, continually chafe at western self-reference and self-consolidation. Emerging from beyond established cultural borderlines, such texts assert a *verbal recalcitrance* or irreconcilability, an 'enunciatory disorder' as Homi Bhabha puts it: a strangeness which antagonistically and creatively interrupts western forms of understanding, such as the assumed conflation of biology and biography in the writing of the south.[36] It is not enough therefore simply to coat such resistance with the now over-familiar and still under-examined, though relatively safe term hybridity.

The mention of disorder and creative interruption finally returns me to what I mentioned earlier with regard to the wayward intricacies of Roy's writing, which I then had to bracket: the 'ambiguous unclassifiable consistency' of her writing, to adapt a quotation from the text itself (*GST* 30). The poems and the poetic exercises in prose of Naidu and Roy respectively, their stilted and skittish burlesques, and the evasive or over-stylised arabesqueries of their language, demonstrate a subtle subversion that at once co-operates with and exceeds the definitions criticism imposes. There is something chillingly composed in a poem of Naidu's like the two-part 'Songs of my city' from *The Bird of Time*. Different voices obediently perform a pastiche of a many-textured spice-rich

India which, in each one of the paired poems, comes to rest on images of silence and confinement, or death.[37]

Differently though connectedly, Roy's writing persistently works at unsettling and undoing the English language. Strange attractions are created between words through rhyming and alliterative patterns. Grief-stricken, the mother Ammu's eyes are 'a redly dead', a 'deadly red' (*GST* 31). Having reached the age at which her mother died, the central character Rahel too is at 'a viable, die-able age' (*GST* 3, with many repetitions). Most predominantly, the childish play on language of the seven-year-old twins at the centre of the story shockingly literalises conventional actions and sayings, including phrases from Kipling ('we be of one blood, thou and I'), exposing hidden cruelties. At the film of *The Sound of Music*, the Orangedrink Lemondrink Man 'moved Esta's hand up and down [his penis]. First slowly. Then fastly' (*GST* 103). Ammu, forced to leave Ayemenem after the discovery of her love affair, has to 'pack her bags and leave. Because she had no Locusts Stand I' (*GST* 159). As the narrative voice remarks: 'only the Small Things were said. The Big Things lurked unsaid inside' (*GST* 173). Throughout, the novel insists on this co-existence; the sometimes forgotten interaction of great and little 'gods', of grand and *petit* forces. In a country such as the one Rahel comes from, 'various kinds of despair competed for primacy': 'That Big God howled like a hot wind, and demanded obeisance. Then Small God (cosy and contained, private and limited) came away cauterized, laughing numbly at his own temerity' (*GST* 19).

In Roy as in Naidu, personal despair is caught up in and only seemingly dwarfed by 'the public turmoil of a nation'

Notes

1 Rudyard Kipling, 'The Ballad of East and West', *The Definitive Edition of Rudyard Kipling's Verse* (London: Hodder and Stoughton, 1989), pp. 234–8.

2 Naidu's poetry appeared in four collections published between 1895 and 1917: *Songs* (1895), *The Golden Threshold* (1905), *The Bird of Time* (1912) and *The Broken Wing* (1917). The 'little Indian princess' is W. B. Yeats's term, according to Maud Gonne, *A Servant of the Queen* (London: Victor Gollancz, 1938), p. 331.

3 Edmund Gosse, 'Introduction', *The Bird of Time: Songs of Life, Death and the Spring*, by Sarojini Naidu (London: William Heinemann, 1912), p. 7.

4 Gosse, 'Introduction', pp. 4–5.

5 Gosse, 'Introduction', p. 5.

6 Sarojini Naidu, *The Golden Threshold*, intro. Arthur Symons (London: William Heinemann, 1905), was dedicated to Gosse and brought together the poems written since his intervention.

7 Gosse, 'Introduction', p. 6.

8 Makarand Paranjape (ed.), *Sarojini Naidu: Selected Letters 1890s to 1940s* (New Delhi: Kali for Women, 1996), pp. 44–6.

9 See also, for example, Susie Tharu and K. Lalita (eds), *Women Writing in India: 600 B.C. to the Present*, vol. 1 (New Delhi: Oxford University Press, 1991), pp. 329–40.

10 Arthur Symons, 'Introduction', *The Golden Threshold*, by Sarojini Naidu, pp. 9–10, 18.

11 Here I follow Arif Dirlik's definition: 'North connotes the pathways of transnational capitalism, and South, the marginalized populations of the world, regardless of their location'. See Arif Dirlik, 'The postcolonial aura: Third World criticism in the age of global capitalism', in Padmini Mongia (ed.), *Contemporary Postcolonial Theory* (London: Arnold, 1996), p. 311. 'South' can also be read less metaphorically in that the rich countries of the world tend to be concentrated in the northern hemisphere.

12 Robert J. C. Young, *Colonial Desire* (London and New York: Routledge, 1995), pp. 27–8.

13 See Graham Huggan, *The Postcolonial Exotic: Marketing the Margins* (London and New York: Routledge, 2001), in particular in this context chapter 2, 'Consuming India'. Huggan styles Roy as a prominent instance of the rise of 'Indo-chic'. See also Maya Jaggi, 'An unsuitable girl', *Guardian Weekend* (24 May 1997), pp. 12–18; Padmini Mongia, 'The making and marketing of Arundhati Roy', unpublished conference paper, University of Barcelona, Spain, September 1997; Sara Suleri, 'Woman skin deep: feminism and the postcolonial condition', *Critical Inquiry*, 18 (1992), 756–69. The more or less simultaneous production and publication of this critical work in the 1990s, including my own essay on which this chapter is based, suggests that at least some mechanism of critical cutting-down-to-size is present within postcolonialism's inflated market in exotic goods.

14 Arundhati Roy, *The God of Small Things* (London: Flamingo, 1997). Page references will be included in the text along with the abbreviation *GST*. Before 18 October 1997, the time of the Booker Prize ceremony, the novel was already reputed to have sold 500,000 copies in 18 languages.

15 See Shirley Chew, 'The house in Kerala', *Times Literary Supplement* (30 May 1997), p. 23; Alex Clark, 'Fatal distractions', *Guardian* (19 June 1997), p. B4; Michael Gorra, 'Living in the aftermath', *London Review of Books* (19 June 1997), pp. 22–3; Stephen Moss, 'A contest won in a vacuum', *Guardian* (15 October 1997), p. 3.

16 As confirmed in the *New Yorker* magazine's Golden Jubilee issue (23/30 June 1997), which carried a centrepiece photograph of most of India's prominent writers in English, with Rushdie, accompanied by Roy, in the foreground.

17 See, for example, Emmanuel S. Nelson, 'Arundhati Roy (1960–)', in Jaina C. Sanga (ed.), *South Asian Novelists in English: An A-to-Z Guide* (Westport, CN: Greenwood Press, 2003), pp. 218–22; 'Interview', *Vrij Nederland* (Amsterdam, 18 October 1997), pp. 18–19. Latterly, on the back of Roy's success, a number of Indian women (in most cases first) novelists have sprung into prominence, among others, Kiran Desai, Manju Kapur, Ameena Meer and Shauna Singh Baldwin.

18 See 'CV: David Godwin', *Independent* (20 October 1997), p. B5.

19 See Gillian Beer, quoted in *Guardian* (15 October 1997), p. 3; and Alice Truax, review of *The God of Small Things*, *New York Times Book Review* (25 May 1997), p. 5. See also Floris van Straaten, 'Wreedheid als sleutel tot de liefde' (Amsterdam, 17 October 1997), p. 10.

20 Moss, 'A contest won in a vacuum', p. A3 and Truax, 'Review', p. 5.
21 Or, though to a lesser extent, from the time of the acclaim for Naidu's earlier com-
    patriot Toru Dutt (1856–77), whose work was also taken up by Gosse.
22 Gosse, 'Introduction', pp. 7–8.
23 Gayatri Spivak, *Outside in the Teaching Machine* (London: Routledge, 1993), p. 277,
    and 'Neocolonialism and the secret agent of knowledge', interview with Robert
    Young, *The Oxford Literary Review: Neocolonialism*, 13 (1991), 226–7, has used the
    term *new orientalism* to describe the homogenising, de-contextualising effects of
    late twentieth-century multiculturalism. As will become evident later in this
    chapter, I prefer neo-orientalism because of its verbal analogy with neocolonialism.
24 In *The God of Small Things* this exuberance is accentuated of course by its famously
    erratic capitalisation.
25 See only, as a case in point, the host of critical studies of postcolonial women's
    writing cited in the bibliography to this book.
26 Here I take catachresis to refer to the contingency of reference or potential defor-
    mation inherent in any metaphor. See Gayatri Spivak, *A Critique of Postcolonial
    Reason: Toward a History of the Vanishing Present* (Cambridge, MA: Harvard
    University Press, 1999), for example, pp. 14, 188.
27 See Huggan, *The Postcolonial Exotic*, pp. 1–33, but especially pp. 5–7.
28 In this sense Terry Eagleton's line describing the persistence of total systems in a
    postmodern world can be applied to postcolonialism: 'The term "post", if it has any
    meaning at all, means business as usual, only *more so*'. See Terry Eagleton, *The
    Ideology of the Aesthetic* (London: Blackwell, 1990), pp. 380–1.
29 Aijaz Ahmad, *In Theory: Classes, Nations, Literatures* (New York and London: Verso,
    1992), p. 33.
30 Dirlik, 'The postcolonial aura', pp. 294–320.
31 See Jon Mee's speculations on the ideological work done within India by the Indian
    novel in English: 'After midnight: the Indian novel in English of the 80s and 90s',
    Postcolonial Studies, 1:1 (April 1998), 127–14, especially pp. 132 and 134.
32 Paul Hamilton, *Historicism* (London: Routledge, 1996), pp. 178, and 149–50. For
    their comments on postcolonialism's neocolonial complicities, see also: Ania
    Loomba, *Colonialism/Postcolonialism* (London: Routledge, 1998), pp. 245–58, and
    Bart Moore-Gilbert, *Postcolonial Theory: Contexts, Practices, Politics* (New York and
    London: Verso, 1997), pp. 3–4, 17–21, 185–203.
33 This is the kind of material that is almost too knowingly satirised in Hari Kunzru's
    The Impressionist (London: Hamish Hamilton, 2002), especially the second part,
    'Rukhsana'.
34 See Aijaz Ahmad's remarkable 'rave' review of Roy's 'overwritten' narrative,
    'Reading Arundhati Roy *politically*', *Frontline* (9 August 1997), pp. 103–8. Despite
    the novel's alleged sentimentality, misrepresentations of south Indian
    Communism, and failures in realism, he sees it as fully embodying its social world
    and as doing so in the medium of a decisively vernacular English.
35 Spivak, *Outside in the Teaching Machine*, p. 277; and see also her *A Critique of
    Postcolonial Reason*, p. 173. My view of contextualised temporalities as necessarily
    accompanied by verbal recalcitrance can be compared with Spivak's observation

that historical contextualisation remains self-consolidating of the west unless married to 'critical reading'. For a useful overview of the different interpretative axes inscribed or ascribed by postcolonial criticism, see Stephen Slemon, 'The scramble for post-colonialism', in Chris Tiffin and Alan Lawson (eds), *De-scribing Empire* (London and New York: Routledge, 1994), pp. 15–32.

36 Homi Bhabha, *The Location of Culture* (London: Routledge, 1995), pp. 126–7.

37 Sarojini Naidu, 'Songs of my city', in Elleke Boehmer (ed.), *Empire Writing: An Anthology of Colonial Literature, 1870–1918* (Oxford: Oxford University Press, 1998), pp. 314–15.

10

Tropes of yearning and dissent:
the inflection of desire in Yvonne Vera
and Tsitsi Dangarembga[1]

To build something new, you must be prepared to destroy the past.
(Yvonne Vera, *Butterfly Burning*)[2]

This chapter seeks to bring into juxtaposition two Zimbabwean women writers and a question of same-sex sexuality: its configurations of desire, its vocabularies of aspiration. It thus extends this book's overall concern with women's representation into the area of women's sexuality, especially in so far as sexuality remains the dark secret of the Third World nation. Queer sexuality, in point of fact, probably still constitutes what could best be termed a virtual non-presence, or at least a covert silencing, an 'unsaying', in postcolonial discourses generally and in African writing in particular.[3] It is a surprising omission or occlusion considering that, since the 1960s, postcolonial theory and criticism have grown up in tandem with the emergence of a politics of identity and cultural difference, and are deeply informed by discourses of rights and of resistance to a variety of forms of oppression. It can only be hoped that the recent concern in African philosophy and criticism with bodies as *sites* of protest will eventually bring a welcome change of focus in the field, including a new concern with desire as a possible mode of resistance.[4]

In the African sphere, despite the frequently urgent discussion of how to go about constructing independent identities in relation to the contexts of modernity, fiction has to date kept noticeably, perhaps strategically, silent on questions of gay selfhood and sexuality. This silence is particularly pronounced in women's writing, especially when we take into account women's levels of dissatisfaction with the structures of power inscribed within heterosexual relationships. Conventionally, as hardly needs spelling out, the decorum if not the taboo surrounding the airing or outing of gay/lesbian sexuality in African writing has generally been explained with reference to African social norms, cultural nationalism and the status quo ('it doesn't happen, it's not done'). The 2003 conflict within the worldwide Anglican community on the ordination of homosexual priests, for example, which was strongly resisted by African and other Third World clergy, reiterated if not reinforced widely held views that homosexuality is a western perversion, or even a foolish indulgence.[5]

With respect to African women specifically, many of whom live with the day-to-day reality of female genital surgery or 'circumcision' across areas of North, West and East Africa, speaking of sex rights or the claims of the desiring female body can be emotionally painful and, in consequence, ethically untenable. It would appear that spaces for the articulation of women's pleasure as self-contained or woman-specific are not easily forged and a tangible sense of taboo, of the unsaid, prevails. As Juliana Makuchi Nfah-Abbenyi writes, a theorisation of women's pleasure as exclusive to women is not only socially problematic, perceived as driving a wedge between men and women, but is also seen as politically reductive, having the potential to impact prejudicially upon women's rights struggles.[6] Writers and critics from other non-western vantage-points, such as South Asia (for which, see the conclusion), might well concur, pointing to the host of cultural determinants which in their contexts act as qualifiers and limits to (homo)sexual self-realisation, certainly to the founding of *identity* on the basis of sexual preferences.[7]

Within this context of so-called 'culturally challenging practices', to quote Nfah-Abbenyi, it becomes clear why the two most prominent instances of lesbian desire in Anglophone African women's writing to date, both curiously from the 1970s, have both been critically discounted on the grounds of deviance. The two 'same-sex moments' are Marija's pass at Sissie in Ama Ata Aidoo's *Our Sister Killjoy* (1977), and Selina's seduction of Gaciru in Rebekah Njau's *Ripples in the Pool* (1975).[8] While acknowledging a certain opportunism on Sissie's part, Oladele Taiwo in a descriptive (and prescriptive) 1984 reading of Aidoo's novel, for instance, describes Sissie as finally doing the decent thing as regards Marija, that is, rejecting her, for the reason that to be lesbian is an 'anathema' 'at home'. Aidoo is chided, however, for her temerity in suggesting, no matter how partially, that the friendship between Marija and Sissie implies that women can do without men: 'If such a situation is tenable in Europe, it has no chance of succeeding in Africa'.[9] Marija's deviant Europeanness therefore is cast as at once sexually and morally, and even perhaps racially or culturally, corrupting.

However, as Taiwo's anxiety to deny the 'situation' betrays, Aidoo's interpretation of the relationship via the narrator Sissie's responses is far more subversive than his comfortable judgements give her credit for. Sissie tends to view Marija's desire for her as part of her exotic and finally disposable otherness, which is concentrated in the figure of the succulent plums that she daily gives her. Yet her initial reaction to Marija's gaze, which is repeated close to the point of her departure, is to imagine the 'deliciousness' of the affair they might have had, had she been a man. For Sissie, while masculinity is bound up with power, in particular the power of refusal (which she does eventually wield), the vocabulary of her imagined desire also concedes a certain self-forgetting and exhilaration, unmistakably pictured as attractive. The anecdote of the two African girls in bed together which forms part of her stream-of-consciousness on the night of Marija's attempted seduction is moreover highly ambiguous as to whether their playfulness is unnatural or un-African; it, too, is once again not unenticing. For these reasons it is understandable that, at the point where the two women say goodbye to one another, Sissie is suddenly unable to find words for the emotion that rises up between them, while she at the same time discourages herself from feeling aversion.[10]

As regards same-sex desire in Rebekah Njau, Selina's affair is unsurprisingly stigmatised by a male character in the novel as 'not the normal type of love'.[11] In that Selina's fractured personality is deviant on several other counts also, the narrative appears to reject what it simultaneously also acknowledges, by projecting a cluster of wayward desires on to her, as if she were a scapegoat. Picking up on these signals, even a recent sympathetic reading by Celeste Fraser Delgado of Selina as a complex site of ambivalent womanhood cannot avoid viewing her case and hence her sexuality as, within its context, pathological.[12] Njau herself has noted in interview that she was confronted with a certain resistance from readers of *Ripples in the Pool*: they felt the book 'wasn't her' (the specific reason for this is not stated).[13] 'Lesbianism', observes the critic Mary Modupe Kolawole, self-consciously speaking for 'ordinary Africans', is after all 'a non-existent issue [in Africa] because it is a mode of expression that is completely strange to their world-view'.[14]

Such silences, sidesteps, censorings and stigmatisations in writing and criticism form the context of this chapter; however, it takes as its central stimulus Yvonne Vera's fervent suggestion in the preface to her edited short story collection *Opening Spaces* (1999) that the woman writer's 'response to … taboo is vital and pressing'.[15] She associates this sense of urgency with the important concern to focus on characters' 'internal, psychological worlds'.[16] By way of illustration she underlines, as Tsitsi Dangarembga herself has done in interview, that *Nervous Conditions* (1988) opens with the shocking breaking of a familial taboo in the form of Tambu's comment: 'I was not sorry when my brother died' – words subversively placed in the mouth of a woman.[17] *Opening Spaces* itself breaches several taboos relating to women's lives: stories broach the subjects of back-street abortion, reverse racism, uxoricide and death by AIDS. Same-sex love, however, the book does not touch. After that interesting moment of emergence in the two mid-1970s novels, the issue has seemingly not openly resurfaced – or not been permitted to resurface – either in Anglophone African women's writing, or in criticism. And yet, still drawing words from Vera's preface, 'the kinship which survives among women in the midst of betrayals and absences' remains itself a pressing topic to which to testify – and one of its forms of course is gay.

As regards the two writers who stand at the centre of this chapter, Dangarembga and Vera herself constitute for my purposes a strategic pairing: as Zimbabwe's two most prominent women writers they are also linked in their contemporaneity. Neither has, admittedly, explicitly addressed gay sexuality in her work, no doubt for some of the social reasons outlined. I have chosen them, however, because both writers have in noted ways widened the boundaries of what it is possible to say about women, their desires, phobias and aspirations, as the quotations above suggested. As I will explain further, my definition of queer writing therefore will attach not so much to character representation as such, or to content or theme, but to a particular searching and interrogative *approach* to relations between women, and to women's sexual identity. It will attach therefore to an aesthetic: to an elaborately detailed or, alternatively, experimental and poetic voicing of those relations, even if these are not in any obvious way sexual. Queerness, I will suggest, can find expression as a questing and/or questioning that takes as its medium a restless and (till now) nameless bodily desire, and, in some cases, is encrypted in metaphor and other poetic effects. I will ask, in other words, whether a queer sexuality may be covertly encoded in these writers' texts in the form of special friendships and special expressions of friendship between women. Moreover, the pairing of the writers, reinforced by their relative isolation in the male-dominated, homophobic context of Zimbabwe, brings out not only the parallels between them, but also the contrasting views they have taken on relationships between women. Whereas Vera tends to be more interested in women in *isolated* positions, links *between* women form the foundation of Dangarembga's narrative.

Zimbabwean literature of course represents no exception in the field of African writing as concerns its avoidance of same-sex sexuality – that is, bar a few texts that touch on male homosexuality. In a precise case of writing holding a mirror to reality, Zimbabwean fiction generally repeats the prohibitions on, and consequent invisibility of, gay sexuality in social and cultural life, which Mark Epprecht and Oliver Phillips, among others, have discussed.[18] The Zimbabwean constitution is an exemplary text in this regard for its silence on sexuality (as opposed to race or religious belief) as grounds for freedom from discrimination. Marechera certainly confirmed the anti-patriotic charges against him as a writer when he included an unprecedented lesbian brief encounter in *Mindblast* (1984), which he described as a 'terrible ecstasy' and as delicious self-completion. Yet the official prohibitions do not exactly correspond to a society-wide silence. Engaging the discussion of whether homosexuality is un-African, or indeed un-Zimbabwean, the writer Chenjerai Hove, in a comment on the banning of the Gay and Lesbian Association of Zimbabwe from the 1997 Harare International Book Fair, made a telling, language-based intervention. (Although new research questions his etymology) he powerfully observed: 'There is a Shona word, *ngochani*, to describe homosexuals . . . No society bothers to name that which does not exist, imagined or real'.[19] Significantly, however, in the very same comment, he undercuts his own advocacy by associating homosexuality with aberration and moral ugliness.

As Hove observes, the Zimbabwe government denial of homosexuality was, however, resoundingly exploded by the trial of former President Banana in the late 1990s for the homosexual abuse of his employees. Yet, since Banana has universally been represented in Zimbabwe as deviant, this again has worked to maintain if not to reinforce the taboo surrounding the expression of queer sexuality. Indicatively, many of Mugabe's electioneering speeches in the 2002 presidential election campaign used homosexuality as a sign of unnaturalness and un-Africanness with which to brand enemies of the state, whether the Movement for Democratic Change or Tony Blair.[20]

In so far as it is a charge which keeps repeating itself, I will pause briefly at this point to cite once again the equation of gay sexuality with un-Africanness, but I will do so basically in order to put it to one side. As I said at the outset, this chapter is not directly concerned with representations of sexuality between women, repressed or not, therefore it avoids the assumption that there is a queer African sexuality out there, that may be reflected in writing. Leaving that question begging, it is not my concern to prove or disprove the empirical existence of lesbian relationships in Zimbabwe. Rather I want to consider writing as a site of *potentiality* for the emergence of sexual expression by women, and in particular of the expression of forms of love between women: for the emergence, that is, of a poetics of queerness. As Eve Sedgwick writes, queer readings are less concerned with how feelings should be than how they *change*, and, following on from this, how their encodings change. Such aesthetic prioritising favours the non-programmatic, the non-specific, desires that are not necessarily resolvable into distinct object choices.[21]

Along lines articulated by Judith Butler, I want therefore to address (queer) sexuality chiefly as a mode of being *dispossessed* of the self and *disposed to* others; hence as a widening of possibility, especially of creative possibility, whether for love or sociality, here in the context of interrelationship between women.[22] Adapting from Butler's concept of sexual being as defined through the experience of ecstasy, of being 'beside oneself', individuation (or rights, or autonomy) in a same-sex situation places prime importance on the ethic of existing for the other, for the other-in-relationship: on 'a field of ethical enmeshment with others'.[23] It is this kind of individuation through love between women peers, even between women friends in an apparently a-sexual relationship, to which I believe the writing of Dangarembga in particular subversively testifies, in spite of itself. As such, her writing provides a powerful alternative scenario of social and political interrelationship to that of the oppressor/oppressed binary that remains so dominant in political discourses – and in the political arena – in Zimbabwe, in Africa, and elsewhere in the postcolonial world.

If for Butler queer desire signifies a different form of sociality through being-for-the-other, Eve Sedgwick, while broadly agreeing, goes further to explore what forms that sociality and widening of possibility might take – forms which I eventually would like to relate to Vera's as well as to Dangarembga's writing. Seeking an alternative to the hermeneutics of suspicion which, following Ricoeur, Sedgwick sees as dominant in queer epistemology, she proposes instead reparative readings – readings interested in accretion and juxtaposition rather than in exposure; in surprise and contingency rather than in the prevention of surprise. Queerness therefore, she suggests, may be discovered in the experimental and not in the normative, in the contextual rather than the trans-historical, in truculent, wayward or even unfixed varieties of female–female passion rather than in the conventional plot of lesbian identity uncovered or repatriated. As in Melissa Solomon's reading of Henry James's *Portrait of a Lady* (1881), queerness may be found, for example, in a female–female relationship in which a woman achieves subjecthood, or gains access to knowledge, through interaction with another. The passion for the female other is the dialectical ground on which identity is sought and achieved.[24]

This interpretation can be connected with what Florence Stratton, in a discussion of, mainly, Nwapa, Emecheta and Bâ, calls the convention of paired women in African fiction. Stratton's *Contemporary African Literature and the Politics of Gender* is pre-eminently concerned with the inversion of the sexual allegory in women's writing (wherein men have authority and women represent powerlessness).[25] With its eye fixed on certain social proprieties, however, her study does not extrapolate that concept of inversion, or the connotations of pairing, into the area of sexuality. Yet Stratton's comments on the frequent 'coupling' of women characters in African women's writing can nonetheless be productively pushed in the direction of Sedgwick and also Solomon's suggestions. The 'familial or social juxtaposition of two [often related] female characters', she writes, 'acts as a corrective to the [traditional] image of women which men writers valorize, for it is the radical not the conservative sister or friend, the one that challenges patriarchal authority, who is rewarded in the narrative'.[26] African cultures as interpreted by women inscribe ways in which women reach forms of self-fulfilment in interaction with, or in self-aware contradistinction to, the experience of other closely related women.

The Tambudzai–Nyasha pairing in *Nervous Conditions* is, as Stratton recognises, a complicated variant of this trope, in that the initially bold Nyasha is bodily punished for her rebellion. It is a further elaboration of the trope, however, that their togetherness is *for both* the site on which the resistant self achieves expression. Obioma Nnaemeka corroborates this reading when she speaks of the sharp distinction in African women's narratives between the debilitations of heterosexual love 'in marriage and outside of it', on the one hand, and 'on the other hand, the affirming and empowering friendship between women inside and outside of marriage'. 'Friendship [between women] has splendours that love knows not', as Mariama Bâ has written.[27] Relatedly, in Vera's 2002 novel *The Stone Virgins*, discussed more fully in the next chapter, the intimacy of the two sisters Thenjiwe and Nonceba, though truncated by murder, is described as closer and more compelling than that of heterosexual lovers. The sister is 'her own breath flowing into her body': 'before [Thenjiwe's lover] occupied all the places in her mind Nonceba, her sister, had already been holding her hand quietly and forever'.[28] In the light of these quotations, the question as to why the valencies of female friendship, both non-sexual and, possibly, sexual, have not been more thoroughly explored in African social spaces becomes perhaps even more pressing. As is widely known, polygamy is widespread in African societies and therefore, as in the zenana, women have long lived together as peers and competitive/non-competitive 'sisters'.

Opening spaces in Yvonne Vera

Like her *Opening Spaces* anthology, Yvonne's Vera's fiction has, subsequent to the retelling of the *mhondoro* Ambuya Nehanda story in *Nehanda* (1993), confronted in painfully lyrical ways strong taboos concerning women, and their healing after violation. The taboos include infanticide in *Without a Name* (1994), incest and sexual abuse within the family in *Under the Tongue* (1996), and self-induced abortion and self-immolation, a kind of African *sati*, in *Butterfly Burning* (1998).[29] Moreover, aspects of the forbidden and unspoken are encoded in at least two of her titles: both *Without a Name* and *Under the Tongue* signify silencings and suppressions, much as does that notorious expression 'the love that dare not speak its name'. At the same time, significantly, these are titles which can be construed as figures for female desire, that is, an internal and internalised desire, or a desire folding in on itself like a butterfly's wings. That Vera has not to date addressed face-on the subject of same-sex desire must therefore have to do with her concentrated preoccupation in several of the novels with the silky textures of a particularly erotic heterosexuality. As *The Stone Virgins* confirms, it could indeed be said that Vera is one of the more explicitly erotic of the literary African writers working today. This does not, however, close down the significations of what might be termed the excess of sexual yearning in her narratives – on the contrary. Especially in *Under the Tongue*, in Vera's fictional worlds survival is characteristically achieved by women through dialogue with other women, in particular with women family members, across the generations: 'women . . . do not arrive at their identities negatively, but interactively'.[30]

Taking into account that the defiance of prohibition forms a layered subject in Vera's work, I have chosen to focus in this chapter on the particularly strenuous yearnings of *Butterfly Burning.* Set in 1946–48, the novel offers a vivid dramatisation of a young woman's frustrated longing for self-realisation – for a selving, that is, as other to a man, and other to the submission to desire with a man. In a powerful scene this yearning is unambiguously brought to a point of crisis in the presence of another woman, the charismatic, enigmatic and ultimately destructive shebeen owner Deliwe. It is she 'who first inspires in Phephelaphi dreams of independence and free self-expression'.³¹ By the end of the novel, it is true, Deliwe comes to represent female heterosexuality in an especially vindictive form. Yet it is important to note that Phephelaphi's lover Fumbatha seeks Deliwe out only after Phephelaphi has already turned away from him, directing her shapeless, urgent longings towards a largely undefined elsewhere – virtually a Lawrentian beyond.

It is a characteristic feature of Vera's writing that body parts, especially those belonging to lovers, and those in pain, are – like music and labour – often depicted in synecdoche, as disconnected from whole bodies, and thus in some manner as disavowing association with conventionally fixed genders or sexual identities. Bodies themselves insistently 'long for flight, not surrender', and disconnect from the earth.³² When in the anticipatory paragraphs that end chapter 4, Phephelaphi distances herself from Fumbatha, she is pictured as 'in flight like a bird', 'brimming with a lonely ecstasy' (*BB* 29). Such images of floating, rising and straining away from the earth find their terrible fulfilment first in the image of the industrial accident at the oil tank, and finally in her suicide by fire: 'she can fly . . . She is a bird with wings spread'. Yet this terminal ecstasy significantly does not connect to any fixed shape of love, or specific love object, not even that of her own body (*BB* 16–17, 129). Ceaselessly mixing abstractions and unadorned plain nouns, fascinated with repetitive, non-object-related activity, and the movements of music, Yvonne Vera's style offers a peculiarly appropriate vehicle for the articulation of such yearning.

Phephelaphi's open-ended longings briefly alight, butterfly-like, in Deliwe's shebeen room, in a scene that occurs almost exactly halfway through the novel (*BB* 52–7). Following the loss of her nurturer mother and separation from her birth mother, she is said to be 'dearly' charmed by Deliwe, her force, her independence: 'the sun rose and set with Deliwe'. (*BB* 52) Given that Deliwe has no interest in her and that Fumbatha mistrusts Deliwe, these curious constructions can be explained only if the shebeen owner is seen as some ultimate of freedom, some boundary which Phephelaphi wishes to exceed. The younger woman's attraction is heatedly described as 'the bliss, the ecstasy, the freedom spreading its wide wings over Phephelaphi's body as she stood watching her'. Appropriately, considering the nature of her quickened desire, Phephelaphi dresses herself in a stiff, white flared skirt like a butterfly's wings to visit Deliwe's house late at night. Now, for a while, the yearning that occupies Deliwe's room comes to rest on the sensuous forms of her male visitors.

However, the ambient kwela music unsettles any such identification, and again unlocks a fluid, powerful yearning, one that is both associated with the memory of Getrude her nurturer mother and continues to leave a powerful trace, a furrow, after she has come to terms with the memory.

The presences of Deliwe and music act as catalysts in what is represented as the process of Phephelaphi's simultaneous breakdown and coming-into-her-own, her 'finding something else', which demands that she visits Deliwe twice more (*BB* 59). Though the chronology of the narrative is fragmentary, as far as the narrative progression is concerned it is after these visits that Phephelaphi takes steps to expand her opportunities. She wishes to realise her dream to train as a nurse. Her heart, it is said, 'rises in an agony of longing' at this prospect of a 'movement forward . . . into something new and untried'. The description of her forceful longing or yearning is worth quoting in full:

> Fumbatha could never be the beginning or end of all her yearning, her longing for which she could not find a suitable name. *Not a male hurt or anything like it* . . . She wanted to do something but had no idea what it could be, what shape it offered for her future.
>
> She could not stop the longing even though she heard the water lapping against the edges, against the rim, as though she was some kind of river and there were things like flooding which could take place inside her body. It was full desire because she liked the lapping on the rim and the liquid falling down her arms, falling, down to her knees. (*BB* 64, emphasis added)

Responding to a comment by one of the men at Deliwe's, Phephelaphi feels that what is important is not to be loved but to love oneself: 'She wanted a birth of her own' (*BB* 68–9). It is only when she can feel that she is 'all the loving that there could be' that she will 'seek something more which perhaps only another can provide, and love a man simply because she could'. Significantly, the desired other or loved-one gains a gender only in the second half of this sentence. What is desired seems to bear an unmasculine shape.

Phephelaphi therefore is a study not merely in unfulfilled but in open-ended desire. Yearning, restless, she moves away from the role of heterosexual lover, and destroys in herself, too, with her self-induced abortion, the easily essential-ised identity of mother which might have bound Fumbatha to her. Her sexual energy, her identity, her sociality, is directed beyond, to a yet-unnamed else-where. As the novel's ending searingly confirms, she is the self-consuming but-terfly of the title, straining to fly, but eventually turned in on itself, its patterns perfectly infolding. Figures comprising image-and-reflection, or inversion, can be read, as Hugh Stevens among others intriguingly points out, as traces of queer desire, that which loops back on itself without ever attaining resolution or articulation.[33] With her 'secret and undisclosed' passion, Phephelaphi, we learn, wants to be 'something with an outline'; and the outline to which her consciousness and bodily form repeatedly return is that of the butterfly. Even after the abortion she is: 'Folded into two halves, one . . . dead, the other living' (*BB* 109). She chooses to die because she cannot maintain these two halves in equilibrium, she cannot live with the betrayal of the two people who had become most important to her, Fumbatha and Deliwe (*BB* 123).

You *and* you: Tsitsi Dangarembga

Diana Fuss and Judith Butler have both observed that homosexual production, including identity production, can be regarded as analogous with mime or ghost-writing. Homosexual production constitutes a self-reflexive performance, an impersonation of normative heterosexual identities, which exposes the construction that makes up any sexual identity.[34] Throughout the tale that Tambudzai tells in *Nervous Conditions*, as the first sentence of the narrative immediately emphasises, she is an impersonator. Indeed, her narrative is interleaved with doubles (Chido–Nhamo; Lucia–Ma'Shingayi; Ma'Shingayi–Maiguru, and so on). Tambu herself comes to stand in for what her brother would have been, the educated first child of the family. She is both him and not him, just as she will later act as the good or obedient version of her cousin Nyasha. She is quintessentially a boundary figure, as well as a surrogate.

It is not my task here to go into the different and changing configurations of women–women relationships through which this *Bildungsroman* complicates both the category of woman, and the oppositions between tradition and modernity, Africa and the west, the family and the individual. Susan Andrade, for example, reads the novel's dual trajectories of 'self-development' in Fanonian terms as figuring a standoff between the self-aware native (Nyasha) and an emergent national subjectivity (Tambudzai).[35] I do want to explore, however, how the central female subjects in the novel support and back each other up, and how their intricate choreography of coming together tracks pathways of desire which, as in Vera, *exceed* any normative microcosmic tale of national self-emergence. In particular Tambudzai's narrative dramatically demonstrates how the colonial reduction of selfhood – the deprivation, as Nyasha says, of 'you of you, ourselves of each other' – can only be withstood through specific, directed strategies of resistance, one of which entails friendship, another sisterhood (*NC* 200).

The bond connecting Nyasha and Tambu belongs in the domains at once of friendship and family. They are cousins, who, after an initial period of mutual alienation following Nyasha's upbringing in England, a period during which they are intently involved in scrutinising one another, come together in an intimacy which Tambu openly describes as her 'first love affair'. In their shared room, their beds arranged in parallel, these two girls – both separated from their backgrounds by the 'deep valley' Tambu also discerns in her uncle

Babamukuru, both, as they mutually confess, culturally intimidated – explore together the risky 'alternatives and possibilities' Nyasha first represents for Tambu (*NC* 37, 78, 64, 75). These are the at-once-questioning-yet-loving terms that Tambu uses elaborately to describe their relationship:

> In fact it was more than friendship that developed between Nyasha and myself. The conversation that followed was a long, involved conversation, full of guileless opening up and intricate lettings out and lettings in. It was the sort of conversation that young girls have with their best friends, that lovers have under the influence of the novelty and uniqueness of their love, the kind of conversation that cousins have when they realise that they like each other in spite of not wanting to. (*NC* 78)

Based on a fundamental sameness, or the mutual recognition of self-in-other of cousinhood (they are 'split selves', as one critic comments[36]), their relationship extends beyond girlhood friendship and involves, significantly, a shift or 'reincarnation' in Tambu's identity whereby she becomes increasingly more like Nyasha, a creature of ambiguity. Conversely, though it is Tambu who speaks often of the dangerous confusions that Nyasha represents, she herself manages to avoid the havoc and self-damage of rebellion. It is Nyasha, instead, who 'responds to challenges' and the inconsistencies of life in the colonial mission with Tambu's early intensity, to the extent of using her own starving body as a protest. Nyasha's 'strange disposition', Tambu writes, in language that could encode other possibilities, resists the starkness of 'black-and-white' certainties: she '[hints] at shades and textures within the same colour' (*NC* 92, 164).

In *Nervous Conditions*, classically, a woman achieves a new, challenging subjectivity through close interaction with a slightly older peer, another woman. In a narrative preoccupied with the question 'what is a woman?', the two friends/cousins/foster sisters explore together and reflect back at each other flexible, autonomous images of self. They achieve an impassioned sociality:

> Nyasha gave me the impression of moving, always moving and striving towards some state that she had seen and accepted a long time ago. Apprehensive as I was, vague as I was about the nature of her destination, I wanted to go with her . . . I did not want to spend . . . whole weeks away from my cousin. (*BB* 152)[37]

What is particularly important about this statement of at once respect and love is that it underlines how the cousins' mutual discovery and exploration is specifically realised through their bodily proximity and mutual bodily awareness, as well as through their striving, as in Vera, for a not-yet-defined beyond. It is indicatively when they are separated, following Tambu's departure for the Sacred Heart College, that Nyasha begins to break down and her anorexia becomes more severe. At moments of deep conflict and pain, such as after the fight between Babamukuru and Nyasha, they unembarrassedly cuddle up together in bed (*NC* 119).[38] Even after they have been apart for a while, a short while before her breakdown, Nyasha asks if she can 'get into bed' again with Tambu, explaining, 'I just wanted to see if you would let me' (*NC* 200). There seems to be in that request some sense that what is asked for is not conventionally natural or self-evident, and may well be refused. At the school dance, watching people dancing, Tambu qualifies the word 'couples' with 'heterosexual': again it is an acknowledgement that there may be forms of being together, or lying together, other than the normative (*NC* 111).

Conclusion

I have attempted to suggest that tropes of same-sex love and yearning for love offer a medium – though not only a medium – through which new forms of identity and desire in African women's writing may be explored. Queer sexuality, in other words, can be seen as a paradigm, even if disguised or embedded, through which to articulate a still-unrealised striving for self-realisation or an ethically invested expression of desire. This, in the Zimbabwean texts I have looked at, often takes place in the eyes of another same-sex subjectivity, a woman friend. Following from this my reading would propose that, even if unlikely or culturally inappropriate, it is important to try to open out and to speak this paradigm, in the interests of widening women's possibilities for articulation, witnessing and self-healing. Now that the overcompensatory mechanisms of a defensive African masculinity, and its accompaniment, the celebration of a symbolic but circumscribed motherhood, is more fully understood as an often coercive form of postcolonial nationalism, it is perhaps more than time to begin to develop an epistemology of African queerness. If, as Charles Sugnet cites Lindsay Pentolfe-Aegerter,[39] 'African' and 'woman' are contested terms both undergoing continuous revision in the postcolonial context, then a malleable, restorative aesthetics of queerness would be the first to recognise this.

Notes

1 I have laid stress on the term *yearning* in entitling this chapter as it neatly captures the force of longing, a force that is at times almost objectless, both in Dangarembga and (especially) in Vera. However, as bell hooks has commented, in the introductory essay, 'Liberation scenes: speak this yearning', to *Yearning: Race, Gender and Cultural Politics* (London: Turnaround Press, 1991), pp. 1–13, yearning also has a political dimension. She writes: 'Surely our desire for radical social change is intimately linked with the desire to experience pleasure, erotic fulfilment, and a host of other passions'. She might have added that it is perhaps in homoerotic desire that that intimate link is most complexly embedded. Indeed, speaking of Langston Hughes, she observes that, where the full recognition of a black homosexuality may

be 'dangerous and denied', homosexual longings are balanced between expression and containment, producing the (codified) 'rarefied intensity of desire' that emerges in a context of repression (p. 197).

2 Yvonne Vera, *Butterfly Burning* (Harare: Baobab Books, 1998), p. 20. Page references to this edition will henceforth be included in the text along with the abbreviation *BB*.

3 Robert Young's impressively compendious *Postcolonialism: An Historical Introduction* (Oxford: Blackwell, 2001) makes no reference to historical struggles for homosexual rights, no doubt because this area remains both contentious and context-bound as a site for political identity formation. I should like to acknowledge here discussions with Alison Donnell about erasures and non-sayings around same-sex sexuality in postcolonial studies, and her own forthcoming work in this area with respect to the Caribbean.

4 See, for example, Achille Mbembe, *On the Postcolony*, trans. A. M. Berrett *et al.* (Berkeley: University of California Press, 2001).

5 Such views were widely expressed, for example, at the time of the New Hampshire consecration, on 2 November 2003, of the first openly gay bishop in the Anglican Church. See Rory Carroll, 'Two views from the pulpit – in just one church', *Guardian* (3 November 2003), 4. However, see Ifi Amadiume's suggestion in *Male Daughters, Female Husbands: Gender and Sex in an African Society* (London: Zed Press, 1987) that female–female 'marital' relationships for Igbo market-women past their childbearing years have traditionally been not only accepted but encouraged within the community.

6 Juliana Makuchi Nfah-Abbenyi, *Gender in African Women's Writing* (Bloomington: Indiana University Press, 1997), pp. 25–8.

7 Here I might draw an example from the situation of an early twentieth-century South Asian woman of letters that is comparable to contemporary conditions to a certain extent, certainly in terms of the prevailing restrictions on libidinal self-expression. In *India Calling*, her 1935 career memoir, India's first woman lawyer Cornelia Sorabji styles herself as a tough-minded 'Man of Action'. In her work as an advocate for women in purdah she proudly represents herself as subjecting her unworldly clients to an openly scopophilic perusal, all in the name of her implied British audience's imperial and anthropological interests. She would have been horror-struck to hear such scrutiny described in terms of the desiring male gaze, though to the contemporary critical eye it may well invite those terms. Working under empire, her first priority was to conform to western ideas of propriety, to the persona of the unflappable, rational, Oxford-educated observer. Her example strongly demonstrates that no reading of desire, perhaps especially women's desire, can be dissociated from the cultural, political and economic conventions which inform and/or disallow its expression. See Cornelia Sorabji, *India Calling* [1935], ed. Elleke Boehmer and Naella Grew (Nottingham: Trent Editions, 2004).

8 Ama Ata Aidoo, *Our Sister Killjoy* (Harlow, Essex: Longman Drumbeat, 1977), and Rebekah Njau, *Ripples in the Pool* (London: Heinemann, 1975). Aidoo's novel was, significantly, completed some nine years prior to its eventual publication. On its

overall 'deviance' as an African realist text, see Rosemary M. George, *The Politics of Home: Postcolonial Relocations and Twentieth-century Fiction* (Berkeley: University of California Press, 1996), p. 233.

9 Oladele Taiwo, *Female Novelists of Modern Africa* (London: Macmillan, 1984), pp. 24–6.

10 Aidoo, *Our Sister Killjoy*, pp. 61, 64, 66–7, 76, 78.

11 Njau, *Ripples*, p. 182.

12 Celeste Fraser Delgado, 'MotherTongues and childless women', in Obioma Nnaemeka (ed.), *The Politics of (M)Othering: Womanhood, Identity and Resistance in African Literature* (London and New York: Routledge, 1997), pp. 130–46.

13 See Adeola James, 'Rebekah Njau', in James (ed.), *In Their Own Voices: African Women Writers Talk* (London: James Currey, 1990), p. 105.

14 Mary Modupe Kolawole, *Womanism and African Consciousness* (Trenton, NJ: Africa World Press, 1997), p. 15.

15 Yvonne Vera, 'Preface', in Vera (ed.), *Opening Spaces* (Oxford: Heinemann, 1999), p. 5.

16 Vera quoted in Carita Backstrom, 'In search of psychological worlds: On Yvonne Vera's and Chenjerai Hove's portrayal of women', in Maria E. Baaz and Mai Palmberg (eds), *Same and Other: Negotiating African Identity in Cultural Production* (Stockholm: Nordiska Afrikainstitutet, 2001), p. 79.

17 Tsitsi Dangarembga, 'Between gender, race and history: Kirsten Holst Petersen Interviews Tsitsi Dangarembga', in Anna Rutherford and Shirley Chew (eds), *Into the Nineties: Postcolonial Women's Writing* (London: Dangaroo, 1994), p. 345; and her *Nervous Conditions* (London: The Women's Press, 1988), p. 1. Page references to *Nervous Conditions* will be included in the text along with the abbreviation *NC.*

18 Mark Epprecht, 'The unsaying of indigenous homosexualities in Zimbabwe: mapping a blindspot in African masculinity', *Journal of Southern African Studies*, 24:4 (1998), 631–51; Stephen O. Murray and William Roscoe (eds), *Boy Wives and Female Husbands: Studies in African Homosexualities* (New York: St Martin's Press, 1998); Oliver Phillips, 'Zimbabwean law and the production of a white man's disease', *Social and Legal Studies*, 6:4 (1997), 471–91. The literary texts which acknowledge male homosexuality include Nevanji Madanhire's *If the Wind Blew* (1996), and Charles Mungoshi's short story 'Of lovers and wives' in *Walking Still* (1997). Thanks to Drew Shaw for pointing these out to me.

19 Chenjerai Hove, 'Fires burn . . .', *Shebeen Tales: Messages from Harare* (Harare: Baobab Books, 1997), pp. 123–4. On the uncertainty concerning the provenance of *ngochani*, see Murray and Roscoe (eds), *Boy Wives and Female Husbands*, pp. xvi, 197–8, 201–2.

20 See, for example, the speech reported in the *Herald* of 6 March 2002 in which Mugabe said: 'Anyone who is gay is a mad person and if we get to know, we charge them and they will go to prison. So that culture, is it a religion, I don't know, it's not our culture and we can't force it on our people. We don't want to import it to our country, we have our own culture, our own people'. Mugabe is also on record for having said that God created Adam and Eve not Adam and Steve. See Rory Carroll, 'Two views from the pulpit', p. 4.

21 See Eve Kosofsky Sedgwick's introduction, 'Paranoid reading and reparative reading', to Sedgwick (ed.), *Novel Gazing: Queer Readings in Fiction* (Durham, NC and London: Duke University Press, 1997), p. 3.

22 Judith Butler, 'On being beside oneself: on the limits of sexual autonomy', Amnesty International Lecture, University of Oxford (6 March 2002); published in Nicholas Bamforth (ed.), *Sex Rights* (Oxford: Oxford University Press, 2004).

23 Compare Emmanuel Levinas, *Ethics and Infinity*, trans. R. A. Cohen (Pittsburgh: Duquesne University Press, 1985).

24 Melissa Solomon, 'The female world of exorcism and displacement', in Sedgwick (ed.), *Novel Gazing*, pp. 445, 446, 449.

25 Florence Stratton, *Contemporary African Literature and the Politics of Gender* (London and New York: Routledge, 1994).

26 Stratton, *Contemporary African Literature*, p. 97, and see also pp. 117 and 143.

27 Obioma Nnaemeka, 'Urban spaces, women's places', in Nnaemeka (ed.), *The Politics of (M)Othering*, p. 170. The following quotation from Bâ is used by Nnaemeka.

28 Yvonne Vera, *The Stone Virgins* (Harare: Weaver Press, 2002), p. 42.

29 Vera's novels previous to *Butterfly Burning* were all also published by Baobab Books in Harare, in 1993, 1994 and 1996, respectively.

30 Ranka Primorac, 'Borderline identities in novels by Yvonne Vera', *Journal of Commonwealth Literature*, 36:2 (2001), 88.

31 Ranka Primorac, 'Iron butterflies: notes on Yvonne Vera's *Butterfly Burning*', in Robert Muponde and Mandi Taruvinga (eds), *Sign and Taboo: Perspectives on the Poetic Fiction of Yvonne Vera* (Harare: Weaver Press, 2002), p. 102.

32 See Vera, *Butterfly Burning*, p. 4, and the whole of chapter 2.

33 Hugh Stevens, 'Introduction: modernism and its margins', in Hugh Stevens and Caroline Howlett (eds), *Modernist Sexualities* (Manchester: Manchester University Press, 2000), p. 6.

34 Diana Fuss, 'Inside/out', in Fuss (ed.) *Inside/Out: Lesbian Theories, Gay Theories* (New York and London: Routledge, 1991), p. 4; Judith Butler, 'Imitation and gender insubordination', in Fuss (ed.), *Inside/Out*, pp. 13–31.

35 To explore such aspects further, see for example the essays collected in Anne E. Willey and Jeanette Treiber (eds), *Negotiating the Postcolonial: Emerging Perspectives on Tsitsi Dangarembga* (Trenton, NJ: Africa World Press, 2002), in particular Susan Z. Andrade, 'Tradition, modernity and the family', pp. 25–59; and Heather Zwicker, 'The nervous conditions of nation and gender', pp. 3–23. See Zwicker p. 22 for corroborating evidence of the Zimbabwean state's officially sanctioned homophobia.

36 Jane Wilkinson, *Talking with African Writers* (London: James Currey, 1992), p. 192.

37 See also *NC* 138.

38 Maiguru, Nyasha's mother, however, is not happy about such cuddling.

39 Charles Sugnet, '*Nervous Conditions*: Dangarembga's feminist reinvention of Fanon', in Nnaemeka (ed.), *The Politics of (M)Othering*, p. 42.

11

Beside the west:
postcolonial women writers in a
transnational frame

Man's history has to be built by the united effort of all the races in the world, and therefore this selling of conscience for political reasons – this making a fetish of one's country, won't do. I know that Europe does not at heart admit this, but there she has not the right to pose as our teacher. (Rabindranath Tagore, *The Home and the World*)[1]

Introduction: the postcolonial and the global

Contemporary readings of the *postcolonial* in literary and cultural critique often see the concept as connected in complex ways with a globalised world distinguished by transnational capital flows and widely ramifying technological networks. The *transnational* in this respect is taken as signifying the movements of peoples, signs, goods and capital that overarch or bypass the nation. According to this view, the postcolonial, like the transnational or the global, refers to multicultural, cross-border activities and commitments, combining a focus on issues of migrancy, diaspora and nomadism, with its seeming converse, a concern with questions of home and belonging. The postcolonial world by this reckoning is culturally wired like the globalised world; its systems of cultural exchange, too, are market-driven and commodified. The tacit admission is, however, that its centres of power remain concentrated, as they do, in the western metropole.

As is illustrated by my intentional confusion above of terms of description and analysis, the reading of the postcolonial as symbiotic if not at points coincident with the global can present problematically in so far as it passes itself off as diagnosis. The particular, characteristic forms of the postcolonial are elided or explained away on the basis of their alleged analogies with the global. The confusion is further compounded by the view of postcolonial*ity*, as opposed to its close verbal analogue, critical postcolonialism, as a global regime of cultural value governed by late capitalist systems of commodity exchange, as in the definition of Graham Huggan.[2] An influential outlook on the postcolonial thus correlates *processes* of globalisation with *paradigms* of cultural critique. It converts certain 'global effects' (of cultural ambiguity, hybridity, and the like), which are by no means widely accepted as applicable across the world, into normative definitions of a global, and postcolonial, condition.

This chapter does not aim to engage in a debate on whether to support or reject such explicatory definitions, although I should say that my concern is always to see the postcolonial as *oppositional* to neocolonial, global discourses rather than as collusive with them. At the same time, however, precisely because of the apparently neat conceptual fit between the contemporary understandings of the postcolonial, the transnational and the global, I should like to investigate the overlap more critically than widely accepted assumptions generally allow. I want to do so in particular by asking the question of how nationalist concerns, too, impact upon that fit. Does the national cut across, disallow or co-operate with the transnational? Such an investigation can probably be most effectively carried out by way of a comparative and symptomatic reading of two differently placed writers (both previously introduced in this book), who share transnational, or at least trans*local*, *and* nationalist preoccupations: the Zimbabwean Yvonne Vera and the New Delhi-located Arundhati Roy. Placing the two in dialogue as regards these preoccupations will achieve two main aims. First, it will implement what I have already alluded to as the interactive, cross-border dynamic of postcolonialism. Second, it will encourage 'the crucial articulation of sameness *and* difference' that is fundamental to postcolonial critical enquiry, which a generalising global or transnational focus may not adequately address.[3] Eventually, this reading should go some way to providing a critical if inevitably oblique commentary on the epigraph from the anti-nationalist internationalist Rabindranath Tagore which appears above; to suggesting, that is to say, that valorising one's country may be one way of participating in a wider global exchange.[4]

It is worth saying that to set the *non*-metropolitan Vera–Roy pairing in a comparative framework is perhaps especially appropriate in that it activates a specific political and historical definition of the transnational, which correlates, too, with more progressive formulations of the postcolonial.[5] The transnational, or *inter*national, in this sense additionally denotes the interaction and exchange of news, information, cultural influence, etc., *between* peripheries, 'between' readerships, communities and cultures of the Third World, or, as here, between writers, so at least nominally cutting out the western metropole as a venue of the exchange. To be sure, the mention of a comparative framework can appear to hark back to the at times narrow, contrastive structures of more conventional comparative literary studies, often confined to literatures in European languages, which embrace certain early versions of postcolonial studies.[6] In practice these frameworks tended either to over-relativise the different poles of the comparative, or to enforce commonalities on the basis of joint experiences of colonisation and decolonisation. If nothing else, the English language, even if adapted, modified, and so on, was regarded in readings like these as providing a definitively western medium on the basis of which the comparative might be established. Such readings, in short, were perforce routed by way of European regimes of cultural value, even if covertly so. As against such extremes, I would want to suggest that a dialogic, margin-margin comparative method should, at least ideally, minimise the intervention of the metropolitan go-between. Especially as both Vera and Roy concern themselves not so much with transnational issues as with the question, succinctly put, of the 'women's nation', a comparative linkage should help prepare the ground for a politically motivated critique of an overvalorised global transnationalism, and of the postcolonial as normatively cross-border.

As this might imply, the attempt to plot preoccupations in common between Roy and Vera is to an extent made possible by the fact that both write with an awareness of the pressure of neocolonial forces upon local lives. Representing different regions of the decolonised world, they speak of how these spaces have been stereotyped and peripheralised in relation to the west and even, in Roy's case, to one another – where, say, Africa signifies savage darkness to India as well as the west. Both writers, too, identify locally – decidedly so – yet both also gesture across frontlines, cross-nationally, especially in their efforts to foreground women's feelings and causes. Even if inadvertently, both Vera and Roy activate that description of the postcolonial as entailing cultural dialogue across national borders.

Simultaneously, however, despite such characteristically postcolonial involvements, both writers have continued to commit themselves, although often subtly and critically, to that political entity which has loomed large in processes of decolonisation as in postcolonial readings – the nation, and the house, home or enclosed room as its favoured surrogates.[7] Although evidently aware of how national structures have conventionally marginalised women, the two writers ultimately settle for the (recast) nation, if at times in a by-the-bye fashion, as establishing a legitimate political space, certainly one from which to negotiate with anonymous global/transnational forces. Even if fascinated by spatial movement and cultural change, they also – the more so – assert the importance of location and locale – the rooms, stores, verandahs, villages, where women's lives unfold. As will become apparent in the course of the chapter, the force of the cross-national comparative method will thus be ironically – and indicatively – to ground the two writers more firmly in their own particular cultural and national spaces.

Transnationalism for women

Earlier readings in this book have noted that postcolonial women writers from Africa, India and elsewhere in the (Third) world, intent upon speaking their

identity through narrative, have been hard-pressed to write a space for themselves either within or even on the margins of the postcolonial nation.
However, by engaging with their condition as women *vis-à-vis* that nation, or
in relation to a nationally circumscribed space, these writers have succeeded
even so in addressing issues of belonging that have *both* national *and* translocal
resonances, on occasion establishing cross-border affiliations as they proceed.

With this in mind, it is worth spending a moment looking more closely at
feminist postcolonial understandings of the cross-national or translocal.
(These terms are less obviously tied to the operations of multinational corporations than is 'transnational' although translocal links, too, can be forged
through globalising processes of cultural dissemination. 'International' of
course denotes a crucial Marxist legacy of internationalist organisation which
has historically, however, often sidelined women's issues.) In what ways have
feminist critics of women's writing found in the cross-national and diasporic
a hospitable axis on which to place their reading of this work? To attempt this
question should give a perspective on the hegemony of the transnational in
postcolonial criticism; those ways in which the postcolonial novel today,
defined as diasporic and multilingual, yet often Eurocentric in reference, is
seen in contradistinction to the 1960s novel of decolonisation based in the
nation. By way of bringing these queries round full circle: is it the case, as this
study may itself imply on several occasions, that the nation's exclusion of
women has contributed (along with postmodern theories of identity as fluid
and multiple) to the retreat of the nation and the rise of the transnational as a
horizon of expectation for postcolonial women writers and critics?

The contemporary understanding of the transnational/translocal is obviously closely informed not only by policies and processes relating to globalisation, but by theories of migration and diaspora. These, while addressing the
historical movements of people, are founded upon a critique of fixed origins
and ethnic absolutes: in Avtar Brah's words, diaspora 'takes account of a
homing desire, as distinct from a desire for a "homeland"'.[8] As Paul Gilroy
influentially argues in *The Black Atlantic*, cunningly shifting postcolonial and
cultural studies preoccupations from 'roots' to 'routes', modern black identities were developed in motion, through the transmission of peoples and cultural influences, through encounter and dialogue, rather than by way of a
competition between static entities.[9] One of the advantages of this shift away
from looking at identities as based on essences and set material conditions is
that it encourages the discussion of subjectivity, especially national subjectivity, as interactive as opposed to *sui generis*. The transnational axes of diaspora
and migration instate a valuable relationality between national formations,
and, as suggested, encourage comparative, interdisciplinary readings of
national cultures and literatures. Importantly for women, national identity,
like identity in diasporic contexts, is according to this perspective seen as multi-

ply inflected in relation to the different constituencies of class, religion, race, gender, language, generation, that may pertain. In the view of Doreen Massey, diaspora emphasises that the normative division of geopolitical space into the bounded, historically linear entity of the nation has to be opened out in relation to other juxtaposed and co-existent modes of spatialisation.[10]

It is here, in the area of the crossover between spaces and subjectivities, that women writers find particular affinities with the transnational and/or the translocal. In *Postcolonial Representations*, a comparative study of cultural *métissage* in women's writing, Françoise Lionnet has boldly examined the potential and significance of such relationality for women. While she does not use the term 'transnational' as such, her concern is to develop a qualifiedly 'universal' feminism that involves making constant negotiations between and across boundaries, and between the particular and the universal, in order to address the dissymmetries of power that impact on women's lives. Without disavowing the nation (which inhabits her frame of particularity), she insists on a dialogue between 'the nature and function of feminism as a global process and the social function of femininity within different cultural contexts'. This is in order, ultimately, to arrive at an intersubjective though locally grounded political space for women, where reciprocity becomes possible (an assertion of sameness as well as difference), as well as, ideally, the achievement of 'a consensus about the possibility [for women] of sharing certain beliefs'.[11] Whereas the assertion of the particular and the absolute within the nation tends to collapse the other's experience into the self's, the translocal/transnational not only allows but stimulates that other focus.

Lionnet's observations relate to Yvonne Vera and Arundhati Roy's work, in that both writers are concerned to structure their narratives to evoke women's intersubjectivity and to represent women in interrelationship. At significant points in Vera women's voices are interlinked or superimposed the one upon the other. In *The Stone Virgins* (2002), for example, as Nonceba is recovering from her wounds in hospital, images of her dead sister intertwine in her memory with remembered snatches of their conversation. In *The God of Small Things* (1997), too, Rahel's memories of her childhood frame Ammu's stream-of-consciousness as she registers her growing desire for the *dalit* Velutha. At the same time, however, Roy and Vera's novels are firmly grounded within distinct, bounded geographies, as if as a quiet reminder that the postcolonial nation and region – Zimbabwe or India, Matabeleland or Kerala – remain important sites of identity-formation and mobilisation. To put the case more strongly, these writers experiment with alternative, heterogeneous constructions of community which, however, remain characteristically nationalist in certain key respects.[12] As the globalised margins have not yet been allowed to arrive at the global system's centre – they appear to agree – the nation cannot be disbanded as a viable space for political self-expression.

Before commenting in more detail on their significant continuation of the *national* within the trans*national*, I will first look more closely at questions of self-representation, location in space and interrelationship as interpreted by these two writers. I will comment on Vera's second and fifth novels, *Without a Name* (1994) and *The Stone Virgins*, prominent in her oeuvre for their vivid spatialisation of women's experience. By contrast, her first novel *Nehanda* (1993) offers a mythopoeic (and explicitly unlocalised) rendition of the eponymous voice of the spirit-medium of the 1890s land wars or *chimurenga*, and *Under the Tongue* (1996) is the deeply internalised narrative of a victim of incest. *Butterfly Burning* (1998), also strongly spatialised, was discussed in chapter 10. Thereafter, shifting away from the topic of Arundhati Roy's reception in the west, which was the focus of chapter 9, I will offer an intertextual commentary on her first and to date only novel *The God of Small Things* and of her non-fictional polemic against transnationalism.

Large nations, small gods

Many recent commentaries have noted that the postcolonial novel in English, in particular the Indian novel, is profoundly transnational or perhaps more accurately *inter*national in terms of its informing traditions, intertextual structures of expression and modes of reception. It is in consequence of this 'internationalism' that critics have rushed to nominate the epic-size, promiscuously allusive Rushdiesque Indian novel in English as *the* desirable, hybridised other to the reviled purism of the west.[13] Although Zimbabwean fiction in English has always been more nationally centred than, say, Indian or even Nigerian writing (hence the controversy over Marechera: see chapter 8), it, too, has been international in its make-up, certainly with respect to its implied audience, and even in its social realist commitments. The writing of both Roy and Vera complies with these 'international' terms of description. Roy's novel, for instance, engages intertextually with Rushdie's manner and style. Vera, meanwhile, who like Roy has lived and studied in the west for a period of time, and whose novels arguably 'dialogue' with Zimbabwean writers like Marechera, Hove and Mungoshi, concentrates on voicing women's historical pain, an issue which, with local modifications, relates women-centred politics across the world.[14]

Therefore, although their writing does not demonstrate transborder, cross-ocean or indeed intra-Third World preoccupations in any consistent way, parallel developments and convergences in relation to particular thematic and stylistic concerns can be traced. To pinpoint such a commonality, they may both be said to explore how women's identity is formulated and reshaped in interaction with male imaginings of identity, and with shifting, often contested, conceptions of space and historical change. While they may not be centrally concerned with Fredric Jameson's allegory of the Third-World nation,[15] they are broadly involved in the fictional revision of different axes of the post-independence social imaginary, of which national subjectivity may be one. If their closest point of identification is thus in effect a negative space, that is, their avoidance of the conventional national allegory, their practice can even so be compared on the grounds of their shared concern to rework the national space from their own particular political perspectives as women.

Gillian Rose's still invaluable theory of women's space sheds further light on this idea of shifting and multiply located identity. The emphasis in her work on constelled *locales* and on diversified space as resistant to homogeneous, 'masculine' space, importantly nuances transnationalism's possible association with the system of global capitalism.[16] In particular, she observes that masculine – and for this she also reads western – forms of knowing are based on the linked premises of exhaustiveness and exclusivity: the west knows everything possible, and everything worth knowing. How then, she asks, is this discourse of engulfing exhaustiveness to be broken open? How should other forms of definition be made to apply? She offers two related pathways – pathways which connect with Brah and Massey's earlier formulations. First, Rose asserts the important existence of other axes of social identity. While this may be self-evident, the point is useful for underlining the need to explore intersections and imbrications *between* these axes. Second, she suggests, it is possible to create new possibilities for identity beyond the conventional same/other dualism by allowing for self-articulation across *gradations* of difference. In short, like Brah and Lionnet, she invites postcolonial and feminist critics to view difference *relationally*. As this implies, Rose conceptualises such shifts of power spatially, as an explosion of the centre-margin picture and the recognition instead of dispersed and diverse spatialities – those the peripheralised have tended to occupy. Borrowing a phrase from Teresa de Lauretis, Rose conceives of identity as a constellation of elsewheres, or, in Rosemary M. George's conceptualisation, subjectivity or 'home' is at once dispersed and resituated.[17]

To relate these ideas to Vera and Roy, a key common element linking their fiction is that each narrates the breaking of social, familial and national taboos, and women's consequent loss. *Without a Name* tells of rape followed by infanticide; *The Stone Virgins* of acts of horrific murder and mutilation committed as part of a civil war. *The God of Small Things* speaks in richly decorative prose of incest (again) and cross-caste sexual trespassing. In each one of these tales, the shift of women's experience to centre stage displaces, indeed replaces, the national imaginary from the foreground. The here and now is the alley, the room, the secret-house verandah, the store verandah, wherever the central characters are able, often precariously, to locate themselves (in literally peripheral spaces). Alongside this, the novels if in very different ways demonstrate an awareness of the global or translocal forces that impinge on, at times violate, these private, internal spaces. Considering how they thus witness to different kinds of cross-border interchange, transgression and self-division, the following question emerges. Is it possible to see these texts as beginning to constitute women's subjectivity as a constellation of elsewheres, that is, as coinciding with the nation, impacted by the global, yet ramifying beyond these spaces also?

In *Without a Name*, as in *Butterfly Burning* or *Under the Tongue*, Yvonne Vera is concerned to retrieve a women's discourse (often, literally, spoken), from the interstices of the heroic narrative of the nation and of the male (and colonial) domination which underpins it. While Nyenyedzi, Masvita's lover in *Without a Name*, grounds his personal understanding of the nation upon an unconditional loyalty to the land, conventionally a male medium in Vera, Masvita the central character wanders half-dead and homeless *across* the land.[18] Her rape by a freedom fighter has alienated her from this space as mythic, ancestral ground. Indeed, her rapist so identifies with the cult of the people as the land's children that he is described as having 'grown' from the earth. He also, chillingly, calls her sister ('Hanzvadzi'). Yet, far from her opposition to the 'father'-land serving as a position of strength, Masvita's wounded incomprehension of what has happened as anything other than brute violence condemns her to a sterile condition of victimhood. Hers is a desperate, destructively translocal search for a sense of autonomous selfhood. She views history and the spaces she travels through piecemeal – not relationally. In the later novel *The Stone Virgins* women as both victims *and* survivors are drawn willy-nilly into the arena of public, national, male-authored history. The novel's title refers, significantly, to San paintings in the Motopa hills in western Zimbabwe depicting virgins sacrificed before the burial of a king. In this novel the pain of history is, arguably, transcended, not through evasion but by means of confrontation, negotiation, and the slow process of healing which follows.[19]

In *Without a Name* Masvita's act of killing her baby by breaking its neck is the last and most 'frightful' in a series of dispossessions from home and tradition that began with the rape which conceived it. Her inability to claim the (male) child, signalled by her failure to name it (and so give it a lineage), is because the moment of its conception for her, too, represented the loss of 'her name', a rupture with the past and the obliteration of memory (*WN* 29, 75, 79–80).[20] It is only upon her final return to her village, when her elderly mother welcomes her by name and thus reclaims her into the interconnected matriliny, that the recovery of memory seems, even if momentarily, to become possible. Vera's intention, as she has herself said, is to insert individual narratives, including women's narratives, into the 'big history the historians write about'.[21] While this statement would appear to dislodge women from their traditional iconic yet subsidiary role *vis-à-vis* cultural nationalism, it is significant that Masvita the aberrant mother, self-excluded from the past and the land, can *even so* be read as symbolic of that nation's unfruitful, alienated condition pre-independence.

The role she plays is of course deeply negative, yet Masvita *as symbol* is in this sense broadly comparable with the Mother Africa figure of more traditional nationalist narratives. Like the nation she, too, is degraded, betrayed, violated, exploited: '1977. It was nothing to see a woman . . . with a baby fixed spidery on her back' (*WN* 36). Masvita is doubly representative, at once of the nation *and* of the displaced underclass of abused, rootless women in the nation, whose life-stories are disruptive of the conventional story of national unity. She is in fact at her most symbolic at those points where her condition emblematises contradiction. She is the nation that cannot offer its people a home; she represents the debased state of freedom in a country where women are oppressed in the name of independence, and where 'Revolution' is most fully experienced, at least in the city, as a commercial brand-name (*WN* 46, 26–7). Bearing her dead baby like 'a hole' on her back, Masvita epitomises the people's dispossession, first by colonialism, then by war (*WN* 86). She has 'lost her centre', 'the past [has] vanished' (*WN* 3); she attempts to split herself to escape her pain: 'She wanted one other of her' (*WN* 19). Produced out of these absences Masvita's deed of infanticide is an almost predictable culmination of her dislocation: the sabotage of the national family at its root.

However, as a *woman's* act the murder is also intended as an impossible strike for freedom, impossible because Masvita's identity is already split and in spatial limbo, stripped of 'fixed loyalties' – and the act is of course fundamentally destructive (*WN* 25, 34, 95–6). The single moment of transcendence which weighs against this is when, on hearing *mbira* music on the bus back to her home village, she experiences a passing feeling of benediction. It is a transitory moment, literally experienced in transit (*WN* 69). Forced to exist in an open-ended nomadic future, Masvita begins effectively to elect for this provisionality. She has learned to mistrust fully formed ideals, as well as rounded 'hand-held' consumer dreams: 'It was better to begin in sections', she feels, 'not with everything completed and whole' (*WN* 45–6, 81). The thickly stitched apron in which she winds her dead baby is picked up from a street-seller she happens to pass. Again and again her subjectivity is shaped as she goes along, negotiated in *ad hoc*, provisional ways, moving between the city and the village (*WN* 55). By implication, therefore, Masvita's groundlessness, in so far as it constitutes her 'space', is established as the medium of women in this particular postcolonial nation – a medium in which they lack or are denied a centre.

Given my concern to plot translocal movement in relation to national belonging (or the lack thereof), it is important to note that Masvita's rootless medium is far removed from the transitional spaces of the transnational migrant. By this I mean the migrant represented in postcolonial discourse as straddling countries in a state of inventive plurality.[22] Masvita, like the masses of women whose situation she signifies, does not have the autonomy or resources that would allow this kind of multicultural plenitude and playfulness to be either achieved or expressed. She represents, after all, the nation suspended in a condition of negativity. Although some of her wanderings are putatively translocal, her experience queries the value of such cross-borderline links, the more so in that the novel identifies a transnationalised freedom with the widespread delight in the city at the availability of Ambi skin-lightening cream (*WN* 26–7).

Like *Without a Name*, *The Stone Virgins* moves between the poles of the city, Bulawayo, which it tenderly maps, and Kezi, 'a rural enclave' two hundred miles away, situated in the 'other world' formed by the sacred, tumbling rocks of the Matopo hills.[23] In this novel, however, differently from *Without a Name*, the women characters are pictured as rooted within their environment, or as in a state of becoming so, whereas the men, in particular soldiers and former guerrillas, are adrift, bereft of meaning, constrained by the 'ceiling' of history (*SV* 74). As this might suggest, despite its cryptic encodings of its controversial subject matter, *The Stone Virgins* represents Vera's most historically realist work to date and a new fictional departure.

To sketch the salient details of its historical background, the novel is set around 1982/83, some two years after independence, the time when rivalries between the two nationalist forces which had battled for control of Zimbabwe, Robert Mugabe's ZANLA and Joshua Nkomo's ZIPRA, once again flared into the open. The conflict drove some former ZIPRA guerrillas, like Vera's brutalised, 'mind-scalded' Sibaso, formerly a cultural nationalist, now the Kezi woman Thenjiwe's killer, back into the hills, this time no longer supported by local communities. For its part Mugabe's government responded with the creation of a hit squad, the 5 Brigade, to crush Matabeleland's dissidence. Brutal atrocities occurred, most of them perpetrated upon civilians, which are reflected in the novel in the destruction of Mahlatini and his store, Kezi's hub of social interchange (*SV* 24–5). Rural settlements like Kezi, always 'at the mercy of misfortune', become, as the character Cephas observes, 'naked cemeter[ies]' (*SV* 26, 143).[24]

As this context suggests, Vera is concerned throughout *The Stone Virgins* heavily to qualify the valorised meanings of 'independence', 'nation', 'land', by plunging her characters without apparent explanation into horrifying situations of civil conflict and physical torture. Even the shreds of idealism that in the earlier novel clung to these terms are obliterated. The mutilated Nonceba, Thenjiwe's younger sister, alone survives the agonies inflicted upon the community. For the rest, the expectations of independence, with which Mahlatini the store-owner fully identified, are exposed as a useless dream that cannot give protection from killers who act in the name of the established national government. When Thenjiwe is decapitated by a killer who attacks her from behind, she incarnates the fate even of bold, self-possessed young women, even perhaps the confident female ex-combatants pictured on the store veranda, 'the most substantial evidence of survival there is, of courage, of struggle' (*SV* 53). The former freedom-fighter Sibaso, sheltering in the stony hills, his own mind turned virtually to stone by his 'voyage into tragic spaces', his imagination 'encumbered', becomes her seemingly motiveless murderer as well as Nonceba's assailant (*SV* 47, 74). As an authorial interjection inserted into one of his monologues puts it: 'Independence, which took place only three years ago, has proved us a tenuous species, a continent which has succumbed to a violent wind, a country with land but no habitat. We are out of bounds in our own reality' (*SV* 74). An independent history, which once seemed to hold out a bright promise, has betrayed people on all sides. Internal division has broken the nation apart.

Yet, as is predictable in Vera's work, just as intimacy can signify both physical transport and the closeness of torture, so history, like the nation, like the city of Bulawayo itself, appears in contradictory guises. Nationalist history works with the heaviness of a killer's hand, yet it may also have the 'weightlessness' (as in Kundera's lightness) of a dead spider.[25] When Sibaso returns by accident to the cultural nationalist text *Feso* that inspired his youthful dreams, the spider perfectly crushed between its pages embodies this weightlessness, this slightness and delicacy (*SV* 111). National independence may seem compromised, yet in the city independence allows Africans 'to go ... and leave, as they please' (*SV* 9). The new flag of the new nation is soiled, yet 'flaps' freely in the wind (*SV* 154). Moreover, independence allows Cephas, Thenjiwe's former lover, to bring her mutilated sister Nonceba to the city and establish for her an unthreatening, familial home at its very centre, where she can live while rebuilding her life, while receiving the medical treatment that will reconstruct her face.

As this might imply, in *The Stone Virgins* there is little that is more contradictory than the forms through which a national history is manifested. In so far as Vera habitually erases causal links between events, the violent irrationality of history that lays communities to waste expresses itself in particularly acute ways. At the same time, however, Cephas, who helps reconstitute Nonceba's life, who seeks to retrieve the past, is significantly not only male but a historian, who interprets history positively, as reconstruction. He 'works for the archives of the National Museums and Monuments of Zimbabwe' (*SV* 163), his particular project to rebuild the great home or kraal, kwoBulawayo, of the great nineteenth-century chief Lobengula. As he himself urges: a 'new nation needs to restore the past' (*SV* 165). His archival work, too, leads him back to Kezi and reveals Nonceba's plight. In this respect the process of national coming-into-being brings about regeneration as well as divisiveness.

For Yvonne Vera the heaviness of history's contradictions falls upon women's bodies. As is strongly implied in the close pairing of the sisters – Thenjiwe who is brutally killed, Nonceba who is maimed but survives – women give expression to the nation's history in both its restorative and destructive guises. The impacts of history violate and obliterate women, and exploit their vulnerability (Thenjiwe, for example, chose to live unprotected and alone). Yet the community may also 'owe [women] a destiny', where destiny signifies how the 'pattern and progress' of community life is shaped (*SV* 54). As they rebuild society, or simply remould their own lives, women *themselves* put into operation and identify with the restorative processes of history, as does Nonceba. It is in this matter of *choice* that national embodiment by women in Vera, especially in this later work, differs fundamentally from the objectification of women figures in earlier post-independence writing. Such choice, the power to 'define the world differently', is perhaps most fully expressed by those female soldiers who hang out at Mahlatini's store. Self-confident if 'unquenchably' saddened by their combat experience, they initially approach independence circumspectly as 'respite from war', not as outright victory.[26] They delay, too, in removing their camouflage. They are idealised figures, certainly, but they are also seen as less prone to sexual anxiety and delusion than the men in the community, and they are not associated with any one particular locale. In spite, or perhaps because, of how their own histories are 'disturbed' and fragmented, they symbolise the fate of the entire country. They not only define the shape of independence but are even able to identify themselves with the hope of a whole 'broken continent' (*SV* 49–55).

By drawing out these different suggestions of national identification and translocal movement, I have tried to propose that Yvonne Vera neither repudiates the nation nor, even more radically, does she reject the idea that women's lives may stand as emblems for the fate of the nation. Writing in the context of Zimbabwe's history of independence struggle, women in her view can be the interpreters of the nation's destiny, just as their bodies provide an accurate gauge of its (pre- or post-independence) condition. By contrast, transnational networks are barely mentioned in *The Stone Virgins* other than where their cultural fall-out in the form of African American jazz, or a wider-than-indigenous variety of cut flowers on pavement stalls, extends the range of escapism and fantasy available in the city's streets. For Nonceba the survivor of history, all fantasy is first to be nurtured within the sheltering space of her city flat, from the window of which the fluttering national flag is visible.

In Arundhati Roy the contrast between the gods of the 'small' – the personal, the domestic – as against those associated with bigger 'things' – national history, social regulation, transnational enterprise, patriarchy – makes an obvious if silent allusion to Jean-François Lyotard's distinction between the grand and *petit* narratives of history.[27] In *The God of Small Things*, a tale of damaged lineages and dispossession, it is predictably in relation to the smaller, peripheral spaces that the lives of women, children and *dalits* are plotted.[28]

Despite this, however, the 'vast, violent . . . public turmoil of a nation' keeps impinging: 'Worse Things' trivialise the small by contrast.[29]

In brief, *The God of Small Things* tells the story of the twins Rahel and Estha's implication in their cousin Sophie Mol's death, and their subsequent lifetime of multiple loss (of speech, family, each other). Their story repeatedly circles round its focal event, delayed till the final chapter, of their mother Ammu's doomed affair with the 'Untouchable', the carpenter Velutha. Virtually throughout, the 'drifting' adult Rahel, the 'two-egg twin' from whose point of view much of the action is narrated, feels emptied by her sorrow, trapped outside her own and the nation's history (*GST* 15–19, 52). Like her divorcée mother an inhabitant of 'penumbral shadows between two worlds', Rahel negotiates her fragile subjectivity in repeated painful encounters with the unexpected and the interstitial, the 'Unsafe Edge' and 'Blurry Ends', of that which lies outside convention (*GST* 3, 44). 'India's a Free Country', says her twin Estha with unconscious irony just before they set out on their fateful journey across the Meenachal River that will lead to their cousin's drowning and their mother's disgrace: it is the twins' single direct reference to the country they live in (*GST* 197).[30]

The small circle of the novel's Syrian Christian family (self-enclosed like the surrounding community), with its Plymouth car and 'tangerine' radio, its bourgeois privileges and international economic and educational contacts, is, if marginal to the Indian nation, nevertheless comfortably plugged into the networks of an overarching 'anglicised cultural imperialism'.[31] It was this very 'neo-imperial imaginary', along with the novel's elliptical structures of entice-ment and delay, that no doubt made for its global marketability.[32] At the same time, however, the narrative maintains a critical watch on its possible collusion with transnational regimes of cultural value. As a paradigm of this watchful-ness, the children's forbidden playground, the multivalent 'History House', once the dwelling of Ayemenem's own 'Kurtz' and called the 'Heart of Darkness', is said to signify 'history' (that is, 'important' European history) to the children precisely because they are locked out of it (*GST* 52–3).[33] It is the same building that, in the novel's present, has been converted into a five-star hotel with, on display, the restored house of Kerala's first Marxist Chief Minister (*GST* 67, 125–7). Here, too, abbreviated Kathakali performances are held for tourists – performances which do, however, help the traditional players to make ends meet. Inadvertent and/or forced complicity with global trade and commerce, these strongly contrasted images suggest, is all too inev-itable in a world where both colonial and anti-colonial structures are converted into commodities, into a 'toy history'.

The commercial and cosmopolitan complicities of Roy's novel are thus offset both by its *enunciatory resistances*, as was seen, and by what Alex Tickell has called 'the sophisticated debate over agency' – relative to its transnational but also national axes – which is conducted throughout.[34] Beginning with Ammu's comment, *à propos* of Brutus's role in *Julius Caesar*, 'you can't trust anybody', and – the unstated corollary – that there must always be someone to blame for a crisis (*GST* 83), *The God of Small Things* tirelessly worries at the problem of responsibility: the fact that it is the twins' grand-aunt Baby Kochamma who betrays the lovers; that a terrified Estha is the one who identifies Velutha to the police. The central question, who does what to whom, which the novel repeatedly poses, is a further way of reflecting the broader metatextual question concerning the work's possible global or transnational complicity back upon itself. Throughout, too, the individual and the community are positioned within criss-crossing causal webs of transnational as well as national interrelationship, which commit them to particular actions and choices. Bodies and desires, as in the repeated reference to the 'Love Laws', are strongly conceived as political.[35] Local interdictions, the novel emphasises from the start, are the product of a long history of cultural encounter that has flowed across Ayemenem in successive waves (*GST* 32–3). Indicatively, although the national entity of India seems remote, the circumstances of the twins' birth (during a blackout occasioned by the 1962 war), like the fate of the local Maoist Communist Party, are shaped by India's cross-border interactions, in both these cases with China (*GST* 40, 68). It is in relation to such forces that 'Estha and Rahel [learn] how history negotiates its terms and collects its dues from those who break its laws' (*GST* 55). As in *Vera*, the impact of history on the individual can wound as well as redeem; as in *Vera*, too, this redemptive quality is subtly interleaved with the restorative charge of a sentimental nationalism.

Roy's sense that local needs are pressed by national and international demands, that small turmoils lock into larger ones, is more starkly articulated in her anti-globalisation polemical writing, collected as *The Algebra of Infinite Justice* (2002), which reflects back on the role played by national history in her novel.[36] Exposing the contradictory destructions inflicted by multinational corporations, and the postcolonial nation's co-operation with these in the name of national pride, her non-fictional collection both probes the benefits of transnational linkups to the Indian national community, and sheds light on the emotional and imaginative make-up of her ideal Indian nation.

On the face of it, the *Algebra of Infinite Justice* essays seem as hostile to the nation as to, say, dam-building multinationals. Writing in 1998, appalled at how India's nuclear capability was touted as a demonstration of national potency, Roy in 'The end of imagination' delivers a counter-blast, an assertion of women's identity as situated outside any nation defined in chauvinistic terms. If protesting against the bomb, she writes, 'is anti-Hindu and anti-national, then I secede. I hereby declare myself an independent, mobile republic. I am a citizen of the earth. I own no territory. I have no flag. I'm female . . .

Immigrants are welcome' (*AIF* 19). The statement is of course strongly reminiscent of Virginia Woolf's 1938 declaration that, given the domination of
nation-state hierarchies by male professionals and masculine concepts of
power, she wanted no part in them. In other of the essays, deploring the rise of
fundamentalism and its association with the worst excesses of nationalism,
Roy takes a similar line, but gives it a twist. She cynically notes that 'the Greater
Good of the Nation' is defined as that which promotes multinational development, privatises natural resources and enriches the corporations involved. 'At
times there's something so precise and mathematically chilling about nationalism', she observes: that is, when it does its arithmetic with transnational
markets, purchase orders and the lifting of import restrictions in mind (*AIF*
71, 118, 133–4).

Yet when Roy delights in India's diversity and celebrates the Indian land as
offering a counterpoint to all that she deplores, it is evident that she does retain
an unmistakably national pride in her country. She appears to share the worry
of Avtar Brah, among others, that transnationalism is so tightly associated with
cognate concepts such as translocation, dislocation, displacement, that the
words nation and location which it internally embeds can dissolve out of focus.
Roy's own India with its 'fissures running vertically and horizontally', and the
Indian people with their capacity for tireless, poorly rewarded protest (*AIF*
77–81, 82), manifest to her the positive alternative not only to the monolithic
nation, but, crucially, to the depredations inflicted by global capitalism. Giving
vent to such sentiments, Roy like Vera allows herself to countenance, even if
mostly implicitly, a redefined nationalism. She holds up a feminised 'India',
consistently addressed using the feminine pronoun reminiscent of Nehru's
writing, as an alternative to the cynical, transnationally networked, post-
independence 'Nation'. In a direct reference to *The God of Small Things* and its
circumspection with regard to the 'public turmoil of the nation', she writes that
the twenty-first century may demand the 'dismantling of the Big' – big bombs,
dams, ideologies, heroes and, presumably, also nations – in favour of the small.
'Perhaps right now, this very minute, there's a small god up in heaven readying
herself for us . . . It sounds finger-licking good to me' (*AIF* 48–9). Yet at the
same time she invokes a 'we' – of a people, a community, a nation reduced in
stature – as the ground of solidarity from which protests may be mounted and
anti-KFC jokes enjoyed (*AIF* 63). On occasion she allows herself to speak in
resonantly nationalist terms: 'this is my land, this is the dream to which the
whole of me belongs, this is worth more to me than anything else in the world.
We were not just fighting against a dam. We were fighting for a philosophy. For
a world view' (*AIF* 159). Presumably she means the Gandhian world-view of
sustainable development and village co-operation, defended by the weapons of
the weak, and vehemently opposed to the caste laws interdicted, too, in *The
God of Small Things*.

'To slow a nation, you break its people. You rob them of volition' (*AIF* 121): it becomes increasingly more clear across the length of *The Algebra of Infinite Justice* that Roy, again like Vera, thinks strongly in terms of two different nations. On the one hand is the capitalised Nation, monolithic, chauvinist, neoliberal, revivalist, in cahoots with multinational companies and the World Bank, which she names the 'transnational multignome', the new Rumpelstiltskin, and reviles outright. Yet on the other hand there is a feminised India, the lower-case nation or people, defined relationally, in mainly familial terms, and from below – analogous with Vera's restorative nation – which she is happy to reinstate *(AIF* 162). Certainly, as her own political activism suggests, this nation can be mobilised on behalf of minority groups, including women – groups disadvantaged both by tradition (the Love Laws) and by the transnationalism associated with globalised capital (the outsourcing of service industries, the relocation of multinational industries to the developing world). Significantly, however, this nation, too, is constituted in cross-border, translocal, even positively international ways (through activist networks, environmental causes, participation in the same biosphere). For Roy it would seem that the two conditions – nationalist loyalty and translocal connection – are interdependent, symbiotic. Such interdependence to her can work for both good and ill.

Conclusion

As my juxtaposition of Yvonne Vera alongside Arundhati Roy suggests, the two writers agree in their affirmation of small, private *as well as* larger public spaces as sites where women's politics can be located. Importantly, however, the importance of these sites is qualified *in relation to* one another, such that something like a 'constellation' of spaces, of the woman's nation as balanced against local and translocal links, crystallises into shape.[37] In both their writing, home, such as it is (Nonceba's flat, the Ayemenem family house), is seen as the intersection of different modes of inhabitation, the product of different narratives of history. And the nation – reclaimed rather than merely endured – is turned into one of its incarnations.

Both Arundhati Roy and Yvonne Vera therefore in their different ways calibrate the transnational with the national, and the other way about. Their texts pay attention to how transnational horizons and translocal journeys usefully disperse some of the more unitary and restrictive definitions of the nation and fragment its enclosing borders. Neither attempts anything resembling a national epic or allegory, such as authored by male writers from Mungoshi to Chinodya, from Rushdie through to Ghosh. But they do interestingly explore the impact of the nation or postcolony on women by taking the risk of representing women's stories *as synonymous with* the nation's. This is even though the narrative modes they adopt – of the confession, of the collage of recovered memory – are immediately more modest, private, hidden, intimate, than those of the conventional national story.

Both writers point out that internal quasi-/national dissent as well as transnational forces can disrupt homogeneous national spaces and identities (to the extent indeed that it may in certain instances make more sense to speak of the *postcolony* than the nation in relation to their work). In *Without a Name*, Masvita's psychic dispossession is a function of nationalist conflict as well as of colonial displacement. In Roy, by contrast, the adult Rahel's sense of being removed from her history is partly occasioned by changes the global tourism industry has brought to Ayemenem. In this case, in the face of transnational incursions, the local provides a site where memory can be regrouped and family relationships restored. Yet for both writers the nation, too, reclaimed for women as a differential space, as has been seen, can become a ground on which their subjectivity – relational, multiply located – may be expressed; a political vantage point from which demands for social justice and equality can be voiced.

By keeping the possibility of a liberatory or *women's nation* alive, but without sacrificing relationality, writers such as Vera and Roy reject the rhetoric of negativity through which the nation is almost always conventionally addressed in a postcolonial discourse that privileges diasporic border crossings, dialogic migrancy, and so on. Qualifying the transnational with the translocal *and* the national, their work queries definitions of the postcolonial not only as normatively transnational, but, by the same token, as *adequately subversive* of the global hegemonies that it itself underpins. In plainer terms, by exploring the different modes through which resistance, identity and home may be expressed, their novels deconstruct the one-dimensional equation of the postcolonial and the transnational, *and* probe its politics also. Work like theirs helps frame the question: if the postcolonial novel is exclusively viewed as participating in the transnational flows of a globalised world, does it not then merely furnish an acceptable cultural front for neoliberal market forces?

Notes

1 Rabindranath Tagore, *The Home and the World* [1919], trans. Surendranath Tagore, rev. R. Tagore (Madras: Macmillan India, 1992), pp. 224–5.

2 See Graham Huggan, *The Postcolonial Exotic: Marketing the Margins* (London and New York: Routledge, 2001), pp. 5–7.

3 See Rajeswari Sunder Rajan, *Real and Imagined Women: Gender, Culture and Postcolonialism* (London and New York: Routledge, 1993), pp. 1, 79, for her argument in favour of a postcolonial comparatism.

4 For a more extensive critical commentary on Tagore's internationalism as in fact nationalist in its make-up, see Ashis Nandy, *The Illegitimacy of Nationalism:*

Rabindranath Tagore and the Politics of Self (New Delhi: Oxford University Press, 1994).

5 As in my own *Empire, the National and the Postcolonial, 1890–1920: Resistance in Interaction* (Oxford and New York: Oxford University Press, 2002). See also Fredric Jameson and Masoa Miyoshi (eds), *The Cultures of Globalisation* (Durham, NC and London: Duke University Press, 1998), on paradoxes in contemporary understandings of the global.

6 Susan Bassnett, *Comparative Literature: A Critical Introduction* (London and New York: Routledge, 1993).

7 See Inderpal Grewal, *Home and Harem: Nation, Gender, Empire and the Cultures of Travel* (London: Leicester University Press, 1996).

8 Avtar Brah, *Cartographies of Diaspora: Contesting Identities* (London: Routledge, 1996), p. 16.

9 Paul Gilroy, *The Black Atlantic: Modernity and Double Consciousness* (London: Verso, 1993). See also Kadiatu Kanneh's critical account of Gilroy in her *African Identities: Race, Nation and Culture in Ethnography, Pan-Africanism and Black Literatures* (London and New York: Routledge, 1998), pp. 62–4.

10 See Doreen Massey, 'Imagining globalization', in Avtar Brah, Mary J. Hickman and Mairtin MacanGhaill (eds), *Global Futures: Migration, Environment and Globalization* (Basingstoke: Macmillan, 1999), pp. 27–44.

11 Françoise Lionnet, *Postcolonial Representations: Women, Literature, Identity* (Ithaca and London: Cornell University Press, 1995), p. 2.

12 As Jon Mee, 'After midnight: the Indian novel in English of the 80s and 90s', *Postcolonial Studies*, 1:1 (April 1998), 127–41, puts it, women writers strive to 'have their say' about who constitutes the nation. See in particular pp. 132 and 134.

13 Amit Chaudhuri, 'What the postcolonial Indian novel means to the west', *TLS*, 5031 (3 September 1999), 5–6. On Indian writing as influenced by colonial and cosmopolitan 'transactions', see also Harish Trivedi, *Colonial Transactions: English Literature and India* (Manchester: Manchester University Press, 1995); Tabish Khair, *Babu Fictions: Alienation in Contemporary Indian English Novels* (New Delhi: Oxford University Press, 2001).

14 On Vera's intertexts, see, for example, Ranka Primorac, 'Iron butterflies: notes on Yvonne Vera's *Butterfly Burning*', and Emmanuel Chiwome, 'A comparative analysis of Solomon Mutswairo and Yvonne Vera', in Robert Muponde and Mandi Taruvinga (eds), *Sign and Taboo: Perspectives on the Poetic Fiction of Yvonne Vera* (Harare: Weaver Press, 2002), pp. 108 and 179–90, respectively.

15 Fredric Jameson, 'Third-World literature in the era of multinational capitalism', *Social Text*, 15 (1986), 65–88.

16 Gillian Rose, *Feminism and Cultural Geography: The Limits of Geographical Knowledge* (Oxford: Polity Press, 1993).

17 Rosemary M. George, *The Politics of Home: Postcolonial Relocations and Twentieth-century Fiction* (Cambridge: Cambridge University Press, 1996), explores the re-siting of the concept of home, and indeed of critical theories themselves as sites for reconceptualising home. Following Chandra Mohanty's injunction to relocate concepts of the self and belonging away from the west, George offers home,

in the lower case, as, in her terms, a flexible, inclusive, diversified alternative to capitalised 'Home', that is to say, identity conceived in a western, national framework.

18 Yvonne Vera, *Without a Name* (Harare: Baobab, 1994), pp. 30–3. Page references will henceforth be cited in the text along with the abbreviation *WN*. See Robert Muponde, 'The sight of the dead body: dystopia as resistance in *Without a Name*', in Muponde and Taruvinga (eds), *Sign and Taboo*, in particular pp. 122–6.

19 The point is made by Terence Ranger in his essay on the figuration of history in the novel: '"History has its ceiling": the pressures of the past in *The Stone Virgins*', in Muponde and Taruvinga (eds), *Sign and Taboo*, pp. 203–16.

20 See Meg Samuelson, 'Re-membering the body: rape and recovery', in Muponde and Taruvinga (eds), *Sign and Taboo*, pp. 93–100.

21 See Jane Bryce, 'Interview with Yvonne Vera, 1 August 2000', in Muponde and Taruvinga (eds), *Sign and Taboo*, p. 223.

22 See, for example, Michael Gorra, *After Empire: Scott, Naipaul, Rushdie* (Chicago: University of Chicago Press, 1997).

23 Yvonne Vera, *The Stone Virgins* (Harare: Weaver Press, 2002), p. 14. Page references will henceforth be cited in the text along with the abbreviation *SV*.

24 See Ranger, '"History has its ceiling"', pp. 203–16. See also Josephine Nhongo-Simbanegavi, *For Better or Worse? Women and ZANLA in Zimbabwe's Liberation Struggle* (Harare: Weaver, 2000).

25 On Vera's citation of Kundera, see Samuelson, 'Re-membering the body', p. 94.

26 For a comparable representation of women combatants, see Vera, *Under the Tongue* (Harare: Baobab, 1996), p. 101.

27 Jean-François Lyotard, *The Postmodern Condition: A Report on Knowledge*, trans. Geoff Bennington and Brian Massumi (Manchester: Manchester University Press, 1983).

28 See Avadesh Kumar Singh, 'Self or motherhood: is that the question?' in Jasbir Jain and Avadesh Kumar Singh (eds), *Indian Feminisms* (New Delhi: Creative Books, 2001), pp. 118–32. In the same collection, Mohini Khot, 'The feminist voice in Arundhati Roy's *The God of Small Things*', pp. 213–22, points out that against the backdrop of closely knit matrilineal networks in Kerala, Roy represents women starkly as isolated monads.

29 Arundhati Roy, *The God of Small Things* (London: Flamingo, 1997), p. 19. Page references will henceforth be cited in the text along with the abbreviation *GST*.

30 As Chaudhuri, 'What the postcolonial Indian novel means', pp. 14–15, says, Indian writers, especially perhaps writers in the vernacular or *bhasha*, 'do not necessarily write about "India" or a national narrative . . . but about cultures and localities that are both situated in, and disperse the idea of, the nation'.

31 See Khair, *Babu Fictions*, pp. 142–3.

32 Huggan, *The Postcolonial Exotic*, p. 77; Aijaz Ahmad, 'Reading Arundhati Roy politically', *Frontline* (9 August 1997), 103–8.

33 In interview Roy has elucidated that the 'Heart of Darkness' reference, even while something of a 'laughing' throwaway, draws attention to the stories of those who live in darkness, who are meant to have no stories. See Praveen Swami, 'When you

have written a book you lay your weapons down', interview with Arundhati Roy, *Frontline* (9 August 1997), pp. 106–7.

34 See Alex Tickell, 'Arundhati Roy's postcolonial cosmopolitanism', *Journal of Commonwealth Literature*, 38:1 (2003), 76.

35 Brinda Bose, 'In desire and in death: eroticism as politics in Arundhati Roy', *ARIEL*, 29:2 (1999), 59–72.

36 Arundhati Roy, *The Algebra of Infinite Justice* (London: Flamingo, 2002). Page references will be quoted in the text together with the abbreviation *AIF*.

37 As Nana Wilson-Tagoe, 'History, gender and the problem of representation', in Muponde and Taruvinga (eds), *Sign and Taboo*, pp. 155–78, too, emphasises, the individual's experience of history is transformed in relation to changes in the collective's sense of history, and *vice versa*.

12

Conclusion:
defining the nation differently

In some notable instances, as has been seen, women writers work to transform the male lineaments of the postcolonial nation. In others, they attempt merely to decipher and to modify its structures of privilege. Although the topics and texts discussed in this book have varied widely, the foregoing chapters have been linked by their shared concern with the strategies used by novel writers, women but also men, to recast the colonial and patriarchal symbolic legacies embedded in many versions of post-independence nationalism. These strategies, which are often interlinked, have included what has been called *literalising* inherited gender-marked tropes – concretising and ironising them – and also *reconfiguring* them in different ways, not least through the deployment of testing, teasing or disruptive narrative styles.

The question left open, however, is whether this recasting and reconfiguring represents a divestment from the nation-state on the part of writers – those who are often set up as the unofficial dreamers of national dreams. Or, alternatively, does it signify an effort to rework national belief to assume a different, more inclusive and progressive form? Is nationalism a discourse that can be challenged, dismantled and rethought even as the necessary efforts are made towards the accommodation of its Third World realities, as R. Radhakrishnan has put it?[1] Can its idealising tendencies be calibrated with reference to the day-to-day contexts through which it is expressed in the world? And if so, can it be rethought in a feminising or more woman-centred direction, so as to acknowledge the discriminations it has helped propagate in the past, and revise or disaggregate its masculinist inheritances from the ground up? Some feminist theorists of nationalism would indeed insist that anything other than a comprehensive overhaul would merely produce another version of the traditional national family drama in which the father is positioned 'on top'. Nationalism, they contend, must work to incorporate a gender-aware imperative if it is to be rethought in a fully liberatory and transformative way.

In their attempts to reappraise national symbolic histories and the narrative forms into which they are cast, women writers extending from Flora Nwapa in the 1960s to Arundhati Roy in the new twenty-first century have, my readings indicate, tended to take the approach of redress rather than out-and-out reconfiguration. To generalise grossly for a moment – they have explored in particular the iconic home and family as the preserves of the traditional values beloved of the nation, dramatising how women's roles and responsibilities have shaped this private sphere. They have shown how family relations and spaces have, despite a binary legacy of gendered symbolism, overlapped in a variety of ways with the male-controlled public sphere of the nation-state, more intricately and densely so than Jameson's theory of the national allegory, for one, allows. Consider, for example, the case of Emecheta's Debbie Ogedemgbe the civil war soldier (chapter 6), or, more substantially, the attempts by writers like Arundhati Roy and Yvonne Vera to shape the nation from a woman's perspective (chapter 11). By probing and nuancing images of the gendered nation, by 'interrupting nationalist discourse with a women's vocality', writers like Emecheta and Roy have powerfully demonstrated how 'small' familial and domestic realities impinge on the large questions of the nation-state. The public narrative of the nation both is, and is not, separate from the *petit récits* of grand/mothers', aunts' and daughters' lives.[2] As in the case of the civilian women who during Zimbabwe's liberation war deftly negotiated between the combatants' bases and the civilian 'keep' or compound, women play several roles relative to the new nation, not only as 'mothers of the struggle' and providers, but as political activists, agents of history.[3]

The Zimbabwean example is apt in this context considering that women writers, like feminist critics of women's writing, appear to encounter a particular difficulty in envisaging roles and spaces through which women might mobilise political power outside of conventional structures, such as that of the nation-state.[4] Given existing hierarchies of privilege, the question is whether it is possible for women to conceive a mode of political leadership that is neither co-opted nor subtly marginalised, nor indeed vulnerable to endless metaphoric expansion (as in 'mothers of the struggle'). While the 'stories of women' explored in this book have outlined many different strategies and subterfuges through which *individual* women wield influence and power, they have also suggested the tentative beginnings of a response to this question in their joint attention to *community*. This is as opposed to the situation of many male postcolonial writers, such as those discussed in chapter 8, whose response to the neocolonised nation or postcolony has been (no doubt understandably) bleakly pessimistic. Flora Nwapa, Bessie Head, Tsitsi Dangarembga, Manju Kapur, Arundhati Roy in her political writing, all at one or other point affirm the power of the *collective*, of women in solidarity, community or colloquy with one another. Moreover, they emphasise the importance not simply of community as such, but of translocal connections of support and interchange *between* communities. They claim the prerogative of *defining the nation differently* – as do Yvonne Vera's women combatants on the verandah of Mahlatini's store in *The Stone Virgins* – not as a single-cell entity, but as gangliar, operating through exchange, network, juxtaposition and interrelationship.

As the final chapter of this book demonstrated, the writer-activist Arundhati Roy provides an emblematic instance of such *defining otherwise* when she rejects the cultural chauvinism of the corporate, privatised Indian nation-state while at the same time acclaiming what she sees as the real India, the feminised land and 'her' people'. The stories through which women narrate their subjectivity, like the diverse groups and communities through which they may seek to wield power, are characterised by such iconoclastic, *heterogeneous identifications* – moulded, too, by where the women situate themselves along the axes of differentiation of race, religion, region, sexuality, class and nation. Through the medium of their layered narratives featuring networks of interrelationship and friends in powerful pairs, woman writers may lay claim to several social spaces at once – spaces which also intersect with the 'scattered hegemonies' (in Caren Kaplan's phrase) of the transnationalised world. As in the woman-centred, yet nation-affiliated work of the contemporary Indian writer Manju Kapur, as in Roy, women reclaim the nation by working with and within these networks. This book will close with a comparative reading of Kapur's two novels (to date), which will epitomise a particularly compelling if controversial way in which the (re-)engendered nation might be reclaimed as a structure of feeling, if not of passion, for women.

Yet, in order that the concept of the constellated-yet-national postcolonial collective not be seen as exclusive to women, just as gender is something not pertaining to women only, it is instructive to draw on an alternative image of the nation, or a nation-of-sorts, from Achebe's *Home and Exile* (2000).[5] Traditional Igbo cultural and political life, Achebe writes in this memoir, was based on a conglomerate system of co-operative villages, the complicated workings of which were embodied within (and illustrated by) its 'intricate and vibrant [market] network'. This decentred network, through which goods, news and new ideas for songs were constantly exchanged, was one, he further notes, for which women had responsibility. Neatly weighed against his story of the 'girl at war' featured in my introduction, Achebe's sketch of an internally networked nation, enshrining community values yet incorporating individualism, and part-managed by women, traces another pathway towards a concept of the nation with which women might choose to identify.

But why do I insist upon testing the viability of that seeming historical impossibility, the 'woman's nation'? Is it not the case that, regardless of the communal and/or postcolonial incarnation it may assume, the nation is inimical to women's self-determination and is therefore to be rejected as a woman's space? From the evidence of postcolonial women's writing the answer to this last question would appear to be no. No, women in the post-independence and neocolonial world do not on balance choose to rid themselves of the nation. Their preferred country – to quote Virginia Woolf one last time – is not the cosmopolitan (and inevitably Eurocentric) 'whole world'. What is instead the case, especially in the context of increasing globalisation, is that women tend to explore and attempt to *adapt* the nation as a site through which their particular relational brand of politics may be organised. They may of course choose to break down the embedded structures of the *state* as the organising principle of political culture. But at the same time the nation – *their* nation – becomes a crucial interface between, on the one hand, market-driven, frequently hyper-exploitative transnational relations, and, on the other, local issues and venues, which have a tendency to become inward-looking, obsessed with cultural authenticity, resistant to change.[6]

Despite the globalisation of national economies and of communication technologies, political, social and cultural management in the world today remains divided along national borderlines, as Samir Amin and Neil Lazarus among others contend.[7] The nation-state continues to be an important agent in the world political order, a countervailing force to transnationalism: it retains the power to regulate the operations of capital and, culturally, to delimit some of the more serious outrages of fundamentalism. Of course, as numbers of women critics, Deniz Kanyoti and Natasha Barnes among them, have argued, the achievement of postcolonial national independence has, to this day, nowhere brought the concomitant liberation of women citizens.[8] Transitions from colonial and other authoritarian rule are often forged by way of 'elite pacts' between men. Yet it remains the case – contradictory as this may seem – that nationalism holds an undying attraction for many women, especially in new or post-independence nation-states. As Djurdja Knesevic writes of the Croatian context, or Mamphela Ramphele of the South African, the nation encourages a sense of *belonging to*; it provides channels through which women can mobilise and take part in public debate.[9] Symbolically, too, albeit in a backhanded manner, the nation can be seen as invoking the prominence of women's roles in the imagining of a community in ways that postcolonial women writers from Buchi Emecheta through to Carol Shields have found enabling.

Given that from the point of view of women political and cultural freedoms cannot be expected as the natural harvest of independence and must therefore be claimed, the nation continues to be for women – as for other minorities – an unforgoable or irrefutable means through which to forge such claims. And if there are admittedly multiple instances of the nation-state failing to deliver on its promises of freedom for all groups, the difficulties of the nightmare-ridden postcolony must be set in the context of the continuing neocolonial domination of the Third World by the west (and of excessive post-independence idealism). When all is said and done, nationalism, with its defining attributes cross-hatched out of myth and historical legend, provides a new civil society with a usable past and a serviceable set of cultural identities. True, the nation in many instances intolerantly identifies itself in contradistinction to an 'other' and therefore quickly raises enemies, yet globalisation, too, is arguably based on very similar premises, as the current global war on terror chillingly demonstrates.[10] In fact it is probably the case that the forces of globalisation disallow diversity and sabotage claims to rights far more thoroughly than the nation ever did.

If, finally, in contradistinction to the uniformity imposed by transnational capital, the modern nation channels what both Anthony Smith and Perry Anderson acknowledge as the overpowering drive within cultures to establish collective meaning, do we not then uncover further persuasive grounds for recuperating the seeming oxymoron of the 'women's nation'?[11] By way of the reading of Manju Kapur which follows, I will ask whether the nation has not paradoxically come into use for women as a refuge and site of sisterly, even homoerotic, resistance – a resistance not only to global market forces from without but to religious fundamentalism from within. Does the nation not provide a base where valuable cultural and libidinal solidarities for women may be claimed and recuperated?

'First realise your need': Manju Kapur

Manju Kapur specialises in the telling of ordinary, apparently insignificant women's stories – stories that provide extended footnotes, pitched from a woman's perspective, to the official narrative of Indian nationalism. *Difficult Daughters* (1998) and *A Married Woman* (2003), her two published novels, each take the tale of an individual woman's *Bildung* from young adulthood through marriage, work and motherhood as their central narrative strand.[12] Fulfilling a principle of the *petit récit*, the novels' narrative structure is comprised in each case of short snapshots or snatches of day-to-day life, including letters, diary entries and first-person interjections from one or other of the main characters, often set up like monologues in a play. Significantly, as in Vera and Roy, both novels concentrate on the articulation of personal emotions and feelings, in particular on erotic self-fulfilment.

However, where in *Difficult Daughters* a personal *jouissance*, or women's self-expression generally, is placed in a marginal position in relation to the authoritative narratives of the traditional family on the one hand, and the coming-into-being of the nation on the other, in *A Married Woman* the situation is, intriguingly, reversed. Here the narrative of erotic (specifically and subversively of homoerotic) self-awakening is identified, even if implicitly, with the increasingly embattled narrative of secular nationalism. My concluding paragraphs will revolve around this fascinating shift of focus in Kapur – one that intertwines intriguingly with the May 2004 shift in the fortunes of the Congress Party. For, if the taboo *petit récit* of a liaison between two women, a widow and a wife, is offered as a protest against communalism, what does this say about women's revised relationship with the secularist, formerly hegemonic nation?

In *Difficult Daughters*, set during the years preceding Partition in the cities of Amritsar and Lahore, Kapur movingly evokes the multiple frustrations encountered by the central character Virmati in her efforts to educate herself and establish a domestic space she can call home. Struggling to integrate her aspirations for learning (initially identified as a masculine terrain) and her desire for a love match, Virmati endures and survives a clandestine abortion, a socially condemned affair, self-chosen marriage, and the difficult position of second wife. Unlike her decisive, politically involved friend Swarna Lata (but *like* the diverse 'national' daughters discussed earlier), Virmati spends long periods of time 'soft' with compliance, languishing in her incapacity to assert herself, in particular *vis-à-vis* her domineering if well-meaning lover (*DD* 236).

Yet, although she is often alienated and alone, Virmati's story is not singular, as the title *Difficult Daughters* itself suggests. Her narrative is woven into a lineage of three generations of daughters, extending from Kasturi, Virmati's mother, through to Ida, Virmati's daughter and the novel's narrator, each one of whom grows alienated from *her* mother while negotiating between the poles of 'Education versus marriage' (*DD* 38, 57). By thus probing daughter–family relations, Virmati's story refracts the divisions between mothers and daughters as correlates for the political partition in the country at large. In this novel daughters' lives *do* parallel national history, though negatively so. Virmati in her wrangling with tradition and authority reflects the turmoil in the public political world, though she is also positioned, paradoxically, as peripheral to national debates. Daughterhood signals 'difficulty' therefore, not only in so far as it denotes rebelliousness, but because daughterhood – traditionally subordinate and dependent – itself represents a difficult or painful position. Moreover matrilineal links, however full of potential, by no means guarantee a continuity of communication across the generations (*DD* 190, 203–4). After her marriage Virmati is symbolically cast out of her mother's house and forced to find her own way. Her punishing exile ends only when the massacres of Partition make her family's continuing rejection untenable.

It is a sign of Virmati's marginality that events surrounding the struggle for Indian independence and the creation of Pakistan are relayed in the novel by way of external report, at times almost as an official voice-over. Harish the Professor, Virmati's married lover and then, much later, husband, interprets the progress of the Second World War and its implications for India through occasional commentaries paternalistically intended as educative. At the end of the novel Nehru is quoted speaking with heavy, retrospective irony of a free and inclusive India (*DD* 252). Other than this we are preoccupied with the affairs of Virmati's heart and her conflicted quest for education – that is, her negotiation, central to many Third World women's lives, between the apparently opposed points of tradition and modernity, which repeatedly threatens her social position and her peace of mind. Rather than being in any sense a building block of her identity therefore, the nation at first features mainly as a subject her lover brings up in conversation. In this sense Virmati sets to one side the male-identified nation as much as she is set to one side or excluded by it.

Towards the end of *Difficult Daughters*, Virmati, a married woman at last, exiles herself from her marriage to continue her education in Lahore. Rather than being perverse, this balancing of options has become her preferred mode of being (*DD* 169, 231, 235–6). She now *elects* to occupy a split space-time or domestic limbo, separate from her husband. From the beginning her dogged attempts to cope with the demands of love against independence have committed her to a series of successive confinements in intractable situations and enclosing, stifling rooms. The 'small' Lahore house where she goes to work on her MA is but the latest in a succession of imprisoning places: the godown, 'poky' student room, two-room hill cottage, and the dressing-room that is the only available place to conduct her married life (*DD* 231, 80, 105, 168). Faced throughout with new beginnings, degrees, teaching positions, she attempts with each new bid for escape to put the past behind her, '[blanket] everything in oblivion' (*DD* 182, 125). Yet with every door she closes, a new confining room appears to shut her in. She becomes reconciled to her difficult choices therefore only by living out a kind of modern schizophrenia, in effect a self-partition, choosing to occupy tenuously linked locations in her unconventional role as a wife who remains a student.

If *Difficult Daughters* is to be read as a *re*inscription of the male-authored nation and the history of middle-class self-determination from which it derives, it is significant that Virmati's story effectively undermines the structures of western-origin romance. In a romance plot the narrative closure provided by marriage conventionally connotes the successful achievement of national and/or bourgeois class identities: take, for example, the ending of E. M. Forster's *Howards End* (1910) or indeed of Ngugi's *A Grain of Wheat* (1967).[13] By contrast, marriage merely brings Virmati a new phase of emotional agitation and discomfort, as well as professional compromise and continuing social embarrassment. Kapur's romance plot carries an alien, even ridiculous imprint in so far as the Oxford-educated Professor, a reader of Wordsworth, is a classic mimic man who sees Virmati as his Romantic 'other soul' and Pygmalion-like tries to remake her in his image. In an emblematic, tragicomic scene during the final, critical stages of their courtship, Harish explains to Virmati the touching significance of a picturesque hill tomb commemorating the loyalty of a colonial wife who survived her medical officer husband by several decades. Virmati's response is literal, cynical and uncompromising: "'Silly woman! . . . Staying for thirty-eight years. Just because her husband had died there'" (*DD* 177). For a woman, unlike for a man, she perceives, marriage and parenthood do not equate with public success, or the accession to an important national or civic role. All the same, just as she rejects the compromises of classic romance, so, too, does she elide the conflicts of emergent India when she is pregnant, choosing to bask in a dry swimming pool, an anomalous island in the storm. For her both romance and the nation signify the unwelcome surrender of self to the collective will.

It is of course true that Virmati's dogged attempt to survive against all odds while at the same time erasing the past can be read at one level as an extended metaphor for the fate of Pakistan, and to a lesser extent India, at Partition. *Difficult Daughters* itself, although a daughter's rather than a national son's story, would according to this reading emblematise the nation and fulfil the terms of Jameson's hypothesis 'writ small', as Susan Andrade would put it. To support this interpretation, the social and political situation in Lahore as well as in Amritsar at times mirrors Virmati's personal state. This is made explicit when she comments: 'I fret about my petty, domestic matters, at a time when the nation is on trial. I too must take a stand. I have tried adjustment and compromise, now I will try non-cooperation' (*DD* 239). Simultaneously, however, Virmati feels increasingly cut off from the city, as she does from her past – and as Lahore indeed is from the Indian nation (*DD* 232). The obvious analogy is with Saleem Sinai's amnesia over the creation of Pakistan in Rushdie's *Midnight's Children* (1981).

Yet to see Virmati's life as bearing the weight of the national symbolic is to erase the tensions, contradictions and accidents from her meandering story. One of the more resonant of these tensions occurs at the very end of the novel when, overcome by the tragedy of Partition, it is Harish who refuses the name Bharati (India) for his daughter, a name Virmati suggests. Exclaiming that rather than being born his country has descended into atavism, he rejects the national narrative as treacherous, and in so doing decisively breaks the metaphoric link of submissive woman and emergent nation. Instead their daughter is given the name Ida, 'two letters short of India'.[14] In other respects, too, the novel deliberately falls short of attempting to represent the 'public turmoil' of the nation. It offers by its own admission a women's story based on personal history and, though it concedes that women may be interpellated by the national cause, it warns that unless they have political and social power they should be wary of any such link.

If *Difficult Daughters* steers a path around the national imaginary, although always with reference to it, *A Married Woman*, despite its provocative homoeroticism, is by comparison firmly committed to the success of the secular nation. Even if it at times questions its political efficacy, it takes its imperatives of social justice seriously. Largely set in the sprawling suburbs of Delhi in the late 1980s and early 1990s, against the historical background of the Babri Masjid crisis in Ayodhya, the novel follows more or less the same line of development as *Difficult Daughters*, tracking an individual woman's life from young adulthood into maturity. In this case, however, the emphasis, certainly at first, is on the monadic individual and the nuclear family, rather than the individual's relations to the extended family or to tradition. Written in part while the author was abroad, *A Married Woman*'s tale of the middle-class quest for self-improvement and self-pleasuring is recognisably informed by western values of individualism and of personal desire as a viable site of self-realisation. A related westernised focus colours the language which is less conversational than in *Difficult Daughters*, less grounded in the untranslated Hindi signifiers which were a localising feature of the earlier novel: *almirah*, *tikki*, *gol gappa*, *samagri*, and so on.

Brought up on a diet of 'mushy novels', Astha the eponymous heroine of *A Married Woman* (her name – ironically – means 'faith'), is from the beginning in quest of 'true love' (*MW* 8). At the same time she feels drawn to the 'safe and secure' – it is this tendency which will ultimately determine her decision to stick with her unsatisfactory but financially stable marriage to the businessman Hemant Vadera. After a few romantic mishaps she finds considerable erotic satisfaction in the early days of her attachment to him, an attachment benignly choreographed by their families. Already at this early point, the central character's development begins to diverge from, while also intertextually commenting on, that of Virmati in *Difficult Daughters*. There, individual choice in matters of love led to repeated emotional betrayals and deferred desire. Here, an arranged marriage brings delayed but real sexual gratification (*MW* 46), and proves to have considerable holding power, surviving the rearing of two children, life with the in-laws, work outside the home for both partners, and Hemant's suspected one-night stands.

The greatest test which the marriage faces, however, is Astha's desire for self-fulfilment and some measure of autonomy away from the family, a goal which she conceives of in canonical western feminist terms as being true to herself, an escape from feeling misunderstood, 'throttled, and choked' (*MW* 109, 167). She is 'fed up with the ideal of Indian womanhood, used to trap and jail' (*MW* 168). The singularity of her quest is offset by the fact that the relationship with Hemant is viewed by virtually everyone other than Astha herself as based, correctly, on wifely self-sacrifice, as against the phony marriages of mutual convenience allegedly contracted by non-resident Indians in America (*MW* 40–1). As with the woman-loving undertones of Vera and Dangarembga, Kapur in this novel is interested in those female potentialities that exceed the possibilities for relationships sanctioned within the confines of the traditional family and its analogue, the nation-state.

Astha's painting, her primary vehicle of self-expression since childhood, is raised to new heights of inspiration when she becomes involved in political protests against the Hindu fundamentalist movement aimed at razing the Babri Masjid in Ayodhya. Built by Emperor Babur on the site, it is said, of a destroyed Hindu temple, the birthplace of the god Ram, the mosque is eventually pulled down in late 1992, as the novel reports at its end, and becomes the flashpoint of serious communal tensions across India (*MW* 290–1). The first step in the politicisation of Astha's art occurs when, in response to a request from an activist, Aijaz, she writes a dramatic script about the Masjid's history for a theatre workshop (*MW* 110–11). The second step comes not long after with the Muslim Aijaz's death at the hands, it is presumed, of Hindu fundamentalists. Astha's paintings are then sold to raise money for the Manch set up in his memory. Even if circumscribed by family commitments and her husband's resistance, Astha's agency as an artist, it becomes clear, is given direction by this political activism, and her social awareness in turn primes her for exercising a new-found autonomy as her friend Pipeelika's lover. '[Painting] represented security, not perhaps of money, but of her own life, of a place where she could be herself' (*MW* 149–50).

Within the pro-secular terms laid down by the novel, it is significant that a cultural movement pitted against fundamentalism is directly responsible for drawing Aijaz's widow Pipee and Astha together in a self-delighting, intensely physical affair. As *A Married Woman* itself suggests, the Babri Masjid crisis from its beginning denoted for Congress and other secularist nationalist parties a serious crisis of confidence in the brand of non-sectarian politics that had sustained the Indian nation since independence. They found to their shock that they did not in fact have a sufficiently powerful purchase on the nation's cultural capital, certainly not one powerful enough to mount an adequate countervailing force to withstand the upsurge of religious feeling which animated the fundamentalists. Astha's throwaway line, 'I don't need religion, whatever I am', spoken in response to her mother's growing devoutness, is a marker of this widespread secular disengagement (*MW* 85). Ayodhya demonstrated that at the level of mobilising the spiritual and private domains of society (those areas of culture and belief conventionally presided over by women), fundamentalist nationalism had the distinct edge over secular state nationalism with its rationalist emphases on self-determination and democratic rights.

It is into this lack within the Nehruvian tradition and, by extension, within the market-driven nation-state, that the woman-centred passion and respect shared by Astha and Pipee is strategically allowed to flow. The novel explicitly chooses *not* to mobilise religious belief of any description, even though its heroine is called Astha.[15] Its alternative to the strong affective hold of religion is an emotionally invested, mutual relationship, especially though not exclusively intimacy between women, the kind of relationship that is relatively unspoken in the Indian women's novel in English. The women's feelings (and the fact they are reciprocated) are set up in contradistinction to, on the one hand, the fullness represented by a communal sensibility, for both women and men, and, on the other, the unbridled individualism represented by India's economic neoliberalism, which is Hemant's domain.[16]

To deflect the charge that her alternative domains of intimacy are merely western and middle-class in derivation (as of course was Nehru's modernising nationalism), Kapur significantly chooses not to describe Astha and Pipee's relationship in terms of a conventional western vocabulary of lesbian queer or homoerotic desire. In this way she strategically sidesteps, if perhaps not entirely convincingly, the widespread controversy which films such as Mira Nair's *Kamasutra* (1996) or *Fire* by Deepa Mehta (1996) met, both of which showed graphic erotic exchanges between women.[17] If anything, the novel's language of female love is decorous, modest, even chaste. At the height of the affair there is much lingering description of the women's (largely non-western) clothing, of dupatta, sari and blouse tantalisingly revealing and concealing, of the delight of touching arms, breasts, fingers, the focus remaining on the upper body. Intercourse itself is conceived of in terms of an abstracted 'mind-fucking', Hemant's sceptical term for what he believes women in love share – literally visualised by Astha as intercourse in the head (*MW* 218).[18]

In terms of the politics of the relationship, too, this sexual reserve or relative conservatism is corroborated: there is no significant disruption of conventional heterosexual identity-formation. Pipee insists all too soon on becoming the dominant partner, so repeating the power differential between Astha and her husband and precipitating the breakdown in their affair (*MW* 233, 234). Astha never uses the words lesbian or woman-loving of herself. She is not given to looking into her sexuality to that extent. She also avoids any allusion to adultery and finds the prospect of leaving her family to set up with Pipee unthinkable (*MW* 232). To Pipee's disapproval, and eventual indifference, their love is always subsidiary to the marriage with Hemant. It is a diversion, not a rival to that socially established bond: 'So far as her marriage was concerned, they were both women, nothing was seriously threatened' (*MW* 232). For the lovers to spend time together, they must occupy, uncomfortably, the hidden, child-free spaces of Pipee's flat.

As the references to women's domains and hidden space will have suggested, Kapur rouses the suspicion that to locate a sufficiently powerful cultural alternative to religious nationalism, she must make a move reminiscent of the masculine nationalist discourses of the past. Yet, given prevailing prejudices, she must do so in a circumscribed, perhaps even compromised, always-already co-opted way. As in Tagore or Bankim, she offers private, feminine space as the central locus of the cultural nation. A creative, self-realising love between women is set up in contradistinction to the self-abnegating love of the divine. But this is not all. Problematically but perhaps unavoidably, Kapur goes one step further by not only eroticising but homoeroticising this love – a step which commits her to raising or rousing the stereotype of the secret, allegedly lesbian passion of the eastern woman. Despite her precautions she runs the risk, in other words, of basing the cultural heartland of the nation within the *ne plus ultra* of orientalist discourse, the colonial 'phantasm'.[19] The activist Aijaz in fact draws a direct analogy between Pipee's love for other women and the strong ties shared by women in the zenana (*MW* 129).

It is a sign of the historical and moral difficulty that women's erotic mobilisation represents in *A Married Woman* that the narrative is committed to so many complex, contradictory conflations, which function either as tactical diversions or as a mode of self-censorship. Astha's is but is not a gay relationship. It is but is not conceived in westernised terms. It is within a domestic space, though an alien, sterile one, that her affair runs its course. It is when she is politically conscientised that Astha becomes aware of Pipee's erotic interest in her, yet her involvement with Pipee also distracts her from the Ayodhya tragedy and eventually leads her back to the solitary, if politically preoccupied, activity of painting. Kapur references a whole matrix of cultural resources to which different configurations of the Indian nation have traditionally had recourse: home, the mother (Astha), the widow (Pipee), the realm of the private, the harem, the *Kamasutra*, symbolic art. And yet, such is her sense of crisis concerning the future of secular nationalism that she pushes these well beyond their conventional meanings into both radical and taboo areas. There is a connection here with Tsitsi Dangarembga's *Nervous Conditions* (1988), where the loving friendship between the cousins Nyasha and Tambu builds an alternative space of interactive self-identification for women, one which does not, however, reject the bourgeois story of nationalist coming-into-being.

Indian women, Inderpal Grewal observes, have historically resisted hegemonic nationalist formations 'by rearticulating [the home] as a site of struggle rather than of resolution'.[20] Astha comes closest to rearticulating fundamentalist formations from the site of her subversive love affair when she and Pipee briefly join a Yatra or pilgrimage across India in the train of a religious 'Leader', organised to demonstrate belief in the united motherland (*MW* 157–8, 184–6, 193, 246 ff). Although Pipee has professional reasons for her participation, and both women are happy about the opportunity of spending time together, the Yatra soon inspires in Astha a different sort of excitement, stimulated by the symbolic geography of the trip. At the beginning, for example, the lovers stand together at the southern tip of India, viewing with interest the Vivekananda Rock (*MW* 256–7). Later, during time she has to herself, Astha begins to reflect on the diversity of India and what it signifies ('The Oneness underlying The

Difference' (*MW* 258)). She is generally delighted to discover new areas of the country. It is as if, as she concedes to her diary, she has fallen into the rhythm of the Yatra Leader's thoughts (*MW* 258); as if, indeed, she were plotting an alternative sentimental journey away from her lover and towards the mythic nation. While taking pains to distinguish her India from the Bharat Mata worshipped by fundamentalists (who, as she recognises, enchance their masculinity in serving the nation), she begins implicitly to position herself as the daughter of a nation intriguingly defined in masculine terms. Back in Ayodhya she has already allied herself with a network of affiliation to 'Gandhiji, father of the Nation' (*MW* 198, 203).[21] Now she finds that the nation's trumpeted qualities of 'patience, tolerance, love and resignation' are qualities she seeks in vain in Pipee (*MW* 260). Unsurprisingly, the Yatra represents both the culmination point and the end of their relationship.

As Astha's pilgrimage suggests, in Kapur a homoerotic plot is made to cooperate even if in unlikely ways with an edgy – sceptical yet emotive – narrative in defence of the secular nation (*MW* 216). Whereas previously a concern for the propriety of the nation might have denied any such alliance, now a concern for its survival as a unified polity – as unity in diversity – encourages the co-operation, especially considering that the greater evil from the point of view of democratic freedom, and middle-class respectability, is fundamentalism. Nationalism, Kapur appears to suggest, is mobilised most effectively around some powerful emotion – if not religious, then erotic or homoerotic. After all, given the *Kamasutra*, who is to say that the homoerotic, far from being outlawed, is not central to the nation's cultural makeup? Far from detaching sexual self-realisation from political activity, a typical move in the bourgeois novel, in *A Married Woman* the union of the lovers, even at its most discreet, champions values associated with the secular, national context.[22] To adapt a comment made about Hinduism by one of the characters in the novel: 'The [Indian nation] is wide, is deep, capable of endless interpretation. Anybody can get anything they want from it, ritual, stories, thoughts that sustain. But first you have to realise your need' (*MW* 85).

If, as Tsitsi Dangarembga once said, the 'gender question is always second to the nation question', then it may be when postcolonial women writers begin to realise their emotional and political needs *at once* within and *besides* the nation that opportunities will be framed for that *always* to be dismantled.[23] Certainly, it is only when male co-participants in the nation recognise that women like men are in quest of symbolic vocabularies of entitlement through which to lay claim to the nation's public and imaginary spaces that women may finally come into their own as both national citizens and storytellers. Only then may the gendered configurations of the nation begin to shift.

Notes

1 R. Radhakrishnan, 'Nationalism, gender and the narrative of identity', in Andrew Parker *et al.* (eds), *Nationalisms and Sexualities* (London and New York: Routledge, 1992), pp. 77–95.

2 The term *petit récit*, derived from Jean-François Lyotard's critique of the grand narratives of modernity, is defined as a modest, locally based, at times fragmentary or stochastic tale, opposed to the so-called grand narrative of the official, male-authored and -authorised nation. It comes to hand as a particularly appropriate way of describing the non-authoritative stories women, in particular here women writers, might tell. See Jean-François Lyotard, *The Postmodern Condition: A Report on Knowledge*, trans. Geoff Bennington and Brian Massumi (Manchester: Manchester University Press, 1984).

3 See the Zimbabwean women's testimonies collected in Irene Staunton (ed.), *Mothers of the Revolution: The War Experiences of Thirty Zimbabwean Women* (London: James Currey, 1990).

4 On the feminist difficulty with conceptualising female leadership and authority, and indeed with the notion of women representing other women, see Nancy Hartsock, *Money, Sex and Power* (Boston: Northeastern University Press, 1983); and Rajeswari Sunder Rajan, *Real and Imagined Women: Gender, Culture and Postcolonialism* (London and New York: Routledge, 1993), especially pp. 116–22;

5 Chinua Achebe, *Home and Exile* (Oxford and New York: Oxford University Press, 2000), pp. 5–7. See Laura Chrisman's reading of Achebe's critique of contemporary 'cosmopolitical' thought in 'The killer that doesn't pay back', *Postcolonial Contraventions* (Manchester: Manchester University Press, 2003), pp. 157–63.

6 On the problematics of a feminist politics of location in the homogenising transnational context, see Caren Kaplan, 'Politics of location as transnational feminist critical practice', in Inderpal Grewal and Caren Kaplan (eds), *Scattered Hegemonies: Postmodernity and Transnational Feminist Practices* (Minneapolis: University of Minnesota Press, 1994), pp. 137–52; and Caren Kaplan, *Questions of Travel: Postmodern Discourses of Displacement* (Durham, NC: Duke University Press, 1996), especially p. 146.

7 See, for example, Samir Amin, *Capitalism in the Age of Globalisation* (London: Zed Press, 1997), and Neil Lazarus, *Nationalism and Cultural Practice in the Postcolonial World* (Cambridge: Cambridge University Press, 1999), pp. 29–51.

8 Natasha Barnes, 'Reluctant matriarch: Sylvia Wynter and the problematics of Caribbean feminism', *Small Axe*, 5 (March 1999), 34–47; Deniz Kanyoti, 'Identity and its discontents: women and the nation', *Millennium: Journal of International Studies*, 20:3 (1991), 429–23.

9 See Djurdja Knesevic, 'Affective nationalism', and Mamphela Ramphele, 'Whither feminism', in Joan W. Scott, Cora Kaplan and Debra Keates (eds), *Transitions, Environments, Translations* (London and New York: Routledge, 1997), pp. 65–71, and 334–8, respectively. See also Simon Gikandi, 'Globalization and the claims of postcoloniality', *South Atlantic Quarterly*, 100:3 (Summer 2001), 626–58.

10 For a critical view of the nation that targets its tendency to other, see Christine Levecq, 'Nation, race and postmodern gestures in Ishmael Reed's *Flight to Canada*', *Novel: A Forum on Fiction*, 35:2–3 (Spring/Summer 2002), 281–98.

11 See Anthony Smith, *Nationalism: Theory, Ideology, History* (London: Polity, 2003), and Perry Anderson, *The Invention of the Region 1945–90* (San Domenico: European University Institute, 1994); and the review by Tom Nairn, 'It's not the economy, stupid', *TLS*, 5223 (9 May 2003), 24.

12 Manju Kapur, *Difficult Daughters* (London: Faber, 1998), and *A Married Woman* (London: Faber, 2003). Pages references will henceforth be cited in the text along with the abbreviations *DD* and *MW* respectively.

13 Compare Doris Sommer, *Foundational Fictions: The National Romances of Latin America* (Berkeley: University of California Press, 1991), which contends that the progress of love in Latin American romance novels mirrors the processes of consolidating the nation-state. So, too, in key works of African fiction. As well as *A Grain of Wheat*, Ben Okri's *The Famished Road* features a tightly knit nuclear family whose travails 'write small' trouble in Nigerian society at large. At the end of Shimmer Chinodya's *Harvest of Thorns* (1989) and of Mongane Serote's *To Every Birth its Blood* (1981) symbolic women are pictured big with child or as giving birth.

14 Pallavi Rastogi, 'Manju Kapur', in Jaina C. Sanga (ed.), *South Asian Novelists in English: An A-to-Z Guide* (Westport, CN: Greenwood Press 2003), p. 123.

15 Astha's name is offset by her lover's unusual secularist name Pipeelika, meaning ant: with regard at least to names, their relationship signifies a juxtaposition of belief and non-belief. Pipee's marriage to Aijaz, it is also worth noting, is cross-communal, Hindu–Muslim. Throughout, religious faith is generally represented either as atavistic or as reduced to overmystified ritual.

16 On the appeal of a communal sensibility for women, see Sangeeta Ray, *En-gendering India: Woman and Nation in Colonial and Postcolonial Narratives* (Durham, NC and London: Duke University Press, 2000), pp. 6–7.

17 Chitralekha Basu, 'A meeting of minds', *TLS*, 5212 (21 February 2003), 23.

18 To adapt from a description which is given of Astha's poems, such same-sex 'mind-fucking' is like 'her own experience endlessly replayed' (*MW* 79).

19 See Inderpal Grewal, *Home and Harem: Nation, Gender, Empire and the Cultures of Travel* (London: Leicester University Press, 1996), pp. 5–7; and also Partha Chatterjee, *The Nation and its Fragments: Colonial and Postcolonial Histories* (Princeton: Princeton University Press, 1994), p. 147.

20 Grewal, *Home and Harem*, p. 7.

21 *A Married Woman* does, however, criticise the Congress Party's concessionary handling of the build-up to Ayodhya (*MW* 111).

22 There is evidence to suggest that among urban, middle-class Indians, religious affiliation is becoming itself increasingly private, individualised, 'secularised'. At the same time, the growing sense is that women should not have to 'de-sex' themselves to gain access to the wider space of the nation. See, respectively, Maya Warrier, 'Processes of secularisation in contemporary India', *Modern Asian Studies*, 37:1 (2003), 213–53; and Nilufer E. Barucha, 'Inhabiting enclosures and creating spaces:

the worlds of women in Indian literature in English', *ARIEL*, 29:2 (1999), 93–107. See also Nancy Armstrong, *Desire and Domestic Fiction: A Political History of the Novel* (Oxford: Oxford University Press, 1987).

23 See Kirsten Holst Petersen, 'Between gender, race and history: interview with Tsitsi Dangarembga', *Kunapipi*, 16:1 (1994), 347.

Select bibliography

Abrahams, Peter. *A Wreath for Udomo* [1956]. London: Faber, 1979.

Achebe, Chinua. *Anthills of the Savannah*. London: Heinemann, 1987.

—— *Girls at War and Other Stories* [1972]. London: Heinemann, 1986.

—— *Home and Exile*. Oxford and New York: Oxford University Press, 2000.

—— *A Man of the People*. London: Heinemann, 1966.

—— *The Trouble with Nigeria*. London: Heinemann, 1987.

Afshar, Haleh, ed. *Women, State and Ideology: Studies from Africa and Asia*. London: Macmillan, 1987.

Ahmad, Aijaz. *In Theory: Classes, Nations, Literatures*. New York and London: Verso, 1992.

Aidoo, Ama Ata. *Our Sister Killjoy*. Harlow, Essex: Longman Drumbeat, 1977.

Akbar, M. J. *Nehru: The Making of India*. London: Viking, 1988.

Alexander, M. Jacqui, and Chandra T. Mohanty, eds. *Feminist Genealogies, Colonial Legacies, Democratic Futures*. New York and London: Routledge, 1997.

Amadi, Elechi. *The Great Ponds* [1969]. London: Heinemann, 1982.

Amadiume, Ifi. *Afrikan Matriarchal Foundations: The Igbo Case*. London: Karnak, 1987.

—— *Male Daughters, Female Husbands: Gender and Sex in an African Society*. London: Zed Press, 1987.

Amin, Samir. *Capitalism in the Age of Globalisation*. London: Zed Press, 1997.

Anderson, Benedict. *Imagined Communities: Reflections on the Origin and Spread of Nationalisms* [1983]. Rev. edn, London: Verso, 1991.

—— *The Spectre of Comparisons: Nationalism, Southeast Asia and the World*. London and New York: Verso, 1998.

Anderson, Perry. *The Invention of the Region 1945–90*. San Domenico: European University Institute, 1994.

Andrade, Susan Z. *The Nation Writ Small*. Durham, NC: Duke University Press, forthcoming.

Appiah, Kwame A. *In My Father's House: Africa in the Philosophy of Culture*. London: Methuen, 1992.

Ardener, Shirley, ed. *Defining Females: The Nature of Women in Society*. London: Croom Helm, 1978.

——ed. *Perceiving Women*. London: Malaby, 1975.

—— *Women and Space: Ground Rules and Social Maps*. London: Croom Helm, 1981.

Armstrong, Nancy. *Desire and Domestic Fiction: A Political History of the Novel*. Oxford: Oxford University Press, 1987.

Awolowo, Obafemi. *Awo: The Autobiography of Chief Obafemi Awolowo*. Cambridge: Cambridge University Press, 1960.

Awoonor, Kofi. *The Breast of the Earth*. New York: Nok Publishers International, 1975.

Azikiwe, Nnamdi. *My Odyssey: An Autobiography*. London: Hurst, 1970.

Baaz, Maria E., and Mai Palmberg, eds. *Same and Other: Negotiating African Identity in Cultural Production*. Stockholm: Nordiska Afrikainstitutet, 2001.

Bakhtin, Mikhail. *The Dialogic Imagination*. Ed. Michael Holquist. Trans. Caryl Emerson and Michael Holquist. Austin: University of Texas, 1986.

—— *Problems of Dostoevsky's Poetics*. Ed. and trans. Caryl Emerson. Minneapolis: Minneapolis University Press, 1984.

Balakrishnan, Gopal, ed. *Mapping the Nation*. London: Verso, 1996.

Balibar, Etienne, and Immanuel Wallerstein. *Race, Nation, Class: Ambiguous Identities*. Trans. Chris Turner. London: Verso, 1991.

Bamforth, Nicholas, ed. *Sex Rights*. Oxford: Oxford University Press, 2004.

Banerjee, Hari. *Sarojini Naidu: The Traditional Feminist*. Calcutta: K. P. Bagchi and Co., 1998.

Barber, Karin, *I Could Speak Until Tomorrow: Oriki, Women and the Past in a Yoruba Town*. Edinburgh: Edinburgh University Press, 1991.

——and P. F. de Moraes Farias, eds. *Discourse and its Disguises: The Interpretation of African Oral Texts*. Birmingham: University of Birmingham, 1989.

Barrow, John, ed. *Cook's Voyages of Discovery*. London: A. C. Black, 1925.

Bassnett, Susan. *Comparative Literature: A Critical Introduction*. London and New York: Routledge, 1993.

de Beauvoir, Simone. *The Second Sex*. Trans. H. M. Parshley. Harmondsworth: Penguin, 1979.

Benstock, Shari, ed. *The Private Self: Theory and Practice of Women's Autobiographical Writings*. Durham, NC and London: University of North Carolina Press, 1988.

Bhabha, Homi. *The Location of Culture*. London: Routledge, 1995.

——ed. *Nation and Narration*. London and New York: Routledge, 1990.

Bloom, Harold. *The Anxiety of Influence: A Theory of Poetry*. Oxford: Oxford University Press, 1973.

Boehmer, Elleke. *Colonial and Postcolonial Literature* [1995]. Rev. edn, Oxford: Oxford University Press, 2005.

—— *Empire, the National and the Postcolonial 1890–1920: Resistance in Interaction*. Oxford and New York: Oxford University Press, 2002.

—— *Empire Writing: An Anthology of Colonial Literature, 1870–1918*. Oxford: Oxford University Press, 1998.

Boose, Lynda E., and Betty S. Flowers, eds. *Daughters and Fathers*. Baltimore: Johns Hopkins University Press, 1989.

Booth, James. *Writers and Politics in Nigeria*. London: Hodder and Stoughton, 1981.

Brah, Avtar. *Cartographies of Diaspora: Contesting Identities*. London: Routledge, 1996.

——Mary J. Hickman and Mairtin MacanGhaill, eds. *Global Futures: Migration, Environment and Globalization*. Basingstoke: Macmillan, 1999.

Brathwaite, Kamau. *Mother Poem*. Oxford: Oxford University Press, 1977.

——*Sun Poems*. Oxford: Oxford University Press, 1982.

——*X/Self* (Oxford: Oxford University Press, 1986).

Brennan, Timothy. *At Home in the World: Cosmopolitanism Now*. Cambridge, MA: Harvard University Press, 1997.

——*Salman Rushdie and the Third World*. London: Macmillan, 1989.

Brossard, Nicole. *These Our Mothers: Or the Disintegrating Chapter*. Trans. B. Godard. Toronto: Coach House, 1983.

Brown, Judith. *Nehru: A Political Life*. New Haven, CN: Yale University Press, 2003.

Brown, Lloyd. *Women Writers in Black Africa*. Westport, CN: Greenwood, 1981.

Brown, Susan, ed. *LIP from South African Women*. Johannesburg: Ravan, 1983.

Burton, Richard. *Love, War and Fancy: The Customs and Manners of the East from Writings on the 'Arabian Nights'*. Ed. Kenneth Walker. London: Kimber, 1964.

Butler, Judith, Ernesto Laclau, Slavoj Žižek. *Contingency, Hegemony, Universality*. London: Verso, 2000.

Cabral, Amilcar. *Return to the Source*. New York and London: Monthly Review Press, 1973.

Cairns, David, and Shaun Richards. *Writing Ireland: Colonialism, Nationalism and Culture*. Manchester: Manchester University Press, 1988.

Camara, Laye. *The African Child*. Trans. James Kirkup. London: Fontana, 1980.

Chatterjee, Partha. *The Nation and its Fragments: Colonial and Postcolonial Histories*. New Delhi: Oxford University Press, 1993.

——*Nationalist Thought and the Colonial World – A Derivative Discourse?* London: Zed Press, 1986.

Chennells, Anthony, and Flora Veit-Wild, eds. *Emerging Perspectives on Dambudzo Marechera*. Trenton, NJ: Africa World Press, 1999.

Chrisman, Laura. *Postcolonial Contraventions: Cultural Readings of Race, Imperialism and Transnationalism*. Manchester: Manchester University Press, 2003.

Christian, Barbara. *Black Feminist Criticism: Perspectives on Black Women Writers*. Oxford: Pergamon Press, 1987.

Cleary, Joe. *Literature, Partition and the Nation-State: Culture and Conflict in Ireland, Israel and Palestine*. Cambridge: Cambridge University Press, 2002.

Cliff, Michelle. *No Telephone to Heaven*. London: Minerva, 1987.

Coetzee, J. M. *Foe*. Harmondsworth: Penguin, 1986.

Connor, Steven. *The English Novel in History, 1950–1995*. London and New York: Routledge, 1996.

Cook, David, and Michael Okenimkpe. *Ngugi wa Thiong'o*. London: Heinemann, 1983.

Corrigan, Philip, and Derek Sayer. *The Great Arch: English State Formation as Cultural Revolution*. Oxford: Blackwell, 1985.

Daly, Brenda O., and Maureen T. Reddy, eds. *Narrating Mothers: Theorizing Maternal Subjectivities*. Knoxville: University of Tennessee Press, 1991.

Dangarembga, Tsitsi. *Nervous Conditions*. London: The Women's Press, 1988.

Davies, Carole Boyce, and Anne Adams Graves, eds. *Ngambika: Studies of Women in African Literature*. Trenton, NJ: Africa World Press, 1986.

——and Elaine Savory Fido, eds. *Out of the Kumbla: Caribbean Women and Literature.* Trenton, NJ: Africa World Press, 1990.

Davies, Miranda, ed. *Third World – Second Sex.* London: Zed Press, 1986.

de Mel, Nelufer. *Women and the Nation's Narrative: Gender and Nationalism in Twentieth-century Sri Lanka.* Colombo: Social Scientists' Association, 2001.

Deshpande, Shashi. *Collected Stories.* Vol. 1. Ed. Amrita Bhalla. New Delhi: Penguin India, 2003.

Dodd, Philip, ed. *Modern Selves: Essays on Modern British and American Autobiography.* London: Frank Cass, 1986.

Donaldson, Laura E. *Decolonizing Fictions: Race, Gender and Empire-building.* London and New York: Routledge, 1992.

Donnell, Alison. *Twentieth-Century Caribbean Literature: Critical Moments in Anglophone Literary and Critical History.* New York and London: Routledge, 2005.

——and Pauline Polkey, eds. *Representing Lives: Women and Autobiography.* Basingstoke: Macmillan, 2000.

Dubey, Madhu. *Black Women Novelists and the Nationalist Aesthetic.* Bloomington: Indiana University Press, 1994.

Dwyer, Rachel, and Christopher Pinney, eds. *Pleasure and the Nation: The History, Politics and Consumption of Public Culture in India.* New Delhi: Oxford University Press, 2004.

Eagleton, Terry. *The Ideology of the Aesthetic.* London: Blackwell, 1990.

Emecheta, Buchi. *Destination Biafra.* London: Fontana, 1982.

——*Gwendoline.* London: Collins, 1989.

——*Head Above Water.* London: Fontana, 1986.

——*The Joys of Motherhood.* London: Heinemann, 1979.

Enloe, Cynthia. *Bananas, Beaches and Bases: Making Feminist Sense of International Politics* [1989]. First edn, Berkeley: University of California Press, 2000.

Fanon, Frantz. *Black Skin, White Masks* [1952]. Trans. C. L. Markmann. London: Pluto, 1986.

——*Studies in a Dying Colonialism.* London: Earthscan, 1989.

——*Towards the African Revolution.* Trans. Haakon Chevalier. London: Penguin, 1967.

——*The Wretched of the Earth* [1961]. Trans. Constance Farrington. Harmondsworth: Penguin, 1985.

Farah, Nuruddin. *Maps.* London: Picador, 1986.

Finnegan, Ruth. *Oral Literature in Africa.* Oxford: Oxford University Press, 1970.

First, Ruth, and Ann Scott. *Olive Schreiner: A Biography.* London: The Women's Press, 1989.

Franco, Jean. *Plotting Women: Gender and Representation in Mexico.* London: Verso, 1989.

Fraser, Robert. *Ben Okri: Towards the Invisible City.* Tavistock, Devon: Northcote House, 1992.

Freud, Sigmund. *On Sexuality.* Trans. James Strachey. Penguin Freud Library. Vol. 7. Harmondsworth: Penguin, 1986.

Fuss, Diana, ed. *Inside/Out: Lesbian Theories, Gay Theories.* New York and London: Routledge, 1991.

Gates, Henry Louis, Jr., ed. *'Race', Writing and Difference*. Chicago: University of Chicago Press, 1986.

Gellner, Ernest. *Nations and Nationalisms*. Oxford: Blackwell, 1983.

George, Rosemary Marangoly. *The Politics of Home: Postcolonial Relocations and Twentieth-century Fiction*. Cambridge: Cambridge University Press, 1996.

Gevisser, Mark, and Edwin Cameron, eds. *Defiant Desire: Gay and Lesbian Lives in South Africa*. Braamfontein: Ravan Press, 1994.

Gibson, Nigel, ed. *Rethinking Fanon: The Continuing Dialogue*. New York: Humanity Books, 1999.

Gikandi, Simon. *Reading Chinua Achebe*. London: James Currey, 1991.

Gilbert, Sandra M., and Susan Gubar. *The Madwoman in the Attic*. Yale: Yale University Press, 1984.

Gilroy, Paul. *The Black Atlantic: Modernity and Double Consciousness*. London: Verso, 1993.

Goldberg, David Theo, and Ato Quayson, eds. *Relocating Postcolonialism*. Oxford: Blackwell, 2002.

Gonne, Maud. *A Servant of the Queen*. London: Victor Gollancz, 1938.

Gordimer, Nadine. *Writing and Being: The Charles Eliot Norton Lectures*. Cambridge, MA: Harvard University Press, 1995.

Gorra, Michael. *After Empire: Scott, Naipaul, Rushdie*. Chicago: University of Chicago Press, 1997.

Grewal, Inderpal. *Home and Harem: Nation, Gender, Empire and the Cultures of Travel*. London: Leicester University Press, 1996.

——and Caren Kaplan, eds. *Scattered Hegemonies: Postmodernity and Transnational Feminist Practices*. Minneapolis: University of Minnesota Press, 1994.

Griffin, Susan. *Women and Nature: The Roaring Inside Her*. London: Harper, 1975.

Gunner, Elizabeth, and Mafika Gwala, eds. *Musho!: Zulu Popular Praises*. Johannesburg: Witwatersrand University Press, 1994.

Gurnah, Abdulrazak, ed. *Essays on African Writing: A Re-evaluation*. 2 vols. Oxford: Heinemann, 1993.

Habermas, Jurgen. *The Postcolonial Constellation: Political Essays*. Ed. and trans. Max Pensky. London: Polity, 2001.

Hamilton, Paul. *Historicism*. London: Routledge, 1996.

Hartsock, Nancy. *Money, Sex and Power*. Boston: Northeastern University Press, 1983.

Harvey, David. *The Condition of Postmodernity*. Oxford: Blackwell, 1989.

Head, Bessie. *Maru*. London: Heinemann, 1987.

——*Serowe: Village of the Rain Wind* [1981]. London: Heinemann, 1986.

Hobsbawm, Eric. *Nations and Nationalism since 1780: Programme, Myth, Reality*. Cambridge: Cambridge University Press, 1990.

——and Terence Ranger, eds. *The Invention of Tradition*. Cambridge: Cambridge University Press, 1983.

Holst Petersen, Kirsten, ed. *Criticism and Ideology*. Uppsala: SIAS, 1988.

——and Anna Rutherford, eds. *A Double Colonization: Colonial and Postcolonial Women's Writing*. Aarhus: Dangaroo, 1986.

hooks, bell. *Yearning: Race, Gender and Cultural Politics*. London: Turnaround Press, 1991.

Hove, Chenjerai. *Bones*. Oxford: Heinemann, 1988.

—— *Shebeen Tales: Messages from Harare*. Harare: Baobab Books, 1997.

Howes, Marjorie. *Yeats's Nations: Gender, Class and Irishness*. Cambridge: Cambridge University Press, 1996.

Huggan, Graham. *The Postcolonial Exotic: Marketing the Margins*. London and New York: Routledge, 2001.

Hurston, Zora Neale. *Their Eyes Were Watching God*. London: Virago, 1987.

Hutcheon, Linda. *The Politics of Postmodernism*. Rev. edn, London and New York: Routledge, 2002.

Innes, C. L. *Chinua Achebe*. Cambridge: Cambridge University Press, 1990.

—— *Woman and Nation in Irish Literature and Society: 1880–1935*. Hemel Hempstead: Harvester Wheatsheaf, 1993.

Jacobus, Mary. *Reading Woman: Essays in Feminist Criticism*. New York: Columbia University Press, 1986.

Jain, Jasbir, and Avadesh Kumar Singh, eds. *Indian Feminisms*. New Delhi: Creative Books, 2001.

James, Adeola. *In Their Own Voices: African Women Writers Talk*. London: James Currey, 1990.

James, Stanlie M., and Abena Busia, eds. *Theorising Black Feminisms*. London and New York: Routledge, 1993.

Jameson, Fredric. *The Political Unconscious: Narrative as a Socially Symbolic Act*. London: Methuen, 1981.

—— *Situations of Theory: Essays 1971–1986*. 2 vols. London: Routledge, 1988.

—— 'Third-World literature in the era of multinational capitalism'. *Social Text* 15 (1986), 65–88.

—— Masoa Miyoshi, eds. *The Cultures of Globalisation*. Durham, NC and London: Duke University Press, 1998.

JanMohamed, Abdul. *Manichean Aesthetics*. Amherst, MA: University of Massachusetts Press, 1983.

Jayawardena, Kumari. *Feminism and Nationalism in the Third World*. London: Zed Press, 1986.

Kabbani, Rana. *Europe's Myths of the Orient*. London: Macmillan, 1986.

Kafka, Phillipa. *On the Outside Looking In(dian): Indian Women Writers at Home and Abroad*. New York: Peter Lang, 2003.

Kanneh, Kadiatu. *African Identities: Race, Nation and Culture in Ethnography, Pan-Africanism and Black Literatures*. London and New York: Routledge, 1998.

Kaplan, Caren. *Questions of Travel: Postmodern Discourses of Displacement*. Durham, NC: Duke University Press, 1996.

Kapur, Manju. *Difficult Daughters*. London: Faber, 1998.

—— *A Married Woman*. London: Faber, 2003.

Kaunda, Kenneth. *Zambia Shall Be Free*. London: Heinemann, 1962.

Kearney, Richard. *Myth and Motherland*. Belfast: Field Day Theatre Company, 1984.

—— *On Stories*. London: Routledge, 2002.

Kenyatta, Jomo. *Facing Mount Kenya: The Tribal Life of Gikuyu*. Intro. B. Malinowski. London: Secker and Warburg, 1938.

——*Suffering without Bitterness: The Story of the Founding of the Kenyan Nation.* Nairobi: East Africa Publishing House, 1968.

Khair, Tabish. *Babu Fictions: Alienation in Contemporary Indian English Novels.* New Delhi: Oxford University Press, 2001.

Kiberd, Declan. *Imagining Ireland.* London: Cape, 1995.

Kolawole, Mary Modupe, ed. *Gender Perspectives and Development in Africa.* Lagos: Arrabon Academic Publishers, 1998.

—— *Womanism and African Consciousness.* Trenton, NJ: Africa World Press, 1997.

Kristeva, Julia. *Desire in Language.* Trans. Léon S. Roudiez. Oxford: Blackwell, 1987.

——*Nations without Nationalism.* Trans. Léon S. Roudiez. New York: Columbia University Press, 1993.

Kunzru, Hari. *The Impressionist.* London: Hamish Hamilton, 2002.

Kuzwayo, Ellen. *Call Me Woman.* Johannesburg: Ravan Press, 1985.

Lash, Scott, and Jonathan Friedman, eds. *Modernity and Identity.* Oxford: Blackwell, 1992.

Lazarus, Neil, ed. *The Cambridge Companion to Postcolonial Literary Studies.* Cambridge: Cambridge University Press, 2004.

—— *Nationalism and Cultural Practice in the Postcolonial World.* Cambridge: Cambridge University Press, 1999.

—— *Resistance in Postcolonial African Fiction.* New Haven, CN: Yale University Press, 1990.

Levinas, Emmanuel. *Ethics and Infinity.* Trans. R. A. Cohen. Pittsburgh: Duquesne University Press, 1985.

Lindfors, Bernth, and C. L. Innes, eds. *Critical Perspectives on Chinua Achebe.* London: Heinemann, 1979.

Lionnet, Françoise. *Autobiographical Voices: Race, Gender, Self-portraiture.* Ithaca and London: Cornell University Press, 1989.

—— *Postcolonial Representations: Women, Literature, Identity.* Ithaca: Cornell University Press, 1995.

Lloyd, David. *Anomalous States: Irish Writing and the Post-colonial Moment.* Dublin: Lilliput Press, 1993.

Loomba, Ania. *Colonialism/Postcolonialism.* London: Routledge, 1998.

Luthuli, Albert. *Let My People Go: An Autobiography* [1962]. London: Collins, 1987.

Lyotard, Jean-François. *The Postmodern Condition: A Report on Knowledge.* Trans. Geoff Bennington and Brian Massumi. Manchester: Manchester University Press, 1983.

McClintock, Anne. *Imperial Leather: Race, Gender and Sexuality in the Colonial Contest.* London and New York: Routledge, 1995.

——Aamir Mufti and Ella Shohat, eds. *Dangerous Liaisons: Gender, Nation and Postcolonial Perspectives.* Minneapolis: University of Minnesota Press, 1997.

Madingoane, Ingoapele. *Africa My Beginning.* Johannesburg: Ravan Press, 1988.

Magona, Sindiwe. *To My Children's Children.* Cape Town: David Philip, 1990.

Mandela, Nelson. *Long Walk to Freedom.* London: Abacus, 1995.

Marcus, Laura. *Auto/biographical Discourses: Theory, Criticism, Practice.* Manchester: Manchester University Press, 1994.

Marechera, Dambudzo. *The Black Insider.* Ed. Flora Veit-Wild. Harare: Baobab Books, 1990.

—— *The House of Hunger* [1978]. Oxford: Heinemann, 1989.

—— *Mindblast* [1984]. Harare: The College Press, 1989.

Massey, Doreen. *Space, Place and Gender*. Oxford: Polity, 1994.

Maughan-Brown, David. *Land, Freedom and Fiction: History and Ideology in Kenya*. London: Zed Press, 1985.

Mbembe, Achille. *On the Postcolony*. Trans. A. M. Berrett *et al*. Berkeley: University of California Press, 2001.

Meer, Shamin, ed. *Women Speak: Reflections on our Struggles 1982–1997*. Cape Town: Kwela, 1998.

Mies, Maria. *Patriarchy and Accumulation on a World Scale: Women in the International Division of Labour*. London: Zed Press, 1986.

Mohanty, Chandra Talpade. *Third World Women and the Politics of Feminism*. Bloomington: Indiana University Press, 1991.

Moi, Toril, ed. *French Feminist Thought*. Oxford: Blackwell, 1988.

Mongia, Padmini, ed. *Contemporary Postcolonial Theory*. London: Arnold, 1996.

Moore-Gilbert, Bart. *Postcolonial Theory: Contexts, Practices, Politics*. New York and London: Verso, 1997.

Morey, Peter. *Fictions of India: Narrative and Power*. Edinburgh: Edinburgh University Press, 2000.

Mosse, George. *Nationalism and Sexuality: Respectability and Abnormal Sexuality in Modern Europe*. New York: Howard Fertig, 1985.

Moussaieff, Jeffrey, ed. *The Complete Letters of Sigmund Freud to Wilhelm Fliess, 1887–1904*. Trans. Jeffrey Moussaieff. Cambridge, MA: Harvard University Press, 1985.

Mukherjee, Meenakshi, ed. *Rushdie's* Midnight's Children: *A Book of Readings*. Delhi: Pencraft International, 1999.

Muponde, Robert, and Mandi Taruvinga, eds. *Sign and Taboo: Perspectives on the Poetic Fiction of Yvonne Vera*. Harare: Weaver Press, 2002.

Murray, Stephen O., and William Roscoe, eds. *Boy Wives and Female Husbands: Studies in African Homosexualities*. New York: St Martin's Press, 1998.

Naidu, Sarojini. *The Bird of Time: Songs of Life, Death and the Spring*. Intro. Edmund Gosse. London: William Heinemann, 1912.

—— *The Golden Threshold*. Intro. Arthur Symons. London: William Heinemann, 1905.

Nairn, Tom. *The Break-up of Britain: Crisis and Neo-Nationalism*. London: New Left Books, 1977.

—— *The Enchanted Glass: Britain and its Monarchy*. London: Radius, 1988.

Nandy, Ashis. *At the Edge of Psychology*. New Delhi: Oxford University Press, 1982.

—— *The Illegitimacy of Nationalism: Rabindranath Tagore and the Politics of Self*. New Delhi: Oxford University Press, 1994.

—— *The Intimate Enemy: Loss and Recovery of Self under Colonialism*. New Delhi: Oxford University Press, 1983.

Nasta, Susheila, ed. *Motherlands: Black Women's Writing*. London: The Women's Press, 1991.

Nehru, Jawaharlal. *An Autobiography* [1936]. Rev. edn, London: The Bodley Head, 1942.

—— *The Discovery of India* [1946]. New Delhi: Oxford University Press, 2002.

Newell, Stephanie, ed. *Writing African Women: Gender, Popular Culture and Literature in West Africa*. London: Zed Press, 1997.

Nfah-Abbenyi, Juliana Makuchi. *Gender in African Women's Writing*. Bloomington: Indiana University Press, 1997.

Ngugi wa Thiong'o. *Barrel of a Pen* [1983]. London: Heinemann, 1986.

—— *Decolonising the Mind: The Politics of Language in African Literature*. London: Heinemann, 1986.

—— *Detained: A Writer's Prison Diary*. London: Heinemann, 1981.

—— *Devil on the Cross*. London: Heinemann, 1982.

—— *A Grain of Wheat*. London: Heinemann, 1967.

—— *Matigari*. London: Heinemann, 1989.

—— *Penpoints, Gunpoints and Dreams: Towards a Critical Theory of the Arts and the State in Africa*. Oxford and New York: Oxford University Press, 1998.

—— *Petals of Blood* [1977]. Cape Town: David Philip, 1982.

—— *The River Between* [1965]. London: Heinemann, 1978.

—— *The Trial of Dedan Kimathi* [1976]. London: Heinemann, 1985.

—— and Ngugi wa Mirii. *I Will Marry When I Want*. London: Heinemann, 1982.

Nhongo-Simbanegavi, Josephine. *For Better or Worse? Women and ZANLA in Zimbabwe's Liberation Struggle*. Harare: Weaver, 2000.

Njau, Rebekah. *Ripples in the Pool*. London: Heinemann, 1975.

Nkrumah, Kwame. *Autobiography of Kwame Nkrumah*. London: Panaf Books, 1973.

Nnaemeka, Obioma, ed. *The Politics of (M)Othering: Womanhood, Identity and Resistance in African Literature*. London and New York: Routledge, 1997.

Nwapa, Flora. *Efuru* [1966]. London: Heinemann, 1987.

—— *Idu* [1970]. London: Heinemann, 1987.

—— *Never Again* [1975]. Enugu: Tana, 1986.

—— *One is Enough*. Enugu: Tana, 1981.

—— *This Is Lagos and Other Stories*. Enugu: Tana, 1986.

—— *Wives at War and Other Stories*. Enugu: Tana, 1984.

Nyamubaya, Freedom T. V. *On the Road Again*. Harare: Zimbabwe Publishing House, 1986.

Nzegwu, Femi. *Love, Motherhood and the African Heritage: The Legacy of Flora Nwapa*. Dakar: African Renaissance, 2001.

Okri, Ben. *The Famished Road*. London: Cape, 1991.

—— *Incidents at the Shrine*. London: Fontana, 1986.

—— *Infinite Riches*. London: Phoenix House, 1998.

—— *Songs of Enchantment*. London: Jonathan Cape, 1993.

—— *Stars of the New Curfew*. London: Secker and Warburg, 1988.

Olney, James, ed. *Autobiography: Essays Theoretical and Critical*. Princeton, NJ: Princeton University Press, 1980.

—— *Metaphors of Self: The Meaning of Autobiography*. Princeton, NJ: Princeton University Press, 1972.

Paranjape, Makarand, ed. *Sarojini Naidu: Selected Letters 1890s to 1940s*. New Delhi: Kali for Women, 1996.

Park, Mungo. *Travels in the Interior of Africa.* London: The Folio Society, 1984.

Parker, Andrew, Mary Russo, Doris Sommer and Patricia Yaeger, eds. *Nationalisms and Sexualities.* New York and London: Routledge, 1992.

Quayson, Ato. *Strategic Transformations in Nigerian Writing.* Oxford: James Currey, 1997.

Ramphele, Mamphela. *Across Boundaries: The Journey of a South African Woman Leader.* New York: Feminist Press, 1997.

——*A Bed Called Home: Life in the Migrant Labour Hostels in Cape Town.* Cape Town: David Philip, 1993.

Ray, Sangeeta. *En-gendering India: Woman and Nation in Colonial and Postcolonial Narratives.* Durham, NC and London: Duke University Press, 2000.

Rose, Gillian. *Feminism and Cultural Geography: The Limits of Geographical Knowledge.* Oxford: Polity Press, 1993.

Rowbotham, Sheila. *Women, Resistance and Revolution.* Harmondsworth: Penguin, 1972.

Roy, Arundhati. *The Algebra of Infinite Justice.* London: Flamingo, 2002.

——*The God of Small Things.* London: Flamingo, 1997.

Roy, Parama. *Indian Traffic: Identities in Question in Colonial and Postcolonial India.* Berkeley: University of California Press, 1988.

Rushdie, Salman. *Imaginary Homelands.* London: Granta, 1991.

——*Midnight's Children.* London: Cape, 1981.

——*The Moor's Last Sigh.* London: Cape, 1995.

——*Shame.* London: Cape, 1983.

Rutherford, Anna, and Shirley Chew, eds. *Into the Nineties: Postcolonial Women's Writing.* London: Dangaroo, 1994.

Ryan, Louise, and Margaret Ward, eds. *Irish Women and Nationalism: Soldiers, New Women and Wicked Hags.* Dublin: Irish Academic Press, 2004.

Sage, Lorna. *Women in the House of Fiction.* London and New York: Routledge, 1992.

Said, Edward. *Orientalism.* London: Routledge and Kegan Paul, 1978.

——*The World, the Text and the Critic.* London: Faber, 1984.

Sanga, Jaina C., ed. *South Asian Novelists in English: An A-to-Z Guide.* Westport, CN: Greenwood Press, 2003.

Sangari, Kumkum, and Sudesh Vaid, eds. *Recasting Women: Essays in Indian Colonial History.* New Brunswick: Rutgers University Press, 1990.

Sartre, Jean-Paul. *Black Orpheus.* Trans. S. W. Allen. Paris: Présence Africaine, 1976.

Scarry, Elaine. *The Body in Pain: The Making and Unmaking of the World.* Oxford and New York: Oxford University Press, 1985.

Schipper, Mineke, ed. *Unheard Words.* Trans. Barbara Potter Fasting. London: Allison and Busby, 1985.

Schreiner, Olive. *The Story of an African Farm* [1883]. London: Virago, 1989.

Schultheis, Alexandra. *Regenerative Fictions: Postcolonialism, Psychoanalysis and the Nation as Family.* Basingstoke: Palgrave Macmillan, 2004.

Scott, Joan W. *Gender and the Politics of History.* New York: Columbia University Press, 1988.

——*Only Paradoxes to Offer: French Feminists and the Rights of Man.* Cambridge, MA: Harvard University Press, 1996.

——Cora Kaplan and Debra Keates. *Transitions, Environments, Translations*. London and New York: Routledge, 1997.

Sedgwick, Eve Kosofsky, ed. *Novel Gazing: Queer Readings in Fiction*. Durham, NC and London: Duke University Press, 1997.

Senghor, Léopold S. *Poèmes*. Paris: Editions du Seuil, 1973.

——*Selected Poems*. Trans. John Reed and Clive Wake. Oxford: Oxford University Press, 1964.

Serote, W. Mongane. *Selected Poems*. Ed. Mbulelo Mzamane. Johannesburg: Ad Donker, 1982.

Shields, Carol. *Unless*. London: Fourth Estate, 2002.

Showalter, Elaine, ed. *Speaking of Gender*. London: Routledge, 1989.

Sinha, Mrinalini. *Colonial Masculinity: The 'Manly Englishman' and the 'Effeminate Bengali' in the Late Nineteenth Century*. Manchester: Manchester University Press, 1995.

Sisulu, Elinor. *Walter and Albertina Sisulu: In Our Lifetime*. Foreword by Nelson Mandela. London: Abacus, 2003.

Smith, Anthony. *Nationalism: Theory, Ideology, History*. London: Polity, 2003.

Smith, Sidonie, and Julia Watson, eds. *De/colonising the Subject: The Politics of Gender in Women's Autobiography*. Minneapolis: University of Minnesota Press, 1998.

Sommer, Doris. *Foundational Fictions: The National Romances of Latin America*. Berkeley: University of California Press, 1991.

Sorabji, Cornelia. *India Calling* [1935]. Ed. Elleke Boehmer and Naella Grew. Nottingham: Trent Editions, 2004.

Soyinka, Wole. *Collected Plays I*. Oxford: Oxford University Press, 1973.

——*Myth, Literature and the African World*. Cambridge: Cambridge University Press, 1976.

Spivak, Gayatri Chakravorty. *A Critique of Postcolonial Reason: Toward a History of the Vanishing Present*. Cambridge, MA: Harvard University Press, 1999.

——*In Other Worlds: Essays in Cultural Politics*. London and New York: Routledge, 1988.

——*Outside in the Teaching Machine*. London and New York: Routledge, 1993.

Staunton, Irene, ed. *Mothers of the Revolution: The War Experiences of Thirty Zimbabwean Women*. London: James Currey, 1990.

Stead, Christina. *The Man Who Loved Children* [1940]. Harmondsworth: Penguin, 1974.

Steady, Filomena, ed. *The Black Woman Cross-culturally*. Cambridge, MA: Schenkman, 1981.

Stevens, Hugh, and Caroline Howlett, eds. *Modernist Sexualities*. Manchester: Manchester University Press, 2000.

Stratton, Florence. *Contemporary African Literature and the Politics of Gender*. London and New York: Routledge, 1994.

Sunder Rajan, Rajeswari. *Real and Imagined Women: Gender, Culture and Postcolonialism*. London and New York: Routledge, 1993.

——*The Scandal of the State*. Durham, NC: Duke University Press, 2003.

Tagore, Rabindranath. *The Home and the World* [1919]. Trans. Surendranath Tagore. Madras: Macmillan India, 1992.

—— *Nationalism.* London: Macmillan, 1917.

Taiwo, Oladele. *Female Novelists of Modern Africa.* London: Macmillan, 1984.

Tharu, Susie, and K. Lalita, eds. *Women Writing in India: 600 B.C. to the Present.* 2 vols. New Delhi: Oxford University Press, 1991.

Theweleit, Klaus. *Male Fantasies.* Minneapolis: University of Minnesota Press, 1987.

Tiffin, Chris, and Alan Lawson, eds. *De-scribing Empire.* London: Routledge, 1994.

de Tocqueville, Alexis. *Democracy in America.* Ed. J. P. Mayer. Trans. George Lawrence New York: Doubleday, 1969.

Trivedi, Harish. *Colonial Transactions: English Literature and India.* Manchester: Manchester University Press, 1995.

Urdang, Stephanie. *And Still They Dance: Women, War and the Struggle for Change in Mozambique.* New York: Monthly Review Press, 1989.

Vail, Leroy, and Landeg White. *Power and the Praise Poem.* London: James Currey, 1991.

Vanamadi, R. *et al*, eds. *Critical Theory and African Literature: Calabar Studies in African Literature.* Vol. 3. Ibadan: Heinemann, 1987.

Veit-Wild, Flora, and Ernst Schade, eds. *Dambudzo Marechera 1952–1987.* Harare: Baobab Books, 1988.

Vera, Yvonne. *Butterfly Burning.* Harare: Baobab Books, 1998.

—— ed. *Opening Spaces.* Oxford: Heinemann, 1999.

—— *The Stone Virgins.* Harare: Weaver Press, 2002.

—— *Under the Tongue.* Harare: Baobab, 1996.

—— *Without a Name.* Harare: Baobab, 1994.

Walker, Alice. *The Temple of My Familiar.* London: The Women's Press, 1989.

Werbner, Richard, and Terence Ranger, eds. *Postcolonial Identities in Africa.* London: Zed Press, 1996.

Whyte, Christopher. *Gendering the Nation: Studies in Modern Scottish Literature.* Edinburgh: Edinburgh University Press, 1995.

Wilkinson, Jane. *Talking with African Writers.* London: James Currey, 1992.

Willey, Anne E., and Jeanette Treiber, eds. *Negotiating the Postcolonial: Emerging Perspectives on Tsitsi Dangarembga.* Trenton, NJ: Africa World Press, 2002.

Williams, Patrick, and Laura Chrisman, eds. *Colonial Discourse and Post-colonial Theory.* Hemel Hempstead: Harvester Wheatsheaf, 1993.

Wills, Clair. *Improprieties: Politics and Sexuality in Northern Irish Poetry.* Oxford: Clarendon Press, 1993.

Wisker, Gina. *Post-colonial and African American Women's Writing.* Basingstoke: Macmillan, 2000.

Wolpert, Stanley. *A Tryst with Destiny.* Oxford: Oxford University Press, 1996.

Woolf, Virginia. *Three Guineas* [1938]. London: Hogarth Press, 1986.

Yelin, Louise. *From the Margins of Empire: Christina Stead, Doris Lessing and Nadine Gordimer.* Ithaca and London: Cornell University Press, 1998.

Young, Robert J. C. *Colonial Desire.* London and New York: Routledge, 1995.

—— *Postcolonialism: An Historical Introduction.* Oxford: Blackwell, 2001.

—— *Postcolonialism: A Very Short Introduction.* Oxford: Oxford University Press, 2003.

Yuval-Davis, Nira, and Floya Anthias, eds. *Woman-Nation-State.* London: Macmillan, 1989.

Index

Note: literary works can be found under authors' names; 'n' after a page reference indicates the number of a note on that page.

abiku 139n.18, 142
Abrahams, Peter 23–5, 28
Achebe, Chinua 11, 14–15, 17n.3,
    20n.31, 27–8, 81, 139n.18, 141
    Anthills of the Savannah 54–65, 145–6,
      156n.21
    'Girls at war' 1–3, 29, 65n.18, 115
    Home and Exile 62–3, 209
    Man of the People, A 54
    Things Fall Apart 96, 104n.33
    Trouble with Nigeria, The 56, 57, 59
affiliation, *see* Said, Edward
Ahmad, Aijaz 11, 25, 166, 170n.34
Aidoo, Ama Ata 13, 173–4, 184n.8
AIDS 174
Ali, Monica 71
Amadi, Elechi 96–7, 101, 104n.33
Amadiume, Ifi 64n.17, 96, 97–8, 101,
    104n.35, 105n.39, 184n.5
Amis, Martin 11
Anderson, Benedict 7–8, 10, 22–3,
    39n.30, 51, 66, 70, 83, 85n.15
Andrade, Susan 23, 35, 96, 213
Anglican community 172–3
Appiah, Kwame Anthony 134
Atwood, Margaret 109, 118, 119
autobiography 8, 15, 66–87
Awolowo, Obafemi 69, 72, 78, 79

Awoonor, Kofi 38n.25, 89
Ayodya crisis (India 1992–93) 17, 215,
    216, 218, 221n.21
Azikiwe, Nnamdi 72, 78–9, 80, 83, 84

Bâ, Mariamma 90, 177, 178
Baartman, Saartjie 129, 139n.8
Bail, Murray 146
Bakhtin, Mikhail 39n.29, 50, 94, 165
Balibar, Étienne 7, 38n.24
Banana, President Canaan 176
Bankim, *see* Chatterjee, Bankimchandra
Barthes, Roland 94
Bengal Renaissance 76
Bhabha, Homi 8, 10, 122–3, 145, 165,
    167
Bharat Mata 14, 26, 72, 75, 76, 219
Biafra War (1967–70) 1–3, 17n.3, 54,
    115–18, 124n.21
Biafra War fiction 125n.22
Black Consciousness 74
body 16, 127–39, 172, 197–8
Boose, Lynda E. 109
Brah, Avtar 6, 21n.42, 190, 193, 201
Brathwaite, E. K. 36n.6, 88
Brennan, Timothy 66, 140
Burton, Richard 129
Butler, Judith 14, 28, 176–7, 178

Cabral, Amilcar 8–9
Carey, Peter 12, 146
Chakrabarty, Deepak 9
Chatterjee, Bankimchandra (Bankim)
    26, 38n.24, 217
Chatterjee, Partha 8, 32
Chaudhuri, Amit 161, 205n.30
chimurenga 147, 192
Christian, Barbara 102n.89
Cleary, Joe 8
Cliff, Michelle 16, 136–8, 139n.18
Coetzee, J. M. 130–1
colonial rule 33
Conrad, Joseph 34
Cook, Captain James 129–30
cross-dressing 38n.24, 49, 51–2, 81

Daly, Brenda 120
Dangarembga, Tsitsi 11, 16, 35, 175, 176,
    178, 208, 219
    Nervous Conditions 174, 177, 181–3,
    218
Defoe, Daniel 130
Delgado, Celeste Fraser 174
de Lillo, Don 12
de Man, Paul 67
Desai, Anita 109
Deshpande, Shashi 15, 119
Diana, Princess of Wales 29–30
diaspora 10, 187, 190–1
    see also transnationalism
Diogo, Luisa 73
Dirlik, Arif 166
Dodd, Philip 68
Du Bois, W. E. B. 79

Easter Rising (Ireland 1916) 91
Emecheta, Buchi 15, 17n.3, 89, 102n.89,
    119, 122, 124n.16 and 17, 125n.25,
    177, 210
    Destination Biafra 107, 114–18, 208
    Head Above Water 114
    Joys of Motherhood, The 114, 124n.18
    and 19

Enloe, Cynthia 28
Epprecht, Mark 175

Fagunwa, D. O. 141
family drama, *see* national family
Fanon, Frantz 6, 8, 9–10, 19n.25, 92,
    103n.19, 142, 150, 181
Farah, Nuruddin 16, 89, 133–6, 141
female genital mutilation 47, 105n.37,
    173
feminism 4, 12–14, 119–20, 207
    as universal 191
    western 7, 121, 124n.17
    see also gender; women's agency
feminist criticism 10, 122
figuration 135–6
First, Ruth 110
Flaubert, Gustave 121
Forster, E. M. 213
fraternity 27, 101, 125n.23
    see also national family
Freud, Sigmund 28, 34, 128–9, 138n.5
fundamentalism 210, 211, 216
Fuss, Diana 178

Gandhi, Indira 26, 29–30, 37n.14, 73, 89
Gandhi, M. K. 33, 75, 78, 86n.26, 158,
    201, 219
Garvey, Marcus 79
Gellner, Ernest 7, 23, 36n.3
genealogy 71, 73, 77–81
gender 3–4, 5–6, 7–8, 12, 14, 15, 22–3,
    27–8, 45, 93, 114, 207, 208
    as allegory 30–1, 91–2, 177
    as exoticising 160–1, 162, 163
    and space 31–2, 94–5, 97–8, 101,
    104n.36, 189, 191, 193–4
    syntax 70–2, 84
gender-blindness 18n.14
George, Rosemary M. 193, 204n.17
Ghosh, Amitav 134, 161, 202
Gikandi, Simon 27, 62, 64n.5, 94
Gilroy, Paul 9, 190, 204n.9
globalisation 10, 16, 166, 210
globalised world 187–9

Godelier, Maurice 30
Gordimer, Nadine 8, 18n.18, 109
Gosse, Edmund 158–60, 162
Gramsci, Antonio 55, 123n.11
Gunesekera, Romesh 106
Gurnah, Abdulrazak 51n.6

Haggard, H. Rider 34
Head, Bessie 16, 36, 41n.49, 109, 129, 141, 208
  Maru 127–8
Hindu nationalism 29
Hobsbawm, Eric 9, 22–3
hooks, bell 183n.1
Hove, Chenjerai 16, 141, 145, 146–50, 152, 154, 155, 156n.22, 175–6, 192
Huggan, Graham 160–1, 187
Hurston, Zora Neale 96
hybridity 165, 167
hyper-masculinity 33, 103n.19
  see also masculinity

Idemili (goddess) 1, 55, 60, 64n.14 and 17, 101, 104n.33
Igbo tradition 60, 62, 104n.35, 105n.37
Indian novel in English 20n.36

Jacobus, Mary 128
Jameson, Fredric 11–12, 30, 62, 93, 192–3
Jayawardena, Kumari 6, 14, 90
Joyce, James 9
Julius Caesar (by William Shakespeare) 200

Kamasutra 218, 219
Kamasutra (film by Mira Nair) 217
Kandyoti, Deniz 23, 210
Kanneh, Kadiatu 13, 204n.9
Kaplan, Caren 5, 13, 209
Kapur, Manju 17, 35, 109, 169n.17, 208, 209, 211–19
Kathakali 162, 167, 199
Kaunda, Kenneth 33, 72, 75, 78, 79–80, 81–2, 83

Kenyatta, Jomo 15, 33, 43, 51n.3, 72, 78
Kiberd, Declan 67
Kincaid, Jamaica 109
Kipling, Rudyard 158, 166, 168
Kolawole, Mary Modupe 174
Kristeva, Julia 94
Kunzru, Hari 71, 170n.33

La Guma, Alex 106
Lamming, George 106
Laye, Camara 25, 37n.10, 89
Lazarus, Neil 12, 41n.49, 210
Levinas, Emmanuel 14
Lionnet, Françoise 13, 14, 21n.42, 136, 191
lions 82
Luthuli, Albert 72, 78, 80, 87n.36
Lyotard, Jean-François 198, 220n.2

McClintock, Anne 5, 23
McEwan, Ian 11, 12
Machel, Samora 40n.42
Madizikela-Mandela, Winnie 79, 81, 88
Mandela, Nelson 8, 15, 33, 38n.25,
  Long Walk to Freedom 66, 67, 68–70, 71, 72–3, 74, 78, 80, 81, 82–3
Mandela, Winnie, *see* Madizikela-Mandela
Manley, Michael 33
Marechera, Dambudzo 16, 134, 141, 145, 150–2, 154, 155, 156n.28, 175, 192
  as modernist 150–1
Marxist legacy 190
Marxist theory 59
masculinity 37n.19, 39n.38, 133, 135, 173–4
Massey, Doreen 191, 193
Mbembe, Achille 9, 15, 38n.24, 143–5, 151, 152
Mbilinyi, Maria 34
Mhlope, Gcina 1, 93
migrancy 10, 187, 190, 203
  see also transnationalism
Milton, John 113
Miranda character 109–10, 123n.7

Mohanty, Chandra 7, 121, 204n.17
Mongia, Padmini 164
mother image 38n.25, 88–90, 91, 93,
    103n.22
Mother India (film by Mehboob Khan)
    88–9
Mugabe, Robert 145, 185n.20, 203
Mungoshi, Charles 192, 202

Naidu, Sarojini 15, 16, 72, 73, 76, 86n.18,
    158–63, 167–8
Naipaul, V. S. 106
Nairn, Tom 33–4, 39n.32
Nandy, Ashis 74
Natarajan, Nalini 26
nation
    as allegory 11–12, 30–1, 92, 103n.18,
        192–3
    as dream-construct 141–3
    imaginary 7, 15, 149
    as metaphor 20n.36, 140
    and modernity 31–2
    in retreat 190, 202–3, 209–11, 219
    as story 10–11, 16, 17, 20n.31, 25–6,
        27, 37n.17, 55, 59, 62–3
    and woman 4, 5, 6, 9, 15, 18n.12,
        19n.20, 194–5, 198, 214
    as xenophobic 9–10
    see also pan-nationalism;
        transnationalism
national family 14–15, 28–9, 38n.24, 73,
    91, 106–10, 112, 113, 221n.13
    and anxiety 37n.19
    bourgeois 31–2
    rewritten 106, 112, 113, 122–3, 207
national liberation 44–5, 91–2, 208
national resistance 6, 9, 33
Negritude poetry 24–5
Nehanda (spirit-medium) 73, 146–7,
    148, 192
Nehru, Jawaharlal 15, 67, 68, 69, 71, 72,
    73, 74–7, 80, 83, 86n.27, 88, 89, 201,
    212–13, 217
neo-orientalism, *see* postcolonialism
Nfah-Abbenyi, Juliana 13, 173

Ngcobo, Lauretta 90
Ngoyi, Lilian 80
Ngugi wa Thiong'o 11, 14–15, 29, 42–53,
    91
    Devil on the Cross 43, 45, 46, 48, 50
    Grain of Wheat, A 44, 46, 47, 48, 78,
        213
    Matigari 42, 46, 48, 49–50
    Petals of Blood 42, 45, 46, 47, 48
Nivedita, Sister (Margaret Noble) 38n.25
Njau, Rebekah 173, 174
Nkrumah, Kwame 15, 68, 72, 78–9,
    80–1, 83, 84
Nnaemeka, Obioma 177–8
Nwapa, Flora 15, 35, 36, 90, 94, 104n.29,
    105n.39, 114, 115, 118, 177, 208
    Efuru 60, 88, 95–102
    Idu 95–102
Nyamubaya, Freedom 89
Nzegwu, Femi 105n.37

Okigbo, Christopher 1
Okri, Ben 16, 139n.18, 141–3, 145,
    152–4, 155
    Famished Road, The 134, 135, 153–4
Olney, James 85n.6
Ondaatje, Michael 10

Padmore, George 79
Pan-Africanism 29
pan-nationalism 33–4, 89
Park, Mungo 129
Partition (India/Pakistan) 17, 212, 213
performativity 10, 56, 69, 122–3, 141,
    152, 181
postcolonialism 5, 6, 9–10, 12, 13, 187–9,
    203
    and comparatism 188–9, 190
    as neo-orientalist 158–71
postcoloniality 165, 187–8
postcolonial novel 27, 35, 192
postcolony 15, 143–5, 151, 152, 202–3,
    208, 210–11
postmodernism 165, 170n.28, 190
Presley, Elvis 161

Quayson, Ato 155n.4

Ramphele, Mamphela 73, 210
Ray, Sangeeta 5, 13, 23, 38n.24
Ricoeur, Paul 177
Rooney, Caroline 148
Rose, Gillian 193
Roy, Arundhati 16–17, 35, 89, 161–4,
    165, 169n.16, 188, 189, 191–2, 208,
    215
    Algebra of Infinite Justice, The 200–3
    God of Small Things, The 167–8,
    198–200, 203, 205n.33
Rushdie, Salman 10, 11, 12, 134, 161,
    165, 169n.16, 192, 202
    Midnight's Children 23, 25–6, 29,
    36n.4, 71, 94, 106, 213
    Moor's Last Sigh, The 37n.13
    Shame 25–6

Said, Edward 91, 102n.16, 164
Sangari, Kumkum 5
sati 33, 120, 121, 125n.33, 178
Scarry, Elaine 132
Schreiner, Olive 106, 107–8, 110–11, 113,
    119, 122
Scott, Joan W. 30
Sedgwick, Eve 177
Selvon, Sam 106
Senghor, Léopold 24–5, 36n.9
Serote, Mongane 38n.25
sexuality 16, 30, 172–86, 216–19
Shelley, Percy Bysshe 113, 124n.14
Shields, Carol 15, 210
    Stone Diaries, The 118
    Unless 118–22
Sisulu, Albertina and Walter 67, 80
Smith, Anthony 22–3, 211
Solomon, Melissa 177
Sorabji, Cornelia 184n.7
Soyinka, Wole 55, 81, 89, 93, 115, 141,
    155n.4, 157n.37
Spivak, Gayatri 1, 13, 14, 20n.32, 62,
    139n.11, 167, 170n.23 and 35

Stead, Christina 15, 116, 118, 122,
    123n.12
    Man Who Loved Children, The 107,
    109, 111–14
Stevens, Hugh 180
Stratton, Florence 5, 23, 30, 51–2n.6, 96,
    177
Sunder Rajan, Rajeswari 23, 37n.14, 90,
    125n.33, 132
Symons, Arthur 158, 160, 162

Tagore, Rabindranath 187, 188, 203n.4,
    217
Tharoor, Shashi 11, 106, 161
Tharu, Susie 32, 39n.34
Thatcher, Margaret 29–30
Theweleit, Klaus 22
Tickell, Alex 199–200
Tocqueville, Alexis de 32
tokenism, 48–9, 58–9
transnationalism 10, 187–203
    see also postcolonialism
Tutuola, Amos 141, 154, 155n.4

Umeh, Marie 116

veil 76, 121, 125
Vera, Yvonne 16–17, 174–81, 188, 189,
    191–2, 193–8, 200, 201, 202–3, 208,
    215
verbal recalcitrance 167, 170n.35

Walker, Alice 89, 93, 102n.89
Wallace, Jo-Ann 111
women's agency 167, 199–200
women's narrative 15, 16–17, 35–6,
    93–5, 106–10, 202–3, 208–9, 214
Woolf, Virginia 91, 201, 210

Xhosa dress 68

Yeats, W. B. 58, 67, 168n.2
Yoruba *oriki* 105n.38
Young, Robert J. C. 18n.14, 184n.3

Lightning Source UK Ltd.
Milton Keynes UK
UKOW06f2333050116

265880UK00006B/134/P